Max Frisch

Perspectives on
Max Frisch

GERHARD F. PROBST & JAY F. BODINE,
Editors

THE UNIVERSITY PRESS OF KENTUCKY

Copyright © 1982 by The University Press of Kentucky

Scholarly publisher for the Commonwealth,
serving Berea College, Centre College of Kentucky,
Eastern Kentucky University, The Filson Club,
Georgetown College, Kentucky Historical Society,
Kentucky State University, Morehead State University,
Murray State University, Northern Kentucky University,
Transylvania University, University of Kentucky,
University of Louisville, and Western Kentucky University.

Editorial and Sales Office: Lexington, Kentucky 40506-0024

Library of Congress Cataloging in Publication Data
Main entry under title:

Perspectives on Max Frisch.

   Bibliography: p.
   1. Frisch, Max, 1911-   —Criticism and interpretation.   I. Probst, Gerhard F.   II. Bodine, Jay F., 1943-
PT2611.R814Z768   838'.91209   80-5181
ISBN: 978-0-8131-6009-2   AACR2

Contents

Acknowledgments	vi
GERHARD F. PROBST Introduction	1
MANFRED JURGENSEN The Drama of Frisch	4
HANS BÄNZIGER Frisch as a Narrator	31
HORST STEINMETZ Frisch as a Diarist	56
LINDA J. STINE "Ich hätte Lust, Märchen zu schreiben": Frisch's Use of Märchen in *Die Schwierigen* and *Montauk*	71
WULF KOEPKE Frisch's *I'm Not Stiller* as a Parody of *The Magic Mountain*	79
KLAUS JEZIORKOWSKI Wilhelm Tell as Peter Jenny: On Frisch's *Wilhelm Tell für die Schule*	93
MARIAN E. MUSGRAVE Frisch's "Continuum" of Women, Domestic and Foreign	109
ROLF KIESER Wedding Bells for Don Juan: Frisch's Domestication of a Myth	119
LINDA J. STINE & HANS BÄNZIGER "Exposed to the other sex": The Problem of Marriage in *Philipp Hotz* and *Graf Öderland*	124
JAY F. BODINE Frisch's Little White Lies: Self-Discovery and Engagement through Skepsis of Language and Perspective	129
GERHARD F. PROBST Three Levels of Image Making in Frisch's *Mein Name sei Gantenbein*	154
GERHARD F. PROBST The Old Man and the Rain: *Man in the Holocene*	166
GERHARD F. PROBST Max Frisch Bibliography	177
Frisch's Biographical Data	224
Contributors	226

Acknowledgments

Permission to reprint book chapters or articles from the following publishers and authors is gratefully acknowledged:

Hans Bänziger, *Frisch und Dürrenmatt* (Berne and Munich: Francke, 1976).

Horst Steinmetz, *Max Frisch: Tagebuch, Drama, Roman* (Göttingen: Vandenhoeck and Ruprecht [Kleine Vandenhoeck-Reihe 379], 1973).

Wulf Koepke, "Max Frischs *Stiller* als *Zauberberg*-Parodie," *Wirkendes Wort,* 1977, No. 3 (Düsseldorf: Pädagogischer Verlag Schwann).

Gerhard F. Probst, "Du sollst dir kein Bildnis machen." Überlegungen zu Max Frischs Roman *Mein Name sei Gangenbein, Colloquia Germanica,* nos. 3-4, 1978 (Berne and Munich: Francke). The article appears here in a revised version.

Jay F. Bodine translated the texts by Bänziger, Steinmetz, and Jeziorkowski; those by Koepke and Probst were translated by the authors themselves.

We would like to thank Transylvania University for its financial support of this project and Alexander M. Gilchrist of the Margaret I. King Library, University of Kentucky, for his most generous and invaluable help in the compilation and repeated updating of the bibliography.

GERHARD F. PROBST

Introduction

Max Frisch (1911-   ) and Friedrich Dürrenmatt (1921-   ) have for more than three decades been considered to be the two outstanding representatives of contemporary Swiss literature. Although both wrote plays that have often been performed in this country, their work as a whole has remained largely unknown to Americans. It is one of the purposes of this book to help remedy this situation, at least as far as Max Frisch is concerned.

It is not our intention to give a detailed Frisch biography here,[1] but a few dates and facts might be of interest to place some of his works in perspective. After briefly studying German literature at the University of Zurich, his home town, Frisch tried his hand at journalism and published his first novel *Jürg Reinhart* during that period (1934). In 1936, with the financial assistance of a friend, he began studying architecture at the Technical University of Zurich, earned his degree in 1941, and worked as an architect until 1954 when his literary success had made him financially independent.

Important other events that were to have considerable impact on his writing included the following: his periodic service as an artilleryman in the Swiss army (1939-1945); his association with Bertolt Brecht after the latter's return from the United States (1947); trips to Berlin, Breslau (Wroclaw), Paris, Prague, Warsaw, and Vienna (1947-1948); a Rockefeller Grant (1951-1952), which gave him an opportunity to visit the United States and Mexico; a second trip to the western hemisphere, which included Cuba (1956); travels in the Arab states (1957); residence in Rome (1960-1965); travels in Israel (1965), the Soviet Union (1966, 1968), and Japan (1969); residence in New York (1971, 1972) and West Berlin (1973, 1974); and a trip to China with Chancellor Helmut Schmidt (1975). Max Frisch received several literary prizes, including the prestigious Georg Büchner Prize (1958) and the Peace Prize of the German Book Trade (1976).

One is reluctant to name Frisch's best works, since such a choice seems to relegate his other works to a status of lesser importance. But on the basis of both critical acclaim and popular success, one must place *Stiller* (1954) at the top of the list. Here Frisch for the first time elaborated on one of his dominant themes, by some critics the central theme of his oeuvre: the search for identity as the questioning of the existence of a self-contained character or personality, its dependence on the reciprocity of interpersonal image-making, and the impossibility of escaping from the roles we assign to each other. Variations of this theme are found in his two other major novels *Homo faber* and *Mein Name sei Gantenbein* and in his plays *Als der Krieg zu Ende war, Andorra, Don Juan,* and *Biographie.* His most successful play, however, is *Biedermann und die Brandstifter (The Firebugs),* which has been called a modern morality play. Although this is certainly suggested by its title ("Biedermann" alludes to "Everyman"), its success is attributed to its being a most fortuitous blend of the theater of the absurd with the Brechtian didactic play as underscored by the subtitle "Ein Lehrstück ohne Lehre" ("A didactic play without a lesson"). In addition to the novel and the drama, Frisch has cultivated a literary genre which in our times of subjectivity has again attained a rather unexpected popularity: the diary. He published his first diary (*Blätter aus dem Brotsack: Tagebuch eines Kanoniers* [Leaves from the knapsack: Diary of an artilleryman] at the beginning of World War II and the second one shortly after the war (*Tagebuch mit Marion*). He expanded the latter diary and published it in 1950 under the title *Tagebuch 1946-1949.* It proved to be the most seminal of all his writings, since it contained themes, motifs, and plots for many of his later works. It also presents descriptions of, and reflections on, life in postwar Europe, expressing Frisch's weltanschauung as well as his aesthetics. The later *Tagebuch 1966-1971* differs from its predecessors in that it deals for the first time in his work and rather extensively with the theme of aging and death. Frisch's three latest works are, in large measure, variations on this theme. *Montauk* (1975) is a fictionalized diary centered around the aging narrator's love affair with a young woman. *Triptychon* (1978), subtitled "Drei szenische Bilder" (Three scenic pictures or paintings), presents death as an agent of eternity, but of an "eternity of that which happened," thus establishing a paradoxically immanent transcendence. Evoking medieval altar paintings and by its title alluding to their tripartite structure as well as to the almost complete lack of plot, *Triptychon* consists of one central "scenic picture" set by the river Styx, flanked, as it were, by two smaller or shorter ones depicting the relationship between the living and the dead. *Der Mensch erscheint im Holozän (Man in the Holocene,* 1979) centers around an old man who is rainbound in a remote alpine valley. This setting is in itself an expressive symbol of the loneliness of old age.

Even a brief discussion of Max Frisch's writings would be sorely deficient if no mention were made of his journalistic work. Not only did he begin his writing career as a journalist, but he continued to use the press to voice his views on the issues of the day. As a trained architect Frisch has repeatedly written about the necessity of urban renewal accompanied by selective preservation of the older parts of cities and about the nature of modern architecture in Europe and on other continents ("Fort Worth: The City of the Future in Texas," 1957; the preface to G. Suter's book *Die grossen*

Städte: Was sie zerstört und was sie retten kann [The big cities: What destroys them and what can save them], 1965). But above all Frisch has constantly involved himself in political issues in the narrower sense of the word. He has spoken out against racial prejudice and pleaded for understanding and better treatment of the foreign workers and their families living in Switzerland. He condemned the Soviet intervention in East Germany, Hungary, and Czechoslovakia as well as the United States' involvement in Vietnam.

The secondary literature on Max Frisch has reached such proportions that the *1979 MLA International Bibliography* shows more entries under his name than for Böll and Grass together. Nobody writing in German today attracts more critical attention. Although some of his works have been treated more than others, there is no distinct favorite. Frisch the dramatist, however, has been studied more than Frisch the narrator.

The relationship between the sexes plays such a central part in Frisch's works that studies of the role or image of women are definitely germane to the interpretation of his oeuvre. Some studies have already been published.[2] One critic (Zoran Konstantović) even stated that the search for identity only appears to be Frisch's dominant theme, his true theme being man's feeling of guilt toward woman.[3]

In compiling this volume of essays, we were guided by three main objectives. The book is a general introduction to the work of this important Swiss writer, particularly since the two books written in English that were of a general nature had been published in 1967 (Weisstein) and 1972 (Petersen). Second, this book contains a few recent studies of special problems, and third, it presents the most comprehensive bibliography of primary and secondary literature published in this country.

---

1. For more information, see the biographical data.

2. See Mona Knapp, "Die Frau ist ein Mensch, bevor man sie liebt, manchmal auch danach ...: Kritisches zur Gestaltung der Frau in Frisch-Texten," in Max Frisch, *Aspekte des Bühnenwerks,* ed. Knapp (Berne: Lang, 1979). M.E. Musgrave, "Kürmann, His Wives, and 'Helen, the Mulatta' in Max Frisch's Biografie: Ein Spiel," in *College Language Association Journal* 18 (1975). L. Köseoğlu, *Die Stellung der Frauenfiguren in den Dramen von Friedrich Dürrenmatt, Max Frisch und Hans Günter Michelsen bis 1968* (Hamburg: Author, 1974).

3. For a more detailed discussion see W. Schmitz, "Frisch-Bilder. Linien und Skizzen der Forschung," in *Max Frisch. Aspekte des Bühnenwerks,* ed. Knapp. In spite of the misleading context provided by the title of the collection of essays (Aspects of the drama), Schmitz's article deals with Frisch's entire oeuvre.

MANFRED JURGENSEN

The Drama of Frisch

For A. Fremd

Max Frisch's first play, *Santa Cruz*, written during August and September 1944, had its premiere on March 7, 1946, at the Schauspielhaus in Zurich. It was preceded by a wide range of early literary sketches, reprinted in the collected works under the title of *Kleine Prosaschriften* (small prose pieces), by the first diary *Blätter aus dem Brotsack* (Pages from the Knapsack, 1939), by the two novels *Jürg Reinhart* (1933-1934) and *Die Schwierigen oder J'adore ce qui me brûle* (The difficult ones or I adore that which burns, 1942, rev. 1957), and by the narrative parable *Bin oder Die Reise nach Peking* (Am or the trip to Peking, 1944).

As early as 1931 Frisch, then twenty years of age, had begun his literary career with an analysis of role playing, both in the theater and outside it. His essay *Mimische Partitur?* (Mimic score?), which appeared on May 27, 1931, in the *Neue Zürcher Zeitung* came to the conclusion that all fiction was derived from some kind of dialogue. It was easy to see that with such a concept of fiction this writer would sooner or later turn to drama as an appropriate form of artistic self-expression. Frisch had discovered quite early that in entering into a dialogue with himself, he would inevitably turn his own preoccupations into dramatic manifestations of a fictional I. Any individual identity could therefore only be involved in role playing; it is forever in search of an alter ego willing to be part of his self-dialogue. Frisch's fictionalization of the I clearly serves the function of self-knowledge. While his literary works may be highly entertaining, they are primarily intellectual, concerned with bearing witness to the reality of man, to the existential problems of individual authenticity.

This fictional form of self-dialogue expressed itself in Frisch's many diaries. From *Blätter aus dem Brotsack* to *Tagebuch 1966-1971*, the author questions himself; as a representative I he calls himself into doubt. In the novels *Jürg Reinhart* and *Die Schwierigen*, Frisch gives an epic account of the same existential dialogue with himself. The literary genre may have changed; his central preoccupation, however, has remained the same: Frisch's subject continues to be the art of self-reflection. In his arabesque *Bin oder Die Reise nach Peking*, the dialogue between ego and alter ego may be followed most clearly. Significantly, Frisch is not interested in any psychoanalytical interpretations of subjective individuality. The other I identifies itself as an expression of existential self-consciousness. Although this alter ego develops more and more into a brotherly You, revealing "the other" as a manifestation of the social I, Frisch's diaries (and their form-fictional applications to novels and, in *Biografie: Ein Spiel* [Biography: A Play], the drama) remain essentially lyrical. Frisch then has made use of all genres in his attempt to realize a fiction of self-dialogue.

The interaction of various genres in the works of Frisch is therefore an expression of different kinds or different states of self-examination. His "Romance" *Santa Cruz* embraces all three genres: Pelegrin and Pedro are narrative personae who at the same time enact (or re-enact) their epic accounts dramatically while they remain throughout the play personifications of lyrical longing. The central theme of the play is that of all Frisch's early works: *Sehnsucht* (longing). What better way to express the longing for another life than in the form of a dialogue with another, a different I? The I itself becomes a dramatis persona: in splitting itself, it realizes the dreams and hopes of a socially identified and personally restricted individual.

But there is another way in which Max Frisch expresses the longing of a limited I: throughout his work, but particularly in its early phase—a period characterized by dramatic lyricisms—he presents the theme of self-realization, the very search for a self, in terms of a pilgrimage, an excursion, a journey. The destinations of such journeys remain beyond the reach of the socially restricted I; they are places of fantasy, dreams, and longing: Peking, Santorin, or Santa Cruz. Frisch introduces a new concept linked to the longing for self-realization: repetition. It too finds its appropriate expression in dialogue; the exchangeability not only of experience itself but also of the very idea, the longing for an experience is a natural consequence of the interchangeability of the personality, of the dramatic splitting of the I. Consequently, the *Sehnsucht*-journey of the I can only be undertaken in the company of the other I: in *Bin oder Die Reise nach Peking* the I is accompanied by its *"Bin,"* i.e., its existential projection of self-realization; in *Santa Cruz* the wandering performer (Vagant) becomes the dramatic symbol of Elvira's and the captain's self-alienation and self-discovery. The two themes of the play which relate to its central issue of self-discovery are repetition and the journey of the self. In his program notes on the occasion of the first performance of *Santa Cruz* in Zurich, Frisch summed up the interaction of these themes: "Santa Cruz, that is the name of a foreign, apparently Spanish, harbor, but one shouldn't look it up on the map—if at all, one will most readily find it in his own experience, in that area of recognition that everyone has already had, of that dream-like, surprising experience of standing before a certain situation in life and knowing: I have already experienced that, I don't know when or where, but basically it's exactly the same, and wherever I go, I will experience it again and again.—That's Santa Cruz." In many ways this drama could be described in the same terms that Frisch applied to *Bin oder Die Reise nach*

Peking: both are "Träumereien" (dream pieces). There is overwhelming evidence that *Santa Cruz* was meant to be a dream play. The wandering performer himself (the Vagrant) is a dream figure; both Elvira and the captain relate to him only in their dreams. Significantly, they are introduced into the play by the wandering performer; only with his help can they enact their dreams. There can be little doubt then that *Bin oder Die Reise nach Peking* and *Santa Cruz* belong, not only historically, to the same period of Frisch's development. It is well known that Frisch habitually expresses certain themes and preoccupations in various, and to him experimental, literary genres (cf. *Gantenbein* and *Biografie* or *Stiller* and *Andorra* or, generally, the "pretexts" in the diaries).

It is all the more remarkable then that this "dream play" *Santa Cruz* incorporates into its enactment of dreams a very acute social conscience. There is no withdrawal from harsh social realities in the dream analysis. "Do you know what I can dream?" asks the proletarian innkeeper's wife in the prologue. The castle is not only an obvious symbol of marriage, of a splendid life where, snowed under by routine, everything is under lock and key; it is clearly also a place beyond reach for the workers and peasants, a place of wealth and of splendid social isolation. The innkeeper's wife informs the wandering performer:

> Our captain! as the people say here. Our castle! And not one of them has ever set foot in the castle in his whole life.

WANDERING PERFORMER: Why not?
INNKEEPER'S WIFE: They don't ever let anyone in.

The ordinary people of the village have no access to wealth; they do not share the profits of their labor. The keeper of the castle is identified as "a man of order." He is the exponent of a particular brand of social order. The wandering performer can only force his way into the castle because he personifies dreams and longings. In that sense, the people of the village share his entry into a realm beyond their reach. It is essential to realize that Elvira and her husband are haunted by the wandering performer not only as an erotic seducer in a purely private sphere; he is (like Jürg Reinhart) also a representative of the opposite social forces: poor and fighting for his freedom. The boat on which the captain hopes to escape to his personal freedom is the pirate boat of the wandering performer. This dream boat and the freedom the inhabitants of the well-kept castle long for are described by the captain's butler in the following terms:

> Such a dirty ship, your Grace?
> *He hastily collects the baggage.*
> Your Grace, I can't stand the sea. In pictures, yes, it has a pretty color, but it stinks, most of the time.

The dream of freedom can only be realized by a change of social structure, by a destruction of the very order the captain and his castle represent.

CAPTAIN: My good fellow, I too considered it differently.
SERVANT: It was such a pretty castle, your Grace, that we could have had there.

Only in dreams can social freedom be realized. Frisch's critics have, on the whole, reacted negatively to this play because it seemed to them to avoid the burning issues of contemporary society. It is the well-known objection to Frisch's alleged subjectivity. No one who has read (or seen) this play, the first of ten, with an open mind can fail to recognize the social dimension of our dreams, of our longings. Frisch shows marriage as the most intimate social relationship, not as a purely private affair. In the same way, our most intimate dreams and ambitions are revealed to be social in character and consequence. The fact that we can share a dream makes our longings too part of an overall, i.e., social, pattern of repetition. As the play ends:

THE LAST FIGURE: I'm the child of your blood, Viola, experiencing everything anew, everything, everything beginning again.

Already at this early stage Frisch moves in the direction of the "model theater." One of the most important aspects of his drama *Santa Cruz* lies in its parabolic nature. In that, too, it is a rewriting of *Bin oder Die Reise nach Peking*. On the stage too now the I is on its way in search of its "Bin," its alter ego, its social I—in search of its audience.

Frisch's second play (although the first to be performed on stage), *Nun singen sie wieder* (They're Singing Again Now), bears the subtitle *Versuch eines Requiems* (Attempt at a Requiem). In his own introduction to the printed edition (1946), Frisch spoke of "a far-off sadness" and "the involuntary force of dreams" which prompted and informed this drama. He was very much aware of his own unique position regarding the war; as a Swiss, apparently unaffected by the conflict surrounding his own country, Frisch could only attempt to present the lessons of the war from a bipartisan point of view. This he does in *Nun singen sie wieder* not only by representing both sides of the warfaring factions, but also by enacting the lamentation of his requiem in staging a realm of death where friends and foes are equals.

In dealing with the German dilemma, Frisch analyzes dramatically the dichotomy of *Geist* (spirit) and *Macht* (power). The theme is summarized neatly in an entry in his *Tagebuch 1946-1949* where, under the heading of "Café Delfino" (written during October 1946), we read:

I'm thinking of Heydrich, who played Mozart, as an example of a definite experience. Art in this sense, art as a moral schizophrenia, if one can say so, would in any case be the opposite of our task; and all in all it is questionable whether the artistic and human task can be separated. A sign of the spirit that we need is not primarily a talent representing some plus, but rather responsibility. Especially the German people, who were never lacking in talents, or minds that felt themselves beyond the demands of the common day, the Germans were the ones who supplied the most, or at least the first, barbarians of our century. Shouldn't we learn something from that? (*Tagebuch* 1: 115)

The character of Herbert personifies this moral schizophrenia in an exemplary fashion. Art as a cultural alibi is exposed for what it is: aestheticism, formal rhetoric without humane values. The lengthy discussions between Herbert and Karl in the first part of the play tend to have the effect of set pieces in a Platonic dialogue. It is fair to say that up to *Graf Öderland* (Count Öderland) the argumentative nature of Frisch's plays meant that very little real dramatic interaction took place on the stage. Set speeches, quotations, and montages take the place of dramatic plot and interaction in the traditional drama. Indeed, some of Herbert's reflections read like diary entries; one of his speeches seems to reflect the despair Frisch expressed in his diary on the occasion of the atomic bombing of Bikini—exemplifying the interrelationship between some of the themes in *Nun singen sie wieder* and the *Tagebuch 1946-1949*. In the play Herbert explains: "We reached for power, for the ultimate force in order to encounter the spirit, the real one; but the cynic was right, there is no real spirit, and we have the world in our pocket, whether we need it or not; I don't see any limit to our power—that's the despair." A year later, Frisch reacts in rather similar fashion to the possibility of a total nuclear destruction of the world: "The progress that led to Bikini will yet take the last step also: the deluge will be feasible. That's what's grandiose. We can do what we want; at the end of our progress we're standing where Adam and Eve stood; for us there still remains only the moral question" (*Tagebuch* 1: 67). This is an updated version of the same dilemma which lies at the center of the play *Nun singen sie wieder*: the conflict between spirit and power.

Stylistically, the drama relies heavily on narrative passages with intensely lyrical overtones. In addition, Frisch makes extensive use of quotations which in turn are used as leitmotivs. In juxtaposing identical passages spoken by opposing forces, he literally plays out one viewpoint against the other without seeming to take sides himself. Examples are the spring motifs, the tulip bulbs, the title theme "They're singing again now," the priest's statement "My place is here," the lyrical descriptions of the countryside ("The dark fields are gaping after light and they're frittering away manure out there, the horses are steaming."), the hateful accusation of German and Allied soldiers "They're devils . . . they're devils," and the teacher's desire "I just wanted to see them once: face to face." Frisch uses them not merely for characterization; he interrelates them, combines and redesigns them, until they amount to a kaleidoscope of prejudice, anguish, and despair. These leitmotivs accumulate to a reflective statement per se; the exchange of dialogue is more like the self-reflection of a diary. Max Frisch stages his own thoughts on the war, uses the theater as a pretext for a visualization of the self-reflective dialogues in his diaries. No wonder that in his comments on the play he wrote: "The place where these scenes take place always emerges from the spoken word. Scenery should be present only to the extent that the actor needs it and in no case would it attempt to simulate reality. For the impression of a play must remain preserved throughout" (*Ges. Werke* 2: 137). The place of action clearly is Frisch's own consciousness and his conscience. One theme which seems to have been overlooked by most critics is the theme of all Frisch's early works: *Sehnsucht* (longing); the longing for a better world, a meaningful life as well as the longing of fiction, of illusion, of all art. In that sense, Frisch's theater itself is an expression of the author's *Sehnsucht*, more than a full relization of all the potentials of the stage. Eduard's speech in the third scene of the play clearly sums up Frisch's concept of the piece, a concept he retained right up to one of his last dramas, *Biografie: Ein Spiel.*

EDUARD: I believe in illusion. Even that which never occurs in the world, even that which one cannot grasp with his hands and cannot destroy with his hands, even that which occurs as a desire, as a longing, as a goal going beyond everything existing at hand. . . .

All theater, all fiction is in this context a rehearsal, an attempt to play out possibilities that cannot be realized outside the realm of art. The theatrical rehearsal held a deep fascination for Frisch. It is significant that his *Probe*-concept (testing in rehearsal) is, by its very nature, related to the montage of quotations. Play, *Spiel*, then, is the interaction of quotations used as self-characterizations, quotations of a self which can never be defined but only rehearsed.

One theme that proved to be of major significance for many of his later works, Frisch introduces as a dream: the Rip van Winkle folktale, a legend by Washington Irving. In fact, then, Frisch quotes this modern literary myth; it is a quotation, however, with variations. Among the Allied soldiers one reports:

Yesterday I had an abominable dream. . . . Our flying bedstead caught on fire and we all jumped out, one, two, three, four, five; I've dreamed that a lot already: it's as if the parachute didn't want to sink down to earth at all, and at last I land each time in my hometown, a town as on Sunday, you understand, a little desolate, boring, strange, more or less as if one were coming back centuries later; the streets that one knew, the plazas, suddenly it's a meadow and the goats are grazing on it; but the coffee house is standing open like a ruin, your friends are sitting inside, they're reading the newspaper, and on the little marble table is moss, moss; no one knows who you are, no common memories, no common language and so forth . . . an abominable dream.

It is not difficult to recognize the American legend in this description of a nightmare. Frisch also wrote a radio play entitled *Rip van Winkle* and, more importantly, revived the myth in his best-known novel *Stiller*. In addition, the short tale *Schinz* in his *Tagebuch 1946-1949* offers yet another variation of the Rip van Winkle theme. To my knowledge, its early appearance in the play *Nun singen sie wieder* has been virtually overlooked by all Frisch critics and scholars.

In Frisch's drama, dreams and nightmares, hopes and longings, projections and flashbacks all form part of a moral, intellectual, and existential totality. From the earliest diary *Blätter aus dem Brotsack*, the subsequent novel(s) of Greece, and the "dreamings in Prose" *Bin oder Die Reise nach Peking*, there is a natural progression to the "Romance" *Santa Cruz* and the "Requiem" *Nun singen sie wieder*.

The characterization of his plays indicates Frisch's own development not only as a dramatist but also as a writer of growing political awareness. His next play *Die Chinesische Mauer* (The Chinese Wall) bears the subtitle "A Farce." Again, broad use is made of quotations as a structural device. Frisch separates his dramatis personae into "figures" and "masks." Of the former it may be said that they relate specifically to the play concept; they are in fact introduced in the first speech of "Der Heutige" (The Present-day Man) as figures of the play. Frisch again plays them out against each other; in the place of a traditional dramatic conflict there is a figurative exchange of beliefs, attitudes, and views. We are dealing here with purely figurative speech quoted by the theater; or, better, with figurative language quoting the stage. None of these figures are dramatic characters controlled by a personal psychology. The masks, on the other hand, are rather more obvious and direct quotations, either from history or from literature. They are, as the present-day man states in the first scene of the play, "figures that populate our brain, and to the extent of being figures of our thinking, . . . still alive throughout." Ultimately, then, both "figures" and "masks" fall under the heading of Frisch's play concept.

The play begins with a visual quotation of the Great Wall of China. In describing it, the present-day man quotes from the encyclopedia. If this drama in its most literal sense is a play and the dynamics of this play are provided by a structural interaction of quotations, its immediate and ultimate theme is history. Frisch's more recent play *Biografie: Ein Spiel* applies the same logic to the history of an individual. In *Die Chinesische Mauer* Frisch follows the principle of the encyclopedia: he quotes from history and stages a conversation piece which, even under the designation of a farce, remains a playful exercise, lacking the dimensions of a dramatic realization. It must be obvious that the very choice of theme dictated the limitations of this play. If it is the paywright's intention not to write about one particular period in history but to embrace the entire course of European civilization, his presentation can only take the form of selective quotations.

But Frisch does not simply quote from literary or political history. Frequently he quotes himself. The most striking example is the repeated warning of the present-day man: "The deluge is feasible.... That is: we stand before the choice whether there should be a humanity or not." Readers of the *Tagebuch 1946-1949* are familiar with the corresponding entry (written in 1946, the same year as *Die Chinesische Mauer*): "The deluge is becoming feasible.... It depends on us whether there is humanity or not." The Nanking of his play is clearly a quotation and variation of the Peking in *Bin oder Die Reise nach Peking*. Furthermore, the dilemma of Hwang Ti, summed up in the Exclaimer's statement "The world is ours," the entire power-versus-spirit theme which forms the highlight of *Die Chinesische Mauer*, is unmistakeably a representation of the central conflict in Frisch's earlier play *Nun singen sie wieder*. Here too he relates the power/spirit trial of strength to a purely aesthetic concept of culture. Hwang Ti's master of ceremonies, Da Hing Yen, declares the conscience of the present-day man as poetic and awards him the "golden chain around his neck"—a national prize for cultural achievement: "What would it be—the most powerful empire in this world, victorious over all barbarians—what would it be without the streaming glory and decoration of its spiritual forces? That's why it's an old custom for us to reward and honor the spiritual forces that we have listened to with joy." Significantly, this award and its announcement are themselves a quotation. Not only Brecht was to experience this kind of honor; the capitalist West has found its own form of reconciling spirit and power: the countless industry prizes to writers and artists speak for themselves.

Another striking quotation from an earlier play by Frisch occurs toward the end of *Die Chinesische Mauer*. In the twenty-third scene Napoleon, the Inconnue, Pilatus, Phillip of Spain, Don Juan, Brutus, Cleopatra, Columbus, and Romeo and Juliet reappear in a highly stylized form of self-quotation.

Frisch describes their appearance as follows: "Entrance with the polonaise of the masks. They move in the manner of a play clock; each figure has its word when it gets to the front and then it further turns around itself." Their self-quotations are, by their very nature, self-characterizations. At the end of his "Romance" *Santa Cruz,* ten visionary dream figures appear to the dead Pelegrin; Frisch gives them the following directions: "While everything around him, the walls of the room and Elvira and the captain who is holding the collapsing woman up, just as he had had to support her once earlier when Pelegrin left her—while all of that is sinking into darkness, music sounds and around him the figures appear." The last of these figures is Pelegrin's child Viola, who says of herself: "She who experiences everything anew, who begins everything again." Napoleon in *Die Chinesische Mauer* opens the play-clock danse macabre with the words: "I'm not supposed to return! they say. I mustn't! What's all that talk?" It is clear, then, that Frisch's use of (self-) quotations is not restricted to themes, ideas, and characterization; it applies as much to the formal structure of the play. Only in the overall composition of figurative and masklike alienated quotations does it find its ultimate identity.

One form of quotation lies at the very center of this play: it is the theater quoting itself. This occurs in the obvious sense that major characters address themselves directly to the audience to reveal their theatricality. In the case of Mee Lan, her speech *ad spectatores* culminates in the appeal: "You all think you could show me something? You think that I don't notice that I'm dressed up? And you who are grown-ups and know everything, do you believe yourselves that, for example, Father always knows best? I'm not stupid. You think I don't notice that everything here (this throne, for example! even bobby-soxers catch on to that) is theater?" It is interesting to note that she already reverses the traditional order in accusing the audience of acting ("show me something"). The concept of theater is clearly extended beyond the limits of the stage, as is expressed in the corresponding definition of the play as a farce. Her father Hwang Ti in turn offers a different kind of duality when he enters into a dialogue with the audience: "You with your dramatics! I have to smile. Go out and buy your newspaper, you down there, and on the front page you'll see my name. Because I don't let them knock me down; I don't hold on to dramatics." Clearly, Frisch's concept of the theater here is a sociopolitical analogy, an extension of pretense, role playing, and make-believe. Theater and "reality" (i.e., history) interact in their respective quotations. If we are arguing that in Frisch's *Chinesische Mauer* the theater is quoting itself, it is necessary to add that this kind of self-quotation can only take place in a confrontation with history. What Goethe expressed in reference to himself, "I have become historical to myself," now applies to the consciousness of our whole century, to the totality of modern literature.

Frisch's protagonist, the present-day man, can only be understood in these terms. He is then above all a representative of modern, contemporary theater—and as such a forerunner of the later Frisch-protagonists (Stiller, Faber, Gantenbein) who are all authors, producers, and directors of their particular brand of a "theater of the self." Nothing could be more misleading therefore than the attempts of various Frisch critics to psychoanalyze this concept of a theatrical self-rehearsal. In Frisch's works it is always a social and political, not merely a private, individual; an individual in search of his place in contemporary society and history. The identity crisis of Frisch's protagonists is not an expression of a subjective neurosis but a manifestation of an existential crisis. The *Ich* itself has been reduced to a sociopolitical quotation. In a society consisting of a totality of such self-quotations (and in literature of similar quality), Frisch's present-day man despairs at the end of this theatrical piece of history:

THE PRESENT-DAY MAN: We're not going to play on any further!
BRUTUS: What's the reason?
THE PRESENT-DAY MAN: Because the whole farce (as if we could repeat it) is starting over again from the beginning.

In Frisch's concept of the theater we are presented with an existential confrontation: that of man's fiction and his authenticity. In the formal use of quotations he expresses the epitome of this dilemma. It is, of course, a polarity which in one form or another has been the determining factor of human existence from the beginning of time. Authenticity can be a deadly exercise, both individually and collectively. Gantenbein explains: "I thirst for betrayal. I would like to know that I am. Whatever doesn't betray me falls under the suspicion of living only in my imagination, and I'd like to get outside of my imagination, I'd like to be in the world. I'd like to be betrayed in the innermost depths." In the first version of *Die Chinesische Mauer* (1946), Min Ko expresses the dialectics of fiction and authenticity, of violent illusion and self-realization: "It is I, yes. For the first time I know that I really am: they're demanding my head. For the first time I know that I, a poet, can alter the world." Later he comes to identify his fictional I with the voice of conscience; discovering the I in somebody else means socializing and moralizing the identity of an authentic mode of being. The fictional I—and hence all literature—becomes a moral agent. "Min Ko (The Fool): I am the voice that you hear coming out of yourself, nothing more, the voice of your own consciousness, which you're afraid of." In Frisch's second version of the play (1955), he summarizes the intentions of his theater when he adds to the instructions (which are directed not only at the actors): "The masks speak in stylized quotations." This holds true not only for the literary allusions (Cervantes, Shakespeare, Schiller); the entire dialogue of Frisch's play espouses the style of historical, political, social, and, ultimately, existential quotations.

Frisch defined his fourth play, *Als der Krieg zu Ende war* (When the war was over), as belonging to the genre of historical plays (afterword to the edition of 1949). Yet he is anxious to turn historical events into paradigmatic fiction, the "factual event" acquires the moral and aesthetic qualities of a parable. History in this case too came to Frisch in the form of a quotation; revisiting Germany immediately after the war he listens to countless "stories from the so-called Russian period." Thus Frisch experiences this history of the immediate past through "stories," i.e., as fiction. *Als der Krieg zu Ende war* is an "epic drama," both in its nature and in its origin. The first lines of Agnes Anders are not even disguised as a monologue; they are in fact quotations (indicated in the text by quotation marks) of an epic narrative. A great deal depends on how successfully the actress playing Agnes Anders manages to convey in her speech the quality of a quotation. We are witnessing here in the stylistic device of such narrative quotation the genesis of the play. Agnes's role playing includes a constant act of self-alienation; in her epic self-stylization she uses the third person. Of herself and her immediate situation she reports: "One morning, it was a Wednesday, Agnes had to leave the cellar." At the beginning of Act Two this same device is used to recapitulate events which are not presented on stage: "Yesterday Agnes was outside. At seven o'clock when Agnes went up as ever, he was waiting already in his cap and coat." Occasionally her epic report is used as a contrapuntal device in Frisch's orchestration of dialogue. Agnes "freezes" in the middle of a discussion with her husband during which she quotes from Stepan's "stories" and then continues on another level with her narrative construction: "Three weeks earlier, when Agnes went upstairs for the first time, they had sworn to each other that they would not pay for their lives with shame." This statement is now confronted with her conflict of loyalties: her love for Stepan and her marital faithfulness to Horst. All moral conflicts are raised and discussed on this narrative level of the play, hardly ever in the dramatic re-enactment of a historical event. No doubt the influence of Bertolt Brecht was greatest on Frisch during the late 1940s, as the *Tagebuch 1946-1949* verifies. In *Als der Krieg zu Ende war* the alienation effect of Brechtian epic drama has been used for its own ends and, one might add, with considerable effect.

Frisch's second war play is the earliest example of a theatrical treatment of his diary theme "Thou shalt not make unto thee any graven image" (1946). It reintroduces the enemy image of the earlier farce *Die Chinesische Mauer*. The "Mongol dogs" reappear at the very beginning of the play when Gitta watches the Russians entering Berlin and remarks: "Nothing but Mongols!" Later, Horst Anders refers to them as "Russian swine." It is in fact the source of alienation between him and his wife who draws (again in the form of quotation) analogies with the Nazi-terminology of "Jewish swine." The Russians too have their image of the enemy; Ossip calls Agnes "You swine, German, you dung cow, Teutonic." Significantly, it is at this point that his superior officer Stepan intervenes and orders him to be silent. Both Agnes and Stepan endeavor to treat others, including the enemy, as humans; "as if we weren't all of us made of flesh and blood, humans of flesh and blood, you and I" as Agnes puts it to him. Frisch's play ends rather pessimistically. Like the earlier war play *Nun singen sie wieder*, the love of Agnes and Stepan does not suffice to overcome the graven image. Love is affirmed as a source and expression of human recognition, but ultimately it too cannot put an end to man's inhumanity to man. "Love is beautiful, Benjamin, Love above all," says the Russian Orthodox priest at the end of *Nun singen sie wieder*. "Love alone knows that it is not in vain and it alone doesn't doubt." *Als der Krieg zu Ende war* ends on a similar note. Agnes's last lines consist merely of names, the names of the men whom she loved but who would not let her love reconcile their hateful concepts of war and violence.

AGNES: Horst!
   Horst lowers his gun.
HORST: At your disposal—.
   Horst throws his gun to the floor.
STEPAN: Muij uchòdim /We're leaving here/
   Jehuda obeys with effort and exits through the sliding door. Stepan slowly turns and looks back, his face as if drained.
AGNES: Stepan Iwanow—??
   Stepan slowly takes his cap . . . and goes out.
HORST: Where's he going?
   Agnes is silent.
   He's got something planned.
   Jehuda comes with a pack, goes through the room as if it were empty; he picks up the gun from the floor.
AGNES: Jehude—?

Agnes's last words call individuals by their names, but they are no longer individuals; they have reverted to images of prejudice and hate. Frisch's extensive use of quotations as a means of epic drama ultimately leads to his very own brand of theater, the "model piece." In *Biedermann und die Brandstifter* ([Philistine and] the firebugs, 1957-1958), *Andorra* (1958-1961), and *Biografie: Ein Spiel* (Biography: A Play, 1967), Frisch's drama reaches its high point. Although his truly great plays were not written until the 1950s and 1960s, their genesis lies in the development of his early dramatic experiments. A transition to the model and play concept of his later plays is marked by the "ballad in twelve scenes" *Graf Öderland* (Count Öderland). It is based on a lengthy sketch in Frisch's *Tagebuch 1946-1949*, originally written in the year 1946; its first stage version was presented at the Schauspielhaus Zürich in 1951, but the final script was not completed until 1961. Clearly, *Graf Öderland* no longer belongs to the group of Frisch's early plays of the forties, plays which were not only conceived during the immediate postwar period but completed and performed in those years. The influence of Brecht on the young Frisch is most evident in *Die Chinesische Mauer* and *Als der Krieg zu Ende war*. In the years 1947 and 1948 Frisch's contact with Brecht was at its most intense. An entry in his *Tagebuch* from the year 1948 underlines the impact Brecht had on the young Swiss playwright: "Our association goes most smoothly when the conversation, which Brecht always leaves up to the notions and requirements of his partner, revolves around questions of the theater, of directing, acting, questions concerning also the writer's trade, which, handled soberly, inevitably lead to something of substance" (*Tagebuch* 1: 291). Predictably, Brecht showed great interest in *Als der Krieg zu Ende war*, Frisch's renewed attempt to write an epic drama dealing paradigmatically with the events of recent history. It is, as Frisch himself noted, a historical play, dramatically dated perhaps; its epic structure, however, bears the portents of Frisch's political, parabolic model theater. Thus the history of the playwright's own development illustrates the genesis of all fiction. The play as a model is not a stylistic device of "timeless" aesthetics; Frisch's play concept emerges as the highest stage of historical fiction.

"We were both dreaming." This sudden realization by the public prosecutor in the final act of *Graf Öderland* draws an obvious parallel with Max Frisch's first play *Santa Cruz*. Both dramas are "dream plays" which lead to a return of the original dilemma; their conclusions reiterate a status quo which cannot be overcome. They are plays of repetition, suggesting the eternal recurrence of paradigmatic conflicts. In *Santa Cruz*, Frisch explores the dream of reconciling marital faithfulness with a longing for individual freedom. As such the play draws an analogy between the relationship of marriage partners and the individual's limited freedom in society. Frisch portrays marriage as the most intimate social relationship. In *Graf Öderland* the dream has turned into a nightmare: the dichotomy is now between social power and individual freedom. Again the marriage, in this case that of the public prosecutor and Elsa, is in a symptomatic state of crisis; again it is the "order" of this social institution which has become indicative of a deadly order characterizing the whole of society, a society or state that Frisch calls Öderland. It could be said that *Graf Öderland* is a politicized *Santa Cruz*. Frisch's public prosecutor rebels against the very order he himself represents. In his attempt to break out of this social order he merely exemplifies the nightmare of personified power: "Whoever overthrows the present powers in order to be free takes over the opposite of freedom, the power," says the president at the conclusion of the play, "and I completely understand your personal fright." The public prosecutor's only response to this analysis of revolution is his desperate and helpless appeal "I was just being dreamed ... Wake up—now, quickly—now: Wake up—wake up—wake up!" The nightmare of an inescapable social order consists of repetitions of interchangeable patterns of power, of an eternal recurrence of the same status quo.

Of all plays, Frisch's *Graf Öderland* seems the most relevant in our present sociopolitical situation. It is indeed surprising to see that over the last decade of increasing political terrorism in the Federal Republic, only a handful of German theaters have included this play in their repertoire. Yet it clearly deals, in the form of an almost Brechtian ballad or "Moritat," with two of the most challenging issues of contemporary Western society: revolution and anarchy. In a series of didactic scenes (Frisch calls them "Bilder") the play demonstrates the cyclic sequence of revolution and restoration, of anarchy and order. It takes up one of the themes of the earlier war play *Nun singen sie wieder*, when it analyzes the totality of power. "I don't want any power!" exclaims the public prosecutor as revolutionary leader. "I want life!" This then is the central theme of *Graf Öderland*: how to live with power. The longing for freedom—in *Santa Cruz* primarily, though not exclusively, a matter of private self-assertion—inevitably leads to the use of violence, as the fate of the murderer illustrates. Yet his freedom is short-lived; in his renewed attempt to stay free he is himself murdered by the police. Freedom to Frisch seems an almost Kierkegaardian grace, a spiritual concept in conflict with political realities. "I am pardoned," claims the Mörder to a police officer. "Not every one can say that." Characteristically, this grace which the murderer experiences in the form of an amnesty is trivialized, caricatured, and ridiculed by the officer's and his own misunderstanding of the nature of such freedom. Both misunderstand his amnesty as "amnesia," a forgetfulness which characterizes the entire Öderland. "Amnesia, that is a fact," reports the murderer, "in all the land." The restoration of the original pattern of power exemplifies a loss of memory in the people of Öderland, including the former public prosecutor: their dreams of freedom have been forgotten; in their attempt to realize these dreams they have turned them into nightmares. Öderland is the reality of their nightmares, the restoration of an order without which they cannot live. The castle of *Santa Cruz* has become the safety and order of Öderland. Power may change hands but only to reinstate the original status quo; the former revolutionary ends as leader of a new government which proves no less dictatorial, no less "orderly," no less "barren" (Öderland). This play of Frisch's concerns itself with the totalitarianism inherent in power. As soon as any challenge to social power succeeds in the name of freedom, it turns against itself and restores the original pattern of restrictions, laws, regulations, prohibitions, and control over the individual. It is this type of violent order which cannot be overcome by violence, it can only return to itself. Frisch shows the inevitable logic of such a process. He demonstrates that freedom is relative and in fact a concept which is, more often than not, an aspect of power and violence itself. This play then has a political urgency and relevance far surpassing Frisch's earlier dramas, and it is its further development toward a model theater which enables it to exemplify its lesson paradigmatically.

Don Juan oder Die Liebe zur Geometrie (Don Juan or The Love of Geometry) was first written in 1952, later revised in 1961. It re-presents in the form of a comedy several of Frisch's earlier preoccupations. The most obvious theme of the play is the search for an individual identity. *Don Juan*, however, is above all a drama about marriage—in the incongruity of the Don Juan theme and the subject of marriage lies the basis for its treatment as a comedy. In one sense, *Don Juan oder Die Liebe zur Geometrie* continues Frisch's dramatic analysis of marriage and as such stands in line with his earlier plays *Santa Cruz* and *Graf Öderland*. It is hardly a coincidence that *Don Juan* opens with a scene "before the castle" and ends with a mock idyllic scene in the "castle in Ronda." As in *Santa Cruz*, the castle is a symbol of marriage; Acts One and Three take place "before the castle," i.e., prior to Don Juan's wedding; Acts Two and Five show him inside the castle, "im Schloss," i.e., in the process of getting married (Act Two) and in the state of being married (Act Five). Significantly, the only time Don Juan appears in his own environment is in Act Four in which he stages his own theater of the self (Ich-Theater). It is the theatricality of his existence, the socially imposed need for role playing, which makes the stage his personal domain. He is finally caught in a "castle with twenty-four rooms," in a marriage with relative freedom which retains the elements of stylized role playing: he is married to the prostitute Miranda who has been elevated to the status of duchess. As lady and ruler of her castle she combines the attributes of her former prostitution with the pure love of Don Juan's former bride Donna Anna whom she impersonates and ultimately replaces. Frisch characterizes the wife as part whore and part bride, marriage as a "prison in paradisiacal gardens." With this devastating combination the woman finally defeats Don Juan, i.e., the freedom of man. "I'm her prisoner, you know," complains Don Juan to the bishop, "Don't forget that, I cannot leave this castle."

As in *Santa Cruz* and *Graf Öderland*, Frisch's first comedy is preoccupied with the uniqueness of love and personal identity. Both are related but cannot be regulated or institutionalized, as in marriage. "That was love, I believe, that was love," claims Don Juan, remembering his nightly encounter with Donna Anna. "For the first and last time. There is no return." The irony is that his unique experience was possible only because of the anonymity of their love. When Miranda appears to him in the guise of Donna Anna, Don Juan beseeches her: "I deserted you. Why this return? I deserted you." Repetition becomes a theatrical device; it can only occur where masks are employed, where individuals stage their own role playing. Frisch makes more and more use of such theatrical repetitions; in *Biografie* he stylizes the rehearsal as a new form of drama. "How could you still believe that I love you?" Don Juan asks the mask of Donna Anna. "I thought the expectation would never return." It is only because it is in fact Miranda that he can fall for the theatrical misunderstanding "We lost each other in order to find each other forever." It is in the nature of man-woman relationships that confusion and illusion prevail. The lover may only return under a different guise; there is in fact no repetition of love. As Don Juan says at the end of Act Three: the real bride is "she who appeared once again before the confused one so that I would recognize her, and I did recognize her." Yet, as soon as Miranda removes her veil, he discovers his mistake. How then does love identify itself? It must be borne in mind that Miranda and Don Juan do in fact love each other; appropriately enough, both have been prostitutes as well as bride and bridegroom.

Frisch introduces a theme that was to become central in his later novel *Mein Name sei Gantenbein* (Wilderness of Mirrors). It is only through betrayal that the uniqueness of the individual can be identified. Don Juan complains to his friend Roderigo that all women seemed the same to him during his riotous wedding night—except for one. "But she had something, the last woman on this confused night, something that no one else has or will ever have again, something unique that charmed him . . . she was the bride of his only friend." To this friend he admits: "Your name burned on our foreheads and we indulged in the sweetness of perfidy until the cocks crowed."

The authentic I can be experienced wherever it is betrayed or itself betrays. Gantenbein's Christ analogy serves as a further illustration of this. Love, to Frisch, is the unknown, including the unknown qualities and characteristics in the beloved. Lovers then are by definition individuals in search of each other, unknown to themselves. Sexual love is experienced by Don Juan as an eternal repetition of the same, exchangeable emotions: "Not until it's there again do I know: That's how it is, yes, that's how it always was," he confesses to his ladies. Repetition of reality, on the other hand, is a theatrical device; it is a re-enactment of something unique. That is why during the "wild night" of pre-Christian times everyone who participated in the sexual promiscuity also wore a mask. Father Diego reports: "Everybody paired off with everybody when they had a longing, and no one knew during that night whom he embraced. For everyone wore the same mask." Don Juan's life too is turned into a theatrical spectacle, the social consequence of his individual theater of the self. "They're presenting it in the theater now," the bishop informs Juan. He expresses Frisch's own concept of the theater when he declares: "Truth cannot be shown, only invented." Repetition too is such an invention. Ultimately, therefore, authenticity and truth can only be imagined; which in turn must mean that our imagination cannot be merely repetition or reduplication. Thus, one of the key lines of the play is Don Juan's reply to the bishop's inquiry "Have you seen the spectacle in Sevilla?"—the spectacle, that is, of his own life: "I don't make it to Sevilla." As with Santorin, Santa Cruz, or Peking, Sevilla proves for Don Juan a place beyond his reach; it is the stage where he, in all the theatricality of his own role playing, would be at home. Instead, he is "at home" in the castlelike or fortresslike marital bonds to Miranda, forced to play the social roles assigned to them.

Frisch calls his *Biedermann und die Brandstifter* (The Firebugs, 1957-1958), rather flirtatiously a didactic play without a moral (Lehrstück ohne Lehre). In the context of the play, the subtitle is borne out by the closing lines of the Chorus:

> Much is senseless, and nothing
> More senseless than this story:
> Which, namely, once enkindled,
> Killed many, ah, but not all
> And changed nothing at all.

It is fair to say that *Biedermann* is the most Brechtian of all Frisch's plays. Like the later *Andorra* (1958-1961), it offers a dramatic analysis of social behavior. In *Biedermann*, however, Frisch relies rather more heavily on the spoken word than on the kind of theatrical demonstration which makes *Andorra* an altogether more dramatic performance. It is easy to trace *Biedermann* back to its origin as a radio play. In Frisch's *Lehrstück*, unlike Brecht's epic drama, the rhetoric of the argument is not balanced by its sensuous staging. The grotesque humor of *Biedermann* derives almost entirely from linguistic misunderstandings or a particular kind of hypocrisy which expresses itself in language. In the most literal sense, the pattern of this play is predictable. In the first scene Biedermann quotes from his newspaper: "Another one of those door-to-door pedlars (Hausierer), one who nests up in the attic, a harmless pedlar," only to be interrupted by the maid who announces "The pedlar, who would like to speak with you." Even Biedermann's instictive lie "I'm not at home!" linguistically emphasizes the social relationship between the fire raiser and himself. It is as house owner that Biedermann is haunted by the intruders; their anarchic arson is directed against the very concept of bourgeois ownership. Biedermann is willing to treat Schmitz as a beggar in the hope of buying him off, but he is determined to keep him away from his house: "But no one is coming into my house." His concept of humanity is based on house ownership; as he says to the fire raisers: "Finally and at last, gentlemen, I am the owner of this house." It is this combination of ownership and humanism which characterizes bourgeois culture and leads to its ultimate downfall. Biedermann cannot tolerate any questioning or challenging of either of his concepts. By contrast, the revolutionary anarchists maintain "Every citizen is culpable, to be exact, from a certain income level on." It is idle to want to identify more closely the revolutionary program of the fire raisers; they are clearly meant to personify forces determined to destroy bourgeois values. Frisch is at pains not to specify their particular political persuasions, if indeed they have any. Like the intellectual who wishes to detach himself from the violence of a bourgeois overthrow (when it is too late), the fire raisers are clearly meant to be types, identifiable only through their model behavior.

The play is therefore an analysis of social hypocrisy, complacency, and inaction. Frisch draws a bourgeois Biedermann who will not identify himself, even where his attitudes are ludicrously obvious. By contrast, his opponents make no attempt to hide their identities, without being recognized by Biedermann. As so often in the drama of Max Frisch we are witnessing a spectacle of confusion. It is no longer simply individual role playing which leads to deception and frustration; now the theater of the self is replaced by a theater of society. Both the anarchic fire raisers and the bourgeois Everyman are violent; the only difference is that Schmitz and Eisenring do not disguise their intentions. Biedermann on the other hand characteristically reconciles his violence with certain bourgeois values: "I'm too good-natured," he agrees with his wife, "you're right: I'm going to twist this Knechtling's throat around." Unaware of the absurd contradictions of such statements, he can argue: "I don't believe in class differences!" only to continue, "I sincerely regret that right in the lower classes; they're still blathering about class differences."

Biedermann tries to resolve concrete social conflicts by escaping into vague concepts of humanism, themselves a manifestation of bourgeois values. His social attitudes are characterized by vanity and fear. Because he has a guilty conscience about the values he enacts or implies, Biedermann will not identify them. Instead, in his attempts to disguise them, he is anxious to appear to be in agreement with the intruders. "The two gentlemen, namely, still think me to be a fearful philistine," he says to his wife, "who doesn't have any humor, you know, that you can bully and frighten." As Frisch has argued elsewhere, nothing is as philistine as the fear of being a philistine. When Biedermann has a chance to protect himself from the violence of the fire raisers, it is his own guilt—his responsibility for the death of Knechtling—which prevents him from handing the intruders over to the police. He is in fact acting in collusion with the very forces that threaten to destroy his way of life. Significantly, the police officer in a false reference identifies Schmitz and Eisenring as Biedermann's "employees." Together they assure the police that the petrol under Biedermann's roof is in fact hair tonic. Both benefit from the bourgeois system of economic exploitation. As a result of this collusion, Biedermann offers the fire raisers his friendship. As the play progresses, he more and more comes to identify himself with them.

Biedermann und die Brandstifter logically progresses from Frisch's earlier farce *Die Chinesische Mauer*. Here, too, the protagonists address themselves directly to the audience (Biedermann, Babette, Dr. phil., Chor). However, in this *Lehrstück* these speeches serve less as a dramaturgical device of alienation than a directly didactic purpose. As Biedermann says in his address: "You can think about me, gentlemen, whatever you want. But answer this one question for me." Frisch's stage direction at the end of the Dr. phil.'s demonstration to the audience seems almost too obviously didactic: "The academician climbs over the stage apron and sits down in the parterre section." By comparison with *Die Chinesische Mauer* this is a far more provocative play, designed to involve the audience to a much greater extent. No doubt, despite its subtitle, Frisch's *Biedermann* hopes to incite in his audience a willingness to political action. Of his earlier plays, one similarity with *Graf Öderland* cannot be overlooked. Both are "revolutionary plays," both are nonspecific about the political identity of the forces determined to overthrow the social status quo. And as in *Graf Öderland*, the maid announces at the end of the play: "The sky is burning!" Both dramas amount to an appeal for greater political consciousness, for a more articulate identification of social values.

The spectator must be reminded that he is watching a model, as indeed is the nature of theater, Frisch wrote with reference to his best known play *Andorra*. He simply calls it "A drama in twelve scenes." If it stands in the tradition of *Die Chinesische Mauer, Graf Öderland,* and *Biedermann und die Brandstifter*, developing as it does the concept of model theater, it also has at least one other thing in common with *Graf Öderland*: both plays are structurally divided into twelve scenes or "Bilder." The "Bild" holds a special significance for Frisch; it is not simply a dramatic scene but also the graven image toward which his theater directs itself. In the context of the drama of Max Frisch, the "Bild" has a very special dramaturgical significance: it is neither an attempt to represent realistically a place of action nor an antiillusionary device to shock his audience into a state of sociopolitical self-alienation. Frisch speaks of a basic image/scene (Grundbild) for the whole play, which is in fact the market square of his fictitious Andorra. This basic

"Bild" is meant to be ever present throughout the play; all other scenes appear as reflections of this "Grundbild" of Andorra. In other words: Frisch's theatrical "Bild"-concept presents the image of an image. As he directs in his annotations to the play: "All scenes that do not take place on the plaza of Andorra are presented in front of it." The entire drama unfolds as a reflection and projection of the real creator of images: the society based on fear and prejudice called Andorra. It is in this sense that Frisch remarks: "Andorra is the name for a model."

The line of the bishop in the earlier play *Don Juan oder Die Liebe zur Geometrie*, "Truth cannot be shown, only invented," refers specifically to the interaction of prejudice and images staged by society's own brand of theater. It is therefore not only the basis of Frisch's own drama but raises a general question extending far beyond the function of the stage. How can social play acting be revealed for what it is, political role playing in relation to power? With reference to *Andorra*: how can the truth of individual and social role playing be exposed? Clearly, not by imitating it but, according to Frisch, by analyzing the dynamics of this social process. His theater therefore uses "Bilder" which are neither fictional nor antifictional but which offer a critical anatomy of society's own staging of prejudice and persecution of the individual in the name of an image of man based on power and the right of might. *Andorra* is, above all, a play about truth; the staging of it and its "unstaging." It is obvious that Frisch owes a great deal to Bertolt Brecht, yet his own model theater is characterized by its own kind of didactic intent.

Another line from *Don Juan* could be seen as the basis of Frisch's special brand of "epic drama." It is Celestina's lament "Why does truth have it so difficult in Spain?" Again and again Frisch analyzes social distortions, manipulations, and exploitations of truth. It is a truth which, for him, identifies itself most clearly in the uniqueness of the individual. Only the integrity of an individual can bear witness to the truth. Society's treatment of individual beings therefore is indicative of its attitude to truth. A social outsider is almost always an articulate critic of social hypocrisy and violence. Truth in that sense has a difficult time in all societies, not only in Spain, not only in Andorra. What the teacher says to the carpenter lies at the basis of Frisch's model theater: "I see what's there and I say what I see, and all of you see it too." *Andorra* is a play about the difficulty of speaking the truth in a society determined to pretend it does not exist. "They will be amazed when I tell them the truth," claims the teacher. Yet truth is manipulated to such an extent that none of the witnesses who take the stand after their fateful betrayal of Andri (the "other" Andorran) admits to any guilt or part in his downfall. Andri appeals in despair: "How is it that you all are stronger than the truth?" The answer lies in his gradual realization that they can defeat truth by being stronger; their very power can manipulate and destroy truth.

Andri comes up against Andorrans like the doctor who, being a spokesman of Andorran power, can insist from a different angle "surely one can still tell the truth in Andorra." His truth is the truth of ruthless prejudice and resentment, a complete manipulation of facts for the sake of defending his own personal and social interests. Andri's father anticipates the despair of the final tragedy when he askes the Senora: "And if they don't want the truth?" Society cannot be forced to accept the truth of individual rights and the freedom of personal existence. Frisch makes it clear that society must want to face truth, and that only individuals can appeal to it. One of the most significant exchanges in the play takes place between the Senora and Andri. "The truth will judge them," says Andri's mother, "and you, Andri, are the only one here who doesn't have to fear the truth." Andri's reply testifies to his growing awareness of the difference between individual and social truths. "Which truth?" he asks. It is a question that remains unanswered. In his subsequent conversation with the priest, Andri expresses his knowledge of the relativity of social truth.

FATHER: Andri, That is the truth.
ANDRI: How many truths do all of you have?

Andri is the only one who reaches an understanding of truth which is both personal and social. As he says to the priest, "Already now I don't need any more enemies, the truth is sufficient." It is the need for imaginary opponents, antisocial forces, and "enemies" which has taken our societies further and further away from truth. The only other kind of truth an Andorran society can offer is symbolized in the final "Bild" of the play: covered by black cloths and forced into anonymity Andorrans face each other and keep asking "You there. Who am I? ... Who are you? ... Don't you all recognize me?" The so-called blacks are not so much a foreign force intent on invading Andorra as representatives of the dark forces of mass violence and untruth. It is a part of themselves which takes over the control of Andorran society. Social power is forever in need of a scapegoat; any individual who challenges its principles of order must be made an example of. That is the fate of Andri. He is gradually becoming aware of the pattern of individual persecution in the name of a social truth. Frisch reintroduces a theme so prevalent in his earlier plays: that of repetition and recurrence. "What's coming has all already happened before," says Andri to Barblin, expressing his newly gained understanding of the model kind of behavior which surrounds him. The complementary remark from the Andorran establishment is made by the doctor at the opening of the final "Bild"; for him there is no doubt that despite the "invasion" of the blacks, "Everything's remaining as before ... Andorra is going to remain Andorran." That too is an expression of a social pattern, a model of social existence, a paradigm of social survival. It is easy to see then why for Frisch the theme of repetition is linked with his concept of a model theater. Almost all his plays end with a return to the social status quo. They are, to a greater or lesser extent, "Lehrstücke ohne Lehren." In that, however, lies the challenge, even provocation of the drama of Max Frisch.

Biografie: Ein Spiel (Biography: A Play, 1967) is the culmination of all Frisch's earlier dramas. Most of the major themes reappear in this, the most comprehensive play he has written. Here the spheres of private and public life intermingle; the individual identity finds itself defined both by personal and by social forces. The play of biography is no longer merely a theater of the self, nor is it the exclusive domain of society at large. *Biografie* balances the private self-definition of *Santa Cruz* with the public role playing of *Andorra*. Dramaturgically, this means that in Frisch's more recent drama the theater is enacting itself. Instead of subjective self-projections and/or the creation of prejudicial images by society, instead of a private *Ich-Theater* or a socially oriented *Gesellschafts-Theater*, the newer play *Biografie* emerges as total theater. And it is specifically the absence of any dogmatically held view by Frisch or the play itself which makes the theatrical rehearsal the intellectual, moral, and artistic basis of this drama. One important aspect of a rehearsal is of course repetition, a central theme in all Frisch's dramas. Here repetition is neither accepted nor rejected as in so many of his earlier plays; it is simply reconciled with the logic of an all-embracing self-expression. It is in harmony with the very medium of representational self-expression. The stage has become, more than ever before, a realm of self-reflection. As such, it is the center of the play, it is the center of conflict, the essence of our consciousness. In *Biografie* the theme itself is presented as a variation. Max Frisch explores the identity of choice, the private and public existence based on freedom. As such, the play analyzes the mechanics of historical existence, the process of gradual identification. Only this development is inevitable, its influences, both private and public, may alter and are largely a matter of choice. The reconstruction of an individual identity does not demonstrate the fatefulness of its biography, it merely illustrates the inevitability of acquiring any identity. Identity is inescapable; biography, a game played according to its rules. Kürmann's freedom of choice lies in the playful range of his selfdom, his performance in the game is limited by the need to be identified. This play of Frisch's is a sublime comedy about man's imprisonment in his self-styled freedom. If he wants to find himself, he is in need of identification, both privately and publicly; once he is discovered though, he has lost the freedom of continuous individual choice.

The theme of repetition—*Wiederholung*—well known from Frisch's earlier plays, is introduced by a quotation from Anton Chekov's drama *Three*

Sisters. Vershinin's contemplation of a second chance to live his life reaches its peak in his conviction "Each one of us would then endeavor, so I think, above all to not repeat himself.—" Frisch introduces a number of devices which signify the theme of repetition throughout the play. Among them are the piano-playing accompanying a ballet rehearsal next door to Kürmann's residence, the extensive use of quotations and reruns of individual scenes, the symbolic clock work (reminiscent of *Die Chinesische Mauer*), and the recurrence of certain dilemmas in a following generation (cf. Kürmann's son Thomas: "I can't hear it any more: When I was your age! Maybe that's the way it was, just as he says, but it's not like that any more. He's always coming up with his biography!" Or Kürmann's mother being treated in the hospital in exactly the same manner as, later, Kürmann himself: "You see, Mr. Kürmann, you see: Flowers from your son in America. All roses. . . . Such a son." Cf. "You see, Mrs. Kürmann, you see: Flowers from your son in America. All roses. . . . Such a son."). However, it is in his conversation with Krolevsky that the concept of repetition gains a new dimension for Kürmann. At first, it is merely on a private and personal level that he can say to his visitor: "I don't need to repeat myself" and, a little later: "You don't need to repeat yourself either, Krolevsky." At the end of their conversation Kürmann applies his fear of repetition to society at large: "If we can begin once again, we all know what we have to do differently." This is a reference to political behavior, to social opposition, to attempts to alter the sociopolitical structure which determines the lives of individuals. In an exchange with the Registrator, the social and the private spheres intermingle: "You stand under the suspicion of wanting to change the world. No one will come upon the suspicion of your wanting merely to change your biography." In that sense, too, *Biografie* could be defined as a comedy of errors.

It is in the second part of the play that Kürmann begins to sense a uniqueness which remains, but which, ironically, he is unable to accept. Antoinette leaves him after they have spent the night together: "Bygones are bygones," the Registrator records, "she doesn't even insist upon the intimacy of the evening conversation." Kürmann is shocked ("not a word of seeing each other again?") and can only repeat his amazement ("I don't understand it—"). Finally he comes to the conclusion that Antoinette is a unique woman ("eine einmalige Frau"), *einmalig*, that is, in the most literal sense, a woman who does not live repetitions. When he tries to stop her from leaving him, he pleads with her: "We don't even know each other," to which Antoinette replies (rather like Frisch's earlier protagonist Don Juan): "that's what's beautiful about it." In a different context Kürmann too discovers the uniqueness of experience, a reality that cannot be repeated. "Do we have to repeat everything?" he asks the Registrator, "Even the happiness and everything . . . that won't do." The happiness of unique moments in his life, moments of a shared reality, Kürmann cannot relive: "–our happy conversations. . . . How could they be repeated when the secrets have already been used." The identity of such experience calls the entire concept of repetition into doubt. It is in the sphere of social interaction then that uniqueness can be discovered. Repetition can only be overcome in a shared reality, not in an attempt to escape from a socially defined identity.

The clash of social and private life lies at the center of Frisch's comedy. *Biografie*, like so many of Frisch's plays, is a drama about marriage. It is in marriage that the private and social identities merge, it is again the most intimate social relationship. Kürmann's wife Antoinette pleads for a sense of proportion when she asks: "Assume I had slept with a man last night or every time that you imagine it: What then? I ask you, what then? I ask you, Would that then be the destruction of the world by fire?" Destruction of private confidence is juxtaposed here with the total annihilation of all mankind. In the same manner, the following dialogue between Kürmann and the Registrator unfolds:

KÜRMANN: I ask: What transpires in a month?
REGISTRATOR: Summer of 1963. *He looks in the dossier:* "Konrad Adenauer considers his retirement.
KÜRMANN: I mean here, what happens here?

Again, Frisch is intent on showing the relative triviality of Kürmann's private obsessions. Another exchange between Kürmann and his Registrator sounds almost like a certain brand of criticism which has been lodged against Max Frisch himself:

REGISTRATOR: . . . Don't you have anything in your head other than your marriage?
KÜRMANN: Be quiet.
REGISTRATOR: Is that your problem in this world?

It is, of course; Frisch's no less than Kürmann's. How to realize oneself socially has remained the overriding theme of the drama of Max Frisch. It was appropriate then that marriage should play such a central part in his theater. In the discovery of the marriage partner as a complementary alter ego lies the root of a social self-acceptance. The "holy cross" of marriage and the egotistical playfulness of a Don Juan can once again be reconciled and harmonized to a "play" of identity which is both exploratory and enjoyable.

Frisch's latest play, *Triptychon* (1978), appears to be a counterversion of *Biografie*. It analyzes the finality of life from a theatrical realm of death. Not time but death determines the inevitability of an individual biography. This is not a new insight, not even in the works of Frisch; already *Homo faber*

(1957) saw death as the executor of a personal history. Nor is it new that Frisch stages a sphere of death: both *Nun singen sie wieder* (1946) and the epilogue to *Biedermann und die Brandstifter* (1958) cast the dead as reflections of their self-projection in life. *Triptychon* is by no means the play of an old man afraid of death. The subject of death has always been a central aspect in Frisch's dramatic analysis of man's identity.

Triptychon is made up of three, loosely interrelated, "scenes," each with its own dramatis personae (even if a few overlap). It does not claim to add up to a "play"; instead, it offers repeated attempts to relate death back to life: to our social values, to our concepts of science, philosophy, and religion, to our relationships in love, hate, and indifference. Frisch's "death" is a theatrical device, the pretext for a dramatic analysis of human reality, of man's identity, of his self-concept. Despite the religious model from which the work takes its title, Frisch at no stage glorifies or mystifies death. His scenic triptychon is clearly an expression of faith on the altar of the theater. Only the stage can realize death and use it as a means of social analysis. Again, Frisch has made extreme use of the theater, because he knows that it allows him to rehearse, to demonstrate, and to recognize behavior in a concrete, sensuous, and exemplary fashion.

The discovery that unites all three scenes is a secularized eternity of being: death perpetuates our lives. What may have appeared to be a mere coincidence is turned into an inevitable fate. Death makes our life count, it makes it valid. In a rather Nietzschean manner it rules over an eternal recurrence of the same. Theatrical repetition, varied re-enactment through rehearsals, emerges as a lively exercise; life itself appears, by comparison, to be deadly and final. The ultimate triumph of the stage is that it can treat death as a variation, as a technical device, as a rehearsal. Frisch's theatrical realm of death serves the art of self-knowledge; it allows for change, its model demonstration aims at a new understanding, a different kind of being. It does not want to perpetuate our life, such as it is, but strives to alter it. Frisch's theater is an agent of change.

It is significant that as soon as the widow Sophie Proll sees her dead husband Matthis (17), she begins to quote the living (9/18, 9/20) and to misquote the dead (22). The living distort the lives of the dead. In their confrontation the living seem to be dead and the dead very much alive. The extensive use of quotations indicates repetition, even in thought and speech. The priest can only quote his alleged faith and knowledge. In the second scene the clochard, representing the theater (he used to be an actor), constantly quotes from world drama: Shakespeare, Diderot, Strindberg. Death is a process ("La mort est successive," Diderot); in that alone lies its theatricality. The clochard (and with it the theater of Max Frisch) manages to unfold this process, to reveal "the corpse within us" (61). As always with

Frisch, the theater serves the function of enlightening man, not in the form of abstractions or with philosophical pretensions, but as a model, in sensuous analysis. In this way, man becomes more and more identified with the theater—indeed, he is the theater. His life consists of role playing. He is quoting not only classical literature but increasingly his own identity as well. Death is seen as the eternal repetition of the self-quotations we have lived. As the dead Katrin says to the old man: "We're going in circles" (66). Not surprisingly after such knowledge she wishes never to have lived (68). The mother too does not want to live again (71). Death is an enlightening force which reveals life such as it has been lived (68). Yet, even in death, there seems no hope, no redemption: man remains the same, he seems unable to change his identity. The priest keeps comforting the dead, promising them a life beyond death. As Katrin tells Xaver: "we tell each other the same things, nothing new is added" (72). The dead clochard reminds us of the theatricality of the living: his memory is exhausted, he tells us, now others are playing his role (83). Death is demythologized by the theater; it becomes another tool of analyzing and assessing social behavior. Frisch offers a dialectical definition of death: it is both repetition and redefinition. The social dimensions of a death which continues to define our age are unmistakeably articulated in the form of political criticism.

Francine and Roger, the protagonists of the third scene, feel that they were alive only as long as they could rethink the world. Man's inability to change is seen here as a form of social death. With reference to the dead Lenin whom Francine remembers in his mausoleum in Moscow, she laments that we live with the dead who do not rethink (106/107). Repetitions and quotations thus gain an added significance, they are an indication of our unwillingness to change, our inability to think, our deadly existence. As Francine puts it: "we've said it all" (111). Frisch shows in his *Triptychon* how all acts, thoughts, and misunderstandings are repeated in death; death becomes the stage for re-enacting our lives. The finality does not lie in death but in our unthinking life, in our inability to do anything other than repeat ourselves. Life itself is seen as a form of deadly self-quotation. As such, it is unsocial, sterile, uncommunicative. It seems that in both life and death only repetition or silence are possible (cf. 93/94). Significantly, the scenes end in repetitions and self-quotations (114/115) which become synonymous with Roger's suicide.

Not a play dealing with the fear of death then but scenes reflecting on man's seemingly incurable social laziness, his inability to change, intellectually, emotionally, morally. Death in this case can only confirm the triviality of such being. Katrin puts it most explicitly when she says at the end of the second scene: "eternity is banal" (84). What Frisch means as well is that human banality too seems eternal. *Triptychon* has more in common with

Biedermann than may at first appear. It shares above all the lament over man's incorrigible selfishness and his inability or unwillingness to learn, to change, to think dynamically. As such, these scenes must be seen as an appeal to live creatively, socially, and intelligently. The moralist Frisch has written another "Lehrstück ohne Lehre," both in content and form. His scenes do not therefore add up to the total unity of a traditional play concept. In his self-negating didacticism Frisch too has taken refuge in quoting himself. Xaver asks in the second scene: "Why aren't the people living?" (48) And later he repeats the question when he asks Herr Proll: "—did you live?" (80) Both lines repeat the concern of the traveling performer (Vagant) in Frisch's early play *Santa Cruz* (1947). It is difficult not to apply the despair of Roger to Frisch himself: that he too is talking with the dead (99). *Triptychon* was written by a social moralist who, like his clochard, realizes that death is gradual but who sees signs of this death all around him, who does not restrict death to the individual, any more than life. *Triptychon*'s real subject is a social death, in fact: the death of society.

HANS BÄNZIGER

Frisch as a Narrator

Frisch's first major work following his private book burning[1] was *Blätter aus dem Brotsack* (Pages from the knapsack), written during his military service in 1939 and published in 1940. As he relates there, he entered the border guard service as a regular army recruit, convinced that Switzerland was going to be drawn into the war. An apprehension of never being able to return home gave these jottings a greater seriousness than any of his earlier journal confessions. They became the mirroring of an endangered man—much as Gottfried Keller's diary of a century earlier was the mirroring of an enthusiastic politician and lyricist with a bad conscience. As a hundred years earlier, a sobering consciousness forces itself upon the spirit of the time. "In the future all faith will have to prove itself on bare walls" reads one of the first remarks. Camaraderie counts a lot; brotherhood of persuasions, little. The battle in itself would be senseless gods' play, but it had to be fought if the Swiss Confederacy's territory was infringed upon.

History, as observed from a Tercino village, appears to Frisch to be indistinct. When contact with world developments is interrupted, one senses a feeling of being lost. With that experience, one's neighbor counts more— the buddy brushing his teeth or the one needing to go to the infirmary. Even one's superior counts more. Describing the swearing-in of his battery, Frisch shows himself as one who fits into his greater community with a remarkable matter-of-factness. It is an objective integration, no glorification depending upon mystifications of the flag and homeland; shortly before the swearing-in he writes: "We do not want to surrender the infinite, whether it is called God or something else, nor to make an idol, strangling the human element in us, of the earth bequeathed us; we will love our fatherland and defend it, but never worship it."

The military community appears to Frisch to be free of prejudices and bourgeois elements; the recruit loves the bare walls and is occasionally fearful of his return to civilian life. Once again a Swiss writer admits that he is happy about the times that seized him in their iron grip—a Swiss who must have lived a complex bourgois life and was seeking deliverance from the bourgeoisie. This attitude corresponds to that of Albin Zollinger's *Bohnenblust* (Bean blossoming, 1942). It is closer to the times than the attitude of most other Swiss authors—to name only two examples, one could compare Welti's *Steibruch* (1939) or Zemp's *Gedichte* (poems, 1943). Nevertheless, Frisch did not write in the style of a heroic nihilism or with the cold skepticism of most Germans.

In contrast to Meinrad Inglin's closed picture of the *Schweizerspiegel* (Swiss mirror) from the first border occupation, the diary form was appropriate. In the literature of World War II, fragmentary structures were a popular expedient. Unable to encompass the larger contexts, writers hoped to make do with "insights." Here and there, perhaps in Ernst Jünger's *Strahlungen* (Radiations), this assumed moderation became a pose and coquetry. Frisch here presents himself as the keeper of a log book, as a steersman near the maelstrom. Max Frisch prevents any empathy with his cool pose. As a man who had to earn his daily living, he had at first no leisure time to work out all his ideas. He had time only to jot down the most important things in cafés. Almost all the sketches for his later works are found in the diaries. For him the diary was a necessary solution—and hence a natural form. To be sure, like Keller and unlike Gotthelf and Dürrenmatt, Frisch was also personally predestined for this loose form of notebooks.

If the public ever abandons or insults Frisch, he can retreat into himself; thus arose the *Tagebuch mit Marion* (Diary with Marion, 1947) and the enlargement *Tagebuch 1946-1949*. In no way does a fear of censorship force him to write these notebooks of a most private nature; indeed, he is no pronounced moralist. But this style is also determined by something of the spirit of despotism (in Switzerland of certain anonymous powers, of the public opinion) and by something of the needs of an eighteenth-century man to become at one with himself through reflection. There is even a rather direct path from Kierkegaard to the diarist Frisch. To be sure, even in disguise Frisch is a contemporary man directed toward this world and existence; he battles as one engaged in his nonengagement. Only by way of exception do words and thoughts simply fall into his lap; and if they ever do, it is most likely when he profits from being an author with a Swiss passport able to gather impressions more quickly and comfortably. It would seem then that a willingness to absorb new ideas, an openness to anything different, and a sovereignty were a matter of course for him during the mid-1940s, while reflection was a luxury.

Karl Krolow and other Germans have felt his work to be typically Swiss; the peaceful humane tone, the "chronicle-like communication" became possible from a distance. Krolow says also, "Frisch's diary belongs to the type that puts private information—even though it is permitted—in the margins next to the entries and has the trait of being 'public'; 'public' is understood here in an extended sense, even traceable in the author's tendency toward the parable, toward an 'exemplary' consciousness, a certain chattiness that draws conclusions. To his public aspect belong also the cities, the landscapes, the people of these landscapes that Frisch often records precisely as in a snapshot, macabre and tender scenes, colors, lights, but also gray-covered views, fittingly paltry, masculine melancholy that cannot be held back but rushes on to the next note which stands there all the more luminous and plausible."[2]

On the other hand, the *Blätter* and the diaries also furnish evidence of a lack of distance, of that which has not been overcome, of that which is serious and private. The sharp reprimand of a captain which the soldier Frisch had brought upon himself (recorded in the *Blätter* and *Tagebuch*) recurs in Stiller.[3] Did this experience remain fixed in his memory so long because, as was frankly admitted in the first notes, Frisch needed compensation for his lack of a father?

Three years following the soldier's book appeared Frisch's first major novel, a work in which a uniform can no longer obscure the difficulties of normal life, in love and in friendship. *J'adore ce qui me brûle oder die Schwierigen* (I adore what burns me or the difficult characters, 1943)— published fourteen years later in a new edition without the first part ("Reinhard oder die Jugend") and with the title *Die Schwierigen oder J'adore ce que me brûle*—is a novel of an artist like Keller's *Der Grüne Heinrich* (Green Henry) and a series of variations on the theme of love like *Das Sinngedicht* (The epigram). The beauty of nature is intact here while men, gripped by the power of love and transitoriness, drift toward their end. Keller's legacy, however, appears on the whole to be unimportant. "A breath of ancient tragedy" (Korrodi) can be felt in the very first chapters and throughout. Jürg Reinhart, the novel's hero who would like to kill his father, does not master the "knot of senseless life" until he destroys himself. Love consumes those who are insufficient. A curse rests upon the family of difficult characters. As men they are not equal to their women; Turandot masters them.

In this novel we encounter various elements in embryo form that are portrayed more thoroughly in later works: the problem of the semi-artist afflicted with wanderlust, the problem of marriage and fatherhood, the problem of the bourgeoisie. It is already evident that besides being the shock of the bourgeois, Frisch is also a keen observer of the viable forces of order. One thinks of the scene in which Hortense's father, an imposing colonel, finishes his correspondence and conscientiously responds to the petitioners, while at the same time indignantly pushing aside Jürg Reinhart's letter with its vain and sensual script. The landlord, Yvonne's husband, is a man of honor, even more so than the artist when seen in the novel as a whole. Among the bourgeois, human relations are still possible; among intellectuals, hardly at all. For them everything is interlude, futility, senseless repetition. The young artist is pained by the heritage of the western world because it points out his impotence.

Reinhart respects those elements that burn. In the self-characterization of Stiller, that is called a weakness for radicalisms. In this novel, at least, he cannot come to terms with the peaceful and orderly elements. The precise and structuralized quiet life, which makes an existence with others possible, contains too little for him that is not conditioned. In his next prose work we read the expression of the same idea: "Whoever does not give his earth over to fire so that it burns—how should there ever develop a spirit in him?"[4] That is spoken by a saint in an area behind the Chinese wall while he has a courtesan on his knees.

There are difficult characters everywhere: in Greece and Dalmatia, but especially in Switzerland. There, after the years of the industrial boom, and where the heritage of the diligent industrialists, entrepreneurs, and old-established families becomes a definite restraint for a multifaceted man like Reinhart, it is difficult to inject new ideas into life. The flame that wants to burn cannot find any fuel for its fire; the man who wants to love cannot find any friendship. Thus the prevailing tone of the novel is one of sadness and disappointment. The structure of society is too difficult for the individual to survey in order to find his proper station; the gap between individual and society is too deep to form a creative activity with others.

Die Schwierigen was no better or worse than hundreds of similar novels of those decades. The narrations in the imperfect tense (passages that Frisch takes over into *Stiller* will be indicatively in the present tense), the conventional juxtaposition of interesting figures, and the elaborate landscape descriptions arouse the suspicion that Frisch lacks the spontaneity of the epic writer. There is a close similarity here to Zollinger's novels, which appeared a short time earlier.

Bin oder Die Reise nach Peking (Am or the trip to Peking), appearing in 1945 and written during the previous year while Frisch was on vacation, now no longer strings together the plastic and linear experiences of the various self-sufficient novel figures, but rather plays—for the first time this narrative characteristic of Frisch's is clearly shown—with forms of perception, with identity and time. To Bin's question about how one experiences anything at all, Frisch has the first-person narrator respond "You said it yourself: the things that we consider memory are present." Every plot can be categorized in this manner in terms of the characters and time expanse.

Bin appears as the force in one's own existence that is often overlooked, as that aspect which peers over the shoulder of the ego. Already in the introductory chapter where a stranger obstructs a marshal's decisions, that becomes evident. Both the facade and the core of the personality, the conscious and the unconscious, the foreign and one's own native element, the "I" and the "Am," the waking aspect and the dream, belong to one's existence, to the "I am."

The narrator stands in a state of romantic expectation enticing him out of the narrow circle of his responsibilities. In the course of a spring evening he moves out of everyday existence and up to the Chinese wall to gaze into the land of his longings. With Bin/Am, his "spirit," he chats about youth and happiness and traverses the land of memories with him. Not society but rather the wide expanses of the soul are portrayed.

To be sure, the story deals with a Zuricher from the years of the Second World War, i.e., with an inhabitant of a small modern nation who wants to suspend the narrow borders of his realm and the limitations of his individuality. Bin is a Stiller in nuce, though the theme of a bourgeois estranged from himself still possesses in *Bin* a romantic, harmless form. A spirit joins with Kilian in all bliss of confidence; there is no sense yet of a man standing in contradiction to reason and law and denying his identity. The fields of the unconscious can heal. The role that the narrating protagonist takes reminds him during his distant sojourn that as a bourgeois he has to play out his role— with the mask of a gentleman and of a respected figure in the small theater of the world. He cannot leave the role behind in Peking, since the role is a metaphor and not the result of an existential conflict.

The trip leads away from present-day Switzerland and then back again. Kilian is a soldier who obtained a leave of absence and then returns to his wife and child. Peking is a place of longing he will never reach. But there are also places of longing in Switzerland; they mix in part with the entirely dreamlike landscape; for example, with the house that Kilian built and whose plans are drawn up in the role. But in Switzerland everyday life prevails with its dutiful assiduity. There, one is the slave of his work; there are no princes there as near Peking, only the ordinary people along with the rich ones; "that makes the people common."

This prose piece in a sketch contains the entire masquerade of the *Chinesische Mauer* (The Chinese wall). A breakthrough into the trancendent realm is impossible because this-worldly elements and otherworldly elements are constantly intermixing. Bin is a spirit, not the spirit. He is a vehicle, not a power, not even a diabolical one like Mephisto or Roquairol.

Although the structure of the work is similar to that of a *Märchen* like *Hyacinth und Rosenblüt*—in both creations a person's expectations lead beyond himself—the concrete form of the expectation should not be overlooked. Instead of the blue flower we have a geographical name whose concrete meaning is not considered. Instead of leading toward the interior, Frisch leads us toward the exterior. The trip to Peking is not the eternal return of a Novalis or the *Journey to the Orient* of Hermann Hesse, who, with the image of the Orient or "Land of the Morning," symbolizes the "homeland and youth of the soul," the "becoming one of all times."[5]

The sentence "Longing is our best aspect," which Albin Zollinger had already penned,[6] is a psychological experience in a land of repressions—

evidence once again that Romanticism, which did not occur as a literary epoch in Switzerland, was again being compensated for step by step. Bin is not an actual "doppelgänger" but rather the "second I" whose "suprareality" is recognizable, for instance, when he also smokes a pipe. Doppelgänger figures stem from epochs and areas in which the philosophical principles of identity are modified most stringently—in reality there is not supposed to be any identity of two things or events, even an object is not identical with itself.

In Frisch, accordingly, there appears in moderate, tangible form a quasi-romantic irony, a suicide of feelings. A hymn to wine—that natural means of setting oneself loose—closes with the words:

> O wine, one drinks you like sun and prickling foam, sparks of humor and good spirits, nothing more; and afterward, unforeseen, we are drunk, cheerful from the profundity of your smiling melancholy...
> In other words:
> He doubtlessly drank a little also.

To be sure, the irony functions in *Bin* as a foreign element, more so in any case than that in Saint-Exupéry's *Petit Prince,* published two years earlier. That blissfulness of feeling mixed with tones of Rilke is suspended. The element of ineffability, not as overestimated in earlier centuries, can be recognized in *Bin* as a pose (as in Frisch's early theater pieces). In those years the delight in being different becomes an obsession.

I want to add another word here about nonliterary parallels to *Bin.* Carl Jung in the 1920s, in the same city of Zurich from which Kilian begins his journey to Peking, set forth his theses of the archetypal conditioning of the soul. Peking, to be sure, is not an archetype like the anima of a romanticist; nevertheless, one senses that Jung and Frisch belong together in certain respects. (Frisch also quotes Jung in the program notes for the premiere of the *Chinesische Mauer.*) The recognition of the soul, particularly of its many-sidedness, is common to both of them. Both think it is hazardous to have a soul. "Heaven and Hell are the fates of the soul and not of the civil man who with his nakedness and timidity in a heavenly Jerusalem would not know what to do with himself," said the psychologist once—entirely in the literary sense. The aspect of soul is of the highest value for both Jung and Frisch.

Confessional delimitations are foreign to both Jung and Frisch, especially that of a Protestant either-or. (Jung spoke of Kierkegaard once as neurotic.) They believe that God speaks many languages, including Oriental ones. Not wanting to travel to the east (as Morgenlandfahrer)—Jung often warns against imitating and appropriating eastern practices—they are nevertheless plainly envious of the rich images of the Orient. Whatever is able to release the modern intellectual from his all too enormous consciousness is worthy of respect for them.

The novel *Stiller* was written in 1953-1954 and published in 1954, on a theme of burning topicality. A generation earlier, at the time of Hermann Hesse,[8] the analogous heroes of novels strove to remain true to themselves. They were hypochondriacs; Anatol Stiller attains his goal solely through resignation. He would like to pass as an American and could perhaps be healed by a psychoanalyst.

The novel is reminiscent also of the ancient stories of doppelgängers, of figures who transform themselves, of the motif "clothes make the man," of fairy tale characters who want to be something else, or of those who have slept their time away. Concerning the form, we can speak of an adventure novel, a criminal novel, and an epistolary novel as well as of a novel of state, an educational novel, and a roman à clef. All in all it is decidedly a piece of Swiss literature. Keller's Strapinski, a melancholy, adventurous malcontent is not dissimilar to the sculptor Anatol Stiller; similar also in many respects is Pankraz, sulking at home and most diligent in other lands; the three Seldwyler long to move beyond the borders of their common, accustomed patterns and search for foreign elements.[9]

With this work Max Frisch joins the ranks of great novelists (especially scarce in Switzerland), that group which from time immemorial has always considered as insignificant that which was at first felt as pure and personal in lyrics. Colorful variety, an all-encompassing philosophy, and heterogeneous motifs distinguish the creations of such a novelist. What does it concern the authors if their works are decried by professors as merely successful thrillers? (Max Rychner alluded to as much with great caution.[10]) Every work of this genre has to include something of an odyssey. The tendency toward great dimensions produces the verve of the narration. So it is in *Stiller* also. It is Frisch's first novel—and Swiss literature's first since Schaffner's *Johannes*—with a major rhythm and composition.

The stroke of luck that a Swiss author was again able to make it into the mainstream of world literary events is presumably connected with the new situation of the small nation state. The ocean is no longer farther away for a Swiss confederate than for an Englishman. The continents have, in a sense, moved closer. A man of the Biedermeier epoch, in contrast, could not feel like a cosmopolitan. In the twentieth century the uncanny seems to begin just outside the house door: In the diary sketch "Schinz," a respectable citizen takes a Sunday walk in the forest. There he comes to his senses; he sympathizes with the thinking of the extreme left—and that is more interesting psychologically than politically—becomes a small rebel and then finally an "emigrant." Schinz is in his fifties and has four children. It has been claimed that this sketch is the nucleus of *Stiller*.[11] Is that claim not more valid, however, for Frisch's *Öderland*? Doubt concerning this question is quite revealing.

Many possibilities of existence form the basis of this novel. In the writer's "workshop conversation" of 1961 Frisch stated that "every self that expresses itself is a role." Or in the same context: "With a fixed sum of different events, one could, by simply basing them upon a different fiction (Erfindung) of his self, not only relate but also live seven different life stories. That is uncanny. He who knows it, finds it difficult to live." Stiller's difficulties reflect his complicated disposition.

The novel begins with the border-crossing of a Swiss citizen, with the customs formalities of Stiller returning home, with the very tangible conflict between an artist and the executive authority of the state. Thus, at the beginning, the novel is geopolitically comprehensible. However, Frisch quickly leaves the realms of personal and spatial limitations; it is not his desire to narrate in a linear manner but rather in a boundless, unlimited style appropriate to modern man. The returnee jots down the events in prison. In the narrow space of his cell he seeks to regain his lost time, he has to recognize his reality, i.e., his identity after being unfaithful to it for so long. Until that time he had not wanted to accept himself. The way to the bitter end is portrayed with a simultaneous technique used so often today. With it the involved situation becomes clear more quickly than it would have been possible in a naive, graphic narration.

Walter Jens characterized the book's opening situation as exemplary for the modern novel: "I am not Stiller!"[12] With one sentence the reader plunges into the action; the prison cell remains the fixed point for a novel hero who rambles far afield—it is like the cell of Oscar in Günter Grass's *Tin Drum*.

Anatol Stiller, the Zurich sculptor, lives in a childless marriage with the distinguished ballerina Julika, a born martyr. The couple continues on in an unfruitful manner similar to that of Stiller's hometown. He considers his wife frigid in her magnanimous pride; he considers himself an egotistic failure. He was not equal to the decisions confronting him in the Spanish Civil War nor to the demands of his marriage. (The important role that marriage plays in the development sets this novel apart most clearly from other novels of the mid-century, as well as from Keller's *Pankraz the Sulker*.) The marriage would have been his touchstone, but Julika dies, leaving behind a Stiller humbled and "real." In the probation period he was, exactly like Don Juan, fleeing from himself.

With the themes of unfaithfulness and a suspension of identity, the novel becomes a counter to the civil law codes which require unequivocalness and exact orientation in the time period between birth and death. Stiller is never alone. He lives in distractions, as Pascal conceives them; he does not live as a member of the community, or even of creation itself. In his reductionist endeavors as a sculptor, he has contravened the commandment "Thou shalt not make unto thee any graven image"—as well as by treating his wife primarily as an abstract form and not as a human being. "It is an important question whether there is not something inhuman in the venture of modeling a living human being. It is an essential concern for Stiller," says the prosecuting attorney in his epilogue. And the prosecuting attorney has already been designated as Stiller's spiritual adviser in disguise. Stiller's sin is the ancient, Promethean hubris. The same prosecuting attorney asks this man, who seemed so taken up with himself at the beginning and who now at Lake Geneva is sobbing for his wife: "Why did you come back from your Mexico? Precisely because you experienced as much. You two are a pair. ... Rise again! Your old dear nonsense, Stiller, permit me to tell you: your murderous pride—you as the savior of both your selves!" He is the same type of man as the woodland spirit (Waldgänger); a being that wants to transfigure himself but is not capable of it.

Kurt Marti claims that the novel's psychological questions are transparently theological,[13] a perspective that needs to be stressed. Stiller suffers from a nonbelief in what at one point in the novel is designated as an overtaxing of the self, and in that sickness of time (Zeitkrankheit) which is the downfall of so many people. Stiller wants to resuscitate himself and to create images. He wants to emerge from his nullity; for that reason he does not recognize his identity. He recognizes himself as a prisoner of his hope. The prisoner's following notation, a postscript that lies at the basis of the entire novel, is the question of how modern man can be redeemed: "I actually only hope," says Stiller, "that God (if I approach him) will make me into a different, namely, a richer, deeper, more valuable, and meaningful personality—and that is exactly what it is, I suppose, that keeps God from assuming a real existence for me; that is, from becoming recognizable and capable of being experienced. My *conditio sine qua non* is that he will revoke me, his creature." According to Marti, the word *revoke* suggests redemption.

Seen in the context of Stiller, Frisch's earlier protagonists now appear in a different light. Bin, Rittmeister and Rittmeisterin, Graf Öderland and Don Juan were also seeking redemption—as romantics and sufferers of wanderlust—but were not yet ready for a genuine redemption. Not until life and especially marriage, as the embodiment of European life, have developed into anguish to the same extent as for the sculptor Stiller can the necessity arise for God to redeem his creature.

The theological concern in the novel is relatively concealed. The problem of the sexes and of marriage, as always in Frisch, is fairly evident; thus it requires less commentary. On the other hand, the novel as a mirroring of the times and of Switzerland could be subject to misunderstanding. The political glosses in particular have irritated many of the Swiss.

Stiller hates Zurich's lack of historical perspective, its architecture without imagination, the lack of daring (no one suffers at all from the calamitous compromises), the sullen, insipid, petty-minded shopkeepers. Among the architects, the recognized modernist Willi Sturzenegger, who on the basis of his "cheerful resignation" derides all the idealists, is enough to make Stiller ill. A few entries remind one of Goethe's *Briefe aus der Schweiz*: "Perhaps as a prisoner I am especially sensitive to their slogan of freedom. What in the devil do they make out of their renowned freedom? Whenever it might somehow become costly, they are as cautious as any German subject. Indeed, who can afford to have a wife and children, a family with appurtenances as is fitting, and simultaneously have a free opinion and not merely in secondary matters?" Stiller hates the clichéd Switzerland, hates the mummified Switzerland, hates the Swiss's widespread desire as a people for marking out a self-manufactured image of and for themselves instead of living life and enduring as a people.

The reproaches, taken objectively and personally, are anything but new. Only the context is new: That they stem from a Zuricher who does not want to accept himself, who flees from a confining reality to America and experiences there all kinds of movie episodes—and more. Later Stiller accepts not only himself but also Switzerland. The criticism stems from the mouth of a failure, of a would-be Spanish soldier, not from Frisch himself; seldom have his readers noted that.

One simply cannot steal away from the everyday routine of bourgeois married life and then shoot up his wife's Sunday cake after she has remained at home meek as a lamb—as Isidor did, whose story the imprisoned Stiller would like to relate to his Julika. This major theme is recognizable in this abbreviated burlesque, as well as in the *Tagebuch* sketch and most comprehensibly in the radio play *Rip van Winkle* (1953).[14]

Stiller feels himself the prisoner of his hopes and of his wanderlust. The mask of his double and his attempt to leave the borders of his homeland behind are connected with the quandary of a contemporary Swiss romanticist. That is the reason he mocks the Helvetian bourgeoisie and glorifies the powerful aspect of a wilderness, the stupendousness of the American continent. (Walter Faber no longer does that, or rather no longer wants to.) If that were not the case, then Stiller would not be Swiss or at least not a Swiss intellectual. As strange as it may sound, Stiller is more pronouncedly Swiss than tradition-minded Swiss patriots in analogous narratives—precisely because he grumbles about his fatherland. His ill humor stems from the feeling of not being permitted to criticize openly. Frisch said of Albin Zollinger that it was not the lack of public tribute that disappointed him so bitterly but rather the feeling of "speaking into cotton,"[15] that is, of not having any echo and encountering only indifference. That is why artists become resentful toward Switzerland.

Stiller is a European, as little as he boasts of it and as far removed as he is from all formal oratory in favor of Europe. He suffers from that continent of individualists, from that lovely atmosphere with its manifold nuances where there are few opportunities for conspicuous virility and the natural joy of living. As a representative of a complex civilization, he falls under the impression that Europe, not just Switzerland, is like Sleeping Beauty somnolently dreaming that struggle and manhood is still possible only across the seas. Also, only across the seas is the journey to the "Mothers" possible. During his adventure in the Texas cave he encounters the primeval eternal darkness, time as an archetypal phenomenon—timelessness and the life necessity of man's measuring time become terrifyingly manifest—there he progresses inwardly to the point that the voice of his Angel will find him, the voice that will protect him against the nonessential. In the grotto he encounters a skeleton and ultimately becomes the murderer of his "friend." Does Mr. White kill Stiller or vice versa? In any case a doppelgänger is murdered. Like the man in Plato's parable of the cave, he sees the shadow of existence. The grotto is the counterimage of the realms of the intellectuals, of the impotent prattler, and of reproductions.

The mirroring in the cave is something other than portrayal by human hand. As a married European, Stiller falls into entanglements that estrange him from his natural and physical being. Modern society does not allow him to develop and find himself. "We live in an age of reproduction. Most of the things in our personal world view we have never experienced with our own eyes; to be more exact: perhaps with our own eyes but not on the actual spot; were are tele-viewers, tele-hearers, tele-knowers."[16] Hans Mayer maintains that the portrayal of life and literature in the age of reproduction is the actual theme of the novel.[17]

Stiller is not capable of recapturing the lost time, of overcoming his past. A heartless society surrounds the artist; no one has confidence in the "creation as an act of God's charity" (Karl Barth). The prosecuting attorney alone offers real help.

Finally Stiller does find his way into his actual existence. "He began . . . to be in the world"; he anticipates the power and the glory beyond himself. He does not believe in them but waits.

With the novel *Stiller* Frisch proved himself to be a master of composition. Who could have been more successful than Frisch in making the most complicated developments relatable, in shaping the most inner experiences into a form agreeable to all readers? Even Kierkegaard employed certain fictions as a way to outwit the reader. In the foreword to *Either-Or,* alluding to the fiction of editing in "Diary of the Seducer," he says: "The one author comes to the point of sticking inside the other like one of the little capsules in a Chinese capsule game." The path leading from such a capsule game to the narrative technique in *Stiller* was difficult; passable only for someone possessing sufficient joy of form and play. These talents were recognized and praised by Emil Staiger, who was deeply affected by the novel's truthful intention. In his review of the novel, concerning the surprising mixture of various aspects, the dizziness in the description of the past, and the apparent flippancy, he writes: "And not the least of the author's accomplishments is the artistry with which he is able to maintain this extremely difficult, gliding tone, as secret anguish, humor, and derision combine for a prose concert of which we know no parallel in our literature. Just as surprising is how the techniques of the modern novel, flashbacks, simultaneous reportage (and whatever else the various artifices may be called, which are usually nothing other than artifices), become sensible and even necessary. Stiller, a figure representative of a certain spirit of our day, seems to generate the modern form spontaneously and out of his inner self and to legitimize it for the first time." Dürrenmatt, who arrived at a similar conclusion independently of Staiger, wrote: "The one aspect is mirrored in the other, and nothing remains 'true' other than this mirroring itself. It is exciting to follow this through and to perceive the adroitness with which Max Frisch varies and telescopes time and space. And if in the process we are seized by dizziness, then the epilogue of the prosecuting attorney mercifully provides us with a less interesting, but nevertheless, relatively fast footing."[18]

The novel was well received almost everywhere. It established Frisch's world reputation in much the same way that *Besuch der alten Dame* (*The Visit*) established Dürrenmatt's. Karl Korn reveled in the ironic glint;[19] he and other Germans, grinning candidly, dwelt upon Stiller's attacks on Swiss propriety. Karlheinz Braun in his dissertation investigated the extent of the flashbacks in the "narrated time" and the relation of "narrated time" to "narrative time."[20] The investigation of the details—among other things the notation of the various years' playing a role for Stiller, Mr. White, Isidor, the prosecuting attorney, etc.—demonstrate Frisch's exactitude.

Dürrenmatt in his discussion of the novel comments upon Frisch's tendency in his art not to exclude his personal and private life, not to skip over himself. "He is entangled in his work. Frisch is one of those writers who stubbornly refuse to write pure fiction, something that irritates many people all the more as this author apparently could write purer and better fiction than those now doing so." Dürrenmatt declares that the novel *Stiller* arose out of an existential quandary. "The undertaking with no regard other than to portray himself, to mean himself, could annoyingly only be dared in the form of an admission, a confession, related to the nonpersonal background of religion; a religious backdrop suspends the private aspect, as in the case of Augustine and Kierkegaard; however, if this background is removed, as in Frisch, then the confession is no longer conceivable as a book, much less one from which royalties could be obtained; what one admits to a friend cannot be communicated to a reading public if one does not want to lapse into embarrassment."[21]

Following his considerations of novel technique, Dürrenmatt might have commented more thoroughly upon White's judgment of Switzerland—"one of the most enjoyable, but also one of the most important pages of this amazing novel." Although difficult to decipher, the marginal glosses of the manuscript contain primarily Dürrenmatt's reflections on the theme of Switzerland. As I understand it, Dürrenmatt's critique was not completed because a concrete formulation of the theme by him was thwarted during the planning of his "New City." But in spite of the critique's fragmentary character, it is clear that the discussion is an instance of an important literary exchange between two literary friends.

In spite of its sweeping narrative manner, *Stiller* had a tormenting effect, and its ending, more than anything, was one of nullity, a virtual failure. In an odyssey through the soul, there is no comforting naiveté—nor brevity and cheerfulness; the task is to discover the continents of the soul. For that reason it was hoped that Frisch would make a turn toward outward life. This turning outward resulted in the portrayal of a technician, an employee of UNESCO. *Homo faber* (1957) cannot be set at variance with himself, he is no pluralist, he does not torment himself in his inner life and in his homeland but rather becomes caught in the maelstrom of fate; he not only begins to tumble but plunges precipitously. Whereas Stiller was a sculptor, Walter Faber is a technician. As an architect Frisch was acquainted with both possibilities: formation and calculation. Following the novel of productions and reproductions, following the interweaving of inner-life aspects, came a relatively dispassionate report. Following the images of colorful suppressions came the fiction of someone purged: an almost old-fashioned strictness. Walter Faber is sobered and refrains from always wanting to be someone else.

All over the world, mechanisms are being built today that have surpassed even the conceptions of previous centuries. Cybernetics has again raised the question of whether machines can replace human capabilities. Walter Faber believes they can. For himself he doubts being able to experience nature; he films everything, including people, attempting thereby to replace his capacity of memory. (Sabeth asks him what he wants with her when he approaches her with his movie camera.[22]) He claims that any feelings are signs of fatigue; he views a perilous situation from the standpoint of Maxwell's demon. Such sobering moods, however, lack that certain humor of conventional novels. Faber's pride in standing solidly on the ground, of seeing precisely the things people talk about, leads him into error. The conviction that his sense of reality certainly does not make him blind leads him directly into darkness and into death.

His presumptuous miscalculations lead to incest. By no means a saint with a glorious future, Faber meets his daughter Sabeth by pure chance on a return trip to Europe. The determined bachelor, who feels most at home amid the noise of the ship's motor, makes a marriage proposal, almost against his will, to the chic, twenty-year-old coed and then drives with her through Italy. Still he has confidence in his "realities." The Erinyes do not yet appear; at first Sabeth's snake bite does not seem to be fatal, but she dies. The mischief carried out in the night of love—with a lunar eclipse and a consciousness of the hovering, rushing heavenly bodies—kills him as well, the fanatic of probability. Near him stands Hanna grieving over the death of her only daughter.

The representation of the abhorrent becomes all the more credible as Frisch restrains himself stylistically in his report; i.e., he depicts a fifty-year-old man in all his weaknesses. Faber gropes in the darkness. It is not the foundering we are familiar with from dozens of contemporary novels but rather the life of an intellectual bungler. Naturally Faber's bungling is not in his area of specialization but rather in his entire life-style. Instead of finesse, he possesses merely the *ésprit de géometrie* (Pascal); hence the consciously bungled language with the crippled subordinate clauses. (Other than that, it is the language of a so-called role-novel, which was eminently suitable for the radio and had a very successful effect in the memorable reading on Studio Zürich by Peter Lühr). In order to avoid feelings, Faber forces beautiful expressions and tries to keep any sensitivity at arm's length with hurriedly fabricated comparisons. The sea is like tinfoil; the Mediterranean air, like cellophane with nothing behind it; the surf, like beer foam; the black cypress trees, like exclamation points.

Toward the end, the pace of the report becomes more and more breathless. The interspersed returnings to earlier events can hardly be designated any longer as flashbacks; rather there is a hestitation on the part of the narrator in view of the dreadfulness that is breaking into this botched life. In this regard Frisch's work exhibits a previously unknown austerity and dimension. Ash trays, apartment rooms, a soiled shirt, streets, and vehicles become motifs with terrible vividness. Faber, who at the beginning always faithfully films his "episodes" and properly orders his film in-between, at the end in Düsseldorf has to watch the images flash on the screen like shadows of revenge. His sexuality becomes a curse for him; the mother—Hanna, whom he calls a hen in her anxiety—becomes a love trap. In spite of that, nowhere in Frisch's oeuvre is there a woman who acts as humanly and motherly as Hanna, although she never does overcome her egocentricity; it is said of her that she actually wanted to have her child without a father.

Faber stands at war with creation, experiencing it either as a stinking fecundity in Guatemala or as a swamp of sexuality in New York. Creation as culture, as a divine gift, is foreign to him. He is nature's adversary like Don Juan; this time, however, the struggle ends with more than a farce. Faber lives outside the context of social time, and it does not even register with him that he wanted to marry his own child. His horizons are narrow because he lacks perception and good breeding; those horizons could be enlarged only by seeing a higher order. "To be sure, we are not able to see such order," Leibniz said once, "because we are not standing at the right vantage point, just as a perspective painting can best be recognized only from certain positions but cannot present itself at all from the side. Only we have to place ourselves with the eyes of our understanding in that position where we cannot see or stand with the eyes of our body."[23] A statistician and calculator of probabilities will never be able to achieve the "right observation point."

Hanna's life has been bungled by three "technicians": by the chess-playing manager Joachim, by the Communist Piper, but particularly by the seemingly most harmless of the species, Walter Faber. Paradoxically he is an employee of the UNESCO program for underdeveloped countries—as if the civilized world were not even more underdeveloped! (This point appears in the work not as a polemic in the foreground but as a hardly noticeable, tragicomic background.) Hanna recognizes Faber as "underdeveloped" and tells him as much after his sickness. "Discussion with Hanna!—about technology (according to Hanna) as an artifice for arranging the world in such a manner that we do not have to experience it. The mania of the technician to make creation useful because he cannot keep 'her' as a partner, cannot undertake anything with 'her'; technology as an artifice to remove the world as an obstacle from the world, for example, to dilute it by using rapid tempo so that we do not have to experience it. (What Hanna means with all that, I do not know.)" Walter Faber attempted to live without death, was not capable of aging, dealt with life as an addition rather than as a contour (Gestalt). Nowhere is the connection between technology, lack of maturity, and incest so articulate as in these remarks.

Thus it becomes understandable why Faber must use the language of a bungler:[24] he wants to dilute the world by applying rapid tempo so that he does not have to experience it. Even after the misdeed that he perpetrates on his daughter, Faber does not change; or at most, perhaps, in becoming no longer fit due to his stomach ailments or in becoming impotent due to aging. Aging could hardly have a different meaning for him. Only like a flash at the end does the inkling of a real human being spring up in him, in the entry for 0400 hours, the instructions for the eventuality of his death: "Being in the world," he says, means "being in the light ... but especially: holding one's own to the light, to joy."

The sickness that he registered earlier as the nonfunctioning of his body and wanted to eliminate with tablets apparently did change him. His existence, which was played out in airplanes and at improvised stations and reproduced fittingly by his movie camera, was snatched back into the realm of life. In the face of death he is now finally "in the world." The entire report begins with the description of a flight from New York to South America. In an incident in Texas, Faber senses the need to remain behind after seeing his face in the mirror. The loudspeaker, however, calls him: "Passenger Faber, Passenger Faber. ... This is our last call." Could things have gone on without him, with the Super Constellation, with the world? Did the last call sound for him in vain?

Ever since Saint-Exupéry, in whose work flying was still a manly adventure, ever since Gerd Gaiser's *Sterbende Jagd* (Dying hunt), where man still bears relatively human traits, there has probably not appeared any narrative in which flying has received such a sobering portrayal. That is connected with the fact that flying for Frisch is no longer a mythos. Present-day alienation engendered by technology is perhaps more typical for passengers than for pilots. In *Tagebuch I* among the entries for 1946, Frisch makes the remark (it was his second or third flight) that after the first pleasant thrill, flying leaves a "certain emptiness" in a person. The feeling for distance and space is lost. It is magnificent, to be sure, but there is still something demonic about it.[25] A few pages earlier in the diary stand the sentences that can be considered a precursory form for Walter Faber's experience of time: "We live on a moving conveyor belt and there is no hope that we can make up for ourselves and improve a past moment of our lives. We are our past, even if we reject it, no less than our today.—Time does not change us. It merely unfolds us." In conjunction with our narrative: Time does bring forth children, but it does not make men into fathers. That would be called change. Time produces encounters—for Walter Faber they accumulate into a host of coincidences—but not love. Time allows him to remain intent upon exactitude as well as foolish and blind to the interconnectedness of human relations.

Faber reminds us of the tragic myth of Oedipus or even of Daedalus or Wieland (who also committed incest but were creativity's heroes). Faber finds his judgment in Greece.[26] His flights around the world lose their meaning in the face of his death, for a man plunges into his inner self. A man who has lost the keys to his existence—we are reminded of those futile telephone calls in New York and of the futile attempts to get into his own apartment—will be punished by fate. Joined with the motifs of his earlier works such as the *Chinesische Mauer* with its closed inescapability or *Graf Öderland* with its strict inevitability is now the element of ancient tragedy. Here Dürrenmatt's objection concerning Öderland is no longer valid—that Öderland is, namely, too human. Now it is fate that swings the ax. What Werner Beber stated concerning *Homo faber* indeed holds true: "He dealt with 1957 employing the means and methods of 1957."[27] Such works are not mere pretty ornamentation.[28]

After the premiere of *Andorra*, Frisch lived for four years in Rome, the city of great film directors and friendly people, although it can hardly be designated as the center of the world for Frisch and for numerous colleagues in his profession. During this period he undertook various trips: to America, Berlin, Jerusalem, Zurich. The most important parts of the novel *Mein Name sei Gantenbein* (*A Wilderness of Mirrors*), however, porbably came into being in Rome, some sections long before its publication in 1964. One section, "Das Paar," appeared in print in the *Jahresring* 1961-1962.

The atmosphere of the novel is friendlier, more playful, and non-Swiss than in *Stiller*, which started out "I am not Stiller!" It is a long step from this protest to the indifferently placed subjunctive "Mein Name sei Gantenbein" ("Let my name be Gantenbein"). There is no imperative element in this statement but rather the indication of one possibility out of many. It is not the case of a man's attempting his way out of a Zurich prison through rebellion and hating the attempts of a social order to make an identification without love; it is rather the case of a narrator's setting as a prerequisite the nonidentificability of an actual person and trying on stories like clothes. There exists here only the composite self or the implied author, suggested by the book; the fictive figures merge into one another; the self possesses more than one role and it would be nonsense to speak of "doppelgängers" with Enderlin or Svoboda.

Frisch relates in an imaginary interview that after a mild auto accident in a small village he had envisaged glass fragments getting into his eyes.[29] This imagination, this "perhaps," was the point of departure. Real life has no variants and for that reason it is of interest to him to mirror a person in his fictions. That means, however, that the novel has no action or development and manages as it were without the past tense (the German imperfect, "this illusion of historicity"). Indeed, the fiction ends with two scenes that lack all historicity: a corpse floats down the Limmat through the center of Zurich and almost achieves a "floating away without a history"; and at the very end comes a small image of September; the narrator is hungry and thirsty, he likes life. An anonymous and grotesque dreamlike death—at the beginning death appears on the street of a large city, at the end a corpse floats down the Limmat—forms the background for the possibilities of human existence.

In singularly broken vividness, a manifold string of impressions lights up the narrative in rapid fashion. We peer through a kaleidoscope, seeing a series of streets in Paris, New York, and Zurich, and watching cars roll past like toys. Immediately the reader senses that the observers are unessential and that the experiences are impersonal, whether they come from the bartender, Enderlin, or from Gantenbein. The lunatic's dream of meeting Eve naked is the first personal and admittedly impressionable experience. Or the other lunatic's experience of standing naked on a stage—Gottfried Benn had already said that the self was a phantom.

The death of the man in the parked car—thus the novel begins—is described just as dispassionately as Gantenbein's car breakdown in Lengnau in the canton of Berne. The language is dispassionate and casual.[30] The image of the cleaned-out room has a sad effect. A woman leaves her lover. Here Frisch employs weighty metaphors; the empty room is reminiscent of Pompei, the deserted man compares himself with a mummy. One of the major motifs in the novel is love (although the narrator disposes of belief in the individual person as superstititon, like the representatives of the "nouveau roman"). No clearly defined individual can any longer pit himself against love, jealousy, and solitude in a depersonalized world.

Because "stories of the self" can hardly be justified today in the face of the pressing general problems, Frisch treats the private affairs of his characters in a detached manner. He withstood the temptation of allowing Gantenbein to become a political figure.[31] "This is not the time for 'stories of selves.' Nevertheless, human life is carried out or misspent with the individual self, nowhere else" (p. 103). This admission inserted into the novel shows what the author's shamefaced dialectic consists of and why, although not willing to write an anti-novel, he calls into question his stories just the same.[32]

That is a dilemma, not a genuine paradox. Frisch writes in a personal manner precisely in spite of the dilemma although he does not pretend to believe in the relevance of the three personal pronouns; he writes stories although he pictures historicity with its triadic movement of past, present, and future as an illusion; he writes of birth, life, and death, although he is willing to suspend the boundaries of existence. The best passages are a product of the three-dimensional thought that Frisch seeks to overcome with less resoluteness than have other modern writers.

With all depersonalization and demythologizing of the events, a myth in secular form is proffered—that of the blind seer. By means of his blind man's glasses Gantenbein is able to approach closer to other people because he can let them be perfectly free to play their roles; he obtains a more confidential relationship to them because he grants them the validity of their lies.

One listener at a reading of Frisch's in Munich in 1964 said that the satirical story of society's keyhole-peeker[33] was being given another performance in this novel. The attribute *satirical* is disputable, for Gantenbein is depicted as being very patient and empathetic. It remains questionable whether the theme of the discovery of truth (which Frisch discusses in the imaginary interview) can be amalgamated with the lie of simulated blindness.

Due to the tranquillity with which the writer portrays life as a game, with which he distributes roles according to this desire (it is no longer merely the role of an Öderland or of a White), and with which he accepts the lack of action, the expression satire has to be ruled out. The contemplative Gantenbein comes much more to the foreground than the more proficient Enderlin.

In my opinion, the novel's worldwide success is not primarily due to its quality. Frisch is not only in the interesting proximity of the "nouveau roman," but he has also created some episodes that are tailor-made for the movies; he adheres skillfully to the most immediate problems of the modern period. How does one deal with the difficult undertakings of our day? "One speaks about the most recent space flight; thus about the future and humanity; hence, about things that no one is able to see" (p. 55); that sounds as cogent and reconciled as most cocktail-party conversations.

The novel *Gantenbein* has only rarely been rejected outright by the critics.[34] There were no language blunders chalked up against Frisch, something that happened rather frequently in his earlier writings. The entertaining, modish aspect, of which the author in his own commentary says that it was not the purpose of the novel but only an enticement, did not miss its mark. Hans Mayer evaluated the novel rather reservedly; he pointed to Dürrenmatt's *Blind Man* as a possible stimulus, to passages in the diary and in the writer's "workshop conversation" of 1961, to the manner in which the main figure is set up by the narrator, and to the feeling of boredom that sets in during the second part. Toward the end of the novel the reader has the impression of witnessing the trying-on of new clothes, when the one trying on the clothes knows from the beginning that there is no way he will buy them. Marcel Reich-Ranicki defended the work in the same newspaper, *Die Zeit*: Gantenbein was not to be judged morally; "In any case I believe that a three-dimensional, real human figure was not striven for, but more a type of 'Märchen'-figure, generated in the middle of a realistically depicted environment." The formula might be, not as Mayer suggested, namely, homo ludens in the discrepancy between life and narration, but more "the suffering creature between love and death." Hans Egon Holthusen, under the rubric of "The Fifty-year-old Man," spoke of the born storyteller sawing away as literally as possible at the branch on which he is sitting. Frisch, he says, is an expert in the hard, crude devices for making readers (like girls) compliant; certain wild episodes could be designated as anti-Helvetian Helvetianisms.

Among the more important commentaries only Heinrich Vormweg ("Othello as Mannequin") took up a position decidedly opposed to the author. "Even in ready-made suits reality is indubitable. However, this denouement is warped. It has a modernistic timbre resting upon a superficial fallacy." The reader naturally feels cut to the quick, Vormweg says; that lies in a preference for the realm of possibilities we presumably owe to present-day consumer conditions. *Gantenbein,* the number one best-seller of the season in 1964-1965, truly became a consumer article. There were takeoffs in cabarets and comic strips on the man with the blind man's glasses. This attention was something new for Frisch's work.

The author had less success with the filming of one episode. Work on the film, which was originally given the title "The Ashes of a Pipe-smoker," was taken up twice by the Atlas-Gesellschaft in Duisburg in the fall of 1965 but had to be discontinued due to various circumstances. In the spring of 1966 in the Berlin Akademie der Künste, Frisch along with Ernst Schröder presented the work, and soon thereafter the *Skizze eines Films* (Sketch of a movie) was published.[35] It is the story of a man believed to be dead who no longer dares to take part in the lives of those left behind. The theme of resurrection forms a conspicuous parallel to Dürrenmatt's *Meteor.*

The novel *Gantenbein* is the product of a progressive age of reproduction, a virtuoso play with episodes and jugglery; *Andorra* treated the theme of modern solitude—parabolic and also graphic, enlightening—created with the utmost concern. We should not forget how far Frisch had traveled to arrive at these unpretentious, masterly designed works.

Frisch indeed never struggled with a mass of inherited material as Zollinger did but rather always lived in a healthy relationship to literary tradition. The German novel of education, modern odysseys, warmhearted romances, parable games—all these and other forms enriched his work. In all he is a man of restraint and consistent development. At least in *Andorra,* Büchner is as important a model as Brecht.[36] Observing the path from *Die Schwierigen* to *Gantenbein* and from *Santa Cruz* to the latest plays, we can trace the pathmarks of the years of apprenticeship and mastery (which can be distinguished more clearly with him than with Dürrenmatt). From a literary standpoint it is the path from neo-romanticism to engaged realism; from a political perspective it is the path from protest to forbearance or, formualted with greater reservation, to a nonconformance no longer disturbing to anyone. Once he was even given the cautious reproach that one could perceive his good literary upbringing in the "masterly anticipated addition of the possible reactions of refined people";[37] his allusions were earlier often coincidental, not obligatory; the associations did not extend very far. Expressed more positively: Frisch views the reader as a partner and strives for the reader's sympathy. He is incapable of creating epics in the style of some American or Russian writers. In *Tagebuch I* he reflects upon such preconditions of his work (pp. 181, 241, 335).

The provisory nature of his existence is conditioned by the fear of intellect-deadening conventions, of a sterile traditionalism. In the fear of reproductions we need to be careful not to form precipitously an image of our neighbor. Prejudices kill the living relationships among men. (In the name of love modern theologians are also revising their conceptions of God.) As a contemporary he was not closed off to any important questions. He spoke with teachers, wrote about pocket books, took an interest in politics and discussions going on among the continents. In the field of art he mastered architecture, as dilettante he was attracted to painting, he wrote prefaces for art volumes, and won painters for friends.

His work is socially minded. "I also believe that there is much in the world to be changed," he says in his remarks to the third edition of *Öderland*.[38] Radio plays a small part in his work, for he likes "to be present at the clash of work and audience."[39] The public is his partner, at times a stimulating one and at times an annoying one. In his speech for the reception of Zurich's literature prize, he designated the achieving of a correct relationship to one's audience, of forming a marriage with it, as being every bit as important as having talent. Frisch believes that Albin Zollinger was not successful in doing so because Switzerland did not sufficiently recognize him.

Santa Cruz, Don Juan, Stiller, Hotz, and *Gantenbein* deal with the problem of marriage; in these, and in the other works as well, love is never represented in its absolute form but always in its connection to society. Beautiful pairs, paradisiacal innocence, sweet life do not occur. Women are not a fulfillment for Frisch's men but are the proof of their imperfection; nevertheless, again and again man seeks to be redeemed by the woman. Don Juan flees into the abstractions of geometry; Stiller denies himself and lives as White in America because he feels he has failed Julika. Certainly, marriage is not the only goal for Frisch, but it is the center around which his thinking revolved for a long time and around which his characters take shape. In this regard Albin Zollinger was very similar to him. The course of the world in Frisch's writing rarely mitigates the anguish of the lost center. This anguish distinguishes him from Brecht, in whose collective thinking marriage could have no central meaning.

In *Don Juan* a travesty of marriage takes place, Philip Hotz's anger is not sufficient to destroy the marriage. This is ridiculous and grotesque and in no way entertaining. Nevertheless, Frisch as a stylist is generally closer to light entertaining literature than Dürrenmatt—even closer to the belletristics that he has often sharply criticized. "What do our belletristics do?" he asked. "They spin yarns with their lyrical clichés; belletristics are always the scaling down of ideals that have (unfortunately) just passed away and to which no reality corresponds any longer."

In spite of the intent of parody and alienation,[40] Frisch's distance from literary traditions is not all that great, and with an understanding of these connections one is able to orient himself in Frisch's work fairly easily. Zollinger and Brecht have already been mentioned, and the connections to Dürrenmatt are manifest.

The connection with Kierkegaard is more complicated. On the one hand Frisch's understandable restraints hinder him from openly acknowledging this religious writer.[41] Formally, for example in regard to the relationship between life and work, the similarity is evident. It has been claimed that there is hardly a written work into which the author's own life story has been amalgamated to such an extent as in that of the Dane. He writes of his futile love for his fiancée, and with the aid of a fictive editor misleads the reader into rushing after generalities. What must Kierkegaard's passionate desire of choosing "himself" have meant to Frisch the romanticist, carrying his Santa Cruz around in his heart so long? As the motto for *Stiller* stands a passage about the connection of "'self'-choice" with human isolation and "deepest continuity" and another passage about the connection between free will and 'self'-choice. How must these self-torturing reflections have gripped Frisch—the unpretentious (self-effacing) assumption that one is merely an individual on tryout (Probe-Mensch).

His existence is similar to such a tryout. He doubts the constancy of the individual and its identity. The problem of identity, which is also of great interest to epistemologists, psychiatrists, and sociologists, is brought closer to Frisch's readers in a commonly understood form and with the means of irony and montage. (In Kafka the problem was still portrayed in mythic form. Gregor Samsa awakes one morning and is no longer the same as he was, yet he is still the same person.)

Frisch has many friends and enemies. One's relationship to others—to an Andorra that is to be rediscovered in all situations—can in no way be called harmonious. It is the disproportionality of talent with society as Goethe depicted it in *Tasso*. He is the citizen and emigrant together—a citizen with full consciousness of the responsibility accruing to an individualist in a politicized world; an emigrant in all restraint befitting a man who allows himself no arcadia or ivory tower. Sensitive, complicated, critical, he strives for a citizenship whose existence at the present time is more endangered than ever.[42]

1. According to *Tagebuch I*, p. 279, Frisch burned everything he had written, including the diaries, around 1937. That did not include the two novels *Jürg Reinhart* (1934) and *Antwort aus der Stille* (1937), both published by the Deutsche Verlagsanstalt in Stuttgart.

2. Karl Krolow, "Max Frischs Tagebuch," *Dichten und Trachten 13, Jahresschau des Suhrkamp Verlags* (Frankfurt, 1959), p. 65.

3. "The Captain's Reprimand," *Blätter aus dem Brotsack*, p. 21; *Tagebuch*, p. 279; *Stiller*, p. 205.

4. Passages used in *Stiller* can already be found in *Die Schwierigen*, pp. 67–73. They do not correspond word for word as M. Wintsch-Spiess says, but only in certain parts of the descriptions in *Stiller* (pp. 462–64). On the other hand, the scene "Ammann als Architekt" was taken in part word for word from the essay "Das erste Haus," a personal report of Frisch's in the *Neue Zürcher Zeitung*, nos. 1449–86 (Sept. 1942).

5. Hesses "Morgenland" concept: *Gesammelte Dichtungen* in six volumes (Frankfurt, 1952), 6:24.

6. "Die Sehnsucht ist unser Bestes," by Zollinger, *Die große Unruhe* (Zürich, 1939), p. 282.

7. C. G. Jung, *Von den Wurzeln des Bewußtseins* (Zürich, 1954); here from the selections of the Fischer-Bücherei (1957), p. 37.

8. Allusion to the Hesse circle: Frisch dedicated the publication of part of the Diary to Hesse; *Basler Nachrichten* (July 6, 1947).

9. Characters from the works of Gottfried Keller: Strapinski from *Kleider machen Leute*; Pankraz from *Pankraz der Schmoller*; the three Seldwyler from *Die Leute von Seldwyla*.

10. Max Rychner, *Die Tat* (Nov. 27, 1954); cf. also K. A. Horst, "Bildflucht und Bildwirklichkeit," *Merkur* (Stuttgart, 1955).

11; The sketch "Schinz," *Tagebuch I*, pp. 245 ff., seen as the source by M. Rychner in his review of the *Tagebuch* in *Die Tat* (Nov. 27, 1954).

12. Walter Jens, *Deutsche Literatur der Gegenwart* (DTV-edition, 1964), pp. 88, 95.

13. Kurt Marti, "Das zweite Gebot im 'Stiller' von Max Frisch," *Kirchenblatt für die reformierte Schweiz* (Basel, Dec. 5, 1957).

14. "Rip van Winkle," *Kreidestriche ins Ungewisse* (Twelve German Radio Plays since 1945), Moderner Buch-Club (Darmstadt, 1960). In the radio play the main character's name is Anatol Wadel. After the prosecuting attorney's announcement of the verdict, Wadel attempts to strangle his wife Julika.

15. Cf. M. Frisch, "Albin Zollinger als Erzähler," *Neue Schweizer Rundschau* (Oct. 1942), p. 358.

16. *Stiller*, pp. 244–45.

17. Hans Mayer, "Anmerkungen zu Stiller," *Dürrenmatt und Frisch* (Pfullingen, 1963).

18. E. Staiger, "Stiller," *Neue Zürcher Zeitung* (Nov. 17, 1954).

19. Karl Korn, "Ein Mann, der sich selbst sucht," *Frankfurter Allgemeine Zeitung* (Nov. 16, 1954), with the remark that there a "Panopticum of the Swiss bourgeois world" was shown.

20. A fairly comprehensive Stiller bibliography can be found in the dissertation of K. Braun, "Die epische Technik in Max Frischs Roman Stiller, als Beitrag zur Formfrage des modernen Romans" (Frankfurt, 1959), and in Monika Wintsch-Spiess's dissertation, "Zum Problem der Identität im Werk Max Frischs" (Zurich, 1965). Additions are the reference of W. Kayser to *Stiller* in the essay "Wer erzählt den Roman?" *Die Vortrags-*

reise (Berne, 1958), an essay of W. Weideli in the Winter edition of the journal *Présence* (Geneva-Paris, 1955-1956), and the blunt attacks of Karlheinz Deschner in *Talente, Dichter, Dillettanten* (Wiesbaden, 1964).

21. Dürrenmatt on "Stiller" in his *Theater-Schriften und Reden*, with the exception of the remarks concerning Switzerland.

22. See Brigitte Weidmann "Wirklichkeit und Erinnerung in Max Frischs Homo faber," *Schweizer Monatshefte* (Zurich, Aug. 1964).

23. G. W. Leibniz, *Von dem Verhängnis*, ca. 1714.

24. G. Kaiser, *Schweizer Monatshefte* (Zurich, Jan. 1959), speaks of "One of the most difficult tasks of contemporary literature," namely "to have the modern man speak as a person no longer oriented toward his language."

25. *Tagebuch I*, pp. 50, 52, 22; cf. also the essay of Enzensberger "Vergebliche Brandung der Ferne, eine Theorie des Tourismus," *Merkur* (Aug. 1958), and similar material in the essay collection *Einzelheiten* (Frankfurt, 1962).

26. Hermann Böschenstein, *Der Neue Mensch* (Heidelberg, 1958), p. 123; he calls the work a "homecoming novel."

27. W. Weber, "Homo faber," *Neue Zürcher Zeitung* (Oct. 26, 1957), now also along with two other essays about the *Tagebücher* and *Biedermann* in *Zeit ohne Zeit* (Zurich, 1959), pp. 85-101.

28. Concerning *Homo faber* cf. R. Geissler, ed., *Möglichkeiten des modernen Romans* (Frankfurt, 1962), pp. 191-214, with bibliography. See also R. Abirached, *Nouvelle Revue Française* (June 1962), which is somewhat negative; one senses the "de-Switzerlandization" of a Swiss; for him the novel has too much of an allegorical effect. See further the structural analysis of Hans Geulen, *Max Frischs Homo faber* (Berlin, 1965); B. Allemann's critique on the Hessischen Rundfunk (Oct. 20, 1957); the laudatio of C. J. Burckhardt (Veillon-Prize) with the reference to a rare artistry that was able to lead in this case "out of the depressions of antipathy to pure vision"; and B. Herzog, "Von den Liebessorgen älterer Herren," *Schweizer Rundschau* (Sept. 1960).

29. Imaginary Interview, "Ich schreibe für Leser," *Dichten und Trachten* (Frankfurt, 1964), no. 24.

30. Examples of sloppy language: "Man speiste reizvoll," "er fühlte sich nicht besonders," "die Dame foppte ihn schmeichelhaft." *Mein Name sei Gantenbein* (Frankfurt, 1964), pp. 7-8.

31. Interview, "Soll der Onkel auf die Barrikade steigen?" *Woche* (Olten, Aug. 19, 1964).

32. Frisch disputes the claim that his writing has similarities to the nouveau roman (Ich schreibe für Leser); for an opposing view, see W. Emrich in a review of "Goldene Früchte" by N. Sarraute, *Welt der Literatur* (Hamburg, Oct. 1, 1964).

33. *Münchner Merkur* (Oct. 20, 1964).

34. Critiques: Mayer, *Die Zeit* (Sept. 18, 1964); in a review of S. Bellows's *Herzog*, he drew a parallel between the American novel and the Swiss one, *Die Zeit* (April 30, 1965); Reich-Ranicki's reply, *Die Zeit* (Oct. 2, 1964); Holthusen, *Merkur* (Nov. 1964); H. Vormweg, *Der Monat* (Dec. 1964). Worthy of mention among the innumerable other reviews are R. Baumgart "Othello als Hamlet," *Spiegel* (Sept. 2, 1964); P. Hamm, "Entwürfe zu einem späten Ich," *Die Weltwoche* (Oct. 16, 1964); A. E. Hohler, *Tagesanzeiger* (Zurich, Sept. 12, 1964, negative); R. Michaelis, *Frankfurter Allgemeine Zeitung* (Aug. 29, 1964); W. Weber, *Neue Zürcher Zeitung* (Sept. 12, 1964); G. Blöcker, "Max Frischs Rolle," *Süddeutsche Zeitung* (Sept. 5, 1964); A. Krättli, *Schweizer Monatshefte* (Jan. 1965); and finally Peter Schneider's criticism of the reviews by Baumgart, Mayer, Heissenbüttel, Blöcker and Reich-Ranicki, "Die Mängel der gegenwärtigen Literaturkritik," *Neue Deutsche Hefte* (Gütersloh, 1965), no. 107.

35. *Zürich-Transit,* cf. the "Epilogue" in *Zürcher Woche* (Dec. 17, 1965), the Berlin report "Max Frisch als Drehbuchautor," *Neue Zürcher Zeitung* (March 28, 1966), and the review of the text, *Neue Zürcher Zeitung* (May 14, 1966).

36. In numerous motifs, types of scenes, and main thoughts there are parallels; the whitewash motif in *Die Rundköpfe und die Spitzköpfe* and *Andorra,* the motif of smashing furniture in *Die Kleinbürgerhochzeit* and *Hotz.* The stimulus for Brecht's writing *Galilei* and Frisch's writing *Die Chinesische Mauer* was the news of splitting the uranium atom.

37. J. Kaiser, *Dichten und Trachten* (Frankfurt, 1959), no. 13; in *Konsequenzen eines Bildersturms* Kaiser speaks of the remarkable lack of tendentiousness in the work. Various commentators such as Reich-Ranicki and Deschner agree there is no tendentiousness, or even conformity.

38. Notes on *Öderland,* 1961.

39. See *Werkstattgespräche.*

40. See Frisch's epilogue to Hearson and Trewin, *Euer Gnaden haben geschossen* (etchings by R. Searle; Zurich, 1954).

41. Cf. H. Gollwitzer, who refers to both Karl Jaspers and Frisch in his lecture "Gottes Offenbarung und unsere Vorstellung von Gott" (printed 1964, Munich).

42. Concerning Frisch in general, see W. Weber, *Zeit ohne Zeit* (Zurich, 1959) and *Tagebuch eines Lesers* (Olten, 1965); G. Rau, *Preuves* (Paris, Aug. 1958); W. Stauffacher, "Langage et Mystère," *Etudes Germaniques* (1965), no. 3 (on *Stiller* and *Gantenbein*); H. Plard, "Der Dramatiker M. F. ...," *Universitas* (Sept. 1964; contains a few errors); M. Gassmann, "Max Frisch, Leitmotive der Jugend" (Ph.D. diss., Zurich, 1966); H. Karasek's monograph in *Friedrichs Dramatiker des Welttheaters* (Velber, 1966); D. Zatonskij, "Homo Max Frisch," *Inostrannaja literatura* 4 (1966; with a reprint of *Homo faber,* translated into Russian).

HORST STEINMETZ

Frisch as a Diarist

One of the trivialities in Frisch scholarship has been to point out the close connection between Frisch's *Tagebuch* (Diary) *1946-1949* and the rest of his work. To discover the inseparable interweaving of his diary and literary work does not require any great acumen. The interconnection, moreover, has been increased with the appearance of the second *Tagebuch* in 1972. A whole series of dramas is present in the *Tagebuch 1946-1949* in the form of either a conceptual outline or at least a motif inventory; namely, *Graf Öderland, Andorra, Als der Krieg zu Ende war, Biedermann und die Brandstifter, Schinz*. In addition, a great number of individual motifs are found there that are encountered again in almost all the literary works; for example, the motifs of repetition and self-acceptance. Also smaller details that appear later in the works already exist in the diary, such as the angel that Stiller will meet, or observations about jealousy and unfaithfulness that return in *Mein Name sei Gantenbein*. By no means, however, can the *Tagebuch I* be treated as merely a type of motif or content source for Frisch's dramas or novels, nor as, in addition, something like a poetic of Frisch's.

Naturally it has also been noticed how often Frisch uses the diary as both form and motif in other works. *Stiller* as a novel is written for the most part in diary form; in *Homo faber* not only does the "second station" constitute a diary but also the "first station" is to be conceived as a type of diary written subsequent to the events. *Mein Name sei Gantenbein* consists of a self's entry notes that do not, to be sure, appear directly in diary form but can readily be understood as a diary-form style. The dossier used by the recorder-registrar in the play *Biografie* is not, according to the author's stage directions, a diary that Kürmann did keep, although it is one that could exist in his mind. The early piece *Santa Cruz* shows the captain during the writing of his diary; *Bin oder Die Reise nach Peking*, written even before *Santa Cruz*, follows in its layout the structure of a diary, and that is also the outline of the even earlier *Blätter aus dem Brotsack*. This regular resort to diary forms or similar structures unmistakenly points toward the fact that the relationship between Frisch's diaries and literary work is closer and more intensive than is the case with other authors who during their other poetical writing might have kept a diary and published it later—even during their lifetimes. In Frisch there is manifested a relationship that goes much beyond connections of motif and content. Thus Jürgen Schröder correctly determined: "A boundary line between his diaries and other work can hardly be drawn."[1] Actually it is necessary to go a step further, since a boundary cannot be drawn at all. The reciprocal crossover of the boundary not only applies to individual aspects of subject matter, content, and form but also characterizes the structure and essence of Frisch's entire oeuvre. The congruency between diary and work is so great that finally all his literary works have to be defined as components of a comprehensive diary. After all it is inconsequential whether one designates the literary work as sections of the diaries or the diaries as literary products.

An unprejudiced view of the diaries has been obstructed repeatedly by among other things the fact that so many of Frisch's works have been anticipated in motif or sketch in *Tagebuch I*. That has been misleading above all in the sense of understanding it to be a type of idea storehouse. In actuality, however, these sections, partly carried out and partly mere literary projections, have their own function in the *Tagebuch*, serving the elucidation of the problems discussed and portrayed in the diary. For as in *Bin oder Die Reise nach Peking, Stiller, Santa Cruz*, or *Biografie*, there stands in the center of the diaries a man or person, an ego that wants to find information about himself. And the so-called literary inserts are not primarily the first conceptions or formulations that are later completed and merely jotted down or noted at the time of the diary's composition; rather they are attempts to objectify one's own self, they are the expression of the wrestling carried out to delimit the nonself. Used already in *Tagebuch I* as well as later in other works was the "invented example," employed for the elucidation of experiences, for the attempt at objectification in parable form of the elements incapable of direct expression.

Only from the perspective of the later publications, not from the perspective of *Tagebuch I*, do the sketches of *Graf Öderland, Andorra,* or *Biedermann* constitute first drafts or projections. Read in the context of *Tagebuch I*, they constitute alienating self-analyses of the diary-self and descriptions of his relationship to the world. In them are documented the play character and consciousness, and the artistic element, for whose creation Brecht's techniques were already used even before they were reflected upon in *Tagebuch I*.

Therein is revealed the especially close interconnection of the diary form and the techniques of an alienating portrayal. In Frisch they are inseparable. They develop and complement each other, and in a type of reciprocal amalgamation they lead to art forms, to forms of fiction and illusion that are characteristic of Frisch's oeuvre and alone capable of suitably rendering his special themes and problems, of portraying them at all.

At least since the nineteenth century the personal notes of a diary (which was merely the chronologically ordered recording of certain events, experiences, and thoughts of its "keeper") have developed into forms serving many types of literary purposes. Innumerable diaries that only remotely possess a similarity with the original form illustrate the development from a private, intimate journal to a literary medium, to an art form whose publication is planned before being written. However, with regard to the great variety of forms that the genre has assumed in the twentieth century,[2] it is not decisive that even many diaries in the traditional sense have from their inception been planned for publication. Nor is the use of the diary as a form of fiction in the novel or novella a determining factor. This type already had made its appearance in the eighteenth century (Tieck, *Ein Tagebuch*, 1798; diary inserts are found substantially earlier, Defoe, *Robinson Crusoe*, 1719; Richardson: *Pamela*, 1740). It is a phenomenon that developed alongside the epistolary novel and novels containing epistolary inserts. Along with this line of development, which is continued in Frisch's novels, exists the pure diary form, a form ensuing without any direct connection to the novel but still serving, nevertheless, literary purposes. To be sure, with this type the original diary form is subjected to numerous variations and modifications. Due to its very nature, the diary form accommodated itself to this development since its "open form," its loose structure, and its internal and external flexibility make it an ideal vessel for all possible representations, objects, stylistic levels, and intentions without making it necessary to relinquish its characteristic features.

The great range of diary forms can hardly be surveyed today. On the one hand there stands, for instance, a work like *The Diary of Witold Gombrowicz*, which contains an extensive public justification of its author. Parts of the diary were published while it was still being drafted. Gombrowicz depicts his own actions and experiences; his personal perspective is decisive throughout. In this way his work maintained a large part of the diary tradition. On the other hand stands a work structured completely differently: Heinrich Böll's *Irish Diary*, a work that is actually a collection of stories from Ireland. Here the interweaving of the author's person and personality with the narrated material has the most subordinated significance. Peter Boerner thus asks with good reason whether the title *Diary* is justified here.[3]

The diaries of both Gombrowicz and Böll no longer coincide with the layout and intention of the private journal. Gombrowicz uses the form of a personal confession for public justification, which through its very representation as originally private notations intends to gain in credibility. In Böll the connection with the personal, private sphere is in actuality suspended. In *Irish Diary* the diary form is the bond holding the narrative together. It has taken the place of a narrated plot.

Somewhere between these two modern formulations of the diary stand the diaries of Max Frisch. Their exact placement is made even more difficult by the fact that they are put into the context of a special form of the diary. One encounters in almost all observations and investigations of *Tagebuch I* the concept of a "literary diary," which is considered to be a special genre of diary, to which Max Frisch's work also belongs.

All the problems that the diary as literary genre can proffer seem to be combined in Frisch's *Tagebuch I*. It conveys the impression that it was begun and at least in some sections kept as a private diary; at the same time it was from the beginning manifestly written for readers. It is a "writer's workshop," at least it can evoke that impression; on the other hand there is no doubt that it is "artistically constructed," composed as a complete whole. That can be readily recognized in the recurring place names, which have replaced to a large extent the dates characteristic of a diary, and announce with their recurrence as "chapter headings" certain thematic complexes (Café de la Terrasse, Café Odeon). The diary appears full of contradictions—but only as long as it is read as a personal diary of Max Frisch, that is, as long as it is viewed simply as private notations brought into the public eye, notations—as expected in the case of a writer—that have been interspersed with literary inserts, with sketches of literature, similar to poetical études.

The dedication to the reader, however, attempts at the very beginning to hinder such a reading of the book. It warns against understanding the book merely as a traditional diary: "The reader would be doing this book a great favor if he, rather than leafing back and forth according to whim and chance, observed the compositional sequence; the single stones of a mosaic, and such a mosaic is at least the intention of this book, can hardly justify themselves individually" (7).[4] Thus individual passages as isolated sections do not convey the intention of the author; only the book as a whole is capable of achieving the effect. The diary does not thereby reveal the intimate sphere of the author.

Yet an additional fact relativizes the *Tagebuch* as a diary in the usual sense. The author hardly ever expresses a concern about eventually rereading his own notations. This diary was evidently made for his own use in a different sense. When the writer speaks of reading his diary, he almost never does it in regard to himself.[5] More interest is shown for the writing itself, for the act of writing. "Writing constitutes reading one's self" (22) states the central sentence in the section "Of the sense of a diary." And even in the various entries on the theme of writing, writing is emphasized not only in its meaning concerning the activity of an author but directly concerning its existential value for the person writing.

The challenge to the reader to read the book as a whole and not as a traditional diary, as well as the recurring reflections and statements about the sense of writing are keys for the structure and understanding of *Tagebuch I*. They underline the inner structure of the work, whose unity is not to be found in the author's biography or in the chronology of his notated experiences. These statements are at the same time a first indication of the fictionality of the whole.

Frisch himself explicitly stated that his *Tagebuch I* was not to be confused with the "private diary that one once kept as a young man"; here he has used the diary as a "literary form." His *Tagebuch I* went beyond the "log book of chronological events," it was a diary that sought reality not only in the facts but equally in fiction.[6] It is not inconsequential that Frisch avoids the term "literary diary" and speaks of a "diary in literary form." Thus he emphatically indicates the fictional character of *Tagebuch I*, which does not claim to be a literary diary in the traditional sense but rather belongs to literary forms and structures.

How then can the fictionality of a diary be developed when it doubtlessly contains a great number of autobiographical facts? How can the "I" of this diary, which also undeniably exists outside of the work, lose his demonstrable reality and become a fictional figure? The answer can be found in one of the numerous statements of the diary-self about himself: "Every experience remains basically unrelatable as long as we hope to be able to express it with the actual example that befell us. Only that example which is as distant from me as it is from the listener is capable of expressing me: namely, the fictional example. Only what has been poetisized, transposed, transfigured, only what has been formed is, in essence, capable of conveying" (411). With these words the constitutive relationship is sketched out in which the expressive values of fact and fiction stand in relation to the self of the diarist. Facts have only a limited value because the self involved in them cannot appropriately express itself. That is better achieved, if not solely, with the "fictional example." This amounts to nothing other than the fact that the self becomes observable in its true nature only when it uses fiction for self-recognition and self-representation. And that again means that the reader, if he wants to gain insight into the personality of the diarist, cannot refer to or invoke those statements of the writer that appear to agree with a reality beyond the framework of the book. Precisely those passages that apparently contain Frisch's actual experiences are the ones that do not concern the true self and whose reliability is therefore suspect.

To be touched upon only marginally is the problem that arises when the reader cannot with ease distinguish between fact and fiction. The criterion for his decision is gained through comparison with the reality outside of *Tagebuch I*. However, this procedure naturally does not guarantee any correct results. Even where we seem to be dealing with facts from the life of the writer Max Frisch—and in most cases the reader is only able to surmise as much—we could in principle still be dealing with fiction. To give an extreme example: the whole complex of "Letzigraben," the "second" vocation as an architect, could be fiction and interpreted as such, as a "fictional example."

One can easily make a test, as an example, of the diarist's words according to which not the "real" but only the "fictional" sample can express his nature. In the midst of the notes is found an autobiography of the author. This autobiography is mostly limited in its length of seven and a half pages to external dates and locations, such that there emerges a type of brief life story. It is not much more than a sketchy outline of the writer's life's story. Sober, objective, limiting itself almost completely to verifiable facts, the author courteously places the external data of his life at the disposal of those who call for such a biography and expect none other. Absent is the rendering of all personal information. Thus it has not been without secret irony that Frisch scholarship has made thorough use of this "autobiography" to impart specific information about Frisch. It is with yet greater irony that apparently no one has remarked until now in what great contrast the autobiography stands to many other sections of *Tagebuch I*. It portrays an image that corresponds to the requirements of many Frisch readers. Precisely therein lies, however, the distancing of the diarist from this image. The fact is degraded to an image so that in this "autobiography," it is precisely the self of the diary that cannot be found.

Yet there is no lack of obvious indications of the incidental character of this self-portrayal as far as the self of the diary is concerned. Preceding the biography are some sentences printed in italic and parentheses in which the autobiographer speaks of the impossibility of avoiding repetition—which leads to the emergence of an image. In Paris it is impossible to do anything that is not already routine or a cliché: "There is nothing in this city that millions have not already done, seen, painted, written, experienced" (274). Following this sentence are the words leading into the "autobiography": "Thus, directed to myself, I am writing today about myself" (274). Being directed to oneself in this context turns into a glaringly ironic statement, since what follows precisely does not refer to the actual self but rather to that which is not "fictional," that which is true, to be sure, but only of superficial, not essential, significance.

In addition, the text of the autobiography itself contains—in spite of all brevity and objectivity—an indication signaling the relativity of its value. In the short depiction of the first foreign journey undertaken by the journalistic novice, the following is found:

> The trip, the first one out of the country, led ever further, with every article that was published at home or in Germany, across Hungary and the length and breadth of Siberia, Bosnia, Dalmatia, where, soon befriended with German emigrants, I spent a whole

> summer, sailing around for days on end along the coast, exempt from any responsibility, free, ready for every present moment; this is then my actual memory of youth. Later the trip progressed to the Black Sea, which my mother had spoken about so often, to Constantinople, where I became acquainted with the mosques and hunger, finally to the Acropolis and as a wanderer on foot through the center of Greece, where I spent the nights in fields, once also in a small temple. It was, in spite of being darkened by the death of a young woman, a full and happy time (278).

The "actual memory of youth" is designated as the period that stands basically in contradiction with the image of the self-biographer. It is a period of freedom that is incomprehensible through the means of conventional portrayal in a life's story. Through the added description there shimmers something of the longings and desires of the self. In them there appears a contrast to the image otherwise portrayed in the autobiography, an image that the author projects of himself for the purpose of distance for himself and for others.

The autobiography and its "antinomian" relationship to the other parts of *Tagebuch I* shed light precisely upon those sections that seem to be linked with the nonfictional reality. These parts convey a reality that is real in a superficial sense but do not include the "actual" reality nor even at best approach it. Corresponding to the image of the self shown in the autobiography is the image of the world. This image comprises the person's superficial aspects, representing a relative value. It practically forces the diary writer to go beyond it, to replace it with other images more appropriate to reality, if not at least to enlarge upon it. What the diarist is seeking in his depiction of the world and of the confrontation of his inner self with it is "realms of life yet unknown, unexperienced realms, a world that has not yet been described" (241), that lies concealed in or behind the actual reality. Hence the numerous travel impressions—"Under way" (Unterwegs) reads the programmatic heading of a series of entries—hence also the strong hope felt throughout (but thwarted at the end of the book) that the catastrophe of the Second World War might have changed the rigid image of the world along with the conduct of men relative to such a world view. Out of this hope speaks the conception that the present image of the world and the individual is merely provisional; one can and must overcome that world. In this context the hesitant and objective descriptions of life in the ruined German cities, of Theresienstadt, of the sojourns in Poland and Russia are to be movingly felt. Consequently the author refrains from almost any interpretation. He is reluctant to draw conclusions from the image he sees. The image is not permitted to be transposed into the "actual." From the standpoint of the observer, however, there does not become visible any "new world that should be brought to light through epic discovery but rather only the distorted face of the old one that we know and that is worthy of mention only in its aberrance; that is to say, the ruin presupposes that we know, or at least have a sense of, its earlier wholeness, the ruin is almost nothing without the background of its yesterday, it is worthy of mention only by comparison, with reflection" (242). Coming to terms with the world, to which process his autobiography belongs, as well as with all the experiences of the self which affect its existence in the world basically occurs in light of a double perspective. The diary keeper recognizes the parallel between his existence and the image of the world. He writes a diary in order to escape the one-sidedness of these images. Finally, coming to terms with the world takes place for the sake of his own self. The decisive goal is the battle for self-recognition on the part of the essentiality lying behind the, as it were, official autobiography. The diary has its center point in the "thought, whether it would be possible that our life could have proceeded differently" (174).

From this vantage point reality is seen as only one of the possibilities standing open to the self for realization. Therefore, as a fact, the irrefutability of this self-materialization is called into question. In principle it is replaceable with a different reality. In this manner the solidity of reality is diminished. And with it the verifiable reality of the author Max Frisch is relativized to such an extent that it borders on the reality form of fiction according to its essence and constitution as only one realization of different possibilities. It has no more argumentative force than the fiction.

The insight and recognition of this state of affairs establish the point of departure for composing the diary, and simultaneously this insight and recognition are to be substantiated with the aid of the dairy. By writing, forming first of all the images into words, the author is able to see through the provisory value of reality. "Writing amounts to reading one's self." The act of writing has in this context both a negative and a positive aspect. With the rendering of the existing reality, one is first of all in a position to read what one is not. One can only describe the image, depict it as that which is. If, on the other hand, one attempts by means of the writing process to express (directly) the "actual," then the undertaking's dubiousness is revealed in all its severity, and that has to be overcome if writing is to have meaning. Language turns out to be closely affiliated with the image, to be part of the reality that comprehends merely the surface:

> Our concern, the actual, can at best be paraphrased, and that means most literally: One writes around and around it. One encloses it. One makes statements that never contain our actual experience, which remains inexpressable; these statements can only encircle it, as close

and exact as possible; and the actual, the unutterable appears at best as the tension between them.

Our endeavor is presumably to express everything that is utterable. Language is like a chisel that hews everything away that is not secret; and all saying means removing. In that respect it should not disconcert us that everything that comes to words lapses into a certain emptiness. One says what life is not. One says it for the sake of life (42).

In view of this situation, self-understanding presents itself to the writer only in a roundabout way. His only other alternative is to represent the nonreal, in which language also contains, at least in part, other truth. This is the alternative of art, genuine invention, the "fictional example." This alternative offers him the possibility of exemplifying himself in other images. Here also they remain images since here also language forms the basis upon which rest the varying projections of the self. However, the noncommittalness now amounts to freedom; the replaceability becomes an advantage. The examples are, in the true sense of the word, samples. They achieve something of the character of theatrical roles. They resemble theatrical situations, testing, playing, creating the illusion of an artificially projected reality that, though not real, is yet true. Thus it is not coincidental that the diary writer repeatedly speaks of his fascination with the theater. He recognizes in the situation created by the theatrical "framework" what he is otherwise incapable of seeing: people (66).

The fictions in *Tagebuch I* in this manner become proofs for the existence of the true self veiled for the greatest part by images. The numerous so-called literary inserts are thus not to be conceived as the first jottings down of the works of the author Max Frisch but rather as self-projections that express the true self. In any case they are supposed to contribute to suspending (Aufheben) one-sidedness and the falsifying limitation of factual (yet already relativized) life, or at least to make it perspicuous. The unity and totality of *Tagebuch I,* which Frisch in the dedication postulates as something to be accepted by the reader, is brought about by this correspondence between foreground reality and exemplary fiction structured in the manner just discussed. The *Tagebuch I* does not divide into two parts, as it were, with the one comprising a private diary and the other containing literary sketches. Rather they complement each other; together they result in a work of literature.

The close interweaving and homogeneity of the "fictional examples" and of the other entries of *Tagebuch I* are not recognizable solely on the basis of the writer's comments but are demonstrated by the text itself. As a rule the fictional episodes follow sections in which their general theme is reflected upon; and then the simple sequence is usually transformed into a near dialectical relationship. The insight of the reflections is transposed, as Frisch likes to say elsewhere, into a "story" (Geschichte)[7] or, better, into a type of play action. To a great extent this process corresponds in its model form to the conditions and forms of the Brechtian theater. Seen from the factual form of its life, the self alienates itself within the fictions of certain play situations, where its unrealized existential possibilities and variants gain contour. In this manner, as in Brecht, the factualness of supposedly irrevocable occurrences is suspended in favor of an alteration intended to further the truth. For the portrayal of his specific "self" subject matter (Ich-Problematik), Frisch in *Tagebuch I* employs a technique similar to the Brechtian alienation. And he apparently has not fully recognized the significance of the technique developed and applied in this work when he speaks of how enticing it would be to apply Brecht's theory of alienation to the novel as well (294). He has already done what appears to him to be merely an enticing idea.

The fact that the inseparable coherence of the so-called literary insertions and the other sections has not been noticed is all the more surprising when it is set forth with explicit words in more than one place. That happens most distinctly in the well-known section carrying the title "Du sollst dir kein Bildnis machen" ("Thou shalt not make any graven image"). Into this section is interpolated the story of the "Andorran Jew," which is usually interpreted solely as an early prose version of the later theatrical piece *Andorra*. For an understanding of *Andorra* it is customary to refer to the comments in "Du sollst dir kein Bildnis machen." The opposite course, however, is the correct one. In any case, this is the course that should be pursued in analyzing *Tagebuch I*.

With the biblical command "Thou shalt not make a graven image" we are to be warned against marking out or determining another man merely according to the conception we have made of him. In doing so, we limit his possibilities, his chances to be able to change or vary in accordance with those possibilities that lie within him but are not yet realized. We reduce his reality to the image of him that we have projected. In this manner we become the "composers (Verfasser) of others" (33). These thoughts form one of the main theses of *Tagebuch I*, in light of which one can read almost the whole book; moreover, in light of this principle almost all the literary works of Max Frisch can be unfolded. In *Tagebuch I* the diary writer confirms and documents as much in innumerable passages. Again and again he points out the danger of images, their one-sidedness and power of misconception. The autobiography is an indirect certification of it. Just as often, however, Frisch also shows the possibility of breaking through the constraint of the image.

Into this context then is inserted the story of the Andorran Jew, the story of the young man whom all the Andorrans consider Jewish. Because they treat him exclusively as a Jew, in accordance with their image of him, the only possible thing for him to do is to become a Jew. Finally, without its being explained in greater detail, his death comes in a cruel and revolting manner. Not until then do the Andorrans realize that they have destroyed a life by the image they projected of him: "Until one day it turns out that the deceased—something he could not have known himself—was an orphan whose parents were later discovered, and he was an Andorran like one of us" (37).

Reflection and narration complement each other; they relate basically to the same thing. Their relation to each other illustrates by way of example the tie between private, personal entries and fiction. The fiction is a reflection transposed into another image or rather the allegorical shaping of that which was recognized in theory or in an experienced event. The narration is tightly bound to its context and for that reason—and this cannot be reiterated often enough—it is not the first sketch of the later model.

In principle, the later theatrical piece could already have been interpolated into the diary. The dramatic form would not have changed anything in the relevant context.

The "Moritat Graf Öderland," for example, is also found in a theatrical version in the *Tagebuch I*. In this case Frisch has progressed with the drafting of the later work no further than perhaps with *Andorra*. Here also it is a matter of a "fictional example" with which an episode and experience of the diary-self is to be expressed. "Graf Öderland" follows a series of entries that form a thematic unity. The first of them "Aus der Zeitung" (from the newspaper) reports of a cashier who, apparently completely without motivation, slays his family with an ax. The following entry carries the title "Am See" (at the lake). The diary keeper there depicts how he often interrupts his daily drive to work to pass some time at the lake. There, in full view of nature, he recognizes the one-sidedness of his existence, the uniformity and senseless of his well-ordered daily life. He is able to evade all that for short moments at the lake. There he is able to find refuge for a few moments from the administratively structured life, which, to be sure, is also threatening this location: "Now the place ... has become a daily refuge, and whether I am on my way home, exhausted from a sullen day, or again on the way to work, which will be every bit as sullen as yesterday and the day before yesterday, I always feel assurance and expectation as long as I am going toward the water. Someday an officer will come here also, asking for identification; there has to be [some kind of] order!" (70/71) And somewhat further on it reads: "Often while I am sitting here, it amazes me more and more often why we do not simply break out" (72). The possibility of breaking out has taken form in the "newly discovered myth" (as Dürrenmatt calls it)[8] of Graf Öderland, while simultaneously the motif of order and the newspaper story of the cashier's apparently senseless murder are fashioned together with it. The myth becomes an allegorical execution of what was felt by the diarist. The judge (in the later versions he is the prosecuting attorney), as an alienated self of the diary writer and with an ax in his hand, breaks out of the everyday order in hopes of gaining life, i.e., in order to realize his long-suppressed life and existential possibilities. He attempts (in vain) to break out of the rigid images of life and of his own self.

The series of similar examples could be extended without effort. There is, for example, the "Story with the Russian Colonel and the German Woman" (220), which was the nucleus of the later theatrical piece *Als der Krieg zu Ende war* (When the War Was Over). This story again distinctly belongs in the context of the reflections on images and on language: "What it is in the case that captivates me: That it represents an exception, something special, a living contradiction of the rule, of prejudice. Everything human appears as something special. Overcoming prejudice; the only overcoming possible is that found in a love which makes no image. In this special case, it is facilitated by the lack of a language. It would hardly have been possible if they could have encountered or had been constrained to encounter each other in language. Language as receptacle of prejudice!" (220).

Furthermore there is the "Burlesque," the later *Biedermann und die Brandstifter* (The Firebugs), following the depiction of the overthrow of the government in Czechoslovakia in 1948, where the author criticizes the "general self-conceit: that would not be possible with us" (242). There is "The Harlequin, Sketch of a Movie," preceded by some thoughts on death and immortality that are then transposed into a play action. There is finally the "sketch" of the attorney Heinrich Gottlieb Schinz, which among other things can be read as a commentary on the autobiography. While the outer world considers Schinz a "clinical case," he has made a new consequential existential experience; he has, as he says, "encountered the spirit" (Geist) (433). The short story of Schinz appears in a conspicuous place: shortly before the end of *Tagebuch I*. In this manner it not only has the power of suggestion, but it also has a special significance; indeed, in it the general theme of the entire diary is taken up again: the distance that exists between the image of a man and his actual reality. This sketch in this place challenges the reader not to identify the diary keeper with the author Max Frisch. The diary-self is not documented in controllable facts but rather and above all in its attempt to find out "what is possible for us in this life" (32).

The content of the "fictional examples," however, is not only what they show as alienations of the real self or its image. On many other occasions it is also a question of what they demonstrate. Thus, for instance, the author in the Café Odeon encounters a man who "associates his name with a distinct hate" (271) without even knowing the person bearing the name. Immediately before the sketch of Schinz stands a short passage about a sojourn in Arles. It reads:

> I light a cigarette. It could also be a totally different city; one always sits before the puzzle of an ant hill. Do not ask why! They simply go back and forth because they live. They simply live. Beautiful. That is, many do not live beautifully, for example, those in alleys that eternally stink of discharge, but they do not smell it; habituation is everything. In any case they live, they go or sit, they talk together. One is just coming from hunting in the Camargue; he stands the rifle on the wall, orders a coffee, and tells of the bugs that bothered him. Would I like to be this hunter? Or any other citizen of Arles, for instance, the doubtlessly very distinguished man on the left? (429)

Here is described in its essential aspects a point of departure, such as the ones that will later constitute the *Gantenbein* novel.

Also in quite inconspicuous places the basic theme is recognizable again and again. One example is the conversation that the architect Frisch has with a worker at the construction site Letzigraben. It closes this way:

> "Do you know," he says, "I also actually wanted to become something completely different—"
> "Namely?"
> "An artist" (270).

The *also* in the sentence placed in the worker's mouth discloses more about the diary writer than about the speaker. The architect had not mentioned with a single word that he had wanted to become something else. Thus the *also* must be interpreted as an insertion of the diary-self, who recognizes his own problematical question in the statement of the worker and then, in the notation of this conversation, makes him a type of companion who "also" senses the limitations in his life.

Thus, on almost every page the unity of the basic theme and the associated expansion and fictionalization of the author-self can be observed. In this manner *Tagebuch I* is divested of the one-sided, pragmatic character of being the depiction of the thoughts and experiences of an empirical person, and it is transferred into the realm of fiction and literature. Hans Werner Richter is one of the few who have recognized this basic structure, although he also was not able finally to let go of the idea, both that a literary diary is supposed to remain in its very essence a statement of an empirical person and that a disintegration of its basic form is inadmissable:

> Objective? Yes, am I moreover honestly objective? In attempting it, I am already departing from the truth. I am no longer taking notes, I

> am telling tales. I am telling tales for the diary reader, my diary reader of tomorrow. Is that the sense of a diary?
> In many literary diaries I discover this propensity not to note down but rather to tell tales. That is what makes it worth reading to the consumer.
> Max Frisch is an example of that. He writes a novel and presents it as a diary. It is almost always not the novel of his life but rather of how he imagines his life, his thoughts, and his experiences. These imagined conceptions correspond to the conceptions of Max Frisch's reader.[9]

Richter is right to the extent that he determines that the book is directed in its intention toward the readers. That also cannot be any different since we are, to be sure, not dealing with a private diary. On the contrary, we are dealing with literature that is just as much fiction and illusion as Frisch's dramas and novels and that addresses itself to readers just as all literature does. Frisch himself stated these facts unequivocally. In his conversations with Horst Bienek he pointed out that the diary form was "specifically characteristic (eigentümlich) for the author with my name."[10] In such a formulation, strange only at first glance, we can perceive the adequate mirroring of the basic structure of the diary-self. The formulation emphasizes the fact that Frisch is conscious of the special form that he had been able to give to the diary as literary genre. Characteristically Frisch does not speak of a literary diary, but rather of a "diary as literary form." However we might interpret the sentence that the diary form is specifically characteristic for the author with his name,[11] the unusual statement makes one thing evident: the diary writer is not the citizen Max Frisch but rather an author bearing his name. Thus in *Tagebuch I* the same relationship prevails between the author Max Frisch and the diary-self as between the author of a first-person novel and the first-person narrator appearing in it. With Frisch they both merely bear the same name. From this fact came the misunderstanding that *Tagebuch I* was a book of personal notes rather than the fictional work that it actually is, standing in its essential nature closer to the novel than to the genuinely private journal.

1. Jürgen Schröder, "Spiel mit dem Lebenslauf. Das Drama Max Frischs," N. Neumann, J. Schröder, M. Karnick: *Dürrenmatt, Frisch, Weiss. Drei Entwürfe zum Drama der Gegenwart* (Munich, 1969), p. 63.
2. Cf. Peter Boerner, *Tagebuch* (Stuttgart, 1969), esp. pp. 51 ff.
3. Ibid., p. 28.

4. All references in the text refer to the edition *Tagebuch 1946-1949* (Frankfurt, 1958; Zweites Suhrkamp Hausbuch).

5. Even in the case where the author also is compelled to read what he has written—he has to correct parts of the galley proofs—the role of reader is imputed to others, and also when the reader is "a creation of your imagination, not unreal and not more real than the characters of a narration or play" (182). Reading what he has written, even what he has written in his diary, belongs in any case to the category of extraordinary situations: "Reading one's self! I need a lot of Cinzano for that. Which is not to say that writing is not a pleasure! I shall not leave it. But now and then with a galley in one's hands, one does wonder what kind of an interest that should have for others" (181). Thus here also, from the view of the author as writer and from the view of the reader, the accent lies on writing.

6. Horst Bienek, *Werkstattgespräche mit Schriftstellern* (Munich, 1965), p. 26.

7. M. Frisch, *Ausgewählte Prosa* (Frankfurt, 1965; edition suhrkamp 76), pp. 8ff.

8. Friedrich Dürrenmatt, "Eine Vision und ihr dramatisches Schicksal: Zu *Graf Öderland* von Max Frisch," *Über Max Frisch*, ed. Thomas Beckermann (Frankfurt, 1971; edition suhrkamp 404), p. 110.

9. Hans Werner Richter, "Warum ich kein Tagebuch schreibe," *Das Tagebuch und der moderne Autor*, ed. Uwe Schultz (Munich, 1965; prosa viva 20), p. 104.

10. Bienek, *Werkstattgespräche*, p. 26.

11. Cf. esp. the informative discussion by Jürgen Schröder, pp. 64ff.

LINDA J. STINE

"Ich hätte Lust, Märchen zu schreiben": Frisch's Use of Märchen in *Die Schwierigen* and *Montauk*

Max Frisch[1] once replied, rather snappishly, when asked what led to his obvious fondness for the diary form, that such a question was really tantamount to asking someone with a large nose about how he acquired such a love for large noses; he had no special fondness for it, Frisch went on, he simply had his nose.[2] Many studies have dealt with the diary aspect of Frisch's writing.[3] What has been overlooked in such studies, however, is the fact that it is not so much the diary form itself that characterizes his writing style as it is the telling of stories—the diary simply provides Frisch with a convenient format in which to satisfy his "greediness for stories."[4] Although he has turned to various sources for material for this storytelling, the most common and consistent one is the realm of folklore, the world of the *Märchen*.[5] Frisch explored many different aspects of the *Märchen* during the various phases of his literary career, but a fundamental relationship persists which is present in all the genres he uses and at all points in his development. It ranges from his attempt at writing an original *Märchen* at one point (*Bin oder Die Reise nach Peking*, 1: 601-58) to a book poking fun at a revered legend at another (*Wilhelm Tell für die Schule*, 6: 405-70). He has filled his diaries both with familiar *Märchen* motifs and with new tales sprung from his own imagination, one of which he tried repeatedly to rework into a fulllength drama (*Graf Öderland*, 3: 5-89). He has written a novel and a radio play which have at their core a folktale ("Rip van Winkle" in *Stiller*, 3: 359ff) and has, on the other hand, compressed his own complicated philosophy of writing into a two-sentence-long "Märchen" (in *Montauk*, 6: 661). The relationship of the *Märchen* to Frisch's works, then, is as persistent as it is multifaceted. A brief discussion of Frisch's use of the *Märchen* in his first major novel, *Die Schwierigen oder J'adore ce qui me brûle* (1942) and in his latest one, *Montauk, eine Erzählung* (1974-1975) can provide a structural and conceptual framework within which to view this overall relationship.

Die Schwierigen[6] is interesting today less as an independent artistic creation—its philosophy is rather facile and its style highly derivative—than as a first example of many of the themes and techniques which were to recur throughout Frisch's later writing. His use of the *Märchen* provides a good case in point. The second section of *Die Schwierigen* is entitled "Turandot oder das Heimweh nach der Gewalt." There are several significant aspects to his use of this particular *Märchen* material. Most obvious is the fact that he was already turning to the realm of folklore for parallel stories with which to illustrate a point. The trial of her suitors by a hostile maiden is a basic *Märchen* motif.[7] It turns up often in literature; Schiller, for instance, wrote a drama entitled *Turandot* in which he used the original *Arabian Nights* characters as mouthpieces for his own enlightened philosophy. It is characteristic of Frisch's version, and of his later practices, however, that he changed both the characters and the course of the action. Yvonne in *Die Schwierigen* is not Turandot in a twentieth-century setting, as Schiller had transplanted the Oriental princess to eighteenth-century Weimar: she is compared to Turandot (1: 408f)–the *Märchen* is a symbol. And, again in accordance with Frisch's later methods, he does not merely drop the allusion to the Turandot material and let the reader make his own application. He has Reinhart give *his* interpretation of the Turandot tale, according to which Turandot is the embodiment of an unwanted emancipation which men have foisted upon women, an emancipation which leads women to test men out of the sheer frustration over the fact that men allow this testing. The device of having one of the main characters tell a story within the story is a technique which Frisch later perfects;[8] he conceptualizes his theme in terms of a *Märchen* motif and then puts an explanation of its meaning in the mouth of one of his characters, thereby giving the reader an added dimension with which to view the action, by allowing him to contrast the original material with the fictional character's retelling of it.

A logical question is why Frisch chose to have Reinhart refer to the Arabian Nights version of this motif rather than any other of its numerous appearances in folklore or mythology. Indeed, considering the subtitle and Reinhart's explanation of the story, "*Brünhilde* oder das Heimweh nach der Gewalt" would have done less violence to the spirit of the original source. That he turned to the Turandot material instead is a comment on Reinhart's views of life and literature, as well as perhaps an indirect comment on Frisch himself in this period. When Reinhart explains to Yvonne what he means by comparing her to Turandot, he says: "Es spielt in China, glaube ich, und natürlich ist es ein Märchen." Fantasy and reality were two diametrically opposed spheres for Frisch at this time, torn between his career as an architect and his love of writing: literature, or art, seemed able to exist only apart from the real world, in China perhaps, but not in modern Switzerland. The artist could be integrated into society only after he renounced his art; thus, at the end, Reinhart gives up his life as a painter to serve society as a gardener. (By giving up his career as an artist, he is following in the footsteps of Gottfried Keller's *Der grüne Heinrich*, Frisch's self-avowed "bester Vater" at the beginnings of his career.) And like the Heinrich of Keller's first version,

Reinhart cannot reconcile the needs of society with his personal needs. He eventually commits suicide as his only means of escaping the temptation to remain in the world of fantasy.

Frisch's concern with the dichotomy between life and art is easily traceable, if we follow his varying approaches to the use of the *Märchen*. The problem remains constant in the thirty years following the publication of *Die Schwierigen*; Frisch's solutions for the problem, however, did change. Early works, such as *Die Schwierigen, Bin,* and *Tagebuch 1946-1949*, had used *Märchen* in two opposed ways: as representations or illustrations of reality, and, conversely, as examples of escape from this reality. But regardless of which use he put the *Märchen* to, the boundary between the two worlds remained distinct. Later, in *Stiller* to some extent, and especially in *Tagebuch 1966-1971* and *Mein Name sei Gantenbein*, the fictional world became more "real," while the real world was increasingly colored by fantasy. In *Montauk*, this process is completed.

Frisch had suggested the direction his thoughts were taking in a 1971 interview, when asked whether he would now be working on a new diary. He admitted his preoccupation with the problem of reality versus fiction and the connection of the diary form with this theme. And he continued: "First I have a forefront reality. Let us assume I described how I drove with you through Brooklyn and Queens today. . . . And I indicated the exact date and what I had seen in the manner of a report. Then suppose I wrote a reflection or a fictional story. The fiction would then be much more aware of its own fictionality and would therefore be much purer than one I simply invented. . . . All I know is that I would like to spend some time again with pure fiction, either with drama or prose.[9]" What resulted was *Montauk*, the framework of which is a description of the weekend two characters named Max and Lynn spend at a small hotel on Montauk, Long Island. Events of the weekend call forth reflections and reminiscences by the narrator/Frisch about his life to this point, especially to the three important women in his life, his first wife Constance, the writer Ingeborg Bachmann, and Marianne, his present wife. But while the narrator protests again and again that his telling of the framework story is simply an objective report of actual events with nothing fictional added, this claim is made questionable by the narrator's attitude toward the events he reports, an attitude just like that of a modern storyteller to the unproblematic fictionality of the *Märchen* world.

The direction that Frisch's involvement with the *Märchen* followed in the years between *Die Schwierigen* and *Montauk* is not an unusual one. As writers mature, their work typically becomes more abstract. Problems that were once dealt with as external subject matter become an internalized question of form. Thus Frisch's concern with the *Märchen* in *Montauk* becomes more subtle, but it provides no less basic a theme. It provides *Montauk* with an added dimension; the reader's part is written into the novel, in a sense. The work then functions on two levels, the unproblematical and therefore fairy-tale-like world of the frame story and the problematic, reflective level of the narrator, who tells the frame story while at the same time contemplating his reactions to it, an analyzing process which the reader finishes.

Perhaps the two levels of reaction to the *Märchen* world in *Montauk* can be best explained through a brief discussion of the way two other modern authors have used the *Märchen*: Franz Kafka and Thomas Mann. Clemens Heselhaus called Kafka's novellas "antimärchen,"[10] a characterization which probably implies too conscious a use of *Märchen* tradition on Kafka's part but which does point up its importance in Kafka's writings. Kafka's works, Heselhaus claims, are antimärchen because it is precisely the *Märchen*'s characteristic sense of invisible community, the idea that things happen as they should, that is lacking.[11] One can move a step further with this observation. The reason that the world of Kafka's novels seems lacking in sense is that the reader is seeing it only through the eyes of the protagonist. But for all the other characters, the world they inhabit is eminently sensible. Kafka's world could almost be described as the *Märchen* world seen through the eyes of the outsider. His main characters have the "visible isolation"[12] of a *Märchen* hero, but they lack the concomitant invisible community. It is their misfortune to wake up suddenly in a *Märchen* world which they will not or cannot perceive. It is a world that is perfectly rational within itself—if you accept the basic premises. But Joseph K.—like K. or Gregor—is not privy to these premises, and so he is left on the outside, the only sane person in a world gone mad or, from the other viewpoint, the only madman in a perfectly rational universe.

Mann, conversely, creates in Felix Krull a character perfectly in harmony with his environment. His world, though modern, was very much the one-dimensional world of the *Märchen*. Felix was a true *Sonntagskind*, a hero whose passivity only emphasizes the harmonious community of his world— candy and jewels fall into his possession as if by magic, whatever talents are needed he finds, names and appearances and languages are changed with ease. It is possible, despite the obvious differences in philosophy and personality between the two authors, to see in the framework story of *Montauk* something similar to the world Mann created in *Felix Krull*: Frisch's own "Blick zurück ohne Zorn und ohne Selbstmitleid" (*Montauk*, 6: 709) is a fairy-tale reworking of his major themes. Max, like Felix, inhabits an unproblematic world, through which he moves with the ease of a *Märchen* hero. The problems which have occupied Frisch throughout his career—identity, jealousy, transitoriness of life, image-making, and, of course, death—are conspicuous by their absence in the framework story. This Max has time in his one weekend; time for life, but none to worry about its passing; time for new impressions, but not enough to have them harden into habit and prejudice; time to try on new clothes, but not enough to have them settle into the same old wrinkles.

The narrator, however, like the Kafka heroes, cannot understand such a world. He continually marvels at even the most commonplace successes of Max: "Es gelingt nicht alles an diesem Tag. Zwar findet er den Parkplatz (nur in Träumen kommt es vor, dass ich den Wagen nicht mehr finden kann) und der blaue Ford steht an seinem Ort." (6: 651). The narrator is so far from a world in which things happen as they ought that the most normal occurrences are transformed by his observations into *Märchen*-like "miracles"; precisely the attitude of the modern reader, from the perspective of his own complicated world, to the "wonders" of the *Märchen,* wonders which acquire heightened effect because they are simply taken for granted by the characters experiencing them.

Discussing this implied contrast between a real and a *Märchen* world, however, does not exhaust the importance of the *Märchen* concept in the novel; it turns up more openly in a simile expressing a basic conflict arising from Frisch's autobiographical style. In the section headed "Notizen im Flugzeug," we read: "Als Märchen von einem Fischer, der ein Netz einzieht und zieht mit aller Kraft, bis es am Land ist, das Netz, und er ist selber drin, nur er. Er verhungert" (6: 661). It is left to the reader to fill in the missing object of the comparison—*what* is like this *Märchen*? One answer, and a key to a major theme of the novel, could legitimately be writing, as a closer look at this "Märchen" shows. A fisherman who unsuspectingly casts his net only to catch something other than that night's dinner is typical *Märchen* material; one thinks immediately of "Von dem Fischer un syner Fru" (*KHM* #19). It is not so typical, however, in the naive world of the *Volksmärchen*, at least, that this unexpected catch should be the fisherman himself.[13] Nor can *Märchen* tradition explain the second sentence: "Er verhungert."[14] An explanation must take into consideration Frisch's theory of writing, both his reasons for writing *Montauk* (Ich möchte wissen, was ich, schreibend unter Kunstzwang, erfahre über mein Leben als Mann," 6: 633) and his ideas on the reasons for writing in general. *Montauk* is by no means the first place where the idea of writing as a means of gaining self-understanding appears. In *Tagebuch 1946-1949* we find the equation: "Schreiben heisst: sich selber lesen." "Wir können nur," he continues a few lines later, "indem wir den Zickzack unsrer jeweiligen Gedanken bezeugen und sichtbar machen, unser Wesen kennenlernen, seine Wirrnis oder seine heimliche Einheit, sein Unentrinnbares, seine Wahrheit, die wir unmittelbar nicht aussagen können, nicht von einem einzelnen Augenblick aus" (2: 361). There would seem to be an irreconcilable conflict in a writer who considers life to be the omnipresence of infinite possibility[15], but who with equal conviction sees writing as a means of finding out which of those possibilities make up his own life. Success equals failure.

"Der einzige Vorfall, der keine Variante mehr zulässt, ist der Tod," reads a passage from *Tagebuch 1966-1971* (6: 75). Death is the inevitable accompaniment to life's infinite possibility, and it runs like a leitmotiv throughout Frisch's works,[16] till it culminates in *Montauk*, not as accompaniment but as theme. The only passage in *Montauk* where the Ich and the Er, that is the "Märchen" and the "real" world, are identical—and it occurs, significantly, only in the subjunctive—is the episode where Max has accidentally stepped on the brake instead of the clutch and nearly caused a serious accident: "Das wäre es, zwei Verkehrstote, eine junge Amerikanerin (die genauen Personalien) und ein älterer Schweizer (die genauen Personalien), ihr Wochenende an der Küste wäre erzählbar, unser Wochenende" (6: 727). Their weekend would be reportable and would thus be apposite to our weekend, the narrator and the narrated would be one, only if death would end life's infinite variation.[17] Once again in *Montauk*, as is so characteristic of Frisch's style, the spaces between the lines speak more eloquently than the text. The printed lines tell of the happiness of a finite—and fictional—experience of love; the white spaces, the sadness of an infinite resignation.

Thematically and structurally *Die Schwierigen* and *Montauk* show a remarkable similarity in concept. In both works, the full extent of a character's—and novel's—complexity emerges only when the stories he tells and his reasons for telling them are analyzed. The statement Frisch made at the beginning of his literary career: "Man gibt Aussagen, die nie unser eigentliches Erlebnis enthalten, das unsagbar bleibt" (2: 379), might almost be an answer to the narrator's question in *Montauk*: "Dies ist ein aufrichtiges Buch, Leser, und was verschweight es und warum?" (6: 747). For Frisch, now as then, an experience that is written down and described is only one of an infinite number of possible reactions.[18] The true experience that the author wants most to express remains indescribable. All he can hope to do is approach it as closely as possible through circumscription. Thus, Frisch tells story after story in his search for the truth, and whether he chooses a *Märchen* from folklore, as he did in *Die Schwierigen*, or whether he gives a real event *Märchen* overtones, as in *Montauk*, the basic premise and end result are the same: by opposing varying degrees of fantasy, Frisch hopes to suggest through comparison and contrast the one thing words cannot directly express—reality.

---

1. Max Frisch, in a letter quoted by Christa Wolf in "Max Frisch beim Wiederlesen oder: Vom Schreiben in Ich-Form," *Über Max Frisch II*, ed. Walter Walter Schmitz (Frankfurt: Suhrkamp, 1976), p. 12.

2. Horst Bienek, *Werkstattgespräche mit Schriftstellern* (Munich: Carl Hanser, 1962), pp. 26f.

3. See, for example, Rolf Kieser, *Max Frisch: Das literarische Tagebuch* (Stuttgart: Huber, 1975); Heinz Schafroth, "Bruchstücke einer grossen Fiktion: Über Max Frischs Tagebücher," *Text und Kritik* 47/48 (October 1975): 58-69; Horst Steinmetz, *Max Frisch: Tagebuch, Drama, Roman* (Göttingen: Vandenhoeck & Ruprecht, 1973).

4. Max Frisch, "Unsere Gier nach Geschichten," *Gesammelte Werke in zeitlicher Folge*, ed. Hans Mayer and Walter Schmitz (Frankfurt: Suhrkamp, 1976), 4: 262-64. All following references to Frisch's works are from this source and identified in text by volume and page number.

5. *Märchen* is a more comprehensive term than *fairy tale*, including both fairy tales and folktales; I shall use the term *Märchen* in my text for want of an accurate English equivalent.

6. I quote from the 1957 version, 1: 387-601. This is a reprint of Frisch's 1943 novel *J'adore ce qui me brûle oder Die Schwierigen*, from which the first section has been omitted. The omitted section, in turn, was a reworking of Frisch's first published novel, *Jürg Reinhart: Eine sommerliche Schicksalfahrt* (1934), 1: 225-386.

7. Compare, for example, the beginning of "Vom klugen Schneiderlein," *Grimms Kinder- und Hausmärchen* (hereafter *KHM*) #114: "Es war einmal eine Prinzessin gewaltig stolz; kam ein Freier, so gab sie ihm etwas zu raten auf, und wenn er's nicht erraten konnte, so war er mit Spott fortgeschickt. Sie liess auch bekanntmachen, wer ihr Rätsel löste, sollte sich mit ihr vermählen, und möchte kommen, wer da wollte."

8. The best example is his highly intricate use of the Rip van Winkle material in *Stiller*; see my "Chinesische Träumerei–amerikanisches Märchen: Märchenelemente in *Bin* und *Stiller*," *Max Frisch, Aspekte des Prosawerks*, ed. Gerhard P. Knapp (Berne: Peter Lang, 1977-1978).

9. Rolf Kieser, "An Interview with Max Frisch," *Contemporary Literature* 13 (1972): 7.

10. Clemens Heselhaus, "Kafkas Erzählformen," *Deutsche Vierteljahrschrift für Literaturwissenschaft und Geistesgeschichte* 27 (1952): 343-76.

11. See Max Lüthi's discussion of the *Märchen*'s "Allverbundenheit," in *Das europäische Volksmärchen* (Berne: Francke, 1947), esp. p. 64.

12. Ibid., in the chapter on the *Volksmärchen*'s characteristic "sichtbare Isolation, unsichtbare Allverbundenheit," pp. 62ff.

13. For the more complicated and introspective modern writer, however, it seems to be an appropriate result. J.D. Salinger uses similar imagery in one passage from *Seymour: An Introduction* (Boston: Little, Brown, 1959), when he describes a boy catching a fish which he brings home and puts into his bathtub, only to discover that the fish is wearing a school cap like the boy's own, with the same initials sewn inside it. A more striking parallel, considering her prominent role in *Montauk*, is to a passage from Ingeborg Bachmann's "Das dreissigste Jahr": "Er wirft das Netz der Erinnerung aus, wirft es über sich und zieht sich selbst, Erbeuter und Beute in einem, über die Zeitschwelle, die Ortschwelle, um zu sehen, wer er war und wer er geworden ist." *Gedichte, Erzählungen, Hörspiel, Essays* (Munich: R. Piper, 1964), p. 68.

14. I wonder if the image of Kafka's "Hungerkünstler" and the comments it makes on the role of the artist in society entered into this image.

15. First formulated in *Tagebuch 1946-1949*, 2: 360.

16. It has frequently been noted by critics, from early studies like the chapter on leitmotivs in Manfred Jurgensen's *Max Frisch: Die Dramen* (Berne: Lukianos-Verlag Hans Erpf, 1968), pp. 13-25, through the most recent works such as Heinz Gockel's *Gantenbein: Das offen-artistische Erzählen* (Berne: Bouvier Verlag Herbert Grundmann, 1976), esp. pp. 89-122.

17. Gerhard vom Hofe also discusses death from this perspective in his interesting study "Zauber ohne Zukunft," (*Euphorion,* Bd. 70, Ht. 4, pp. 374-97), but I believe *Montauk* is better viewed as the logical development of Frisch's aesthetic principles than as their revision, as vom Hofe claims.

18. Most clearly formulated in *Tagebuch 1946-1949,* 2: 360.

WULF KOEPKE

Frisch's *I'm Not Stiller* as a Parody of *The Magic Mountain*

Writing in "Thomas Mann from a Distance," Reinhard Baumgart observes: "He has hardly found any successors, in contrast to Rilke and Benn, Kafka or Brecht. Nowhere, as far as I can see, has admiration for him emerged from a patient passivity and become productive."[1]

Is this thesis really defensible, even if we limit ourselves to the period after World War II, as Baumgart seems to do? Is such a view not too much determined by an internal German perspective and related to that of the "complete new beginning" of 1945? Furthermore, there is the inevitable counterquestion also alluded to by Baumgart: what is conceivably meant by a "succession" to Thomas Mann, in the sense of a productive confrontation and transformation? I submit that a closer analysis of Max Frisch's *I'm Not Stiller* provides an answer to this question. Several connections have been established between Frisch's narrative works and those of Thomas Mann; connections with *Death in Venice, Doctor Faustus,* and *Felix Krull*;[2] none of them, however, is so obvious as that with *The Magic Mountain.*

It suffices to think of the famous passage about "reproduction" to understand the importance of confrontation with literature for the life of Stiller and thus the book *I'm Not Stiller.* This confrontation takes the form of a sarcastic concern, which stresses the significance of the object by rejecting it and an attempt to establish a distance from it. It is expressed in the form of parody which determines the structure and style of *I'm Not Stiller.*[3] Parody is expressed in many forms and on several levels; it reaches from Stiller's parody of Wild West stories, where Stiller's butt Knobel stands for the gullible audience at large, through that of serious literary models and includes the parodistic use of Max Frisch's own "Thou shalt not make unto thee any graven image." Kierkegaard is also among the examples so used. The nature of this parody can perhaps be most easily illustrated by a comparison of Stiller's Spanish "adventure at the bridge" and Hemingway's *For Whom the Bell Tolls.* Each detail is reversed: Jordan is an experienced expert; Stiller an inexperienced amateur. Stiller is supposed to guard the bridge; Jordan destroys it. Jordan gains love and respect; Stiller's cowardice makes him lose both these and his self-respect also. Both of them are loners, misfits; but while Hemingway describes a critical test for an originally uninvolved

American, Stiller's immature idealism is exposed immediately. The end result in *I'm Not Stiller* is a radical negation of masculinity, of heroism in the style of Hemingway. The "test of man's courage at the front" is turned into its opposite. This parody does not preserve by means of irony, but rather unmasks its object as wrong, untrue, and dangerous.

Especially when considering Thomas Mann, we have to keep in mind that parodies are undertaken with very different attitudes and intentions.[4] Furthermore, we have to consider that Thomas Mann's own procedure was parodistic, so that *I'm Not Stiller* may have to be regarded as a parody of a parody. It is, of course, not really in keeping with the idea of the book to single out and to pursue one such particular relationship, since the web of these relationships and thus of parodies constitutes the nature of *I'm Not Stiller*. But it seems to me that this particular relationship is worth following up, however one may rate its value for the interpretation of the entire work, since it offers an especially illustrative example for Frisch's procedure.

The allusions to Thomas Mann in the book are both incidental and pointed. During his first leave, when Stiller describes Zurich in a relatively friendly mood, he mentions "Thomas Mann's new home" (63)[5] (Mann was in a way Frisch's neighbor when he wrote *I'm Not Stiller*). However, Stiller immediately compares the world-famous Thomas Mann, recipient of all the honors Switzerland can offer, with "all manner of our kind who achieve something outside in the world, until their fame also gradually flatters their own country" (63), who are therefore not at all supported by Switzerland itself when they most need it. This side thrust at Switzerland does not necessarily contain any animosity toward Thomas Mann. But the reader will begin to ask himself more questions when he reads the description of the "reproduction," the proof for Stiller's thesis that "we are tele-viewers, tele-hearers, tele-knowers" (151). Here Stiller says with regard to the "inner life of man": "How the devil am I to prove to my counsel that I don't know my murderous impulses through C. G. Jung, jealousy through Marcel Proust, Spain through Hemingway, Paris through Ernst Jünger, Switzerland through Mark Twain, Mexico through Graham Greene, my fear of death through Bernanos, inability ever to reach my destination through Kafka, and all sorts of other things through Thomas Mann?" (152) The clear aim of the allusion to Mark Twain and Switzerland is Stiller's defense lawyer, the first reader of Stiller's notebooks; the other places which Stiller mentions are those which preoccupy him: Spain, Paris, Mexico, Switzerland, and he likewise enumerates his own problems: fear of death, jealousy, fantasies of murder, the feeling of never-arriving. Stiller pretends to have been in the United States and Mexico during the years after World War II, but he is entirely familiar with the literary fashions in Central Europe. Thus he knows not only about Proust and Kafka but also about the success of Bernanos's *Sous le Soleil de Satan*, Graham

Greene's *The Power and the Glory* (the German translation appeared in 1948), Hemingway's *For Whom the Bell Tolls*, and even Ernst Jünger's *Strahlungen*. The last example, as well as that of Mark Twain, shows that Stiller is quite facetious at times.

How are we to understand in this context "all kinds of other things" in Thomas Mann? In his sculptor's studio Stiller has *The Magic Mountain* as "the only work by Thomas Mann" (320), and he knows this book so well, like all other books in his library, that he can write into his notebook after the hearings at the scene in Davos: "Yesterday in Davos. It is exactly as Thomas Mann describes it" (57). Stiller is playing an American called White who sees Davos for the first time with his own eyes. When he subsequently writes down the "protocol" of Julika's narrative about her disease in Davos, the Thomas Mann reminiscences are getting so obvious that Ulrich Weisstein has called the Davos episode a "pastiche" of *The Magic Mountain*.[6] The most characteristic feature of a pastiche, however, is absent, namely, the mimicry of the style. The Davos episode is not only described with a marked conciseness—only a little over twenty pages without Stiller's visits, in obvious contrast to the epic prolixity of Thomas Mann—it also consciously reverses all motifs aimed directly at Mann. In *I'm Not Stiller* it is the young theologian, a combination of Naphta and Settembrini, who steals the X-ray picture; however, he uses it artfully to demonstrate to Julika how little she knows herself. Hans Castorp reads books himself; Julika gets them explained to her and much more for entertainment than for "education." The rather decidedly Protestant message of the Catholic theologian: "Thou shalt not make an image" is never associated with herself by Julika, but always with Stiller, and thus could be understood as a parody of Frisch's *Andorra* which at that time existed in the *Tagebuch* sketch. In any case the Davos episode shows as well as the postscript of the prosecutor that a molding of the personality by disease, i.e., because of the increased receptivity of the sick person, does not take place; Julika also refuses categorically to enter into the dangerous process of knowledge of the self.

In finding "all kinds of other things" in Thomas Mann, Stiller certainly refers to *The Magic Mountain*. If one considers that the passage about reproduction mentions mostly books which were discussed in the first postwar years, one would think of *Doctor Faustus*; but there is no trace of this relationship. Nor does the *Tagebuch 1946-1949* mention *Doctor Faustus*, even in the passage where Frisch critically comments on the negative attitude with which the Germans received Thomas Mann in 1949. The topic of Germany is generally one of the key areas of the *Tagebuch*, so that it would be logical to find *Doctor Faustus* mentioned. The only significant sentence about Thomas Mann is a quotation. Max Frisch reports his meeting with Albin Zollinger in 1941 and mentions that the latter had praised Thomas Mann as a "master of accuracy."[7] Zollinger can have referred only to earlier books by Thomas Mann.

Among the books mentioned in the reproduction passage, only C. G. Jung and Proust can be found in Stiller's library. No wonder, since Stiller has spent the postwar years in America. Thus the complex "Germany" is eliminated. Therefore we should follow the pointers in the book and look for "all kinds of other things" in *The Magic Mountain*. Even if one discounts Stiller's contemptible tone, "all kinds of other things" can only be understood as deprecation, approximately in this sense: there are lots of other things in Thomas Mann, but not a theme of central importance. That does not have to be taken literally; it only shows that Stiller puts up resistance against Thomas Mann.

There is an external indication that the effect of *The Magic Mountain* is not limited to the Davos episode. Seven notebooks of Stiller correspond to the seven chapters and seven years of Thomas Mann. Stiller's marriage lasts for some seven years, and for approximately the same length of time Stiller is missing.[8] While he writes his seven notebooks, Stiller in his comfortable prison is in reality outside of time, in a "waiting period," and basically he is also outside of Switzerland—and free from himself.[9] After the Spanish civil war Stiller seems to have lost interest in politics, besides not sharing the anticommunism after World War II; but the four central characters—Stiller, Julika, Sibylle, and the public prosecutor—seem to be so preoccupied with their personal affairs that World War II, Auschwitz, and the atomic bomb cannot touch their lives. Some calculation is needed to figure out that the year of crisis with Julika's sickness in Davos, Stiller's affair with Sibylle, and the adventure of the public prosecutor in Genoa is 1945,[10] which at least enables them to travel to Italy, France, and the United States; but the concrete details of the postwar situation which so fascinated the diary writer Max Frisch are completely left out. In spite of all realism, the story of Stiller takes on the character of being removed from time, of a fairy tale. Since on the other hand the situation in Switzerland is described with all references to actual events due to Stiller's juridical confrontation, life in Switzerland altogether is given the atmosphere of a magic mountain, of a society in the mountains without relation to the "plains." After all, the geographic location of *The Magic Mountain* is in Switzerland, although Swiss nationals appear in it only in the roles of "servants." Therefore it cannot be an accident that in Thomas Mann's story the beginning of World War I renders this life in the magic mountain impossible; the story takes place according to the words of the narrator in a past, before the "change of times." Max Frisch's *I'm Not Stiller* reaches into the present and unfolds irrespective of the catastrophes of world history. Would this not suggest regarding Switzerland as a magic mountain, and one that continues in its enchanted existence untouched during the historical crises?

Thomas Mann's magic mountain is not only a place for "Bildung" but above all a place of adventures, and that is of spiritual adventures, as according to Thomas Mann the "Bildungsroman" (novel of development) is nothing but "a sublimation and spiritualization of the adventure novel."[11] Adventures take place in the areas of love, of the subconscious, even of myth—all of this being mutually interconnected—and thus Thomas Mann can associate the comfortable and civilized Swiss sanatorium with the underworld, the witches' mountain, the Venus mountain, and even the castle of the Holy Grail.

What is typical for the magic mountain? Above all its distance from ordinary life and at the same time its secluded nature, which opens new dimensions to man, especially that of death, the access to the "underworld," and also the access to the frightening area of one's own subconscious. The safety valves of the previous life are absent—although middle-class decorum is guaranteed by financial independence, at least for Hans Castorp—and the people affected become a community of the dying. They live in a transitory area outside of space and time, in a forced disorientation, which compels them to reflect on basic questions of life and death.

In *I'm Not Stiller* we find a striking accumulation, even a continual series, of places which are characterized by their distance from the previous life and by their isolation, and which place man into a transitory area where the previous unilinear course of time is suspended, i.e., where disorientation and a reflection on one's position has to begin. One might call such places "magic mountain-like places" and the situations which correspond to them, "magic mountain-like situations." Such magic mountain-like situations begin with Stiller's stay in prison, Julika's sanatorium, and Stiller's studio, where he tries to escape into his work; Sibylle experiences a timeless waiting period in New York; the public prosecutor chances in Genoa into an unknown area and experiences a disorienting confrontation with his subconscious. The chronological time which is filled by these episodes, although usually mentioned or deducible, is normally kept in the background through the accents of the narration; it is the "experienced time" that matters, which is characterized by stagnation or repetition. The magic mountain-like places and situations come in greatest numbers in Stiller's experienced and/or narrated stories: the cargo room of the boat, Isidor's yellow fort in the desert and the seven years until his return home, the plantation in Mexico, Rip van Winkle for whom time stands still while he is in the cave, and the Carlsbad Caverns. In contrast to *The Magic Mountain*, Frisch's characters cannot associate with others in these situations. On the contrary; all magic mountain-like situations in

I'm Not Stiller are confrontations with the self in an absolute loneliness, a fact especially well illustrated by the relationship of the young theologian in the sanatorium with Julika.

The diary writer Stiller is certainly aware of this literary dimension; this can be seen in the passage he wrote about reproduction. But he finds no satisfaction when he discovers literary, psychological, or even mythical references; they rather arouse his sarcasm. Hans Castorp traveled to Davos with a book called *Ocean Steamships* and was alienated there from his practical world. At the beginning, Stiller is condemned to using and living literary clichés, as a victim of reproduction, one who knows reality only secondhand and who tries desperately to break out from sublimation into unfiltered life. But his stories of adventure fall back into literary clichés, and since he himself is aware of it, he stylizes them consciously as trivial literature and his complete success is by no means limited to his guardian Knobel. The cliché corresponds to Knobel's dream of what reality should be like, but it also confuses the defense lawyer Bohnenblust.

The defense lawyer understands the stories as documents of Stiller's physical life, and it is easy for him to prove that the persons "murdered" by Stiller, his father, the husband of the mulatto woman, and the "hair oil gangster" Schmitz, are still alive. Stiller's "murders" correspond to deep psychological wishes and needs, of which he is aware himself. The obvious symbolism of his stories is a trap for Bohnenblust and Knobel. After the story of the cavern in Carlsbad, Stiller gets tired of his success with Knobel. He dissolves the illusion. The result:

> Knobel seems to be a little confused.
> "—are you Jim White?" he asks.
> "No," I laugh, "not quite! But what I experienced myself, you see, that was exactly the same—exactly."
> Knobel seems to be a little disappointed.

What appeared to be an adventure thus becomes a repetition of an archetype and a wish-fulfilling fantasy: expression of psychological processes. Stiller has by no means escaped from sublimated reproduction, not even in cowboy country at the border of Texas and New Mexico. The visit to the cavern with the spectacular stalactites has long since become a tourist attraction, and Stiller's description of its discovery is a result of poetic imagination. If one considers his listener and his sarcastic distance from himself, as well as his knowledge of books, one should be rather careful to consider whether the cavern can seriously be compared to Plato's cave allegory.[12]

Stiller has done everything to escape literature, but with little success. At the same time he fights against the idea of "Bildung" and in his Davos episode he negates the possibility of Bildung through illness. For Stiller, Julika's illness is escape, which only makes her more rigid psychologically. From a literary point of view, *I'm Not Stiller* thus had to become a confrontation with the model of the *Bildungsroman*. Hans Mayer has already stated that the model of the Bildungsroman is valid for *I'm Not Stiller* but only under a radically critical approach.[13] In this context the following relations have to be considered: Max Frisch's first novels *Jürg Reinhart* and *Die Schwierigen* are completely in the tradition of the Bildungsroman, the model being Gottfried Keller's *Green Henry*. Green Henry, just like his predecessor Wilhelm Meister, leaves home to realize his dream of becoming a great artist. At the end both recognize that their idea of being an artist was an illusion, and they find a suitable field of activity in society; Wilhelm Meister even finds great happiness in his marriage.

Thomas Mann has conceived *The Magic Mountain* as a Bildungsroman and at the same time a parody of the Bildungsroman. Already on September 4, 1922, he wrote to Arthur Schnitzler about "a kind of Bildung-story and Wilhelm Meister-tale." In a letter to Felix Bertaux of July 23, 1924, he called *The Magic Mountain* "a kind of modernization of the novel of development and education and also something like a parody of it," and in the letter to Ernst Fischer of May 25, 1926, he confirmed once more: "Already the renewal of the German Bildungsroman on the basis of and under the symbol of pulmonary tuberculosis is a parody."[14] Thomas Mann therefore really intended a renewal of the Bildungsroman following the model of *Wilhelm Meister* but as an expression of the "love for an artistic spirit, whose realization one no longer believes in,"[15] i.e., as a parody. Hans Castorp begins as a burgher like Wilhelm Meister, son of a merchant, but without feeling confined by this origin. His desire for the world which then opens up to him in the Davos magic mountain was completely subconscious and was based, considering his parentage, rather on weakness than on a special talent. He would, however, never go as far as wanting to produce literature or any other art. In Davos his life experiences an unexpected intensification and development through his confrontation with death. He advances into hitherto unknown regions and becomes aware of the basic problems of his age. The result of the process of development is uncertain. The ambivalence that only disease generates higher spiritual life still remains. The fairy-tale world far from the course of time gains a rather ominous power over Hans Castorp; even the much quoted vision in the section "Snow" remains a dream, a vision of a possible future.[16] Bildung in *The Magic Mountain* is extremely problematical. And yet: Hans Castorp does return to the plains a different person than when he went there. The description of his war service at the end shows an ironic distance from the patriotism of Thomas Mann and so many other Germans in 1914; but the reader leaves Hans Castorp with the conviction that this one will prove to be a good citizen. In spite of all doubts and problems the parody preserves the original idea of the Bildungsroman and the value of Bildung. Thomas Mann's parody preserves the model by questioning it. It is therefore in its real nature conservative, directed, however, not toward the past but toward the present and future.[17]

Both for *Wilhelm Meister* and *The Magic Mountain* the confrontation with literature is a constituent element, although in a different manner. While Wilhelm Meister tries to understand *Hamlet* in terms of his own life, Hans Castorp is not even aware that Settembrini quotes Goethe's *Faust*. Nevertheless the reference to *Faust* has certainly to be taken seriously.[18] In contrast to them, Stiller feels confined and handicapped by literary models. His conscious stylization of the American adventures as trivial literature indicates his feelings. Of course not only *The Magic Mountain* is an object of his dislike but also the Swiss tradition from *Green Henry* to the novels of the admired Albin Zollinger.[19] Stiller's notebooks constitute an anti-Bildungsroman which makes reference to previous Bildungsromane just as Thomas Mann made reference to Goethe's *Faust,* and with a double intention: as a radical criticism of the literary model and as a negation of the idea of Bildung itself.

Criticism of the literary model begins already with the person and situation of the narrator. Thomas Mann's narrator, the "whispering conjurer of the imperfect," can narrate his story in "the tense of the deepest past." It is a past without recall. Stiller is a first-person narrator, although of a special kind. What he relates is the attempt of society to force the repetition of the past upon him as his future. As a real first-person narrator he keeps a kind of diary of the events during his time in jail. The past before his stay in America he registers as the narration of other people, not without evoking deeper doubts of their "image" of himself. The American period must be reconstructed by the reader himself from Stiller's "fabrications" and subsequent corrections. An epic continuum like that of *The Magic Mountain* is lacking. The narrator is in his "waiting period" in jail really outside the stream of time and outside the Swiss society which wants to force him to repeat his previous life.[20] The comfortable jail is the origin of the paradoxical contradictions which determine action and structure of *I'm Not Stiller*: the jail on the one hand is a magic mountain outside of time; on the other hand it is the place where the present intrudes upon Stiller. On the one hand it is a reflection of the Switzerland which is not free, moving in predetermined and thus always repeating paths; on the other hand it is Stiller's place of freedom which protects him from being condemned to a repetition of his old self. The jail isolates Stiller, but it makes Swiss society come to him, while later in his "freedom" in Glion he lives completely unnoticed and isolated. It is paradoxical that none other than Stiller's escape into the primitivity and primeval nature of America is related in an obvious literary stylization; that his attempt to escape the excess of Bildung in Switzerland leads to nothing but trivial literary clichés; and that the "truth" about his American adventures has to be found in the "fabrications" of his Wild West stories. Stiller's "Bildung," to use the term with appropriate reservations, is expressed by the ironic distance to his own past in the "minutes" of the narrations of the others, in the equally ironic distance from Switzerland in the "diary," and by the nonliterary episodes from America which, however, follow literary models by being nonliterary. The time continuum is broken up, as far as the chronology of events is concerned. The sequence is structured according to the stages of Stiller's new encounter with himself. Lacking is the view back to the past and the total perspective which in *Wilhelm Meister, Green Henry*, or in *The Magic Mountain* provided the context and meaning of the individual adventures.

In contrast to his early novels, Max Frisch in *I'm Not Stiller* is no longer concerned with young people; the openness of youth which characterizes the Bildungsroman[21] is already past here, and we are dealing rather with people who are identified by profession, marriage, and the judgment of society, people of middle age who experience crises in their social life, both in their professions and in their marriages. Stiller's adventure in Spain did not help him at all to find himself. On the contrary, it gave him the fixation that he always had to prove himself. In the narration of the returning Stiller who desperately fights for a distance from himself, no epic distance and overview can be found. The Davos episode which Julika tells Stiller after his homecoming after seven years, and which Stiller writes down, full of malicious reminiscences of Thomas Mann, exemplifies the attitude of the narrator: Davos, which is for Stiller exactly like Thomas Mann had described it, shrinks to a short episode. The leitmotiv is loneliness as otherwise also with Julika. The encounter with the young theologian breaks off when he begins to talk to her about herself. She does not permit "meddling in vital questions of her life," of which the young man could not possibly understand anything, "and thus [says Julika] it could not become a real contact."

Stiller's minutes do everything to evoke the memory of Thomas Mann: the routine of the hours of lying outside, the X-ray picture, the scenery, the theologian, the flight to the "plain." This is all suddenly interrupted by the conversations with Stiller, i.e., events of the outer world happening at the same time and which Julika cannot escape. In her need for being spared any trouble, she does not understand at all how much Stiller is in need of help. While Julika remains in her previous attitude, which is even reinforced by Davos, the "healthy" Stiller experiences a decisive human crisis. The minutes of Stiller reproduce both Julika's point of view and through parody of *The Magic Mountain* reference to the main problems, perhaps even more: do not the people who have read *The Magic Mountain,* and therefore have a literary

Bildung, expect that people have to behave as in literary models? Is not the reversal of the models caused by the very fact that they are taken seriously and then prove to be false and erroneous? Perhaps Stiller also wants to indicate that Julika had all chances of Bildung which Hans Castorp had in *The Magic Mountain,* but was not capable of using them.

If the book is about the negative effect of literary models in life, the aim of criticism has to be the idea of Bildung as such. This criticism, as far as it is oriented toward *The Magic Mountain,* can best be deciphered from the problem of time, which is suggested by the number seven. Thomas Mann's "soup of eternity," repetition, the stagnation of time does finally form a progression of time with a beginning and an end where past, present, and future are clearly differentiated from each other. The epic narrator fights for his medium, continuity, permanence within change, and he finds it endangered, but also confirmed by fairy-tale time. This is past and gone in *I'm Not Stiller.* He sees his life under the curse of repetition: "Repetition. And yet I know that everything depends on whether one succeeds in ceasing to wait for the life outside repetition, and instead, of one's own free will (in spite of compulsion), manages to turn repetition, inescapable repetition, into one's life by acknowledging: There I am! ... But again and again (here, too, there is repetition) it takes only a word, a gesture that frightens me, a landscape that reminds me, and everything within me is flight, flight without hope of getting anywhere, simply for fear of repetition" (59). Stiller thus fights for the voluntary acknowledgment of the compulsion of repetition, while the evasion of repetition is flight which in turn repeats itself and becomes a sequence of repetitions as flight from repetition. On the other hand Stiller also fights for a freedom from himself, and from the repetition that stands in contradiction to it, a freedom that is not granted to him: "I'm not their Stiller. What do they want with me? I'm an unfortunate, insignificant, unimportant person with no life behind him, none at all. Why am I lying to them? Just so that they should leave me my emptiness, my insignificance, my reality; it's no good running away, and what they are offering me is flight, not freedom, flight means acting a part" (38-39). The contradictions cannot be resolved. Stiller's life, previously marked by the pattern of flight, from Spain, through Paris, Davos, and America, has now left behind the "emptiness," the openness of youth, and is condemned to a confrontation with the self and to repetition. In Stiller there is a "Faustian" urge for transformation and for the redemption of himself and others[22] at work which does not cease after his return and his time in jail. While in the model Bildungsroman the women, seen from a clearly male perspective, are goal concepts and are themselves hardly touched in their existence by the aberrations of the male protagonist, Max Frisch has reversed the situation: the stations of the Bildungsroman are more part of woman's life than of man's life. Stiller destroys Julika because he tries to simulate Wilhelm Meister's society of the tower or Hans Castorp's relationship with Settembrini and Naphta. The postscript of the public prosecutor concentrates on this question. In contrast to the literary classics of adultery *Anna Karenina* and *Effi Briest,* the public prosecutor has learned tolerance, and he has found a new life in the repetition of his marriage with Sibylle, without expecting a transformation from his wife or himself. He lives according to the principle of the diary writer Max Frisch: "Time does not transform us. It only unfolds our nature."[23] Sibylle, who has looked for transformation with and through Stiller, returns to the same life and can have the child that was not possible in her relationship with Stiller.

Stiller's attitude, however, is "overreaching himself," in the view of the public prosecutor, who has become aware of his limits. It is arrogance and sin. Stiller expects from Julika a "transformation"; he wanted to "redeem" her. In this manner he had made her his "creature," whom he wanted to create and form. Stiller's sculpting and especially the vaselike sculpture of Julika thus take on a deeper meaning. "Thou shalt not make an image" refers to the sculptor who forms the woman he loves into a work of art which he creates for himself and out of himself. When Stiller simply says at the end, "She is beautiful," he perhaps sees Julika for the first time as she is; perhaps, however, he can see her only as a work of art and thus really without love. The public prosecutor feels that Julika is exactly as Stiller had described her the first time, and, deeply moved, he adds: "That was exactly how she lay on the deathbed, and I suddenly had the monstrous feeling that from the very beginning Stiller had only seen her as a dead woman; for the first time, too, I felt the deep unqualified consciousness of his sin, a consciousness no human word could obliterate" (403). Julika dies just at Easter, in spring, during the season of beginning, which elsewhere in Max Frisch's work is that of hope, of unlimited possibilities.[24] He reverses parodistically his own symbolism, as he also does with Thomas Mann's symbolism of the seasons in Davos. The final reversal of the expectation of transformation and thus of happiness is especially dissonant, since the signs point to the opposite; the marriage of the public prosecutor has found its "rebirth," Stiller has become "different," and there is no doubt about his striving for happiness. The expected does not take place.

The aftereffect of the doctrine of development and Bildung in the discipline of German studies is in my view shown by the fact that Stiller's failure is generally not accepted by scholarship and criticism. Perhaps the difference will be clearer if we think of the end of *Wilhelm Meister's Apprenticeship Years,* where Wilhelm Meister can be told: "You appear to me like Saul, the son of Kish, who went out to look for his father's donkeys, and who found a kingdom." Whereupon Wilhelm answers, and this is the end of the book, "I do not know the value of a kingdom," said Wilhelm, "but I know that I have obtained happiness which I do not deserve, and which I would not like to exchange for anything in the world."[25] Wilhelm's overreaching of himself has thus brought happiness for him; Stiller's is arrogance, sin, hybris: it results in Julika's death and his isolation from society, the complete renunciation of happiness. The postscript ends with the laconic statement: "Stiller remained in Glion and lived alone" (404). The idea of Bildung is based upon confidence in life and in the nature of man. The adventures of Wilhelm bring happiness for him and society.[26] Even the dissipations of Hans Castorp have positive results for him. Stiller's "Ferme Vaudoise" with its false decorations is the expression of his maladjusted and unfitting situation: he has given up all hope of overcoming the contradictions and his isolation. The ferme is something like an anti-magic mountain. It expresses the disillusionment of the belief in Bildung and development, and that is perhaps what makes it a real parody of Switzerland and its way of life. For man the real alternative is accepting the predestination of man's personality, the tolerance of what we always were, are, and will be. Flight from the world of Bildung, from the reproduction of literary models, however, is not possible. Our freedom could only consist in accepting it and not in attempts of escaping into untouched nature and primitive life à la Hemingway.

In taking the minutes of Julika's narration, Stiller parodies "all kinds of other things" in Davos: the psychological conditions of tuberculosis, disease as the factor to begin a spiritual development, the magic-mountain world of a sanatorium. But Stiller also is in a magic mountain, which is the world of Bildung of Switzerland. He tries to counter its preformed and stagnating being with an open development. What seems to be akin to his personality and a necessary correction of the stagnation in the world of Bildung proves, however, then to be only a new magic mountain which leads him back to Switzerland. He cannot escape Switzerland. Switzerland as a magic mountain reverses Thomas Mann's point of departure: for a Swiss it is not escape—that would be the wide plains of America—but everyday reality, and yet removed from time, outside of history in its nature. It does not intensify life, it stifles it. In the parody of the magic mountain motif is the essence of the satire on Switzerland, which ruins a person like Stiller. He has not, although he fights for his bliss in the sense of Kierkegaard, the confidence of the public prosecutor of being in God's hand.

Thomas Mann is a seducer, since he gives the impression that one man can transform and redeem another man and since he gives a false glamour to the magic mountain. The magic mountain according to him is the place of adventures and tests which the hero of the fairy tale passes victoriously. Stiller's life is under this expectation and because of this has fallen into self-overreaching and sin. If the Bildungsroman is the sublimated novel of adventures, then the anti-Bildungsroman is not only the reversal of sublimation, into "raw" adventures, but above all the proof that the anti-sublimation does not reach a new primitivity, but rather falls into a trivial reproduction of the same sublimated models, and that, in doing so, life itself is questioned or even destroyed. The dominating power of Bildung in the conception of Thomas Mann and others, from which Stiller in spite of all efforts cannot free himself, betrays anything but "patient admiration." Parody has thus become something quite different from "love for an attitude toward art whose realization one no longer believes in"; it is rather the reluctantly concerned recognition of the models of Bildung as life-impeding, even life-destroying, forces. It is the expression of man in the prison of literature as Bildung.

1. *Literature für Zeitgenossen* (Frankfurt, 1966), pp. 151-52.

2. E.g. Ulrich Weisstein, *Max Frisch* (New York, 1967), between *Death in Venice* and *Homo Faber* (67,70), and between *Felix Krull* and *Gantenbein* (82), the latter also Martin Kraft, *Studien zur Thematik von Max Frischs Roman "Mein Name sei Gantenbein"* (Berne, 1969), p. 53. A connection between *I'm Not Stiller* and *Doctor Faustus* is seen by Hans Bänziger, *Frisch und Dürrenmatt* (Berne, 1960), pp. 84-84, and Hans Mayer, "Anmerkungen zu 'Stiller,'" in *Über Max Frisch* (Frankfurt, 1971), p. 34.

3. While critics such as Hans Mayer and Ulrich Weisstein have placed the complex of reproduction in the center of their analyses, there is surprisingly little mention of parody in the literature on *I'm Not Stiller*. Frisch's own sentence is striking: "Thomas Mann is parodying himself," in his afterword to Trewin's *Euer Gnaden haben geschossen* (Zurich, 1954), quoted by Weisstein, p. 172.

4. For the concept of parody, see Wido Hempel, "Parodie, Travestie und Pastiche. Zur Geschichte von Wort und Sache," in *GRM* 46, pp. 150-76; with regard to Thomas Mann's parody, see Viktor Zmegac, "Konvention, Modernismus und Parodie. Bemerkungen zum Erzählstil Thomas Mann," *Thomas Mann und die Tradition*, ed. Peter Pütz (Frankfurt, 1971), pp. 1-13.

5. For English quotes with page numbers, I used the abridged verson *I'm Not Stiller*, trans. Michael Bullock (New York, n.d.); other quotes are my own translation from the German edition Frankfurt, 1969).

6. *Max Frisch*, p. 172, n. 7, for Max Frisch's relationship to Thomas Mann; see also Werner Liersch, "Wandlung einer Problematik," in *Über Max Frisch*, pp. 77-83.

7. *Tagebuch 1946-1949* (Knaur-Taschenbuch, 1965), p. 133.

8. See Karlheinz Braun, *Die epische Technik in Max Frischs Roman "Stiller" als Beitrag zur Formfrage des modernen Romans* (Ph.D. diss., Frankfurt, 1959), pp. 24-25; for Thomas Mann, see Christiane Pritzlaff, *Zahlensymbolik bei Thomas Mann*, Hamburger Philologische Studien, No. 25 (Hamburg, 1972), on the *Magic Mountain*, pp. 27-42; cf. also such phrases as "this old fairy-tale number of years of hardship," which Thomas Mann in his essay on Frederick the Great used with reference to the Seven Years' War.

9. Braun, pp. 91-92.

10. Braun, p. 19.

11. The quote is from Thomas Mann's lecture in Princeton on *The Magic Mountain*; for his conception of the Bildungsroman, see Jürgen Scharfschwerdt, *Thomas Mann und*

der deutsche Bildungsroman (Stuttgart, 1967)

12. Bänziger, pp. 87-88; Mary E. Cock, "'Countries of the Mind': Max Frisch's Narrative Technique," *Modern Language Review* (1970), p. 822; Helmut Pfanner, "Stiller und das 'Faustische' bei Max Frisch, *Orbis Litterarum* (1969), p. 209, sees a relationship to the "mothers" in *Faust*.

13. "Anmerkungen zu 'Stiller,'" p. 37.

14. *Briefe 1889-1936*, pp. 199-200, 214, 256 (my translation); see also Zmegac.

15. This sentence which refers to Thomas Mann's *Gesang vom Kindchen* is quoted by Zmegac, p. 7.

16. Scharfschwerdt.

17. For the sources and the development of Thomas Mann's "conservative" concept of history, see Winfried Hellmann, *Das Geschichtsdenken des frühen Thomas Mann* (Tübingen, 1972). The orientation toward the future after the *Reflections of a Non-Political Man* is based on tradition and duration.

18. Herman Meyer, *Das Zitat in der Erzählkunst* (Stuttgart, 1961).

19. For Keller, see Bänziger, p. 25; in Zollinger's *Pfannenstiel* and *Bohnenblust* the characters are real sculptors. The confrontration with tradition, the return to Switzerland, the contradictory, even tragic, situation of the writer in Switzerland in the case of Byland, also the problems of education would be comparable. The use of the name "Bohnenblust" is a false lead.

20. See especially Braun on this problem.

21. Monika Wintsch-Spiess, *Zum Problem der Identität im Werk Max Frischs* (Zurich, 1965).

22. Pfanner, "Stiller und das 'Faustische' bei Max Frisch."

23. *Tagebuch 1946-1949*, p. 19; Braun, p. 78, Bänziger, p. 98; the sentence may be one of the least noticed key sentences in Frisch's *Diary*. It appears in a paragraph with the title "On the meaning of a diary."

24. Wintsch-Spiess, especially pp. 23-32.

25. Hamburger Ausgabe, vol. 7, p. 610 (my translation).

26. Gerda Röder, *Glück und glückliches Ende im deutschen Bildungsroman* (Munich, 1968).

KLAUS JEZIORKOWSKI

Wilhelm Tell as Peter Jenny:
On Frisch's *Wilhelm Tell für die Schule*

The treatment of the Wilhelm Tell subject has been rather singular. At least of two who have used it—Friedrich Schiller and Max Frisch—it would seem that they had actively and consciously taken up this subject matter on the basis of their own choice and with an inner compulsion to portray their own conceptions, but this is not so. The Tell subject was urged upon them by other, more prominent authors or colleagues, and for Schiller and Frisch it took years before the work assumed final form.

Goethe in 1797 had brought the Tell story back from the last of his three trips to Switzerland and planned to model it into an epos similar to *Hermann and Dorothea*. Nothing became of it and, according to Goethe's statements, he claimed to have formally relinquished the subject matter to Schiller for dramatic development.[1] With Schiller the story remained dormant until six years after Goethe's last Swiss journey when Schiller seriously undertook its dramatic realization—providing a whole nation with the conclusive, and later more and more sacralized, form of its state's founding myth—a literary, political process that is perhaps unique in world literature.

More than one and a half centuries later, a concerned Swiss, Max Frisch, again approached the "sacral" subject of the land, a subject suggested to him by Bertolt Brecht. Again it took a lengthy period of time, almost twenty-five years, before the new "Tell" was completed. It is almost as if he were writing the Tell piece reluctantly, constrained to do it by others.

At the end of October 1947 Brecht had left McCarthy America, one day after his appearance before the House Un-American Activities Committee. Shortly thereafter he arrived in Switzerland, the fifth and last stage of his emigration, which had also been the first in 1933,[2] where he remained until late in 1948. During that year he met often with the young Swiss author and architect Max Frisch.

The two major *Diaries* of Max Frisch have lengthy "Brecht chapters," which indicates the immense impact the older man had on the younger one at least in the late forties—somewhat in contrast to the two brief references to Frisch in Brecht's *Arbeitsjournal*. In his *Tagebuch 1966-1971* Frisch remarks in the 1966 section, reflecting back upon the late forties in Zurich:

For a time Brecht was urging me, as a Swiss, finally to write a Tell drama. It would show that the peasant revolt of the Vierwaldstätte was successful, to be sure, but that it was reactionary vis-à-vis the Habsburg utopia, a conspiracy of pigheads. But a Swiss would have to write that. The thesis, which he made appealing from a theatrical standpoint, is at least closer to the historical truth than the hymn we thanked Schiller for with the Rütli monument. It was just that it appeared to me to be all too capriciously applicable to bailiffs of today. I never knew whether Brecht, when he was crafty, considered his craftiness to be imperceptible.[3]

Brecht had sufficient reasons of his own to bring to the attention of a young Swiss dramatist a subject matter that was held in ownership by a German classicist. Shortly after arriving in Switzerland, Brecht had noted in his *Arbeitsjournal* (December 26, 1947): "reading LUKACS' 'correspondence between schiller and goethe,' he analyzes how the german classicists treated the french revolution. Once again not having our own, we will now have to treat the russian one, I think shudderingly."[4] In the following months of the Swiss sojourn, Brecht quotes occasionally from the Goethe-Schiller correspondence in his *Arbeitsjournal*, in which he focuses attention upon the discussion of 1797 about epic and dramatic poetry. He argues in a highly engaged manner with Schiller's ideas about the reciprocal relation between the epic and the dramatic forms, which is quite understandable for the period from which the "Kleine Organon für das Theater" (Little Organon for the Theater) emerges. Brecht was then deeply involved in reflection upon the problems of the epic theater and the theatrical techniques of alienation. Moreover, he was occupied with his adaptation of Sophocles' *Antigone*, using Hölderlin's translation. Brecht's *Antigone* was presented in the Municipal Theater of Chur in February 1948 and once in a Zurich matinee, both times with Helene Weigel,[5] and then in Berlin the *Antigonemodell–1948* appeared.[6]

Those months in Zurich were thus a fruitful period for both Brecht and the participating Frisch, with Brecht productively taking issue with the Classicists. In connection with Schiller, the thought of the French Revolution immediately suggested itself to Brecht, and implicitly the question was narrowed in Schiller to a perspective of Wilhelm Tell. According to Schiller's words, among other things the storming of the Bastille is portrayed in Tell.[7] Hölderlin, that other German "Classicist" who at the time was persistently occupying Brecht's attention, was later discovered to be the Jacobin of his generation; long before, Brecht had noted in his *Arbeitsjournal* (12/25/1947) concerning Hölderlin's language in Antigone: "It is amazingly radical."[8]

Brecht was in the phase of his most productive reception of the Classicists, a reception that for Brecht during 1947-1948 was more a critical discussion of his times and of the possibility, perhaps already past, of changing societal consciousness, and of the social and political structures in Europe after the total catastrophe of 1945. The Classicists in the dark, postwar years—how are they alterable and how do they show our present conditions to be alterable—are Brecht's focus in his occupation with the Goethe-Schiller correspondence and with Hölderlin. From this source came Frisch's impetus.

To begin with, Frisch's first diaries give an indication of why it took almost a quarter of a century after Brecht's impetus before the prose construction (what else should we call it provisorily?) *Wilhelm Tell für die Schule* (William Tell for school instruction) was finished. In 1948 Frisch notes under the chapter heading "during reading": "The description, the message is epic, not the conflict—the clash with a world that is depicted only to the point necessary for taking issue with it, takes place in drama and there most loudly; the novel that takes issue is already a "Spätlese" epic—the costumed essayism of Thomas Mann."[9] The connection with the "reading" noted in the heading becomes inductively apparent: Frisch is taking part in Brecht's analysis of the Goethe-Schiller correspondence about epic and dramatic poetry, and as a discussion partner he is following the "Little Organon for the Theater" in its progress.

The involvement with the Tell material constitutes for Frisch a "taking issue with it," which the later prose text will demonstrate. Taking issue, however, for the young Frisch of 1948 is possible only in drama, not in narrated prose. He does not treat the subject matter in drama, however—perhaps due to his reserve in face of the Schillerian model and the overwhelming Tell conventions. In 1970 those reservations must have been removed. Now, taking issue with the mythos of the Swiss Republic is no longer possible in dramatic, but rather only in narrated prose. What Frisch had prophesied more than twenty years earlier is finally brought forth: "epic late gleanings" as well as "costumed essayism"—but not so terribly costumed when one considers the extensive note apparatus in the prose Tell. It is rather a parodied essayism and not that far removed from Thomas Mann's travesties—*Joseph, The Holy Sinner, The Beloved Returns: Lotte in Weimar,* and *Faustus.*

In August 1948 under the title "On Writing" another entry appears in Frisch's diaries which refers even more directly to Brecht and opens up the entire prospect directly to the finished *Wilhelm Tell für die Schule*:

> Brecht writes in his *Organon* about the alienation effect, namely, that theatrical alienation should remove from socially influential proceedings the stamp of familiarity that makes them secure against intervention. Furthermore, the spectator is not to empathize; he is to be prevented from being set into a trance. His enjoyment should consist rather in alienation in the play of certain familiar and

customary proceedings so that he views them not in an enraptured but rather in a reflective state, recognizing the alterability, recognizing the special limitations or relativity of an action (plot), savoring the higher enjoyment that we can intervene—and production in the easiest manner and for the easiest manner of existence is (says Brecht) in art. ... It would be enticing to apply all these thoughts to the narrative prose writer also. Alienation effects with linguistic means, consciousness of play in the narration, the open-artistic element which is felt to be estranged by most German readers and is outright rejected as being too artistic (aesthetic) because it hinders sympathy, does not produce enrapturement but rather destroys illusion, namely, the illusion that the narrated story really took place.[10]

The procedure used in the much later prose *Tell* is described in advance and in detail, and even the criticism of the reading public is anticipated in the indication that such procedures are sensed to be alienating and are rejected as demoralizing. That is precisely what later befalls Frisch's *Tell* with the angry critiques in which the illusion "that the related story had 'really' taken place" had indeed been destroyed. Word for word this diary text can be read as an early interpretation by the author of the developments in *Wilhelm Tell für die Schule*.

Frisch is concerned with the revision of a mythos—of the myth of his own republic. And in opposition to all the consolidating and sacralizing tendencies that could allow the Tell complex to become a neurotic complex for Switzerland, Frisch presents the myth along the lines of the Brechtian model as one capable of revision, of solution and discussion. The revision of the myth—Frisch is to be understood in this fashion—is a sign of a viable republic. The capacity for revision is an indication of the viability of the political order; the opposite constitutes a danger.

In my judgment, to make a test of this exemplary case should be a matter reserved to the Swiss. Under no circumstances does it behoove the Germans, well practiced in the production of catastrophes, to promote among their neighbors this probe of democracy.

This capacity to revise myths evinces a healthy tradition among the Swiss. Frisch himself names among others Gottfried Keller, who on several occasions in essays and prose fiction treated the Tell saga. And the debate among Frisch's Swiss contemporaries continues after Frisch's Tell up to the present, becoming, if anything, stronger. Frisch's Tell interpretation consciously joins the tradition of the leftist, politically progressive Tell elucidation and critique that began soon after Schiller's play and reaches beyond Switzerland.

One of the first stages after Schiller is Ludwig Börne's review "On the

Character of Wilhelm Tell in Schiller's Drama," the fifty-second piece of the *Dramaturgischen Blätter* from the year 1828.[11] Some very important accentuations in Frisch's characterization of Wilhelm Tell are already pronounced here: Tell as a narrow-minded Babbit and Philistine, whose horizons are narrowed by the high mountains to the point of insignificance. The general traits of the Swiss in Frisch are those seen by Börne in the character of Schiller's Tell: a petit bourgeois (Kleinbürger), he has a slow mind and a submissive character; he is incapable and undesirous of working for the general good, is lacking in courage and only concerned with securing his private interests; in short, he is a "pedant, . . . school moralist, and keeper of the literal word."

Nevertheless, the difference between Börne and Frisch is significant: Börne's discussion remains within the framework and conditions of Schiller's play. In the dramaturgy of the piece, where it determines the placement and actions of the title figure, Börne sees substantial weaknesses though they are not of great consequence since they indicate for Börne that Schiller's Tell is ultimately not "one of the better theatrical pieces that the Germans have." Lacking in Börne, in contrast to Frisch, is any attempt to go beyond Schiller's drama. Neither the Tell myth nor its tradition is addressed, nor is the critique of Tell enlarged to a critique of Switzerland.

Gottfried Keller goes beyond Schiller's play although he, unlike Börne, is in agreement with the classical version of the myth. Keller's relation to Schiller resembles his relation to idealizing portraits, in which those depicted only too gladly recognize themselves. Granted every aesthetic legitimacy or necessity of idealization, however, for Keller idealization is in no way supposed to delude one about miserable reality. Nevertheless, the idealization does have a utopian value, indicating the direction of a desirable development.

In addition, Keller takes Börne severely to task with his criticism of the character of Schiller's Tell: "If Börne could find only a selfish and philistine monstrosity in Tell, then that is proof for me of how little the sickly sensitivity of the suppressed is fit to grasp the ways of independent men."[12] In parallel with Heine's invective, a slave morality is attributed to Börne—one that is not in a position to comprehend the element: "the strong man is alone the most powerful" in the life disposition of the idealized, free, original Swiss. Keller thus justifies Tell's special and aloof position, often noticed and faulted, as the position of the free and independent. Thus Keller, in great admiration for Schiller's accomplishment, puts the Tell myth at his own disposal and makes it easily adaptable.

Keller had taken part in the unveiling of the Schiller monument on the Mythenstein in the Vierwaldstättersee and reported it in two essays, for Cotta's "Augsburger Allgemeine" and the "Morgenblatt." In the latter of these two essays his impressions become the jumping off point for a grandiose utopian phantasmagoria of patriotic musical theatrical pieces that are reminiscent of Wagner's later conceptions (even to the point of the architecture of the Bayreuth Festival Hall) and anticipate elements of Steiner's Eurhythmics. Keller is aware that Schiller is the instigator of such chains of thought, and this dreaming falls into a time around 1860 when Keller finds himself in the greatest harmony with the political conditions in his fatherland—which was not the case either earlier or later. This amounts to that short blissful time at the beginning of the 1860s, during which *The Banner of the Upright Seven* was written, considered by Keller himself to be one of those idealized national portraits of the type like Schiller's Tell, whose value lies in its pedagogical, exemplary function.

In the middle of the 1870s at the end of his service as a state official, Keller was ocuped again in an official capacity with Schiller's Tell; reluctantly, he agreed to rework the literary section of a widely used school anthology. When the question was whether Schiller's Tell should be represented as previously with long extracts or not at all because the work was otherwise easily accessible, Keller chose the middle course: for the new edition he shortened the Tell excerpt. He believed it was necessary to retain some selection to counter the contemporary tendencies that held it necessary, because of critical conscientiousness, to drop the Tell material due to its fablelike character as seen from the viewpoint of the modern source criticism of positivistic historicism.

Keller's truly great adaptation of the Tell myth, however, lies well before his other treatments of Schiller's drama. It is that famous depiction of a rustic Tell production in the story of Green Henry's youth, upon which Keller reflects at the beginning of his Mythenstein essay. This Tell production definitely belongs to the prehistory of Frisch's *Tell* because with it and well over a century earlier the older Swiss author whom Frisch evidently read with respect, had already put into practice those reflections according to which Frisch considered it enticing "to apply also to the narrative writer" certain principles from Brecht's *Little Organon* in order to make visible "the play consciousness in narrative prose."

Keller's *Green Henry* was an intermediate station from Schiller's drama to Frisch's prose version. We are given the prose depiction of a countrified dramatic production of Schiller's play in shortened version:

> The production was based upon Schiller's Tell, which was readily available in a grade school edition and from which only the love episode between Berta von Bruneck and Ulrich von Rudenz was removed. The people are familiar with the book for it expresses the Swiss way of thinking in a marvelously accurate manner, especially

> Tell's character. ... The larger part of the participants was to portray the populace consisting of shepherds, peasants, fishermen, and hunters and was to move en masse from staging area to staging area where the action was taking place, carried along by those who considered themselves called to a more audacious performance. Young girls took part among the ranks of the people, expressing themselves mainly in the communal singing, while the acting parts were handled by youths. Only what was truly historical was supposed to be presented, eliminating all preparations and dramatic interludes. The historical element, along with the Schillerian characters and dialogue as well as his poetical coloration, was to govern the entire enterprise. The scenes of the actual plot were to be divided up among all the various localities according to their special features, necessitating a festive surging back and forth of the costumed masses.[13]

Unlike Börne, Keller expresses the greatest respect for Schiller's classical version. Schiller's *Tell* is not canonized as untouchable, however; it is rather perceived as alterable according to considerations of time, place, and milieu: it is the prototype, the pattern consisting of adjustable individual elements that are themselves variable. Thus the novel's hero furthers his own personal romance within the theatrical performance by assigning the role of Berta von Bruneck to his adored Anna and the role of Rudenz to himself. Moreover, the portrayer of Tell, "a well-known feisty innkeeper and sharpshooter," has to intervene and to mediate a conflict over cattle tolls that had projected itself from the realm of everyday life into the illusion of the play. The rule of the game is simply to remain conscious of the tensions between the daily life of the rural society with its various interrelations on the one hand and the roles and configurations of portrayed figures in the theatrical production on the other. Such alienating interruptions between the play fiction and the everyday world of the farmers are directly sought out, and the first-person narrator seems to enjoy bringing to our attention those charms of alienation which he, in narrating, again fictionalizes, and which naturally refer to historical developments, namely, Schiller's play and historically documented folk festival presentations in Switzerland. Similarities with Oberammergau's passion plays, especially Daisenberger's conception portrayed since 1860, are present in the alienation of an age-old subject achieved through the configurations of a rustic society.

What guarantees the flexibility of the Tell tradition in Keller, as well as its adaptability (which is a type of alienation) is Keller's Neo-Hegelian conviction of the "dialectic of cultural movement." The past—here the Tell tradition and also Schiller's classical play—is worthy of honor, and only windbags and scamps will contemptuously junk it in favor of the latest fad. The past, however, has to be brought into relation with each new present time and each historical configuration.

Whether and if the past is able to relate is a test of its life potency. In Keller's view there is only a limited number of such archaic themes and configurations. Their wealth and vitality are only evidenced by their dialectical interaction with particular modern forms, with new times, places, and modalities. The Tell complex is the expression of just such an archaic construction; perhaps from the perspective of the historical situation of 1290, it was already in the dialectical process of cultural movement, with the archaic core of the myth lying in the prehistoric past, in Nordic sagas of the apple shot and bold sharpshooter and in other traditions according to which such an individual, bold and free, liberated his people by assassinating a tyrant.

The position of the lengthy passages in *Green Henry* in relation to the Tell saga is thus, first, one of respect for the myth, for its national and social functions, respect for its historical expressions, especially in Schiller's drama; and second, one of a free hand to alter the myth, to actualize it, and to use it as raw material or as a functionally alterable constellation.

Had Keller known of Friedrich Engel's remarks of November 1847 on "The Swiss Civil War," which was probably not the case, he would have been just as much in disagreement with them as he was with Börne's criticism of the character of Schiller's Tell. It has the appearance of a pertinent reference to Engels when there is talk in the Tell chapter of *Green Henry* of a "reproach for pettiness, selfishness, and narrow-mindedness, a reproach made against the Swiss by foreign, namely German, travelers." This reproach appears momentarily in Keller's novel to be justified but is refuted in a committed manner. It is precisely this reproach, however, that is brought forth with sarcastic sharpness by Engels—just a few years before Keller in Berlin wrote the Tell chapter of his novel. Engels's reproach was issued with a sarcastic pungency that even today would offend every Swiss. In decisive places in his *Tell*, Frisch quotes some central passages of Engels's remarks. On the whole, it is these few pages from Engels's hand that appear to be a key text for Frisch's version, for the general leftist reception of the Tell myth, and the main stumbling block for Swiss national conservatism. They are the cardinal turning point for the political estimation of the Tell complex after Schiller.

Engels's drastic pronouncements are to be understood in the context of the Swiss Separatists' War of 1847: The Swiss, according to Engels, are narrow-minded. They do not have blinders—it is much worse—they have mountains in front of their eyes, mountains above which their political and historical horizons have never risen. Proof of that would be their most unjustifiably idealized battle of liberation in the thirteenth and fourteenth centuries:

> The glorious liberation from the claws of the Austrian eagle can but poorly bear close and clear scrutiny. The House of Austria was progressive on a single occasion in its entire career; it was in the beginning of its life span when it allied itself with the petit bourgeois of the cities against the nobility and attempted to found a German monarchy. It was progressive in a most bourgeois (philistine) manner, but it was progressive. And who opposed it most decisively? The early Swiss. The battle of the Swiss against Austria, the glorious oath upon the Rütli, Tell's heroic shot, the eternally memorable victory of Morgarten, that was all the battle of stubborn herdsmen against the forces of historical development, the battle of stiff-necked, stable local interests against the interests of the whole nation, the battle of crudeness against learning, of barbarity against civilization. They were victorious over the civilization of the time, and as punishment they have been excluded from all further civilization.[14]

Here we have an exact reversal of parts and of the Tell-Gessler configuration in Schiller, a reversal that, slightly mitigated, both Frisch's text bore as well as the rather crass staging of Schiller's Tell by Hans Günther Heymes in 1965-1966 in Wiesbaden.

Those characteristics, according to Engels, are Swiss constants projecting into modern times: the Swiss confederates are "dumb but pious," which has led to the enlistment of the young men in foreign armies, the custom of hiring themselves out as mercenaries for foreign powers and tyrants and almost always, according to Engels, on the reactionary side against the progress of world history. Furthermore, according to Engels, with the rise of tourism the Swiss have turned themselves into "the most avaricious and knavish swindlers that exist anywhere."

In the center of this malicious criticism stands Engels's observation: "The greatest pride of these thick-set original Swiss has always been that they have never strayed even a hair's breadth from the practices of their forefathers, that they have maintained unadulterated the simple, chaste, staunch and virtuous customs of their fathers during the course of the centuries."[15]

Here, it seems to me, we have arrived at the core of the entire Tell problem and reception following along leftist lines ever since Schiller. In Schiller, Börne, Keller, Engels, Frisch, and Heyme, that which becomes thematical—with the most varying assessment, to be sure—is the adherence of the Swiss farmers and herdsmen to the "past," to the patterns and orders of their forefathers, to tradition.

Before becoming disturbed about such an evaluation by Engels, one should recognize that it does have a certain foundation even in Schiller's dramatic text. It is almost impossible to count the passages in Schiller where the Swiss, in the midst of their political movement against the Habsburgs, are not concerned so much with innovation at all. They do not in a "progressive" manner desire to set up a modern republican order in opposition to an old feudal one, but rather they are pursuing the reestablishment of the old freedom of their fathers. "We want to be free as our fathers were."[16] It is a matter of a retrogressive "conservative" revolution. These views of the Swiss country people become especially evident in the appearances of old Attinghausen in the Rütli scene. And with the oath upon the Rütli in Schiller's text, the true reason and character of this conservative retrogression becomes evident.

> Yes! There's a limit to the tyrants' power!
> When man, oppressed, has cried in vain for justice
> And knows his burden is too great to bear,
> With bold resolve he reaches up to heaven
> To seize those rights which are for ever his,
> As permanent and incorruptible
> As are the stars upon the crystal round.
> The primal state of nature is regained
> Where man stands face to face with his oppressor.
> When every other means has failed, he has
> As last resort the sword in mortal combat.
> It is our right, in face of violence,
> To guard our own. Our country is at stake.
> For wife and child we pledge our lives, our all![17]

The orientation of Schiller's Swiss is that of natural rights—of the oldest judicial status of man and of his societal forms in general. Here the dialectical character of the natural rights discussion of the eighteenth century, especially in Rousseau, is made manifest; this is a discussion that belongs ideologically to the most decisive factors of the French Revolution and of the foundations of the American Constitution: this fundamental change toward innovation, modernity, and progress in the social and political order is oriented on the primeval, the archaic and paradisiacal equal rights of all men, also before God. To this extent, the thought is easily reconcilable with Christian premises: Before God all men are created free and endowed with the same rights. To this extent, there is no contradiction in Schiller's text when the Swiss farmers conduct a rebellion while being devout. This devoutness becomes, initially in Börne and then decisively in Engels and continuing through Frisch, evidence of the Swiss' reactionary position. The strongest symptom of this reactionary attitude for Engels and Frisch is the "back to the old ways"represented so amply in Schiller. One only needs to block out the natural rights impetus of the rearward directed battle cry—as in Engels, Frisch, and others—and then one discovers in the Swiss countryman the perfect reactionary, the prototype of a devout retrograde orientation. For "devout" includes particularly a preparedness to recognize spiritual, ecclesiastical, or legitimate secular authority; and indeed in Schiller, the devout natural rights orientation for the Swiss comes, in the last analysis, to an inconsistent halt before the authority of the emperor of the Holy Roman Empire of German Nations, whom they are largely prepared to recognize as the highest worldly lord. The freedom that the Swiss in Schiller's play attempt to regain is thus the state of being subject directly to the emperor alone, as in the times of their fathers. In Schiller's text there are points of departure for interpreting this stance as inimical to progress and reactionary. Such points are used by Engels and Frisch; but only at a certain cost. To the same degree in which the Swiss confederates slide down the scales of progress, feudal Habsburg power rises—which especially in the argumentation of Engels requires some rather grotesque contortions. Engels is forced by the mechanics of his criticism of the Swiss to make Habsburg-Austria appear to be progressive, which was by no means the case. The touch of urbanity and the devil-may-care liberalistic turn of mind of the Frischian "Gessler," the probable Konrad von Tillendorf, are entirely absent.

For his criticism of Switzerland, Frisch uses those passages in Schiller where the Swiss appear backward, especially the Attinghausen scene. Frisch's Attinghausen is an old calcified sap who is stubborn and above all hard of hearing. He characteristically hears nary a word when the liberal Viennese emissary, Frisch's "Gessler" or the knight von Tillendorf, tries to make clear that "a certain development can hardly be held back, it is even to be desired." The old man answers as a broken phonograph record to the movements of the Viennese's mouth—always and solely: "like before the King's times"—that is how they want it again. As Frisch makes clear in a note: "as before the time of the still reigning king Rudolf of Habsburg," i.e., as during the interregnum. Thus, for Frisch the retrograde direction of the Schillerian Swiss has degenerated to this sniveling automaton response, the natural rights motive has been dropped.

The limited and reactionary basic attitude of the Swiss has become the focus of the modern Tell reception. In the theater season 1965-1966 Hansgünther Heyme staged Schiller's *Wilhelm Tell* in the Hessian State Theater in Wiesbaden. The production had a widespread shock effect. The Swiss farmers appeared as a brutal reactionary horde and in much more unfavorable light than the bailiff (Landvogt Gessler), the representative of the feudal power Austria-Habsburg. Heyme had the confederate land people dressed in clay-colored garb similar to uniforms, thus evoking a whole series of associations: Were the uniforms khaki-colored like those of the Americans in Vietnam, did they appear like the SA uniforms of the Nazi period, were they to be called earth-colored in order to refer to a blood and earth (Blut und Boden) ideology? There was a series of possible associations, continuing on into politically objectionable and dangerous realms. And the printed program for the production, with its text and collection of quotations, also made the mass actions of the people appear as irrational, brutal, and fascistic. Wherever the masses appeared, lynch justice was not far removed—masses are hordes—and over the whole production lay the aroma of the Nazi Imperial Party Day or of a pogrom mood. This 1965 production lay chronologically in the incubation phase of the protest movement of 1968, when the existential postwar years came to an end and the predominance of the Frankfurt Critical Theory was being articulated with Adorno's Heidegger criticism in the *Jargon of Actuality*; the same change became visible in Böll's *Views of a Clown* of 1963, and the general unrest set to explode in 1968 was beginning to make itself felt. Max Frisch's *Wilhelm Tell für die Schule*, illustrating in its nondramatic form the "prose of the conditions," already lies on this side of the time threshold and can already reflect the experiences of the protest, manifest since 1968.

Frisch's version joins with the perspective of Engels and Heyme to the extent that similarly gloomy aspects of mass reactions, of psychological mass mechanisms, are presented, and they are portrayed again with the Swiss country people. The focal point of this interpretation of mass reactions is in Frisch's scene with the "apple shot," which never takes place, to be sure, not even behind the scenes as in Schiller. Frisch's interests lay in the psychological processes. The knight Konrad, Frisch's "Gessler," is not interested in complications at all. He wants to begin finally his longed-for trip home to Vienna on the very day the annoying notice reaches him that someone had not paid homage to the hat. He is all the more intent upon resolving the tiresome disturbance without a fuss. "The forest people, however, were watching gloomily and uprightly." That is, they are not at all interested in a kindhearted ruling, not because they are so "upright" but rather because they are desirous of something sensational at any price, about which they can become gratifyingly enraged. In any case they want to find some offense. Frisch projects in them a righteous, law-and-order attitude, which is always on the point of changing into a pogrom-and-lynch justice. The Swiss put pressure on the bailiff and escalate the entire conflict to the point where the bailiff must require the apple to be shot. Basically, in Frisch the confederates ask for the shot, confederates who are not prepared to go without their scandal and spectacle. "They had been waiting for a long time for some atrocity and now they had it: a father had to shoot an apple from the head of his child."[18] With this headlinelike formulation, the event that has not yet taken place receives in the minds of the masses by way of anticipation the structuralization of sensational mass media. It becomes an event for the *Bild-Zeitung*, the most prominent, richly illustrated daily tabloid in Germany. What has not yet happened is expected and anticipated in the minds of the sensation consumers in Bild-Zeitung structure. In other words, the mass press is not only a definite form of dressing up events for consumption, it is worse: The mass press represents a form of perception and structure of expectation on the part of the consumer, which the mass press then in the cynical manner of friendly service needs only to comply with, concealing the fact that it was the institution that established this mental anticipation structure in its daily client. Reality is the *Bild-Zeitung*; our structure of perception is the *Bild-Zeitung*. That is the dramatic aspect that Frisch gave to his apple shot scene, the aspect that, after Frisch, Heinrich Böll in his *Lost Honor of Katharina Blum* and still later Günter Wallraff in his book about the *Bild-Zeitung* made more central in their works. The masses create their own press, the press creates its own masses, and both create in correspondence their own events. Reality is only that which can be expressed in headlines—it is in such a scene that Frisch's Tell as well as the books by Böll and Wallraff are recognized as interpretations of the period after 1968. Quite consistently, Frisch's scene ends with allusions to the kickings and beatings at student demonstrations.

Frisch is presenting the alterable myth, the adaptable one. And since for him the myth lives on, and even has a powerful message for modern times, Frisch—like Keller at times—is able to make the vitality of this myth more evident than would be possible in a reverent historical reprise. Frisch's practice is similar to Brecht's procedure of myth adaption in *Saint Joan of the Slaughter Yards*, except it goes further. Whereas Brecht vis-à-vis the Schillerian model remained within the dramatic genre, Frisch, an experienced dramatist himself, abandons the genre defined by Schiller's classical version.

Frisch transposes the myth in an epic procedure that he had carried out in a similar, successful manner before, in the system of a tentative narrative structure in which nothing is ever definite, not even names or the identity and character of the main figures, but rather everything remains revisable, open and susceptible to checks—as in the development as leitmotiv of the identity of his "Gessler." The mobility of his prosaic construction, however, was not sufficient for Frisch. He added an apparatus of annotations that further relativizes the main text. The notes are a parody of the practice of scholarly notes. They are more elaborate and structurally more important in Frisch's piece than in scholarly texts, constituting about half of the total text. In contrast to scholarly usage they have not an additive effect but rather work in a manner that strongly relativizes and ironizes the already ironic main text. They have the function of placing the main text's narrated events, set in the summer of 1291, into a precarious relation with all conceivable time levels of the Tell saga's tradition and aftereffects. The annotations confront the Tell story with its reception under different conditions down through the times—

especially in the nineteenth century (e.g., in Engels and Keller) and in Frisch's time. In the notes, for instance, Frisch confronts the supposedly supratemporal pretensions of the Tell occurrence, its "everlasting national commitment" as in the eyes of the conservative Swiss, with the unenlivened Swiss present time, with the disguised Nazi-sympathy during World War II or the bellicose pan-militarism. The main text, already flexible in itself, becomes all the more indefinite under the influence of the notes. It is the national Tell-monument, as in its Altdorf version, that begins to vacillate, and it crumbles in a most ingenious manner under Frisch's techniques of relativization. With the reciprocal relation of the main text and annotations, Frisch achieved foremost that same quality he noted in his early *Tagebuch* concerning Thomas Mann, doing so from the critical distance of the Brecht-student and in a way very appropriate for the Tell theme: "epic *Spätlese*—the costumed essayism."

Frisch did not stage this playfully elegant and yet very serious Tell inquiry in a vacuum. That is proved by the angry criticism that his *Wilhelm Tell für die Schule* encountered in Switzerland and by the fact that two years following the appearance of his prose work, a large Swiss exposition with the theme *Tell 73* received an enthusiastic response from the artists asked to assist and also with the public in different Swiss cities. The conclusion of the exposition was that the heroic Tell myth of the national conservatives was ripe for revision, as was the Altdorf Tell-monument of Kissling. Switzerland in the early 1970s appears to deal with its national symbol as a type of Tell-mobile-building-blocks. The classical arrangement has been loosened. The parts have become free and adaptable for new configurations and provocations.

One example was the Tell radio play to be heard on a sound cassette at the exposition. In it the author Peter Jenny had done nothing other than placing his own name everywhere in Schiller's Tell text where the name Wilhelm Tell appears: a technique of verbal "minimal art" with amazing alienation potency because, according to the author's description, it makes the idolic character of Tell most obvious by consciously effecting the unconscious identification of the individual Swiss with the crossbow marksman.[19]

In contrast to all criticism from conservative quarters, such procedures are a legitimate and politically wholesome way to deal with the myth, without condemning those who indulge in the myth's monumentic version, as Engel's irreconcilable tirades did. Frisch and *Tell 73* are dealing in a previously tabooed, yet tolerant, fashion with the components of the national symbol, in a manner clearly distinguishable from Engels's fanatically ideologized hate-criticism. And if anyone at all is allowed, the Swiss alone would be entitled to carry out such verbal tactics, not the Germans, who could never demonstrate to the Swiss how one should treat national traditions, but who rather drove hosts of emigrants into their country and then found the tolerance quite natural with which the victims of German intolerance were received there.

Similar to the way the Swiss Tinguely proceeds with the myth "machine," the artists of *Tell 73* and Max Frisch with his prose text erect myth mobiles that playfully move their parts but simultaneously chastize the Swiss of today. The parable quality that is evident in Frisch's other works also makes his Tell a means of demonstration and a typical school example; furthermore, the demonstration procedure is to a great extent that formulated by Brecht for the latter's epic theater. This prose work of Frisch's is not only a simple parable, but it also has the explicitness of an allegory in the overtness with which myth and interpretation are brought face to face in ironic reflection, above all through the annotations. The method is similar to the way the biblical Jesus of Nazareth often supplied his parables with interpretations, making the parables into extended metaphors or allegories. We do not want to overextend the analogy here; however, in Schiller's *Tell* it is evident that in many details the title figure shows definite analogies to Christ and similarities to Napoleon—so that there appears the stylization of a national redeemer saving the country—in a remarkable connection with Goethe's puzzling words registering in Schiller a "genuine Christ tendency" becoming more and more prominent.[20]

This christological attribute appears in Tell even after all of Frisch's ironizing. Frisch's Tell still has an element of the national Jesus also— naturally none the less demythologized than that which contemporary theology displays in the Nazarene's case. Frisch's Tell is deheroized and average; perhaps for that reason he again offers to Swiss confederates and his contemporaries apathethic possibilities of identification. Wilhelm Tell as Peter Jenny, as an average Swiss—that could be what Frisch means.

"Wilhelm Tell for school instruction"—that was the problem that Gottfried Keller had wrestled with in his anthology revision. And he had solved it with pragmatic Swiss sensibleness by not simply throwing out *Wilhelm Tell* or proceeding according to Engel's prescription ("It doesn't matter, the Swiss will be burned"); but rather by changing the selection in the anthology. Frisch consciously made the decision for the Swiss-Keller tradition: not to burn, but rather to revise for the present times. By writing *Wilhelm Tell für die Schule,* he did not decide against Tell's further existence, but rather for a Tell of daily use. The issue concerns a Tell with whom we can live if we let him live. It is evident that "school" for Frisch as also for Keller does not mean merely "school"; it is the school of experiences that we attend daily.

1. Conversations with Eckermann, May 6, 1827.
2. See Reinhold Grimm, *Bertolt Brecht* (Stuttgart, 1971), p. 54.
3. Max Frisch, *Tagebuch 1966-1971* (Frankfurt, 1972), p. 30.
4. Bertolt Brecht, *Arbeitsjournal*, vol. 2, 1942-55 (Frankfurt, 1973), p. 804.
5. Frisch, *Tagebuch 1966-1971*, p. 31.
6. Grimm, p. 55.
7. Schiller, letter to A. W. Iffland, Dec. 5, 1803.
8. Brecht, *Arbeitsjournal*, 2: 802.
9. Frisch, *Tagebuch 1946-1949* (Frankfurt, 1958), p. 241.
10. Frisch, *Tagebuch 1946-1949*, pp. 293-94.
11. Ludwig Börne, *Sämtliche Schriften*, vol. 1, ed. J. and P. Rippmann (Darmstadt, 1964), pp. 397ff.
12. Gottfried Keller, *Der grüne Heinrich*, vol. 1, ed. Clemens Heselhaus (Munich, n.d.), p. 336.
13. Ibid.
14. Quoted in *Karl Marx/Friedrich Engels, Über Kunst und Literatur*, vol. 1, ed. Manfred Kliem (Berlin, 1967), pp. 503f.
15. Ibid., p. 504.
16. Schiller, verse 1449.
17. Schiller, verses 1274-87, translated by William F. Mainland, *Wilhelm Tell* (Chicago, 1972).
18. Max Frisch, *Wilhelm Tell für die Schule* (Frankfurt, 1971), p. 73.
19. *Tell 73, Katalog der Ausstellung*, ed. Peter Killer (Spiegel-Berne, 1973), p. 41.
20. Goethe to Zelter, Nov. 9, 1830.

MARIAN E. MUSGRAVE

Frisch's "Continuum" of Women, Domestic and Foreign

In one of his remarks about Bertolt Brecht, Max Frisch wrote in the *Tagebuch 1966-1971*, "What Brecht brought back from his emigration was immunity to the idea of foreignness; he was neither impressed by the fact that different people have different customs, nor did he feel that he must insist on his own Germanness."[1] Unlike Brecht, Frisch has remained impressed by and interested in foreign lands, foreign ways, foreign peoples, and convinced of the value of travel.[2] Quite early in his career, Frisch wrote that every time he returns from abroad, he notices anew the constraint, the inhibitions, the lack of inborn self-confidence of the Swiss.[3] Just after the war, he suggested that young Germans be permitted to travel at government expense so that they could begin to see things differently. It is, of course, no accident that so many of Frisch's characters, like Frisch himself, are often on the road. Even Professor O, who had once told Walter Faber's university class, "travel is atavistic; the time will come when all traffic will stop, and only newlyweds will drive about the world in a coach, but otherwise no one else," even this man, dying of a wasting disease, his face already a skull-like reminder of mortality, is spending his last months of life traveling.[4]

Frisch has used foreign lands to equate with or to contrast with Switzerland, as in *Andorra*; to contrast with the industrialized, materialistic West, as in *Bin oder Die Reise nach Peking*; or to contrast with European or American decadence, as in *Homo faber*. But often the foreign scene betrays simply the author's pleasure in rendering accurate observations of the exotic. This tendency can be observed in both the fiction and the diaries, an example being the three mulatta girls who are dressed in green silk, "Little animals wearing earrings, silent and lovely, frightful, secretive creatures."[5] Frisch calls them unforgettable, but we never see them again.

Frisch often uses exotic peoples to make or to underline his moral or social criticism. In an article published in 1969, Günter Bicknese wrote, "It is striking that Frisch's sympathy for colored (and other disadvantaged) people springs not only from his humanitarian thought but also and not less from his admiration for the uprightness of these people, for their genuine feeling for life."⁶ Frisch does return to these ideas rather often. At Anastasius Holder's funeral in *Bin*, the narrator thinks how thoroughly Europeans have squeezed human beings and human feelings out of funeral ceremonies, so that the survivors and their grief are superfluous. "I thought, among Negroes it would have been different, not to mention the ancient Greeks or the Chinese! Among genuine human beings, among creative people, it would be different."⁷ Walter Faber's four-day stopover in Havana shows clearly how Frisch attacks North American pretenses and hypocrisy by portraying the beautiful Cuban population, "a mixture of Negro and Spanish ancestry," and specifically contrasts the natural beauty and behavior of the Cuban mulattas with white women "who are unable to admit that they are growing old, their cosmetics even on corpses" (*HF*, pp. 220-21).

Though Frisch's mother once told him with some asperity that he should not write so much about women, for he does not understand them, Frisch has nevertheless created an astonishing number of female characters. Since his females often live depressing lives and meet unpleasant ends, the idea might logically arise that he actually dislikes women.⁸ A spectrum or continuum of women, from those closest to Frisch's own society to those farthest—i.e., non-Swiss, non-European, non-German-speaking, non-white—reveals that most must suffer and that those closest to Frisch's society are often the objects of abuse ranging from mental cruelty to callous neglect to desertion in time of need. Two women even commit suicide.⁹

In a recent essay on Frisch, Zoran Konstantinović approvingly quotes Jean-Paul Weber, who believes that every writer has but one theme which is presented over and over in new form. This theme is present in the writer's subconscious mind and appears in the different works with varied, symbolic value."¹⁰ Frisch's eternal theme is the guilt of men toward women, whether son toward mother, father toward daughter, husband toward wife, or lover toward partner (Konstantinović, p. 146). One remembers Faber's indifference toward Hanna once he has arranged for her abortion, Kürmann's tacit refusal to visit his mortally sick mother until she has conveniently died, and multiple desertions: in *Die Schwierigen, Santa Cruz, Stiller, Homo faber, Biographie: Ein Spiel*, and *Montauk*. Though one is careful not to assume complete identity between persona and author, even with so personal an author as Frisch (as he says in *Montauk*, "I have never described myself, I have only betrayed myself"), it is significant that his favorite painting in the Basel Art Museum states the theme of desertion with archetypal figures: Odysseus, the world traveler, who has loved and left many, is robed in blue, the color of the far horizons, while Calypso, the island-bound goddess, is robed in red, the color of sexual frustration.¹¹ Holder said it most coarsely, "Mountains and women are there to be enjoyed" (*Bin*, p. 44).

It is in the light of Konstantinović's observation that I wish to examine certain of Frisch's female characters, concentrating on those who are legitimate sexual-love objects, thereby eliminating mothers like Mrs. Kürmann, Sr., and daughters like Sabeth, as well as the daughter in *Montauk* with whom Max cannot converse because he cannot think of anything to say. The women who remain can be grouped as follows: 1) white, European, German-speaking, homogeneous background; 2) white, European, German-speaking, double background; 3) white, non-European, non-German-speaking, heterogeneous background; 4) non-white, non-European, Oriental or black background. This last category might seem troublesome, for it could be split into two parts; furthermore, some of the Orientals seem to speak German. But remembering William of Occam's razor, I shall not multiply categories needlessly.

Katrin Guggenbühl, the weak, clinging girl who marries Professor Kürmann in order to do her patriotic duty by having a baby, belongs in the first group. She is a domestic woman of the "children, church, and kitchen" type, perfectly submissive to her husband (which enrages him) and fatally obedient. When Kürmann, during a morning quarrel, tells her, "Go hang yourself!" Katrin does just that. Given an opportunity later to change her fate, Kürmann refuses, saying, "I have become accustomed to my guilt."[12] The "Aryan" Katrin, who seems to have had no psychological defenses or strengths, compares with Inge, in *Die Schwierigen*, who, though her role is larger, has no physical resources. Her system is seemingly exhausted; the fact that she simply dies from no clearly ascertainable cause, like many a nineteenth-century heroine, helps to tie the novel more closely to the previous century than to its own.

With the second group, we come to the so-called mongrels, who, in the folk mind, are stronger, smarter, and more resourceful than thoroughbreds. Julika, in *Stiller*, is half-Hungarian; Hanna, in *Homo faber*, is half-Jewish; and Antoinette, in *Biographie*, is Alsatian, quite literally shuttling between Germanic and Gallic culture and society. Frisch himself is of heterogeneous background, as Hans Bänziger in *Frisch and Dürrenmatt* points out, adding, "In this country, the Swiss who have no German, Austrian, French, or Italian grandparents are the great exceptions."[13]

A masterfully portrayed character, Julika has become an admired and highly successful ballet dancer but has never overcome a pathological need to suffer. When she becomes ill with tuberculosis and must enter a sanatorium, Stiller's abandonment of her is a terrible blow; but she survives his neglect and cruelty, even gaining some insight into her own infantile behavior. When she takes Stiller back, she can at least give of herself, though, to be sure, she is still governed by a need to suffer and repress, if we take her illness to have a strong psychosomatic component, as Ulrich Weisstein does.[14] Since Julika does not solve her conflicts concerning Stiller, her reentry into an unhealthy situation makes her ill again, this time fatally.

Hanna Landsberg, another masterfully portrayed character, survives Walter Faber's mistreatment of her by becoming as hostile and rejecting as he is. She refuses to let Joachim be a father to Sabeth, her child by Faber, and refuses to give Joachim a child of his own, using the same specious argument of political and economic expediency which Faber had used to attempt to persuade her to abort. But Hanna is a more complex and contradictory figure than some critics have perceived.[15] She is, in the first place, modeled upon, but is not identical with, a Jewish girl, Käte, to whom Frisch was once engaged (*Montauk*, p. 114). Since Frisch portrays this romance twice, and since desertion is a constant theme with him, three times involving racial differences, we can assume the importance of the idea to him. At the core of Hanna's behavior is her anger with men, starting, evidently, with that fight in which her younger brother defeated her, after which she directs her prayers to the Virgin Mary and not to Jehovah. Her anger is exacerbated, of course, by Walter's behavior when he learns of her pregnancy; she is unable to see Joachim as he really is but only as a Faber figure. Critics have quite rightly seized upon the relationship of this novel to the Oedipus myth, but they have overlooked its Old Testament elements. The scene in which Joachim's body is found is matched in horror, I think, by Hanna's situation at the end, stripped of everything dear or even needful, and with not even a roof over her head. Frisch is a moral writer; I cannot believe that the echoes of Job (and possibly David and Uriah) are accidental.

Another hostile woman is Antoinette, Professor Kürmann's second wife, but we are given no clues as to the origins of her hostility. She has excellent ego-strength, for when we first meet her, Kürmann is trying to insult her enough to make her go home. Since she has a private reason for staying (a man whom she wishes to avoid is awaiting her outside), she is invulnerable to his efforts. When she and Kürmann marry, she pursues her own goals, never subordinating her interests to his, nor does she permit him to govern her private life. At the end of the play, given a chance to play the game of biography revision, Antoinette leaves Kürmann out of her life without hesitation. But even without this decisive action, her strength has been fully documented; as I have pointed out elsewhere, Kürmann, normally cruel and self-centered, several times adopts a "feminine" role in his interaction with Antoinette.[16] Of the three "half-breeds," only Hanna and Antoinette survive, Hanna with terrible psychological damage, though it must be said that in one rerun of his life, Kürmann murders Antoinette for adultery. None of these relationships is healthy.

With the remainder of the women, marriage does not come into question.

As one who chronicles the ways of the Swiss middle class, Frisch keeps his marriages, for good or ill, within that class. As will be seen, though women from other cultures may attract painfully, Frisch's men use them as a sexual vacation from their grim marriages or other situations at home. If unmarried, they marry at home; if married, they remain married. Ivy and Lynn, the two Americans, who are white, non-German-speaking, and of the usual American heterogeneous background, illustrate the point. Frisch had written, "The wonderful thing about love is just this, that it keeps us prepared to follow a person through all of his possible developments" (*Tagebuch, 1946-1949,* p. 31). But Faber ignores Ivy's personality, is indifferent to her developments, and draws faulty, contradictory conclusions about her as if she were a laboratory specimen. (He thinks of her simultaneously as quite promiscuous and as believing that she must marry every man who beds her [p. 36]. This in New York, at a time when only adultery was grounds for divorce). Ivy continues to excite Faber physically, I think, because he refuses to perceive the woman herself. Though Michael Butler's interpretations of the affair are excellent, he is wrong, I think, in calling Ivy "a puppet programmed with a predatory instinct," for she gives love to Walter and seems to require nothing except reciprocation—precisely what Walter cannot give, for he perceives emotions as dangerous and closeness as threatening.[17] A married, high-fashion model, Ivy has access to other men. She clearly prefers multiple attachments, so that even though she loses Faber, she can replace him. Those who make multiple attachments fear losing love-objects, but the identity of the love-object is relatively unimportant.

Since Max, in *Montauk,* is determined to have no guilt in connection with Lynn, he permits her to be herself, a rather sloppy and disorganized young woman at home but efficient at her job. Without comment, Max tells the reader important facts about Lynn: she likes to lead, pays for her own lunch, meditates twice daily whether he is present or not. She feels no need to become an intellectual nor to pose as one simply because she is dating one. Most remarkable of all, Lynn is permitted to correct Max, to tell him when he is wrong without incurring his anger, vexed silence, or exasperation (p. 110). At the end of the book, it is clear that Lynn has another lover; when she and Max part for the last time, she does not look back, for she has things to do. It is he who secretly watches her until she is out of sight. Though Lynn, in her relationship with Max, does not think in terms of survival, she has, nevertheless, the qualities that would protect her from an exploitive lover: she has an occupation and interests of her own, she has self-assurance, and, since she is young and attractive, she has many sexual options open to her. Max treats her with consideration, but one can hardly imagine Lynn's staying in a situation in which she was abused, unlike others of Frisch's female characters.

The final group of women consists of the true "exotics," in the popular sense of the word. They are non-white and are either Chinese or blacks. Considering the substantial and important sections of *Stiller* and *Homo faber* which take place in Mexico and in South America, one might expect Indian women to figure in the continuum, but they are simply described in passing—an old woman selling orchids, a maiden trailing her arms in the lake, girls wearing North American dresses instead of their own traditional costumes as they flock to the Festival of the Moon. Frisch presents us, actually, with the tourists' Mexico—the floating gardens, the lively open markets, the festivals, the volcano, Paricutín. Frisch's own authentic voice may be heard, I suspect, in those sections where Stiller and Faber describe, with considerable loathing, the flies, the vermin, the stinks, the rotting carcasses, the fecal matter on the streets, the horrible diseases, and the ever-present buzzards. It may be that Frisch does not use Indians as characters because the culture is simply too exotic. He cannot find entry into it.

As for Oriental culture, Frisch does not try to enter it but uses instead a technique borrowed from eighteenth-century Chinoiserie (and more immediately, perhaps, from Brecht): he creates characters and identifies them as Chinese. Since his purpose is not realism in either *Bin* or the *Chinesische Mauer*, he is free to use standard Western ideas about Orientals. In *Bin*, for example, Kilian stops at a palace just to look about. "And it was just as one expects from the Chinese, very polite people who behaved as though it was precisely your visit which they had awaited" (p. 80). Kilian cannot be less polite than his hosts, so he stays, the episode serving to separate him temporarily from his alter ego. In the *Chinesische Mauer*, the Chinese princess is no more specifically Chinese than are Brecht's characters with Chinese names. In *Bin*, Maja is identified as Chinese, but she represents youth and beauty or our memories of first love (pp. 49-49). Since these are all imaginary girls, it is not surprising that for once the mating process in Frisch loses that fatal significance which Bänziger noted.[18]

Unlike Indian and possibly Oriental cultures, black American culture seems to have presented no problem of excessive exoticism for Frisch. From the start, its clear relationship to white Western culture apparently persuaded Frisch that he understood blacks and their milieu. Before ever meeting a black, he was using them as characters. The black oyster seller in *Santa Cruz* is a minstrel show figure, while the black sergeant in *Als der Krieg zu Ende war* is a Hollywood film black, tap dancing, singing, and playing the piano. "Begegnung mit Negern," an essay which appeared shortly before *Stiller* and to which it bears a close relationship, reveals the mistaken ideas and expectations which Frisch had about blacks and black culture. He clearly was not prepared for the fact that black Americans are American, for example, his reactions ranging from sentimental to contemptuous, as I have pointed out elsewhere.[19] Even as late as the *Tagebuch 1966-1971*, Frisch was still making judgments about blacks based upon European standards and newspaper articles that were by no means impartial.[20]

Black women appear for the first time in "Begegnung mit Negern" and *Stiller*. The sort of "double vision" which whites often have upon meeting blacks for the first time and which causes Frisch to sound so arrogant in the essay is used artistically in *Stiller*.[21] Stiller actually does see two Florences: the fantasy Florence is sexy and approachable, she prefers the white man to her black husband, and runs away with Stiller without further ado. The real Florence, however, remains unaware of, or indifferent to, Stiller's passion for her, interacts with him only to reprove him for mistreating the cat, Little Gray, and calmly marries her Joe. Stiller had earlier watched Florence "dance down" five men and had thought, "I understood very well that I could never satisfy this girl" (p. 222). The conflict between fantasy and reality is at least partially responsible for Stiller's abortive suicide attempt (p. 448). Florence, a Lotte to Stiller's failed Werther, visits him once at the hospital (p. 450).

The dancing episode in *Stiller* should be compared with a very similar one in *Bin*, since dancing is a well-known metaphor for sexual activity, one that has been exploited to the full by drama and cinema. Kilian sees a girl dancing untiringly with many men. When she finally asks him to dance, Kilian feels like weeping, like kissing her, like hanging himself. In this case, dancing leads to sexual pairing, for when Kilian starts out again for Peking, he takes Maja with him. Newly introduced to sex by the much older Kilian, Maja seemingly enjoys it but feels no obligation to remain, running away the next morning with a youth her own age. The wry humor here, which rests upon a standard "country girl and city slicker" kind of joke, rests, too, on our knowledge of the middle-class pattern of a woman's marriage and fidelity to the man who takes her virginity.[22] But the implication of (potential) promiscuity, signaled by the multiple dance partners, shows that neither Florence nor Maja is bound by this morality of monogamy. Like Lynn, they have other sexual options open to them.

Juana, in *Homo faber*, and Helen, in *Biographie*, are alike only in being black and in having only small parts in their respective works. Juana is a local-color character, but justifiably so, for Faber is still relating to people on a superficial level; the acquaintanceships which he makes in Cuba, therefore, such as pimps, prostitutes, cab drivers, and bar habitués, are perfect for his stage of development. He has no responsibilities to these people but can simply enjoy being among them, alive and beautiful as they are. Juana, the eighteen-year-old "weekend prostitute" in Batista's Cuba accepts Faber and tries with goodwill to understand his broken Spanish. The fact that Faber, who hates feelings of inferiority, tries to use her language shows that he is giving up some of his attitudes of superiority. As a prostitute in a land where prostitution is legal, Juana cannot be hurt by mental cruelty, defloration, and abandonment as a "respectable" woman might be.

The only educated non-white woman portrayed by Frisch is Helen, who was an eighteen-year-old student at the University of California when she met twenty-three-year-old Kürmann. It is she who made him a man in the physical sense, and he loved her as much as a confused, egocentric man can love anyone. Helen can therefore be compared profitably with Hanna, whom Faber loves in his way.[23] Frisch, incidentally, uses both women to contrast favorably with other women—Hanna with the cosmetics-smeared women sunning themselves on the ship deck, Helen with Katrin and Antoinette.[24] The racial issue is foremost in both love affairs, neither Helen nor Hanna being protected by her lover from insults and affronts. Faber/Frisch is silent when the Nazi official in the Basel-Badische train station says, "And this Jewess, I suppose, reports all the horror stories to you" (*Montauk,* pp. 114-15). As Konstantinović writes, "In any extra-legal relationship, the woman sacrifices much more than the man socially" (ZK, p. 151). Even now there are many who do not regard an interracial romance or marriage as a legitimate relationship, thirty-five years after the Nazi period. If Käte/Hanna could not enter the restaurant, neither could Helen enter the California motel. Neither woman is deceived by a love that accepts the humiliation of the loved one in silence. Käte/Hanna rejects the prospective marriage. Helen's last words to Kürmann are, "You're a coward. I always knew you were."

The conclusions that one can draw from Frisch's horror stories of female relationships with men are these: 1) contact with men is dangerous, potentially destructive, to women; 2) the more conventionally moral the woman is, the more vulnerable she is; 3) a profession and interests of her own, including other men, bestow a modicum of safety; 4) holding on to the memory of the past simply distorts the present; one should make a clean break, therefore; 5) instead of merely reacting to others' words or deeds, women should act. A story that Frisch tells twice, in *Die Schwierigen* and in *Montauk*, illustrates the point: an older woman tells her younger lover that another man has offered to support her, obviously hoping to provoke a flattering reaction, but in any case a reaction that would decide for or against accepting the new relationship (*Montauk,* p. 119; *Schwierigen,* 1: 469-71). The tendency to react rather than act caused the woman to see only two possibilities, whereas the possibilities were manifold. As Krolevsky points out to Kürmann in *Biographie,* once the possibilities are understood, they can become actual.[25]

1. Max Frisch, *Tagebuch 1966-1971* (Frankfurt: Suhrkamp Verlag, 1972), p. 25.
2. Frisch is always conscious of his "Swissness." See Hans Bänziger, *Zwischen Protest und Traditionsbewusstsein* (Berne: Francke Verlag, 1975), for a thorough discussion of Frisch's complicated relationship to his own society.
3. Max Frisch, *Sketchbook 1946-1949*, tr. Geoffrey Skelton (New York: Harcourt, Brace and Jovanovich, 1977), pp. 29, 109.
4. Max Frisch, *Homo faber* (Frankfurt: Suhrkamp Verlag, 1964), pp. 126-27.
5. As was common with Frisch until the 1960s, non-whites, whether male or female, called forth animal comparisons. See Marian E. Musgrave, "The Evolution of the Black Character in the Works of Max Frisch," *Monatshefte* (Summer 1974), pp. 121-22.
6. Günter Bicknese, "Zur Rolle Amerikas in Max Frischs *Homo Faber*," *German Quarterly* 42 (Jan. 1969): 59.
7. Max Frisch, *Bin oder Die Reise nach Peking* (Zürich: Atlantis Verlag, 1945), pp. 40, 46.
8. Twice, in Montreal and Chicago, Frisch was asked this question but has not recorded his answer. Max Frisch, *Montauk*, tr. Geoffrey Skelton (New York: Harcourt, Brace and Jovanovich, 1976), p. 44.
9. One could argue that Agnes, in *Als der Krieg zu Ende War*, is not driven to suicide in the same sense that Katrin, in *Biographie*, is. We might also note that Hinckelman, in *Die Schwierigen*, kills himself when he realizes that Yvonne intends to leave him.
10. Zoran Konstantinović, "Die Schuld an der Frau," *Frisch: Kritik, Thesen, Analysen*, ed. Manfred Jurgensen (Berne: Francke Verlag, 1976), p. 146.
11. The psychological interpretations contained in this paper are the result of my work as a therapist with the mentally ill for eight years.
12. To be sure, Kürmann is not responsible for the fact that Katrin directs her anger inward, toward herself, instead of outward; such patterns of behavior are formed in early childhood.
13. Hans Bänziger, *Frisch und Dürrenmatt* (Berne: Francke Verlag, 1964), p. 29.
14. Ulrich Weisstein, *Max Frisch* (New York: Twayne Publishers, 1967), p. 58.
15. Bicknese, for example, sees Hanna almost as another Inge, representative of the exhausted powers of Europe, a woman resignedly gathering and patching together the shards of the past. Bicknese, "Zur Rolle Amerikas," p. 60.
16. Marian E. Musgrave, "Kürmann, His Wives, and 'Helen, the Mulatta' in Max Frisch's *Biographie*," *CLA Journal* 18, no. 3 (March 1975): 345-46.
17. Michael Butler, *The Novels of Max Frisch* (London: Oswald Wolff, 1976), pp. 99-100.
18. "In most of Frisch's mature works, the mating process has a fatal significance." Bänziger, *Frisch und Dürrenmatt*, p. 14.
19. Musgrave, "Evolution of the Black Character," pp. 122, 123.
20. *Tagebuch 1966-1971*, pp. 406-10; 127-28. Though Frisch doubts the words of the *Neue Zürcher Zeitung*, healthy skepticism about American informants is lacking.
21. In effect, two blacks, a positive and a negative, appear in one. The positive image is the black's real identity—a civil rights leader, a professor, a salesclerk; the negative may be whatever stereotype of black character the white has heard and accepted— the black as comic, as primitive, as brute, as imitative child, as ultrasexual, as carefree exotic. The white's resulting behavior can be strange and contradictory.
22. So far as I know, no one has previously commented upon the connection between the Prince's coarse joke told in whispers at the dinner table and the facts of Kilian's brief romance with Maja.

23. Faber thinks, "I didn't marry Hanna, whom I loved, so why should I marry Ivy?" *Homo faber*, p. 36.

24. The comparison is explicit in *Homo Faber*, implicit in *Biographie*. See Musgrave, "Evolution of the Black Character," pp. 128-29.

25. See Hans Bänziger, "Ab posse ad esse," in *Frisch: Kritik, Thesen, Analysen*, for a brilliant explication of this crux in *Biographie*.

ROLF KIESER

Wedding Bells for Don Juan: Frisch's Domestication of a Myth

Whenever Max Frisch's *Don Juan* play is discussed by the critics, their attention unfailingly focuses on the story of that archetypal protagonist of *Macho* who, as Frisch insists, prefers geometry by far to the fairer sex.

The author, on the other hand, strongly emphasizes that his *Don Juan* has little in common with Tirso de Molina's Glorious *Burlador de Sevilla* since he intends to show "Don Juan as a developing character, which is only possible at the price that he is no real Don Juan anymore but a man who (for one reason or the other) acquired the role of Don Juan."[1]

"The love of geometry" is a symbol for what Frisch considers "a male intellect which is an affront because it is aiming for completely different goals than a woman does and which considers woman from the beginning a sheer episode—with the well-known result, to be sure, that the episode eventually swallows up the whole life."[2]

Frisch wanted his Don Juan to be a "spiritual figure," which means that we find in him the opposite of the traditional genius of sensuality, "the incarnation of the flesh or the animation of the flesh through the flesh's proper spirit," as Kierkegaard put it.[3] "His fame as a seducer (which accompanies him as fame although he does not identify with it) is a misunderstanding from part of the ladies," says Frisch. "Don Juan is an intellectual, although well-built and without glasses. It is indeed his spirituality which makes him irresistible for the ladies of Seville."[4]

Far from being a "libidinous libertine" (Hans Mayer)[5] in the fashion of Casanova, Frisch's Don Juan in fact challenges the laws of nature which divide humanity into two sexes. "His opponent is creation proper." By denying his need for a permanent love relationship with a woman he also forecloses fatherhood: "Don Juan," says Frisch, "is childless, even if there were 1003 children."[6]

By characterizing Don Juan as a "parasite of creation," Frisch depicts him not as a rebel against Christian morality but as a lonely researcher for "the virginal," for paradise lost.

It is, as we know, not the first time that Frisch uses biblical metaphors in his own capricious way. In the *Sketchbook 1946-1949* we find the passage which has become the leitmotiv for Frisch's whole work: *Thou shalt not make unto thee any graven image* where we find the following remarks about love: "That is the exciting, the unpredictable, the truly gripping thing about love: that we never come to the end of the person we love: because we love them; and as long as we love them ... Once we feel we know the other, love is at an end every time, but the cause of that, and the consequence of it, are perhaps not quite as we have always imagined. It is not because we know the other that we cease to love, but vice versa: because our love has come to an end, because its power is expended, that person is finished for us."[7] It is exactly this experience Don Juan has when Pater Diego goes through the vows of matrimony in the strange wedding ceremony. The words he uses are biblical and refer to the scene of recognition after Adam and Eve have eaten from the tree of knowledge:

PATER DIEGO: ... Do you recognize each other face to face?
(DONNA ANNA *is unveiled*) Donna Anna, do you recognize him? Answer.
DONNA ANNA: (*silent, as if petrified*)
PATER DIEGO: Answer, Don Juan, do you recognize her?
DON JUAN: Yes!
PATER DIEGO: Answer, Don Juan, do you recognize her?
DON JUAN: Yes ... indeed ... o yes! (*Trombones*)[8]

We understand that at the moment of consecration of the marriage, love is lost since it is contingent on "recognition" which in German includes the meanings of carnal knowledge as well as perception. Don Juan at this point suddenly understands that the love he felt for the woman he seduced in the park cannot be perpetuated by the graven image forced upon him by the act of marriage.

Don Juan's rebellion against heaven is stimulated by his interest for geometry: something in the creation is out of tune. Don Juan wants to find out, "was stimmt," ("what harmonizes," one of Frisch's favorite expressions.) His attempt to prove that permanent love does not exist makes him particularly attractive in the eyes of each one of the ladies who wants to prove the opposite, namely that she alone is the answer to his heart's desire. Don Juan gives up when transitoriness, "Vergängnis," catches up with him. An aging seducer who considers himself a spiritual figure is an embarrassment. Don Juan plans his escape from the ladies by staging the farce of the Stone Guest. Ironically he ends up where he started: in marriage.

It is perhaps the strange combination of farce (Frisch himself calls his comedy "ein Kostümstück") and venerable literary tradition that has prevented the critics from seeing the play in its own context: Frisch's intention to write a parody of the Don Juan myth is only secondary. Among the notes in his *Gesammelte Werke in zeitlicher Folge* we find the interesting remark that the author during his first journey to the United States worked on a novel with the tentative title *Was macht ihr mit der Liebe*. At the end of the same year he began to work on his *Don Juan* while dropping temporarily his novel-project. Later he caught up with it. It developed into *Stiller*.[9] If we consider the simultaneity of the creation of novel and drama we are able to realize some meaningful parallels.

Already in *The Chinese Wall*, Don Juan appears as one of the figures "who inhabit our brain." "I have just come out of the Hell of literature," he explains and complains that nobody, not even Brecht and his Ensemble, understand him. In *Stiller* we find a parallel reference to literature shaping our consciousness: "How am I to prove to my counsel that I don't know my murderous impulses through C. G. Jung, jealousy through Marcel Proust, Spain through Hemingway, Paris through Ernst Jünger, Switzerland through Mark Twain, Mexico through Graham Greene, my fear of death through Bernanos, inability ever to reach my destination through Kafka, and all sorts of things through Thomas Mann?"[10] Don Juan is faced with a similar problem. How can he prove to the world that he is not identical with the myth which bears his name, and that his interest is geometry rather than women? "I am not Don Juan!" he insists, yet his fame is so overwhelming that not even the frank disclosure of the theatrical mechanisms of his planned descent to hell will shatter his reputation. His only way to gain anonymous privacy is to accept Miranda's offer. As father and henpecked husband he blends with a life of mediocrity, just as Stiller does at the end.

Frisch's treatment of the Don Juan myth makes his hero a close relative not only of Stiller but also of other male protagonists such as Walter Faber, Gantenbein, Enderlin-Svoboda, Kürmann, and all the other expressions of a self in search of identity. Their forefather is Don Juan. With him they share their narcissism, their intellectual male chauvinism and their inability to accept woman as more than an episode in their lives. This is the reason why, with rare exceptions, Frisch's female figures do not live an existence of their own. They are focal points of male attention or stumbling blocks such as Antoinette Stein in *Biografie*, the proverbial "Stein des Anstosses" (stumbling block).

"Le Donjuanism" as Camus defined it in his *Mythe de Sisyphe* is a salient principle in Frisch's interpretation of the relationship between man and woman. When the lover of the clear logic of geometry and admirer of the law that parallels meet in eternity sets out in a Faustian effort to find out what holds the world together in its innermost being, he realizes in the end that his existence is absurd.[11] There are only two choices left for him: death or capitulation. Frisch's Don Juan chooses the middle-class solution. His fall from the sublime to the ridiculous is tremendous yet inevitable. It is not the descent to hell of the classical Don Juan, and the formula that in Frisch's interpretation marriage equals hell is no more than a pun. For Frisch's Don Juan is not "ein glänzendes Scheusal" (a brilliant monster) as Brecht called Molière's seducer,[12] but an existential searcher whose greatest fear is the fear of repetition. Thus marriage is a metaphor for repetition, and one of Frisch's metaphors for a man threatened by it is Don Juan. In *Stiller* we find the following remarks: "Repetition. And yet I know that everything depends on whether one succeeds in ceasing to wait for life outside repetition and instead, of one's free will (in spite of compulsion), manages to turn repetition, inescapable repetition, into one's life by acknowledging: That is I."[13]

Dürrenmatt has said that a story has come to the end when it has taken the worst possible turn. One could say the same about Frisch's comedies. Yet Frisch, in contrast to the eschatologist Dürrenmatt, scorns a theological world view. His game is chess. Don Juan has to lose this game. When he arranges for the elaborate descent to hell, he thinks that he has won the game. But he did not reckon with the queen. "The queen may do everything," Kürmann says in *Biografie* when he tries to explain the rules of chess to Antoinette. Don Juan, as Kürmann, sees his plans crossed by a lady who puts him in a golden cage and finally domesticates him with the announcement of his forthcoming fatherhood. With the famous exclamation "Mahlzeit!" at the end, Don Juan concedes to his chessmate.

Frisch's transformation of a literary myth into a middle-class marriage story does not thoroughly succeed. The author plays with the knowledge of the average theater-goer in reference to Don Juan. Ironically, the intensity of the old fable wins an easy victory over Frisch's intellectual Anti-Hero by putting him under its charm. His position of geometry remains unauthenticated even if the author points out the contingency of that cipher: "It is still too early, it would still be shocking, but sometime one should write a comedy with a noble ending: 'Don Juan Or the Love For the Duino Elegies'—the story of the last Don Juan in our time who dismissed all women because they bothered him in his ten years of waiting [to write] the Elegies."

Frisch also tries in vain to downgrade Don Juan's effectiveness as seducer. We witness a single seduction in the second act, and it is Don Juan who is seduced by Donna Elvira, the mother of his bride, who offers him her bedroom as an escape route. In the fourth act Don Juan assembles his former sweethearts, and their number amounts to thirteen only (even though Don Juan hints that there might be "a few more") thus indicating that Don Juan's success as seducer—thirteen victories within thirteen years—is highly exaggerated. Yet above Frisch's attempted understatement the magic *mille e tre* of the immortal Don Giovanni prevails. Or, as the Bishop says: "What else can the theater do? Truth cannot be shown, only invented."[15]

1. "Nachträgliches zu Don Juan," in Max Frisch, *Gesammelte Werke in zeitlicher Folge* (*GW*), vol. III.1, pp. 170f. The translation is mine.
2. Ibid., p. 168.
3. Cf. Werner Oehlmann, *Don Juan: Dichtung und Wirklichkeit* (Frankfurt and Berlin, 1965), p. 194.
4. *GW*, vol. III.1, p. 168.
5. Hans Mayer, "Don Juans Höllenfahrt: Don Juan und Faust," in *Don Juan. Darstellung und Deutung,* ed. Brigitte Wittman (Darmstadt, 1976), p. 348.
6. *GW*, vol. III.1, p. 171.
7. Max Frisch, *Sketchbook 1946-1949* (New York, 1977), pp. 16-17.
8. *GW*, vol. III.1, pp. 117-18.
9. *GW*, vol. III.2, Anmerkungen, pp. 861-62, 865.
10. Max Frisch, *I'm Not Stiller* (New York, 1962), p. 152.
11. Cf. Rolf Kieser and Doris Guilloton, "Faustische Elemente in Max Frischs 'Don Juan oder Die Liebe zur Geometrie,'" in *Max Frisch. Aspekte des Bühnenwerks,* ed. Gerhard P. Knapp (Berne, 1979).
12. Wittmann, p. 137.
13. *Stiller*, p. 59.
14. *Die Tat*, 18 May 1953.
15. *GW*, vol. III.1, p. 165.

LINDA J. STINE and HANS BÄNZIGER

"Exposed to the other sex": The Problem of Marriage in *Philipp Hotz* and *Graf Öderland*

We will begin our discussion with the later play, *Philipp Hotz*, since in it Frisch presents the complex problem of marriage in simple form, with a playfulness which led one Brazilian critic to comment on the "childlike happiness' with which the author played his theatrical games[1]—a characterization that could certainly apply to very little of Frisch's writing. In his latest works, especially, the shadows of the past begin to grow. The death of his mother (1966) and of Ingeborg Bachmann (1973), his own aging (and approaching death), the increasing notion of guilt: all this is the reverse side of the carefree weekend affair in *Montauk*. And, as the three scenes comprising *Triptychon* demonstrate, even death does not provide a final separation from the problems caused by relationships during life.

Typically, for Frisch, marriage bonds serve to trap a husband who longs for nothing less than an island utopia where he can live that life of adventure which he feels to be the only authentic life-style for him. The shortest and wittiest description of this typical Frischian marital situation is the farce *The Great Rage of Philipp Hotz* (1958).[2] The central situation is that of an intellectual, intent on demonstrating his resolve to escape his too-indulgent wife, who begins methodically to destroy their furniture. (An interesting comparison can be drawn to Brecht's early one-act play *The Marriage (Die Hochzeit*, 1919) where the destruction of furniture similarly represents the relationship of a petty-bourgeois couple. This furniture, in Brecht's play, which has been badly made by the husband—and also made so slowly that the bride is five months pregnant by the time the wedding day can roll around—falls apart piece by piece in the course of an increasingly boisterous wedding reception, while the feelings between bride and groom deteriorate accordingly. At the end, however, in the midst of almost total destruction, the couple fall back upon their lower-class vitality—and their bed—and we know the marriage will survive.

Hotz, on the other hand, has nothing to fall back upon. He did not create his own furniture, or his marriage, and cannot do an efficient job of destroying either. His inner contradictions show up even in his name, which sounds both friendly and abrupt: Philipp, "friendly," Hotz, the name of an eighteenth-century Swiss general and many other dynamic, efficient Zurich families. Moreover, Philipp Hotz is a Dr. phil.–we remember all the other ineffectual Ph.D.'s in Frisch's works, with their title and not much else. As an intellectual, Hotz tries to fit the role and be emancipated. To be married should not mean to own each other, he thinks, but he can never actually reach this rational middle ground. He suffers from either too much imagination (GW IV, 440 "I imagine" like Gantenbein, 441, the illusion with the cupboard) or too little (441, not seeing that Dorli is stronger). While Dorli matter of factly eats her apples, Hotz dreams of manly adventures as a mercenary far away. He does not realize his attempt at imprisoning her in the cupboard has failed. He is not even capable of adultery; he fabricates one that his wife Dorli believes. To Clarissa, with whom he professed to have had this nonexistent affair, Dorli protests: "You can say whatever you want to about my husband or men in general, but there is no man, you know, that would confess to adulteries which never happened, you know, and do it right out in public." "Your husband is a writer," Clarissa answers dryly (448), and the two women go on to discuss shame and privacy, truth and publicity; we see that even in the midst of the laughter Frisch is examining the ancient problem of man versus woman but also of individual versus society. "He no sooner smells publicity," Dorli continues, "than he spouts truths about marriage, for instance, that he could never bring himself to say within our four walls." We see this conflict in Frisch's own life: in the officially signed vitae of his works (as for instance the appendix of *Dienstbüchlein*) he never wrote about his first and second marriage, his children, his divorce. But as literature, in *Montauk*, that all changes. And the conflicts persist; we read Marianne's words (VI, 686): "I have not lived with you as literary material; I forbid you to write about me."

While the names of the characters change, the basic situation remains constant. How, Frisch continually asks, can the needs of men and women be successfully reconciled? In *Der Laie und die Architektur*, written four years earlier than *Philipp Hotz*, Frisch showed the polarity just as clearly. When it came to city planning, the layman was concerned with proper traffic facilities, the woman with finding nice places for the children to play. Frisch attributes a conservative "sandbox-philosophy" to the woman, progressive thinking to the man, and the dilemma caused by the confrontation does not disappear. Permanent sexual relations, in such a world, lead to aporias. Frisch does not assign guilt to any one side and preach change; he simply describes the stalemate, in the hopes that the reader will come out with the solution– "zu fragen bin ich, nicht zu antworten" (I'm to ask questions, not to answer any). In contrast to someone like Walter Faber, who has no appreciation for stability, for marriage, for permanence in society and personal relations, Frisch sees clearly the dangers of progressive ideologies and makes this a major theme.[3]

The story of Philipp Hotz ends, to no one's astonishment, in failure. Philipp, who actually manages a brief escape, is not accepted by the foreign legion because he is nearsighted, and he must thus return to the quiet harbor of his home, to the daily mail, the daily routine, condemned, like Stiller, to be the person his wife and others know him to be. But he is only nearsighted, not blind, and the ending is ironic rather than tragic. The blindness of Walter Faber destroys himself and others—Philipp's nearsightedness allows him to view the events of his marriage selectively and thus endure.

The style of the sketch is light, elegant, and disengaged, a style made possible because the varied and complex problems of marriage, adultery, and divorce are not really presented. Like *Biedermann*, this play is a parable. We do not see suffering or longing, the joy and pain of sexual relations within the farce; we see only clichés and types: the practical, efficient housewife, the would-be *machado*. Philipp destroys his prison exactly as Stiller sets out to destroy his atelier. Stiller, however, wanted to destroy the petrified relics of his own past, and his despair gave the scene a tragic depth. When we watch Philipp supervise the destruction of those clocks and pianos, tables and chairs—all the attributes of a proper bourgeois household—we are inspired to think no more deeply than the sight gags would warrant. Sarcastic bons mots banish all the shadows of real grief and sorrow.

In the *Times* review of a 1963 London performance, a critic commented: "One of its best ideas is to break down the fourth wall by giving Hotz the kind of delirious anger in which men naturally start addressing crowds."[4] And this brings us to the second great fury in the face of the marriage situation, the "great rage" of Graf Öderland.

Here, as in *Hotz*, the first level of symbolism is that of a cuckolded husband longing to break out of a senseless, suffocating marriage. The curtain rises on a fifty-year-old successful public prosecutor standing late at night in the midst of a typical lawyer's study, where everything is as neatly arranged in black and white as are the values of the society it represents. With the very first words of the play, the situation—and the tragedy—can be understood: a voice offstage calls out "Martin," the name of the prosecutor. It is his wife calling, looking for him, fixing his identity both for the audience and himself, forcing him out of his fantasies and back into his accustomed role of responsible husband and citizen. She enters the room and brings him the simplistic answers offered by a routine reality. It's late, he's tired, he's been working too hard, he should take a pill, a vacation—suggestions designed to fit him nicely within the system. The bonds of marriage are too rigid to allow change; there remain but two alternatives—conform or break out. A figurative description which captures quite nicely the way which Frisch's masculine heroes perceive the marriage relationship can be found in the words of Mario, the clairvoyant, as he looks through the study for clues to the prosecutor's whereabouts. He picks up a picture of Martin, the prosecutor, and says offhandedly to Elsa, his wife: "and if I might inquire, who put the esteemed missing person into this little frame? . . . Madame personally? (GW III, 36)." The answer, of course, so obvious as to be unnecessary, is yes.

Frisch contrasts the relationship between Martin and Elsa with that between Graf Öderland, an apocalyptic figure who cuts through the boredom and repression of everyday life with his ax, and Inge, the fairylike child who summons him forth. What the Count values in their fantasy marriage is the total absence of frames and image-making. He tells Inge gratefully: "You don't ask who I am—that's wonderful" (GW III, 26). Suddenly, he realizes in amazement, he has unlimited time.[5] (We think here of the weekend affair in *Montauk* which shares this same type of fairy-tale atmosphere. There, too, the character Max continually stresses how much time is available.) For the Count and Inge, then, in the beginning, the boundaries are no longer valid—the ax sees to that. Hope is not a toy ship on the mantel, as Elsa would have it; on the yacht *Esperanza* Inge and the Count set out to sail to an island paradise somewhere on a borderless sea.

A repressive marriage, however, is only one symbol of the deeper problem facing the public prosecutor. Philipp Hotz's whole goal is to be taken seriously, so as to be able to remain within his marriage; he wants to change the components, not the system. Martin's great rage, on the other hand, is directed against society. He is seeking that existential freedom where he can establish his own authenticity. Such an outbreak has the elements of genuine tragedy, for it is as imperative as it is impossible. Inge's and Öderland's fairy-tale marriage is rudely transferred from Santorin to the sewers when the Count is forced to come back to the world of reality and take the responsibility of functioning within a system. Marriage, for Frisch, as numerous critics have pointed out,[6] symbolizes on a small scale what the concept of Switzerland does on a larger scale—confinement, repression, clichés, repetition, all the problems which beset the individual in society.

In a discussion of *Philipp Hotz* and its presentation in the form of a *Schwank*, Frisch wrote in 1958 that he was trying to describe the problems of the intellectual (symbolized by Philipp) who is driven to do something foolish just so the world (and here he adds in parenthesis "his wife") takes him seriously.[7] The equation world/wife is central to Frisch's philosophy. Woman is always "the Other," everything that man is not, the rest of the world in a quite literal sense. A successful marriage, then, would be the symbol of a successful integration of the individual into society, the impossibility of which gives the tragedy to Frisch's world view. His heroes struggle mightily; Don Juan laments, "What an atrocity it is, that man by himself isn't whole," but the characters always end up powerless to achieve their goal of being both "the yolk and the white of the one shell," as Yeats once described this

Platonic idea. Whether in the reality of a humdrum existence or the fiction of escapist dreams, the coexistence of a fulfilled individual and a successful marriage can never succeed. Permanence in today's world has degenerated into permanent repetition, stability means the triviality of Philipp's morning mail and the despair of Öderland's nightly insomnia. But the alternative, breaking out, brings even greater dangers, so Frisch's heroes, whether alone or within marriage, are condemned to an existential loneliness, "bis zum Verbluten ausgesetzt dem andern Geschlecht" ("exposed to the other sex to the point of bleeding to death"; III, 164) as Don Juan sadly says.

    1. Yan Michalski, *Journal do Brasil*, April 10, 1968 (translation of "Pro Helvetia" performance at Rio de Janeiro. "J'ai eu l'impression que l'auteur, heureux comme un enfant, s'amusait avec quelques-unes des infinies combinaisons possibles du jeu théâtral."
    2. Called a *Schwank* in GW IV, 417 and *Stücke* 2 (1962). The theater bill in Zurich (1968) and the first printing in *Hortulus* 8 (1958): 34, called it a "Sketch."
    3. See P. Pütz, *M.F. Aspekte des Prosawerks*, ed. Gerhard Knapp (1978), p. 127. "Faber begreift sich als futurische Existenz, der jede Art von Stillstand oder Bindung (Ehe) zutiefst zuwider ist." Cf. in the same volume, p. 176, M. Eifler: "Ehe [bedeutet] eine legale Sanktionierung eines Eigentumsverhältnisses"; p. 194 Grimm/Wellauer: Frisch spiegle "ein Versagen sowohl der Ehe und Gesellschaft als auch der Kräfte, die sich gegen sie aufzulehnen wagen"; p. 305 Knapp: die Institution der Ehe durchziehe das schriftstellerische Werk wie eine idee fixe.
    4. London *Times*, 1 June 1963.
    5. GW III, 27: "Das ist alles, woran ich mich erinnere: Ich habe einen Beruf, aber plötzlich stehe ich im Wald, meine Ledermappe unterm Arm, und es ist eine Gegend, die ich noch nie erblickt habe. Und plötzlich habe ich Zeit."
    6. See especially Grimm/Wellauer, 193.
    7. GW IV, 458: "Ich frage mich, ob nicht beispielsweise der Intellektuelle–der arme Mann, der nicht tut, was er redet, und der daran leidet, dass ihm seine Tatunfähigkeit stets bewusst ist, der schliesslich, bloss damit die Welt (seine Frau) ihn ernstnehme, etwas Läppisches tut im vollen Bewusstsein, dass es läppisch sein wird–nicht schwankfähig geworden ist."

JAY F. BODINE

Frisch's Little White Lies: Self-Discovery and Engagement through Skepsis of Language and Perspective

Little White Lies—a coinage most immediately applicable to Max Frisch's novel *Stiller*[1]—can in its ambiguity be used appropriately to characterize the whole of Max Frisch's oeuvre. *Stiller* consists substantially of the cliché-ridden lies of "little White," i.e., of Anatol Ludwig Stiller, a sculptor-dilettante who is "little" because of his pettiness and insignificance, and "White" because he assumes that name while on a voyage of fantasy through the "new world." The "lies" that this artistic, social, and marital failure indulges in are "little white ones"—they are not malicious, but rather further a justifiable purpose. Seemingly inconsequential, although imaginative, they lead to the discovery of the self and its relationship to the modern world. An analysis of these and others of Frisch's "little white lies"—i.e., of the "half-truth" modes of expression in his works, particularly along with his views on language and use of manifold perspectives—illustrates Frisch's concerns: namely, the disclosure of the individual self and of the truthfulness and reality of the self's interaction with the sociopolitical world, leading to a type of engagement.

Doubt, skepsis concerning the respective topic or object of contemplation, a certain reserve or an unwillingness to accept readily and at face value, or a calling of the matter into question—such critical thinking is a pervasive feature of Frisch's literary works and discussions. If the questioning is not evidenced by his protagonists, then it is to be evoked in the audience or reader; it is similar in many respects to Bertolt Brecht's alienation effects, especially in intent and point of application. At times the setting mood of this skepsis is farcical, at other times elegiac, ironic, or slightly more critical and satiric. Along with this general phenomenon a skepsis toward language (discussed by Frisch as well as by his protagonists) has also been mentioned often as a feature of his oeuvre.[2]

Frisch is well aware of the danger inherent in excessive doubting. As developed in Elsbeth Pulver's insightful study of *Sketchbook 1966-1971* (*Tagebuch II*) entitled "Mut zur Unsicherheit" ("Courage for insecurity"),[3] self-doubt can lead to the complete inability to function; however, the courage necessary to call our perceptions into question—not to the point that stultifies endeavor, but to the extent that we are able to recognize and to attempt more equitable and "humane" enterprises as solutions to our problems—only this ability and courage to question will lead to change.

Frisch requires his readers and audience to recognize and to doubt his "little white lies" and then those of our sociopolitical world. In the discussion of Frisch's conceptualizations and portrayals of "little white lies," I shall include examples of his perceptions in some more recent works, especially in his books *Montauk* and *Tagebuch II*. The undertaking is to ascertain the *patterns of skepsis* and the *extent of the parallelism of doubt* on the various levels of his works, in conjunction with the intention of achieving change through self-discovery and social involvement.

By way of generalization there are, closely related in principle and of definite concern to my inquiry, two factors to which Frisch's skepsis concerning a conceptualization and its concomitant portrayal is applied: The validity of a portrayal (in language) is called into question by Frisch on the basis of the perspective employed and the rigidifying, limiting, abstracting nature of the expressive medium—of language itself.

Approaching Frisch's perspectivism first at the level of narrative viewpoint, one should immediately note the question concerning the first-person narrative perspective in Frisch's sketchbooks or diaries. Klaus Schimanski of the GDR, desiring to give further underpinnings to Frisch's criticism in *Tagebuch II* of various imperialistic or exploitative aspects of Western society, disputes the analysis of Horst Steinmetz that the first-person narrator of the sketchbook is not to be equated with the author Max Frisch.[4] Indeed, Schimanski is correct to point out a difference between the diary-type novels and the sketchbooks, a distinction based upon "essential structural elements of the specific narrative technique"; and to be sure, the integration of fictive elements in the sketchbook does not lessen the social implications Schimanski wishes to emphasize.[5] Stiller as well as Walter Faber, the protagonist of *Homo Faber*, and the nebulous narrator of *Mein Name sei Gantenbein* are further relativized or further removed from nonfictional reality than the narrators assuming the name of Max Frisch in the sketchbooks.

Frisch himself, however, has been very explicit concerning the fictional nature of all his narrators. They all—including the first-person narrator in the sketchbooks—present a certain varied perspective differing to some extent from that of the actual Max Frisch; the difference (with a varied perspective on social actuality) is made clear by the different role each narrator carries out. In the well-known interview with Horst Bienek in 1961, Frisch propounded: "Naturally the narrator self (Ich) is never my private self, naturally it is not, but perhaps one needs to be a writer in order to know that every self that expresses itself is a role. Always. In life also."[6] Frisch then expresses this matter as the "discovery that every self, even the self that we live and die, is an invention (Erfindung)."[7] Moreover, in *Tagebuch II* Frisch enlarged directly upon this question: "The difference between the narrative self and the direct self of a diary: the latter can subsequently be carried out only to a lesser extent precisely because it conceals too much of its background, hence it is presumptuous:—it is not a full personality (Gestalt): to a personality belongs also that which it withholds, that which does not interest it at the moment, that of which it is not conscious, etc. (*TB II*, 309-10).[8]

In light of Frisch's emphasis upon the role aspect of his first-person narrators, one also has to question the actuality of the various diarylike narrations in *Montauk*—in spite of the fact that, or precisely because, the narrator using the name Max states: "this is a sincere (aufrichtiges) book, reader / and what does it withhold and why?" (*M*, 197; cf. also 138 and 152). The dedication from Montaigne's *Essays* purporting autobiographical essence is to be understood—as in Montaigne also—ironically (*M*, 5). The modern author and his reader must remain skeptical; Hans Mayer, in his review of *Montauk*,[9] is definitely to be concurred with. As the subtitle *A Story* (*Eine Erzählung*) intimates, *Montauk* would be kitsch if taken unquestioningly and at face value. We and Frisch might long for a bucolic original portrayal, but we are too sophisticated or "sentimental" for a direct return to the "naive." Frisch "would like to describe" his encounter directly ("*möchte* es beschreiben"; *M*, 82) but again explicitly indicates his skepsis about the possibility of such expression: "as if a man could relate himself" ("als *könne* ein Mensch sich selbst erzählen"; *M*, 185).

The relativization or distance from nonfictional reality presented in Frisch's works, however, in no way lessens with the reader-partner (which Frisch calls for; *TB I*, 182 and *ÖP*, 56-67) the individual impact achieved or the various sociopolitical implications expressed. Rather a Nietzschean-like perspectivism (which will become more explicit in the course of the investigation and is especially evident with the juxtaposing of his various works) draws out new viewpoints and new insights and underpins other tenets from a new angle, thus avoiding clichés. These principles have become commonplace in literary scholarship, especially in discussions of narrative viewpoint; but we can well fall back upon them when questioning the actuality or validity of Frisch's insights achieved through the playful experimentation with various first-person narrative perspectives. (In fact, in *Montauk* Frisch also experiments with the juxtaposition of perspectives from the first- and third-person narrative viewpoints.)[10]

Actually, rather than lessening the validity of an insight, the particular role or perspective used to obtain it normally enhances its impact; necessary for a more adequate expression, as in the case of Brecht's alienation techniques, is a certain distance, estrangement, or (trans-)formation, which Frisch also strives for in his fiction: "Every experience remains basically unrelatable as long as we hope to be able to express it with the actual example that befell us. Only that example which is as distant from me as it is from the listener is able to express me: namely, the invented example. Only what has been poetisized, transposed, transfigured, only what has been formed is, in essence, capable of conveying" (*TB I*, 411).

Also to be pointed out in this context concerning perspectives is the problematical relationship for Frisch of stories (Geschichten) with their experiences (Erfahrungen) or their underlying, immediate conceptualizations (Einfälle). In *Gantenbein* (p. 30) and *Montauk* (p. 156) the narrator talks of trying on stories as if they were clothes, the various stories being like various life roles invented to convey the experience realized (*G*, 9, 14); in *Montauk* the narrator goes on to explain: "I have served some particular public with stories. I know, I have exposed (entblösst) myself in these stories past recognition. I do not live with my own story, only with parts of it that I have been able to make literary. There are whole areas missing. ... I have never described myself. I have only betrayed myself" (*M*, 156). The stories convey in part the particular experiences realized but certainly not the complete actuality. Frisch dwells further upon this relationship of stories to individual experiences in the interview with Horst Bienek and in the short discussion "Geschichten."[11] A person's actual experience is not expressed directly but only partially through invented stories, and the stories are not the result of memory: "I never relate how it was, but only how I envisage it would be if I had to experience it again." And then, as Frisch continues, the factor of perspective in experiences—along with the possibility to convey them with higher expressivity in stories—becomes evident. The experience is not the result of occurrences lived through (Vorfälle) but rather of suddenly realized conceptualizations or visualizations (Einfälle) perhaps evoked by the individual inner experience: "An occurrence, one and the same, serves thousands of experiences. Perhaps there is no other means to express an experience than the relating of occurrences, thus, of stories: as if it were the story from which our experience had emerged. It is the other way around, I believe. What emerges is the stories. The experience wants to become legible. It invents itself an event" (*AP*, 8-9). A major point for our purposes is then explicated in the sentences: "How I have experienced myself, that is shown in the play of my imagination. ... By inventing what never was and never will be, my experience is shown more purely, exactly and openly" (*AP*, 9). Although the person's full life, the complete actuality of what was involved or how it actually was, cannot be expressed, still the particular perspective, i.e., conceptualization or inner experience (Einfall, Erfahrung), is conveyed by the invented story—and to be sure, conveyed more purely, exactly, and openly than would be possible with an attempt to describe the experience (not to speak of the total actuality) directly. The encounter of "Max" and "Lynn" in *Montauk* is a story of this type.

On close examination, the stories along with their particular narrative viewpoint, as well as the experiences conveyed by them are all actually perspectives, and only the partial perspective of a fictive story is able to convey adequately the partial perspective of the individual inner experience or conceptualization. These half-truth, little white lies convey for Frisch what is capable of being conveyed and with the greatest possible impact—especially when the sophisticated, skeptical reader (as partner) recognizes them as systematic little white lies.

The second generalized factor contributing to Frisch's skepsis toward adequate expression is in principle closely related to the first; it is found in the rigidifying or fixed nature of the medium used to portray the partial perspective. The image or conceptualization with the fixed nature of its (linguistic) designation delimits, abstracts, and thus deadens the vitality or growth potential of the experience portrayed. The inflexible tendency of the language once employed restricts the realization of the greater, more profound total, or potential experience.[12]

This aspect of Frisch's language skepsis has long been recognized,[13] especially in connection with various passages from *Tagebuch I*, such as: "Thou shalt not make any graven image," i.e., of God and, what for Frisch is included in the commandment, of the vital or divine element in every individual (*TB I*, 37); indeed, language is most often the carrier of a graven image, the vehicle of prejudice ("Gefäss des Vorurteils"; *TB I*, 220). But as Wolfgang Frühwald and Walter Schmitz have pointed out in the commentary on *Andorra* and *Wilhelm Tell*, there is a certain development to be ascertained in Frisch's thinking and portrayal of "graven image problems."[14] In the course of his writings during the fifties and sixties, Frisch appears finally to approve certain aspects of his protagonists' forming (self-)images. Frühwald and Schmitz in this context apply the distinction made in social psychology between stereotypes (which are necessary categories of human perception) and prejudices (those stereotypes that resist any critical examination and re-evaluation). As far as language is concerned, mental *images* are indeed quite necessary in their function as linguistic meaning; like stereotypes they are inescapable. But when they become prejudices or "graven images," they fall under Frisch's ethical condemnation. (This distinction between an image and a graven image, stereotype and prejudice, is perhaps not as explicit in the Luther German "Du sollst dir kein Bildnis machen"—unless one differentiates between "Bild" and "Bildnis" along the same lines of thought.) Thus, as will be shown in the further discussion to be the case also with ideology as well as with language per se, images are unavoidable. They are "little white lies";

although necessary, they need to be constantly reexamined and doubted.

Another passage from *Tagebuch I* that is often cited in discussions of Frisch's language skepsis is the following: "What is important: that which is inexpressible, the white between the words, and these words always speak of the secondary matters, which we do not actually mean. Our concern, the actual, can at best be paraphrased, and that means most literally: One writes around and around it. One surrounds it. One makes statements that never contain our actual experience, which remains inexpressible; and the actual, the inexpressible appears at best as the tension between the statements" (*TB I*, 42).[15] In spite of and because of Frisch's skepsis toward language, a certain valuable expression can be achieved. This is something that should be emphasized more in Frisch studies. Although the actual, total experience is not directly conveyed in language, the particular insight conveyed obtains substantial import and enhanced impact because of a conscious skepsis toward the expressive medium. Only a consciousness of the limitations and pitfalls of linguistic expression enable a truly valid, albeit indirect, expression. The "actual," the "inexpressible," appears in the tension in-between or in the juxtaposition of the various expressions. Perhaps along with doubt "courtesy" (Höflichkeit"; *TB I*, 59-62) or "love" (*TB I*, 37; love is one means of avoiding a graven image) is required on the part of the public, acting as a partner to effect the fullest communicative exchange possible in literature.

This understanding of Frisch's language skepsis is further substantiated:

> Our endeavor is presumably to express everything that is expressible. Language is like a chisel that hews everything away that is not secret, and all saying means removing. In that respect it should not disconcert us that everything expressed in words lapses into a certain emptiness. One says what life is not. One says it for the sake of life. Language functions just as the sculptor does when he guides the chisel, by driving the emptiness, the expressible, on toward what is secret, toward what is vital (das Lebendige). There always exists the danger of battering the secret, and also the other danger of stopping prematurely, of leaving it a block, of not confronting the secret, not grasping it, freeing it from everything that would still be expressible, in short, of not pressing on to its ultimate surface.
>
> This surface of what is ultimately expressible, which would have to coincide with the surface of the secret, this intangible surface, which exists only in the mind and not in nature where there is also no line between mountain and sky—perhaps that is what is called form?
>
> A kind of resounding boundary (tönende Grenze) (*TB I*, 42-43).

Frisch's language skepsis is by no means to be minimized or deemphasized; but it does not obviate the necessity of attempting to express the actual, vital, or secret experience. Quite the contrary, his skepsis demands the attempt at an indirect expression; there is a certain approximation to the truth that is enabled by the very calling of the whole procedure into question. If the direct result of the attempts at expression is not the complete, unattainable actual *truth,* the little white lies inherent in the medium of expression (as well as in the particular perspective portrayed) at least enable the reader-partner to approximate the truth possible of attainment through reconstructions of the *truths*—of the partial, perspectival aspects. As W.G. Cunliffe points out with a quotation of Albert Camus applied to Frisch: "Il y a *des* vérités mais point *de* vérité."[16] Through a type of critical dialectic—the conscious comparison and juxtaposing of various perspectives and attempts at expression—an asymptotic approximation of the truth of the vital, actual *experience* obtains.

This problematical aspect of perspective and expression through language is, of course, a central theme in several of Frisch's works. *Stiller,* for example, includes most explicit statements about the problematical nature of (self-) expression: "One can relate everything, just not his real life" (*St,* 83), which allows the possibility for others to make a graven image of the individual. The terrifying experience that Stiller/White realizes through writing during his detention is: "I have no language for my reality" (*St,* 107). That which he records in his notebooks—"all that is merely paraphrasings. . . . I speak quite unclearly—if I don't simply tell wild lies for relief of tension" (*St,* 85). But these statements do not indicate a complete breakdown in expressivity and portrayal; further along in his jottings Stiller/White states: "It seems I cannot communicate. Every word is false and true, that is the essence of words, and whoever wants to believe all or nothing—" (*St,* 230). The very nature of the linguistic medium, the essence of words includes valid and invalid content. Although the last sentence is incomplete, it is evident that neither all nor nothing is to be accepted as a word's "truth content." The actuality is to be found between the all or nothing of these little white lies and must be ferreted out by reflecting upon them, by calling them into question.

The possibility and necessity of an indirect expression—using the little white lies inherent in both the language and the particular related perspective—is then outlined in almost summary fashion from the Stiller/White viewpoint in a lengthy, important passage in Stiller's seventh and last notebook:

> Yes: —who is supposed to read what I have written in these notebooks! And yet I believe that there is no writing carried on without the idea of somebody reading it, and even if that somebody is the writer himself. Then I wonder too: Can one write without

playing a role? One wants to be a stranger to himself. My reality lies not in the role, but surely in the unconscious decision as to what kind of role I ascribe myself. Often I have the feeling one emerges from what he has written as a snake emerges from its skin. That's it; one cannot write himself down, one can only shed his skin. But whom is this dead skin supposed to interest! The question that comes up again and again, whether the reader is ever capable of reading anything other than himself, becomes superfluous: Writing is not communication with readers, not communication with oneself either, but rather communication with the inexpressible. The more exactly one could express himself, the more purely would appear what is inexpressible, i.e., the reality that besets and stirs him. We have language in order to become mute. Whoever remains silent is not mute. Whoever remains silent does not even have an idea of who he's not.

Why doesn't Julika write? (*St*, 437)

As seen from the perspective Stiller/White achieves, the need for expression is ultimately the need to dis-cover the inexpressible, i.e., one's own reality or one's self—although one does not directly communicate with it. In writing, one takes up and develops a certain role, and as Stiller/White comes to recognize, one's truth or actual reality is not that of the particular role assumed in expressing oneself, but rather in the unconscious decision as to what type of role one will play. In reflecting upon one's little white lies and the expressive process afterward, one is able to achieve a certain insight into at least one facet of one's actual reality or self and to discard that which one is not. In recognizing the relationship between the author's actual self, his narrative stance (the role or perspective at the primary level), and the material or role portrayed (the perspective at the secondary level), the critical reader also becomes conscious of the perspectives and insights of the various roles and role types chosen.[17] The truths and falsehoods of the various acts of expression allow for greater perspective and insight and an indirect approach to the actual reality and self behind the role; the truths and falsehoods simply have to be recognized for what they are—the little white lies being shed as a snake's dead outer layer of skin.

In an earlier formulation in *Tagebuch I* Frisch had explained the self-discovery process in the following manner: Writing is tantamount to reading one's self. . . . Only by certifying the zigzag of our various (jeweiligen) thoughts and making them visible can we get to know our own essence, its entanglements (Wirrnis) or its secret unity, its inescapable character, its truth, that we cannot express directly, not from the perspective of a single moment" (*TB I*, 22). As Stiller/White realized at an early period in his writing (in his first notebook), although he was unwilling to let others prove to him who he is, he does not know the full and complete truth himself (*St*, 86); the freedom offered to him amounts to the condemnation of playing a role having nothing to do with him, and thus he asks: "How is one supposed to be able to prove who he is in actuality? I cannot. Do I even know myself who I am?" (*St*, 109). However, somewhat into his last notebook, after he has gained some experience in self-discovery through writing or indirect self-expression, he recognizes the process of self-disclosure or the relationship of the little white lies to the self and immediately questions: "Why doesn't Julika write?" (*St*, 437).

To be sure, the final view of Stiller is disheartening. At the end of his writing, when condemned by the court to be the "old" Stiller and, more importantly, when constrained from any further self-discovery and self-development by the stultifying relationship with the "silent" Julika, Stiller falls back into accepting a deadening role as his actuality, not a role involving any aesthetic expression such as even sculpturing but an empty one like hollow pottery, a role replete with repetition and cliché.[18] He becomes "silent" also. He does not further his self-discovery, he ceases to write and retrogresses from any reflection and self-discovery he had once carried on.

In the process of indirect self-expression, employing little white lies leading indirectly to self-discovery, Frisch is not pursuing a Cartesian proof of the self's facticity but is rather attempting to reconnoiter the self, to find out what it is like. What results, however, is not a type of solipsism—if for no other reason than Max Frisch's self seems to be concerned with interhuman or social exchanges and relations. If the self manifests itself ever so discreetly in the unconscious decision for a particular role type, which it then portrays in various individual roles, then the type of role and the type of self predominantly disclosed in Frisch's oeuvre is a social one. Indeed, the narrator of *Tagebuch II* suggests he might even have overindulged in social questions, producing a hypertrophy of the political aspect. He asks: "The price for this discretion [the elimination of names and personal data for reasons of tact] : the hypertrophy of egocentricity or in order to escape that: a hypertrophy of political elements?" (*TB II*, 311). After the reflection they necessitate, Frisch's particular truths are again found between two extremes, between the hypertrophy of egocentricity and the hypertrophy of political concerns. The critical reader must decide what the particular truth is in-between. The self writing Max Frisch's works, however, shows itself to be most interested in political and social questions.

Another frequently cited passage from the concluding section of *Tagebuch I* provides further insight into the relationship between the narrative self with its concerns and the social questions often expressed in Frisch's oeuvre. By way of justification for his diary or sketchbook format, Frisch explains that the incidences striking enough to be noticed and then recorded in one's diary ultimately allow one to recognize himself by indicating the self's concerns. And upon examination, even in the random incidences noted in Frisch's "diary," the concerns disclosed are by no means related solely to a solipsistic self. That which the self perceives in the incidences it encounters does indeed reflect back upon the self, as Frisch explicates, but what the self "experiences" also goes far beyond its own private confines:

> Wherever I might go or be, it is not everything present at hand that determines my conduct, but rather what is possible, that part of what is present that I can see and hear. We simply pass by in life on all the rest, no matter how present it is. We do not have an antenna for it; at least not now; perhaps later. The perplexing, provoking aspect of every chance happening consists in our recognizing our own configuration; an incident shows to me what I have an eye for at that moment, and I hear that for which I have an antenna.... Of course it might be suggested that we do not always have our possible hearing open, that is to say that there still might be many incidences that we see and hear past although they do belong to us; but we do not experience any that do not belong to us. Ultimately it is always the aspects incumbent on us that devolve on us [i.e., aspects that we expect and that are expected of us: "Am Ende ist es immer das Fällige, was uns zufällt" *TB I*, 463-64].

Thus while concerned with self-discovery and reading himself while writing, the narrator of Frisch's works can and, as will be seen, ultimately does disclose many other than purely egocentric concerns. Indeed, Frisch unavoidably discovers his self's sociopolitical concerns in the incidences incumbent and devolving on him. "Was ihm zufällt, ist Soziales." Therein are found his "experiences," which will be seen to be of a sociopolitical nature.

Even *Montauk*—the story in which the narrator named Max would like to relate merely his own life and specifically the encounters of a weekend (*M*, 82, 155)—even this supposedly more overt exploration of self-concerns to the exclusion of others is a little white lie:

> Since Lynn has not read anything I have written, I enjoy for once saying the exact opposite: —Politics do not concern me at all. The writer's responsibility toward society and all that talk, the truth is that I write in order to express myself. I write for myself.... Public as partner? I can find more credible partners. I publish then, not because I think it necessary to teach or to convert the public, but rather because one needs in order to recognize oneself at all, an

imaginary public. But basically I write for myself. . . . Lynn does not protest at all; it sounds (even to me) more convincing than expected (*M*, 28-29).

The role of the narrator in *Montauk*—as perceived by separating the "Dichtung und Wahrheit" found there (cf. *M*, 177), with the "truth" lying in-between the two functional extremes of pure egocentricity and pure political engagement—is typical for Frisch's oeuvre because it evidences a self very much taken up with social concerns. Again, a certain doubt or calling of the content into question is required on the part of the critical reader-partner, for what "Max" relates to Lynn is the "exact opposite" of what is actual, and even to Max it sounds more convincing than it is. The book is far from being art for the sake of art and, indeed, much more than mere personal reminiscencing. Even the depiction of the narrator's liaison with Lynn (to what extent is it truth and fiction?) incorporates greater, more weighty considerations than a merely personal amorous adventure—such as in Max's reflections on male chauvinism and the relationship with Ingeborg Bachmann, or on the problematical relationship with the Jewish fiancée from Berlin during the 1930s (one of the central themes of *Homo Faber,* often alluded to and then specifically elaborated upon in *Montauk,* pp. 166-69).

Quoted midway through *Montauk* is what could almost be considered the "moral" of *Homo faber*; the idea—genuinely existing in each moment with full realization of interpersonal relationships and in the face of death—is one that could be perhaps partly misunderstood as a suggestion for purely impressionistic egocentricity: "Being in the world: being in the light. Anywhere . . . driving donkeys, our occupation! — But above all: stand firm to the light, to joy in the knowledge that I am extinguished in the light above bushes, asphalt and sea, stand firm to the times, i.e., to eternity in each moment. Being eternal: having been" (*M,* 103; cf. *HF,* 247). But any purely egocentric existence is called into question immediately before and after the above quotation: "Literature suspends the moment, that is why it exists"; "Life in quotations. . . . He [the narrator] does not forget his role nor the immediate responsibilities that ensue from the role; appointed times, he forgets not even for a moment the world situation. There are all kinds of things he does not forget in this thin present time" (*M,* 103). The very function, if not purpose, of (true) literature is ultimately that of eliminating purely egocentristic existence. Literature, as well as the calling into question of "life [reproduced] in quotations," evokes reflections beyond oneself, beyond the moment. Also, the narrator here is most explicit that his role entails social responsibilities, even political concerns. All these aspects point out the particular type of engagement or suprapersonal concern of Max Frisch and also more specifically of the narrator's self in this, perhaps still the most personal work in Max Frisch's writings. Naive and purely personal narrative simply does not appear in the repertoire of the writer named Max Frisch. The naive wish for the solely personal is immediately sentimentalized in a Schillerian sense, it is called into question. Or to express the point by paraphrasing and altering Frisch's terms from the end of *Tagebuch I*: Das rein, naiv Persönliche ist dem Schriftsteller Max Frisch letzten Endes nicht das Fällige, oder was seinem schreibenden Ich zufällt.[19]

In response to frequent criticism Frisch has long maintained the justification for producing in his writings a certain mixture of concerns—fundamentally the concerns of the individual, often narrative self; and then based upon the self's concerns, the problems of the larger society. There is a definite consistency in Frisch's thinking which allows him to portray both types of concerns, producing also the particular perspective won through juxtaposing both the individual and collective concerns. In his various speeches and interviews, especially during the late 1960s and early 1970s, Frisch often found it necessary to defend his treatment of the individual or self. Especially during that time his portrayal of personal, individual problems as opposed to the larger social ones seemed to many critics to be excessive. He stated his point, however, in an interview with Dieter E. Zimmer in *Die Zeit* in 1967 and then reiterated it two years later with almost the identical words in his exchange with Walter Höllerer:

> The domain of literature? That which sociology does not register, which biology does not register: the individual being, the self; not my self, but a self; the person in all his biological and social limitations; thus the portrayal of the person who is included in the statistics but does not come up in them for discussion and is irrelevant in view of the whole but must live fully conscious of being irrelevant—that is what interests at least me, what seems at least to me to be worthy of representation. The domain of literature: everything that people experience, sex, technology, politics as a reality and as a utopia, but in contrast to science, related to the being that experiences (*Dr*, 34).[20]

In this explication Frisch gives his reasoning not only for portraying the individual self and its experiencing of the world but also for portraying a banal, philistine self, as, for example, Anatol Ludwig Stiller or, more specifically in mind at the time of the above exchange with Walter Höllerer, Hannes Kürmann in *Biographie: Ein Spiel*. Basically Frisch is not to be considered guilty of a return to strictly private concerns, i.e., of the "Reprivatisierung" that Dieter Zimmer and others reproached him with; Frisch's starting point in his works has always been the portrayal of a private, individual self (through the concomitant perspective and indirect disclosure of partial aspects of the narrative self). But Frisch's individual portrayals have never done away with social concerns. On the contrary, those social concerns have simply always been presented from the perspective of the individual protagonist. If the protagonist is a trivial Philistine, that fact has to be taken into consideration in determining the perspective and insights portrayed and their validity.[21] Perhaps particularly modern man, viewed individually, has banal, philistine tendencies. In any case, the intended comedy *Biographie* illustrates the triviality of the variants or changes in his biography that Kürmann most desires—as opposed to more substantial ones discussed there in contrast—and Frisch's insights and intentions are to be found in-between Kürmann's banality on the one hand and a work of direct political agitation on the other (cf. "Anmerkungen," *B*, 119).

The primary domain of literature for Frisch is then that of the individual self. It is summed up in the Höllerer exchange in the following manner: "Is therefore what is private ... irrelevant and not the subject of literature? Then sociology is sufficient. But is it sufficient? Society, even a desirable one, consists of persons who live, and living takes place at the level of the self" ("in der Ich-Form"; *Dr*, 41). Frisch, however, has also been most definite in his views that portraying the private, individual sphere does not exclude sociopolitical concerns: "If we understand the word according to the meaning of the dictionary (personal, not public, domestic), then 'private' is self-evidently a subject of literature—and not only of an apolitical one, but precisely of the literature that has reference to a social situation; indeed, the social situation defines individuals in the 'private' existence" (*Dr*, 40). Consequently, there is to be found in Frisch's works a certain type of engagement, but it is an indirect one, not an immediate political or ideological agitation. The most that Frisch considers possible, as far as actual and effective engagement in literature is concerned, is changing individuals' relations to the world (*ÖP*, 79), i.e., changing one's way of seeing it (perspective). Indeed, for Frisch it is not possible to portray the sociopolitical world in art or literature; that which it is possible to represent is individual poetry ("Poesie"; *ÖP*, 76); portraying an individual's relationship to the world is simply one answer to the "unrepresentability" of the world. Brecht is the prime example Frisch refers to in order to maintain that not the world but at best only a model, such as the Brechtian-Marxist thesis of the alterability of the world (eine Poesie), is portrayed in art, theater, and literature (*ÖP*, 76, 78-79).

Frisch's speech "The Author and the Theater" (1964), the source of the above citations concerning engagement, contains in its conclusion the lines: "If there were no literature, perhaps the world would not go on any differently, but it would be viewed differently, namely as the various profiteers of the day would like to have it viewed: not called into question" (*ÖP*, 87). The type of engagement Frisch advocates is the calling of the world into question. That is the type of engagement that literature is capable of, the type Frisch produces in his works—a calling into question, a skepsis, a series of attempts to view the world differently—a type of engagement which Frisch has often elaborated upon through the years. A 1972 treatment of the topic is the interview by Peter André Bloch and Rudolf Bussmann;[22] an earlier treatment of the question is found in Frisch's speech given at the reception of the Georg Büchner Prize (1958). There Frisch speaks of a truthfulness in portrayal (e.g. *ÖP*, 45–46) and concludes by pointing out the individual role in this type of engagement: "It is a resignation, but it is a combative resignation that links us, an individual engagement in truthfulness, the attempt to produce art that is not national and not international but more, namely an ever to be repeated 'disenchantment' (Bann gegen) of abstraction, of ideology and its deadly fronts, which cannot be battled with individual courage in the face of death; they can only be undermined through the work of each individual in his own place" (*ÖP*, 55).

While the domain of literature for Frisch is primarily the individual self, i.e., the disclosure of the self in its interaction with the sociopolitical world, the actual and proper scope of engagement in literature is also individual for Frisch. It changes the individual's relation to the world, or as expressed in the Bloch-Bussmann interview, it is not directly political, but makes a detour— it is "bewusstseinsverändernd," it creates on the individual level a different consciousness.[23] Direct agitation, or perhaps resulting from that, individual "courage in the face of death" is not what is necessarily efficacious or called for, but rather, in the best tradition of German Idealism, the enlightening labors of each individual in his particular situation.[24]

Further variations of his ideas on engagement are to be found in the later works, but important for the present context is the fact that the individual labors which Frisch advocates here proceed according to the same general principles elaborated upon earlier in the context of self-discovery. Just as the disclosure of self is indirectly approximated through skepsis or calling into question two related factors—the language used and the perspective taken by the self—in like manner, whatever engagement is attainable and efficacious consists, in Frisch's thinking, in the discovery of truthfulness in the sociopolitical world, and that discovery is also indirectly approximated through skepsis, or more specifically, through calling into question the same two related factors—both the language employed and the perspective incorporated in portraying that sociopolitical world.

A certain engagement achieved through the calling of language into question has long been recognized in Frisch's works and explicated in his public statements. In the exchange with Walter Höllerer, for instance, Frisch says, "It is already an engagement when literature tests the language currently used for its reality content" (*Dr*, 39). In the interview with P.A. Bloch and R.

Bussmann he states: "In portraying things how they are experienced, literature calls the common use of language into question (verunsichert die Sprache). . . . I myself am of the opinion that this type of engagement has a greater effect than the direct kind, or 'Agitprop' (literature of agitation and propaganda)."[25] By reflecting not only upon the big lies of immediate politics but also upon the little white lies of sociopolitical language, a greater truthfulness beyond them comes into view.

The way Frisch uses language not only characterizes the various persons or roles in his plays and novels but also illustrates their lack of reflection upon their own and others' use of language and the concomitant blindness or shortsightedness in the sociopolitical context. *Biedermann* and *Andorra* furnish prime examples of such problems; as reflected in their language, Biedermann and the Andorrians perceive neither their own mode of thinking nor the sociopolitical actualities.[26]

Among the numerous studies treating Frisch's varied use of language in his different works, Walter Schenker's has discussed how Frisch achieves a certain "linguistic" alienation effect through definite contrasts between dialect and a "higher," standard or more literary language.[27] While Schenker stresses the alienating effect of Frisch's "Hochsprache" to estrange what is self-understood in dialect, Frisch has pointed out that dialect can also estrange clichés of the "Hochsprache."[28] This and the problematical aspects of unreflectingly accepting imperfect tense descriptions as actuality, of not reflecting upon and doubting what might have the linguistic form of a historical account, are also treated in the interview with Peter André Bloch and Bruno Schoch.[29] Numerous other studies have also dealt with Frisch's varied use of language from work to work and in their way demonstrate the general principle to be found in Frisch's writings of calling language into question.

Frisch has been most explicit about his methods of using language to generate reflection and to disclose a greater degree of truthfulness. As early as 1948, in coming to terms with Brecht's ideas while with him in Zurich, Frisch spoke of "alienation effects through linguistic means, play consciousness in narrative . . . [achieved] by hindering sympathetic identification, not allowing the reader to be carried off in his fantasies, destroying the illusion, namely the illusion that the related story really occurred, etc." (*TB I*, 294). In 1958 in the address "Public as Partner," he speaks of striving "beyond conventional language" (*ÖP*, 59); in 1964 in the speech "The Author and the Theater" he avers:

> The reevaluation in each word—which every literature performs on its own account, namely for the sake of the work's vitality—is in itself a contribution, a productive opposition. Various standpoints of yesterday, although still present, are no longer defensible today because literature has changed their names on the basis of their

reality content, and *that* alters not merely the consciousness of the small class of literature consumers; the reconstruction of vocabulary affects all those who avail themselves of borrowed language, thus politicians also. Anyone who would use certain words today would be unmasked—thanks to literature, which determines the market value of words (*ÖP*, 87-88).

Frisch's 1967 postscript to "Finally it can be said again," his response to Emil Staiger in the "Zürcher Literaturstreit" (Zurich quarrel on literature), speaks of the problematical decisions facing every serious writer in "working out a language that again says something, that would be able to bear up to our experiences in this epoch, that does not simply suspend our skepsis in order to present itself poetically, and does not exchange credibility with wishful thinking" (*ÖP*, 147). Or as the formulation offered to Walter Höllerer in 1969 states it, the actual engagement of literature is, as directed against ideology, a "recherche through language" (*Dr*, 41).

An additional interesting and important problem in Frisch studies can perhaps most readily be approached in the context of Frisch's views on social and political language. The problem is that of Frisch's literary model or standard (Vorbild), of which he says that it has not been recognized and thus that he has perhaps not really approximated it very closely.[30] If such a model is to be located, it is most likely to be found in Bertolt Brecht's tradition[31] and to be concerned with language and truthfulness of (self-)expression. At the very least there are aspects of Brecht's literary tradition which throw further light upon Frisch's thinking and literary intentions in general and upon his use of language in particular.

Over the years Frisch has made surprisingly frequent allusions to others' views on language. Most likely deriving from his association with Ingeborg Bachmann are his very brief mentions of Ludwig Wittgenstein (*B*, 9; and *M*, 48). These references do, nevertheless, evoke questions concerning the limitations and expressibility of language. However, two writers squarely in Brecht's tradition, along with their attitude toward language, are explicitly given prominent mention in Frisch's statements from the first *Tagebuch* on. The two are Georg Büchner and Karl Kraus.

Three times, in 1947, 1958, and 1964, Frisch quotes one particular passage from *Danton's Death*. The formulation in *Tagebuch I* (from 1947) goes as follows: "Our thinking has to become concrete! One has to visualize what he thinks and then endure it, or change his thoughts so that he might be allowed to think them. Georg Büchner in Danton as Danton is led into the prison: 'Follow your clichés back to the point where they are embodied, look around, all that is what you said!' A motto that today is hanging over almost all of Europe. . . . The word and the deed are one" (*TB I*, 194). Suggesting that writers should disrupt the "arsenal of clichés" (Arsenal der Phrasen), Frisch then repeats this quotation in his Büchner-prize speech (*ÖP*, 45, 46) and also in the conclusion of the speech "The Author and the Theater" (*ÖP*, 88).

Karl Kraus is referred to in this last speech in conjunction with Büchner and specifically in the context of Frisch's suggestions to call sociopolitical language into question:

> I know: What Karl Kraus once accomplished in this sense did not preserve Vienna from anything. But perhaps one is too immodest; perhaps it should already be accredited to literature that, for example, a word like war (merely to single out one) is at least in Europe no longer suitable as an enticement. Ministers of war are now called defense ministers. This also, to be sure, again turns into cliché; that is why literature has to remain timely; to the extent that it is alive, it always brings language back to the present state of reality, even the literature that is not "programmatically" engaged, perhaps above all the literature that is not "programmatically" engaged (*ÖP*, 88).

Indeed, Frisch's "program" concerning language is in many respects quite similar to Karl Kraus's. Kraus continuously stressed being skeptical in the use of language, calling it into question, checking the content of especially heraldic clichés by comparing them with the sociopolitical reality.[32] Frisch over the years also makes other frequent mentions of Kraus (*TB I*, 120, 237; *Stücke I*, 397; *D*, 139). Other general points of similarity are the first-person perspective and the form of a literary "journal" (Frisch's *Tagebucher* could in numerous respects be considered the counterpart of *Die Fackel*). As far as a literary sketchbook or periodic comments on the times are concerned, perhaps there are some similarities to Büchner also. There are, of course, many dissimilarities as well. At the very least, Frisch is not open to the charge of hypertrophy of egocentricity as was Kraus, and even in a literary "feud" such as the "Zürcher Literaturstreit," Frisch does not convey personal condemnations as Kraus did, for instance, in the cases of Alfed Kerr, Maximilian Harden, and Hermann Bahr. But the fact that Frisch himself refers to Kraus and to this tradition of a critical attitude toward the use of language at the very least underpins all the more this aspect of Frisch's "program." The little white lies of language need to be reflected upon in order to discover to the partial extent possible not only the actuality on the level of the self but also, again to the extent possible, truthfulness on the level of interhuman reality, truthfulness in the sociopolitical sphere.

Just as language—due to the undynamic, rigidifying, and abstracting nature of linguistic designation—was only able to approximate the whole actual self, in the same manner on the level of sociopolitical reality only partial aspects can be expressed and then only indirectly as abstractions. This is a contributing factor to Frisch's standpoint that not the world but only a partial perspective, a poetical model of it, can be portrayed in art and literature (cf. ÖP, 76, 78-79). The quotations cited above in the earlier context of the self's language are applicable here also in a context where the number of "selves" along with the difficulty of portraying their composite is compounded. And here again the problematical nature of language's little white lies does not constitute any grounds for silence; rather Frisch's type of engagement calls for striving after and approximating various truths and truthfulness.

Also on the level of sociopolitical reality, *language,* the one factor called into question by Frisch's skepsis, is closely related in principle to the second generalized factor, *perspectivism*; indeed, the particular linguistic formulation itself definitely conveys a particular abstracted perspective. What Frisch attempts is to approach ever closer to sociopolitical truthfulness by determining as many perspectives as possible and then calling them into question, putting them into juxtaposition and trying to locate the "truths" in-between.

Thus, as indicated in the conclusion of the Büchner speech quoted earlier (*ÖP*, 55), Frisch's skepsis and engagement is ultimately directed against linguistic "abstraction" and the partial perspectivism of "ideology." As Thomas Beckermann puts it—although it is not to be evaluated in the negative, limited manner Beckermann presents it in—the result of Frisch's production is political engagement as criticism of ideology and language, as "Ideologie- und Sprachkritik."[33]

From the beginning Frisch has been most critical of ideologies, of their partial perspectives, and of the blinder effect of ideological convictions. As he stated in 1948 in *Tagebuch I*: "Whoever has a conviction is able to cope with anything. Convictions are the best protection against living truth" (Wer eine Überzeugung hat, wird mit allem fertig. Überzeugungen sind der beste Schutz vor dem Lebendig-Wahren; *TB I*, 308). Herein is again to be found a similarity to Kraus: It is Frisch's criticism of unquestioned ideology and his failure to meet others' ideological demands that alienated him personally from those calling for direct agitation in literature. His criticism of language and perspectivism amounts to a certain meta-ideology. Rather than producing "literature as propaganda for an ideology," he furnishes with his "Sprachkritik" a checking for the actual content of customary language, and with his "Ideologiekritik" a further engagement in reality" (cf. *Dr*, 29).

But his criticism of ideology does not mean Frisch is oblivious to the necessity for some commonly accepted principles. Certain conventions are necessary. He went on to say in the same passage from the Höllerer exchange just referred to: "We cannot manage without ideology, but it continuously needs a control. Literature provides that—even when it does not come forward with direct political engagement, precisely then" (*Dr*, 29). On the sociopolitical level we cannot do without little white lies either, namely those of ideological perspective; but they need to be questioned, reflected upon, perceived for what they are and controlled.

In carrying out this program of calling ideology into question, Frisch engages in a Kraus-like analysis of mass media and specifically of the press. The chorus in *Biedermann* contains one of Frisch's early formulations of the problem: "He who, in order to know what threatens, / Reads newspapers, / Daily incensed at breakfast / Over a distant event, / Daily supplied with interpretation / Sparing him his own reflecting, / Daily being informed what yesterday happened, / Hardly he perceives what momentarily transpires / Under his own roof" (*Stücke 2*, 120). Individuals become dependent in their thinking upon the analysis of the press, and then the press supplies only a particular, partial and normally unquestioned perspective or built-in ideology, as Frisch illustrates on other occasions, such as in a passage from *Tagebuch II* referring to "*first class* newspapers" (*TB II*, 97-98; my emphasis to stress the Krausian ambiguity); the "partiality" of news reporting is also particularly adumbrated in another section (*TB II*, 275-76). In a longer section (*TB II*, 219-26), a very specific ideological criticism, to single out one, of Western society is developed and an analysis given of how that ideology is maintained with the aid of media (the example is the *Neue Zürcher Zeitung und schweizerisches Handelsblatt* (NZZ, Switzerland's equivalent of the *New York Times*): "The proprietors are dependent upon the working forces, but not on their opinion; on the other hand, the majority is dependent upon the opinion of the proprietors: That gives rise to the proprietors' consciousness of responsibility. It is expressed in almost every NZZ article, often between the lines" (*TB II*, 221). Occasionally Frisch uses the Krausian method of juxtaposing various newspaper items in order to point out the truthfulness found in-between or beyond them (see e.g. *TB II*, 258 for a contrast of rich and poor, the distribution of money in the FRG). Ultimately Frisch's analysis of media impact leads him to a characterization of the predominant ideology as a "bogy/toady [Popanz] of public opinion" and to questioning "How sovereign is the majority" (*TB II*, 226).

One of the particular perspectives Frisch has been developing is that of a greater significance obtained by going beyond the lifetime of the single individual. In aging and in view of death, events take on a different perspective and significance—a "truthfulness" Frisch seems to be dwelling upon more and more. The theme is quite predominant in *Montauk, Der Mensch erscheint im Holozän,* and particularly in *Tagebuch II* with its play upon euthanasia and the "Association for the Rejuvenation of Occidental Society" or "Association for Voluntary Death" (*TB II*, 91-96 and passim). Also, there is no question that the relative predominance of a certain gerontocracy can have great impact on the prevailing ideology and the general social and political conditions. In Frisch's latest drama *Triptychon: Drei szenische Bilder* (1978), the central theme and perspective is precisely that of death; here again Frisch supplies various perspectives, i.e., three main ones in three discontiguous scenes. But there the Lucian-like perspective that death adds to life is also reciprocated, in that life adds a certain perspective to death: If life after death were to be merely a continuation of life here but without tangible pursuits and an end in sight; that is, if there were to be no hope for change, continuous development, and improvement, such eternal life would be eternal banality or eternal death.

Perhaps one of the most important factors making Frisch's oeuvre in general and more specifically his *Tagebücher* immensely valuable for us in our present sociopolitical context is the perspective that this "neutral" Swiss provides in the juxtaposition of Eastern and Western ideologies. Providing such an "in-between" perspective was specifically his intent with *Tagebuch I*, as expressed in his dedicatory appeal to the reader (*TB I*, 7). The insights gained through the individual analysis and comparison of opposing perspectives are, of course, the major purpose of Frisch's observations and criticisms gathered while on his journeys through East and West and conveyed in the *Tagebücher*. Naturally, Frisch does not then refrain from applying these perspectives to his native Switzerland also, thus reaping the ire of those Swiss whose most often previously unquestioned positions and conduct were challenged.

Concerning the treatment of Western Society in the *Tagebücher*, Klaus Schimanski (from the GDR) is correct in concluding that Frisch's criticism of the United States—of its social, economic, and political domination as exemplified especially by the Vietnam-war ramifications at home and abroad—goes beyond the position of a bourgeois critic by delving into the basic structure of Western domination and explotation.[34] Indeed, Frisch's presentation with its unoffensive manner should provide us in the West another occasion to call our often unchallenged basic thinking into question. To be sure, the one definite note of approval Frisch gives to America in *Tagebuch II*, twenty years after the earlier sketchbook with his first experiences of the United States, is the "skepsis: that America is on the right course"; even if Frisch did not encounter in the U.S.A. a criticism of the whole system (eine Systemkritik), America's fear of/for America" itself at least made the individuals more "human" during the later visit (*TB II*, 314).

To be sure, Frisch carries out the same program with the present Eastern ideology and its manner of social, economic, and political domination. And those who are in a position to do so should try to perceive Frisch's travel comments from Czechoslovakia, Poland and the USSR not as simply the confirmation of "anti-Communist cliché-conceptions"[35] but as honest attempts unoffensively to question prevailing thought there. At all costs Frisch avoids cliché; here again skepsis is called for on all levels, the fictional and ideological as well. When the reader ponders: Did Frisch really have an interview with Henry Kissinger the day following the Cambodia invasion (*TB II*, 292-307), or did Frisch really encounter the deposed Nikita Khrushchev (*TB II*, 189-93), the truthfulness of the insight pursued is not affected by the degree of fictionality in the portrayal; but the doubt required for judging that should itself eliminate cliché and lack of reflection. Frisch's message would be for one to call the prevailing ideology into question even if those of opposing ideologies do not; the perspective gained through contrast with them, which Frisch attempts to provide, is of the greatest value in doing so. Thus, "truthfulness" is discovered through skepsis of, and located in-between, the various little white lies of ideological perspectives.

A final view of Frisch's type of engagement is to be seen with the following issues brought up by K. Schimanski:

> It is not possible for further consequences to follow after the clear analysis of his own social system when the writer is in fact *politically* responsible, but does not want to be *ideologically* engaged. Frisch's verdict against every "ideology and its deadly fronts," expressed as early as in his Büchner Prize Speech, binds him to an absolutized intellect-power antithesis, to a historical consciousness in which power and ideology are construed to be downright human-inimical categories, without any differentiation of their particular historical quality, of their purpose and content. As a result of that, the practical effectiveness of political insights and demands is largely paralyzed. The protesting nonconformist is harmless to class society, he becomes an alibi for those whom he assails; they can afford him and use him as a demonstration of an ostensibly unlimited intellectual freedom.[36]

In reply it should first be mentioned that Frisch has readily admitted we cannot do without any ideology (*Dr*, 39), but stressed that it had to be called into question on an individual basis. Thus Frisch's "ever to be repeated 'disenchantment' of abstraction, of ideology" ("immer wieder zu leistender *Bann* gegen *die Abstraktion*, gegen *die* Ideologie und ihre tödlichen Fronten"; *ÖP*, 55; my emphasis) should not be read as Schimanski's "*Verdict* against *every* 'ideology and its deadly fronts'" ("Verdikt gegen jede 'Ideologie und ihre tödlichen Fronten'"; my emphasis). The Büchner speech formulation does not constitute a verdict against all ideology, but rather the call for repeatedly removing the blinders to the abstractions and partiality of ideologies and ideological convictions. However, there is always the danger that a writer exhibiting any amount of engagement, perhaps especially of Frisch's type, will be made into a classic or be assimilated into the culture and paralyzed as to accomplishing his hopes of individual and then collective development. Frisch considers even Bertolt Brecht an example of such cultural assimilation—Brecht having achieved the "conclusive inefficacy of a classic author" (*ÖP*, 73). Perhaps the best Frisch can hope for is that a number of critical reader-partners will continually point out what a complete misunderstanding such "classification" would amount to—a misunderstanding of Frisch and his insights into the individual self and social order. Frisch can ultimately only hope for individual development; that is inherent in his particular type of idealism (cf. *ÖP*, 53).

One of Frisch's "truths" is that "Gewalt" (power or violence; see *TB II*, 83) cannot be ruled out as a last resort for skeptical, awakened individuals. For Frisch its employ might depend upon what cannot be achieved by such questioning individuals without the use of violence; the principles are different than in the application of the state's power or force (see, e.g., "Verhör III," *TB II*, 336-41). As Hans Mayer has pointed out,[37] one of the hidden themes of *Tagebuch II* is that of impotence, in old age and in society. If skeptical, questioning individuals are deprived of all power to achieve development and to effect change, then—Frisch seems to be telling us—the results might not be "eternal" banality, l'art pour l'art, or impotent senility but rather violence. Perhaps Frisch's literature is thus immensely more radical than assumed at first, uncritical sight.

In conclusion, perceiving Frisch's little white lies, necessary as they are at the level of both individual expression and sociopolitical discourse—i.e., calling their language and particular perspectives into question, being skeptical, doubting them—leads to engagement in both the self and the social world; it leads to the disclosure of truthfulness of both self and interhuman reality, and the truthfulness or truths are to lead to action and change.[38]

However, as found in an explanation to Walter Höllerer, Frisch maintains that he does not program his work according to some theory (*Dr*, 21). To a very large extent this very analysis has been an abstraction, a reduction. The question must be asked: "Was verschweigt sie nicht alles?!" (What does it withhold?"; cf. *M*, 197). To be sure, this analysis of Frisch's language views and perspectivism is itself a perspective, a little white lie, not the whole truth either.

1. In Frisch studies the formulation "Little White Lies" was originally used as the subtitle of an unpublished group seminar paper dealing solely with *Stiller* and written by Jay F. Bodine, Cornelia Brandt, Robert Kimbril, and Melinda Sieling (1969). The

citations to Frisch's writings will be given in the main text and refer to the following editions all published by the Suhrkamp Verlag in Frankfurt am Main except where noted: *TB I* (*Tagebuch 1946-1949*; 1950); *TB II* (*Tagebuch 1966-1971*; 1972); *St* (*Stiller*, 1954); *HF* (*Homo Faber*, Bibliothek Suhrkamp, 1957); *G* (*Mein Name sei Gantenbein*, 1964); *D* (*Dienstbüchlein*, 1974); *M* (*Montauk*, 1975); *AP* (*Ausgewählte Prosa*, edition suhrkamp, 1961); *Stücke 1* and *2* (1962); *B* (*Biographie: Ein Spiel*, Bibliothek Suhrkamp, 1969); *ÖP* (*Öffentlichkeit als Partner*, edition suhrkamp 209, 1967); *Dr* (*Dramaturgisches. Ein Briefwechsel mit Walter Höllerer*, Berlin: Literarisches Colloquium, 1969); the translations are my own.

2. Cf. Walter Schmitz's "Nachwort" in *Über Max Frisch II* (Frankfurt: Suhrkamp, 1976), pp. 540–41, 560 n. 13; some previous studies dealing specifically with Frisch's use of language are S.P. Hoefert, "Zur Sprachauffassung Max Frischs," *Muttersprache* 73 (1963), 1–3; W. Stauffacher, "Langage et mystère. A propos des derniers romans de Max Frisch," *Etudes Germaniques* 20 (1965), 331–45; G.B. Pickar, "Biedermann und die Brandstifter: The Dilemma of Language," *Modern Languages* 50, no. 3 (Sept. 1969), 99–106; W. Schenker, "Mundart und Schriftsprache," *Über Max Frisch I* (Frankfurt: Suhrkamp, 1971), ed. by T. Beckermann, pp. 287–99; M. Jurgensen, "Leitmotivischer Sprachsymbolismus in den Dramen Max Frisch," *Über Max Frisch I*, pp. 274–86; K. Braun, "Max Frischs 'Stiller': Sprache und Stil–Zwei Beispielanalysen," *Materialien zu Max Frischs "Stiller"* (Frankfurt: Suhrkamp, 1978), 1: 39–51.

3. E. Pulver, "Mut zur Unsicherheit," *Frisch: Kritik, Thesen, Analysen* (Berne: Francke, 1977), ed. M. Jurgensen, pp. 27–54.

4. H. Steinmetz, *Max Frisch: Tagebuch, Drama, Roman* (Göttingen: Vandenhoeck & Ruprecht, 1973), esp. p. 93; and K. Schimanski, "Ernst genommene Zeitgenossenschaft–subjektiv gespiegelt," *Über Max Frisch II*, pp. 385–97, esp. p. 394: "Es gibt weder vom Inhalt noch vom Kompositionsprinzip her irgendeine Veranlassung, den Verfasser in ein fiktives Rollen-Ich umzufälschen."

5. Schimanski, p. 393 ("Tagebuchromane ...") and p. 391 ("Keinesfalls ...").

6. H. Bienek, *Werkstattgespräche mit Schriftstellern* (Munich: dtv 1965), p. 27.

7. Bienek, p. 28; cf. *Stiller*, p. 436.

8. See the complete section "Vom Schreiben in Ich-Form" (*TB II*, 308–11).

9. Cf. Hans Mayer's review of *Montauk*, "Die Geheimnisse jeweden Mannes," *Über Max Frisch II*, pp. 443–47.

10. See the analysis of G.P. Knapp treating the juxtaposition of the first- and third-person perspectives in *Montauk*, in *Max Frisch. Aspekte des Prosawerks* (Berne: Lang, 1978), ed. G.P. Knapp, esp. pp. 292–97.

11. Bienek, pp. 27–29; Frisch, *AP*, 8–11.

12. Or in the jargon of Saussurian linguistics the point is approximately that the "fixed" signifiant evokes an abstracted signifié that does not correspond to the total experience and growth potential of a dynamic human referent.

13. See e.g. the discussion of Stauffacher or Hoefer (note 2).

14. Frühwald and Schmitz, *Max Frisch. "Andorra," "Wilhelm Tell," Materialien, Kommentare* (Munich: Hanser, 1977), esp. pp. 38–41.

15. If not examined closely and called into question, what could be an insight or single "truth" might be perceived merely as a facile aperçu: "Every thought is, in the moment when we first have it, perfectly true, valid, in correspondence with the conditions in which it arose; but then, when we express the result without being able to express the sum of its conditions, the thought suddenly hangs in the void, saying nothing, and then begins the false aspect when we look around and seek out corresponding ideas (for language, unspoken language also, is never capable of capturing in

one moment everything which we are conscious of during the moment in which the thought occurred—not to mention what we are not conscious of) . . . thus we stand there having nothing other than a result, we remember that the result completely tallied; we relate it to phenomena that would never have resulted in this thought, we go beyond the sphere of its validity since we no longer know the sum of its conditions, or at least we alter it—and already the error is there, the violation, the thorough persuasion. Or briefly: It is easy to say something true, a so-called aperçu that hovers in the realm of the unconditional; it is difficult, almost impossible, to apply that truth, to perceive to what extent a truth is valid. (To be real!)" (*TB I*, 228-29). This passage again outlines the limited capabilities of language as a medium of expression and warns against accepting any partial aspect of the complete actuality (i.e., a perspective) directly and at face value. An aperçu is not the full truth; but upon being called into question and viewed in its proper context, it can become a valuable insight.

16. W. Cunliffe, "Existentialistische Elemente in Frischs Werken," *Über Max Frisch II*, p. 165.

17. Paul de Man, using an analysis of the young Georg Lukács, supplies a theoretical framework quite helpful in recognizing the relationship or various perspectives of author, narrator, and narrated self—a framework most applicable to the problematical relationship of perspectives found in Frisch's oeuvre in general and to this passage in *Stiller* in particular; see "Ludwig Binswanger and the Sublimation of the Self," in *Blindness and Insight* (New York: Oxford Univ. Press, 1971), pp. 36-50.

18. Cf. the two analyses by Hans Mayer and Wolfgang Frühwald, both now found in *Materialien zu Max Frisch "Stiller,"* 1: 238-55, 259-68 respectively, "Anmerkungen zu 'Stiller'" and "Parodie der Tradition. Das Problem literarischer Originalität in Max Frischs Roman 'Stiller.'"

19. Whatever is purely and naively personal is not what is ultimately incumbent upon Frisch or what devolves upon his writing self.

20. Dieter E. Zimmer, "Noch einmal anfangen können. Ein Gespräch mit Max Frisch," *Die Zeit*, 22 Dec. 1967, p. 13; *Dr*, 34.

21. For a more elaborate analysis of this question in *Biographie*, see esp. Hans Heinz Holz, "Max Frisch—engagiert und privat," in *Über Max Frisch I*, pp. 235-60; Holz, however, comes to different conclusions concerning the play's value; he contrasts *Biographie* with *Andorra*, ultimately considering the former a most interesting dramatic experiment but wasted on the petty concerns of a banal, individual protagonist.

22. "Gespräch mit Max Frisch von Peter André Bloch und Rudolf Bussmann," *Der Schriftsteller in unserer Zeit* (Berne: Francke, 1972), pp. 17-35; the present analysis goes beyond the engagement discussion of the Bloch-Bussmann interview by treating the continuity of this and related questions in Frisch's oeuvre and specifically in light of Frisch's skepsis of language and perspectivism.

23. Bloch and Bussmann, p. 19.

24. I.e., "enlightening" himself and then others; for the idealistic tradition and the more specific sense in which "idealistic" is meant here, cf. Friedrich Schiller "Über die ästhetische Erziehung des Menschen in einer Reihe von Briefen," *Schillers Werke, Nationalausgabe* (Weimar, 1962), vol. 20, 9th letter, p. 332: "All improvement in the political sphere should proceed from ennobling the character"—of individuals.

25. Bloch and Bussmann, p. 19.

26. See esp. G.B. Pickar, "Biedermann und die Brandstifter: The Dilemma of Language," *Modern Languages* 50, no. 3 (Sept. 1969): 99-106; and W. Frühwald, "Wo ist Andorra?" *Über Max Frisch II*, 305-13.

27. W. Schenker, "Mundart und Schriftsprache," *Über Max Frisch I*, 287-99; cf.

TB II, 255: one of the things Frisch is "thankful for" is "die Spannung zwischen Mundart und Schriftsprache."

28. P.A. Bloch and Bruno Schoch, *"Max Frisch," Der Schriftsteller und sein Verhältnis zur Sprache* (Berne: Franke, 1971), p. 79.

29. Bloch and Schoch, pp. 68-81.

30. "Spuren meiner Nicht-Lektüre," *Materialien zu Max Frisch "Stiller,"* 1: 341: "In anderen Fällen kenne ich mein Vorbild, das aber nicht erkannt wird; offenbar bin ich ihm nicht nahegekommen."

31. See the book of that title: *Brecht's Tradition* by Max Spalter (Baltimore: Johns Hopkins, 1967).

32. See J.F. Bodine, "Karl Kraus's Conceptualization of Language," *Modern Austrian Literature* 8 (1975), nos. 1-2, pp. 268-314; and Josef Quack, *Bemerkungen zum Sprachverständnis von Karl Kraus* (Bonn: Bouvier, 1976).

33. T. Beckermann, "Einmal möchte er es wissen. Zur Ästhetik des Engagements im Prosawerk von Max Frisch," *Max Frisch* (Munich: edition text + kritik 47/48), p. 34.

34. Schimanski, *Über Max Frisch II*, p. 389.

35. Ibid., p. 387.

36. Ibid., p. 389.

37. Hans Mayer, "Die Schuld der Schuldlosen," *Über Friedrich Dürrenmatt und Max Frisch* (Pfullingen: Neske, 1977), p. 106.

38. Concerning the social import of Frisch's views, note the contrast of these conclusions with those represented by Reinhold Grimm and Carolyn Wellauer in *Zeitkritische Romane des 20. Jahrhunderts. Die Gesellschaft in der Kritik der deutschen Literatur,* ed. by Hans Wagener (Reclam: Stuttgart, 1975), pp. 276-300.

GERHARD F. PROBST

Three Levels of Image Making in Frisch's *Mein Name sei Gantenbein*

The relations between Max Frisch's *Tagebuch 1946-1949* (*Sketchbook 1946-1949*)[1] and several of his later works are manifold and well known. We find in it, among others, first sketches of *Andorra* (T. 35ff.), *Graf Öderland* (T. 73ff.), *Biedermann und die Brandstifter* (T. 243ff.), and *Schinz* (T. 433ff.). In addition, the *Tagebuch 1946-1949* contains reflections of a general nature, revealing Max Frisch's weltanschauung and aesthetics. There are finally certain motifs and themes which in different modifications or variations appear in several of Frisch's writings. The best-known of these is perhaps the one Frisch derived from the second commandment of the decalogue. Under the elliptic title, "You shall not make for yourself a graven image," Frisch ponders the curious relationships between people in general, between lovers in particular, and even between peoples or nations. A loving person, he says, does not make for himself or herself an image of the beloved; therefore "we can say the least what the person we love is like," since it is the nature of love to hold us "in the suspense of the living," to follow the beloved person "in all of his or her developments. . . . Love sets us free from all images, . . . boundless, full of all possibilities, of all mysteries, incomprehensible is the person we love—love alone can bear him so." The end of love is marked by the exhaustion of our strength to adjust to further metamorphoses of the other. We are tired of the mystery, the riddle that every human being represents. "We make for ourselves a graven image. It is without love, it is the betrayal" (T. 31-32).

One would expect Frisch to have treated this theme or motif of image-making in a love story. But he did not do so—at least not right away. He first dealt with it in a social context, albeit only in a sketch: "Der andorranische Jude" (The Andorran Jew, T. 35ff.). But in the diary we read this sketch, which more than a decade later was to become *Andorra*, in which Frisch discusses oracle and myth as image-making and, thus, prepares the reader for a wider application of his concept: "It has been pointed out that the miracle of all prophesy can in part be explained by the fact that the future which appears as an image in the words of a prophet is caused, prepared, eventually made possible or at least furthered by just this image– . . . oracle among the old Greeks." Cassandra is considered partially responsible for the misfortune "which she anticipates in her wailing, whose image she projects." For no matter, says Frisch, whether it is friends, parents, or teachers who have a certain fixed opinion of us, this opinion burdens us like an oracle, "and one cannot rid himself of an oracle until one makes it come true." The oracle could also come true as our reaction against it, in that we become the opposite, "but one becomes it through the other."

Frisch thus comes to a conclusion which he was to treat in several of his works, which might even be considered a key to all of them:[2] "To a certain degree we are really the person that others project into us, be they friend or foe. And conversely, we too are the creators of the others; in a secret and inescapable way we are responsible for the face they show us, responsible not for their talents, but for the exploitation of their talents. It is we who stand in the friend's way whose stagnation worries us, and what is more, it is our opinion of him as stagnant which adds another link to that chain which ties him and slowly strangles him." Frisch expands this interpersonal view of image-making to the ethnological when he writes, "We wish him [the friend] that he might change, o yes, we wish that entire peoples might do so! But this does not mean that we are ready to give up our views of them. We ourselves are the last to change them. We think we are the mirror and only seldom do we suspect how much the other is just the mirror of our unchanging image of man, is our product, our victim" (T. 32-34). Here, then, follows "Der andorranische Jude," a Brechtian parable on anti-Semitism, in which Max Frisch as a Swiss, and thus as "another," implies his sharing the responsibility for the image and thereby the self-image of the Germans.

After this brief treatment of the motif or theme of image-making in the realm of sociology or ethnology, it is, as was to be expected, the private sphere in which Frisch first deals with image-making on a larger scale. It is the novel *Stiller,* which was published in 1954,[3] in which Anatol Ludwig Stiller, a sculptor, and his wife Julika Stiller-Tschudy, a ballet-dancer, have certain fixed views of each other, make for themselves certain "graven images" of the other, and, thus, mutually force themselves into certain roles from which they cannot escape. The same is true of their relationships with friends and relatives. But it is this image-making, the "knowing" of, and "being known" by, others against which Stiller rebels. Therefore, he runs away and symbolically calls himself "White" as if he could thus create for himself an interpersonal *tabula rasa,* freeing himself of all images and of all corresponding roles which he believes paralyze him and hinder the unfolding of his true self. For he thinks that the others have the wrong image of him, force him into an identity and into roles which he resents and which he considers not to be truly his. Only physically breaking out of these roles which belong to those images, stepping off the stage which he refuses to accept as his world, is to give him back the freedom of his personality, the freedom of choosing himself. But neither in the Spanish Civil War nor in America does he find this new identity.

He does not know yet—or he refuses to accept—his "true" identity when upon returning home, he is arrested for a crime which he never committed, but with which his old (and true?) name is erroneously and paradoxically connected. Had Stiller not returned home, would he in the end have succeeded in becoming another? The motto of the novel—two quotations from Kierkegaard's *Either-Or*—seem to put such a possibility into doubt: man cannot escape himself and must learn to accept himself, which is the necessary complement and counterposition of the search for identity and, therefore, is as dominant in Frisch's works as the motif of image-making. Man believes, Kierkegaard says, that he chooses himself, but he only realizes what had been in him. Thus the age-old question about man's ability to change his destiny which Socrates already asked, the dispute concerning freedom of the will, predestination, and grace carried on by Pelagius and Augustinus, Erasmus and Luther is psychologized in the manner of the twentieth century, and as always ends in a draw.

Frisch's next treatment of image-making and perhaps the best-known and most obvious is *Andorra,* a "play in twelve pictures."[4] The central character of the play is a young man by the name of Andri whom most of his compatriots consider to be a Jew. But as his name symbolizes, Andri is an Andorran. Since, however, the "graven image" (T. 35) awaits him everywhere, he gradually adjusts to the image and becomes the "typical Jew." Andri is thus forced into a role from which he cannot and finally does not even want to free himself. Toward the end of the play, Andri is dragged away by "black soldiers" whose resemblance with the SS is obvious in spite of Frisch's "alienated" treatment of his material and of the apparent color symbolism present.

Andorra was first performed in 1961. Three years later appeared Frisch's most successful novel, the undisputed best-seller of the season, *Mein Name sei Gantenbein (A Wilderness of Mirrors).*[5] It seems certain that the final work on *Andorra* ran parallel with the initial stages of *Gantenbein.* But the two works not only share this outward characteristic of their genesis, they also have a common theme: image-making. In a manner similar to that of *Stiller,* however, Frisch treats the more private aspects of image-making in *Gantenbein.* In this novel, image-making whose dominance is clearly signaled in the subjunctive of the title ("My name be Gantenbein") is thematized on three levels.

The first level is the only one discussed so far, i.e., making images of one's fellowman and, thus, limiting him in his personal freedom, in his development, his possibilities, forcing him into certain roles. Man's obsession with the normative, his compulsion to categorize in order to be done with a particular phenomenon, is applied to human beings.

The second level is that of the narrator's image-making. By this, I do not mean the narrator's activity as the creation of verbal pictures, but rather and in a much more limited sense the creation of fictive characters which are "sketches of an I" (G. 109). The narrator who remains quite vague and hides behind the different sketches of himself as Gantenbein hides behind his black glasses creates different "images," i.e., self-portraits in which he plays different roles. These different I's even interact with each other in the different stories, but they all love the same woman. This woman symbolically only takes on different guises, wears different costumes as it were, but always plays herself. After all, she is an actress by profession. On this second level, the interpersonal kind of image-making which characterizes the first, is operative, too.

The third level is also one of aesthetic image-making. The accent, however, has shifted from the narrator to the reader. It is the concretization of the novel by the reader which occurs here and which in the case of *Gantenbein*, as in many contemporary works of fiction,[6] goes beyond the actualization necessary in any reading process and appears as part of the narrative strategy and, thus, as part of the structure of the novel.

On the first level, then, and similar to Barblin who does not accept the general image of Andri whom she loves, Theo Gantenbein tries not to make for himself a "graven image" of his wife Lila. He assumes the role of the blind man, which forces him not to see, or to pretend not to see, many things. Although this pretended blindness has to do with Gantenbein's jealousy, and thus with the narrator's, the important thing is its intended effect: Lila, the actress, who must play roles professionally, is kept free from this obligation in her private sphere. She does not have to play a role which would have to correspond to her husband's image of her. Frisch's antithetical style, an expression of his antithetical mode of thought, shows even in seemingly minor details: Gantenbein's black glasses are intended to create an interpersonal Mr. and Mrs. White, to guarantee his wife's freedom, and to make it possible for him to obey the secularized second commandment of the decalogue.[7] Neither, of course, do the other people with whom Gantenbein comes into contact have to play roles which would agree with his images of them. They are free to behave according to their "true" nature. And it is for exactly this reason again that Gantenbein does not need to form images of them since image-making in most cases, i.e., when no telos is involved, is an attempt to discover the true face behind its many masks, the person behind the persona.[8] This type of image-making partakes of the intent of the novel as a whole—inventing stories in order to discover truth—and reflects Frisch's general view of literature—poetization as a manner of coming to grips with reality, independent from, but in its "Wahrheitsanspruch" in no way inferior to, all so-called mimetic or objective approaches.

But occasionally, as for example in the case of the prostitute Camilla Huber, Gantenbein's "blindness" makes role playing possible. Camilla Huber, apparently unhappy about the conflict between her material well-being and the lack of social status this material well-being would bring with it if she belonged to a different profession, enjoys the role Gantenbein's pretended blindness allows her to play, "she enjoys it not to be seen. She enjoys her part.... A modern woman. A working woman even though Gantenbein will never see her at work, a woman who stands on her own two feet and who drives her own car, of course, her self-earned car" (G. 35). Camilla Huber who paradoxically, it seems, in fiction likes "true" stories only (as does the barman), fabricates stories in real life. Here, too, art appears as "Ersatzbefriedigung," as compensation for that which we desire but do not have. With Gantenbein, she can create a verbal world, imagine possibilities for herself which she otherwise cannot realize. She, thus, becomes an ironical parallel to the narrator.[9]

By pretending to be blind, Gantenbein forces himself into a role that corresponds to this self-image and from which his fellowmen do not release him even when his actions demonstrate that he can see. For as image-making results in role playing, role playing, conversely, results in image-making. Frisch here anticipates a behaviorist principle which the American psychiatrist Eric Berne was to apply in his Transactional Analysis. Contrary to the Freudians, Berne does not consider it decisive to go below the threshold of consciousness and to discover traumatically conditioned repressions in order to remedy many lighter cases of emotional disturbance. Berne and his followers, such as Thomas A. Harris, the author of the bestselling *I'm OK—You're OK*, believe that change is more important than adjustment, what will happen in the future is more important than what happened to the patient in the past. Berne believes the creation of a positive self-image to be decisive, since it will result in a positive image on the part of others and, thus, in a change in their behavioral patterns which will in turn interact with the subject's behavior and create spirals of reciprocity between positive images and positive behavior.[10] These views sound very much like those sketched out by Frisch in his *Tagebuch 1946-1949*, thematized primarily in *Andorra, Stiller,* and *Mein Name sei Gantenbein,* but present in one form or another in practically all his works.

This image-making or the abstention from it which characterizes the relationship between Gantenbein and his wife Lila, then, is situated on the first level, the interpersonal, psychological, work-immanent level of communication, as it were.[11] These images become functional as part of the "sketches of an I" on the second level. The narrator invents self-portraits which are bound to, and take shape in, certain roles. These roles are actualized in stories or episodes which make up the novel. Gantenbein is only one of these portrait/role/stories, albeit the dominant one in which the narrator very soon prefers to see himself ("My name shall be Gantenbein," G. 74) and to which he returns ("I remain Gantenbein," G. 180, 182) after his doubts forced him "to try on" other roles and stories "like clothes" (G. 20). Enderlin, Svoboda (freedom), Philemon, and Ali are the other portrait/role/stories and thus, possibilities of the narrating I.

Beyond this, the relationships between Gantenbein-Lila and Gantenbein-Camilla appear as the two basic possibilities of the man-woman relationship, with the variations of Enderlin-Lila as Gantenbein's wife, Enderlin-Lila as Svoboda's wife, Gantenbein-Lila as Svoboda's wife, Svoboda-Lila as Svoboda's wife, Gantenbein-Lila as Venetian Contessa, Gantenbein/Philemon-Lila/Baucis and Ali-Alil. All these partially marital and partially extramarital affairs with their concomitant stories, however, have one thing in common: the woman is always Lila, and even Alil is a palindrome of Lila. The respective men, however, are possibilities or variations of the narrator's self and even share certain characteristics, habits, experiences with the real author Max Frisch: certain corpulence, bushy eyebrows, pipe-smoking, ping-pong playing, architect, prolonged sojourns in Italy (where the novel was mainly written), United States, Mexico. Enderlin, the scholar who receives a call to a chair at Harvard University but declines because of his affair with Gantenbein's wife whom he does not want to leave, is the first "possibility" to be discarded (G. 145). But the narrator relatively early called him "a strange man" (G. 62)—in the double connotation of the word—said of him that "Enderlin can play no role, since he designed himself in such a way that he must prove his identity through achievements," which, however, never makes anybody trustworthy, for "what convinces are not achievements, but rather the role somebody plays" (G. 107). This Enderlin in whom one is tempted to suspect the author playing the part of the scholar when invited to speak about literature at universities, on television, or before other audiences, is put aside as one of the narrator's possibilities, it is true; he does, however, appear even after his "demise" as a variation of the man with whom Lila as Svoboda's wife has an affair.[12]

Enderlin's death—or rather the possible story of his death behind the steering wheel of his car—opens the novel. But the novel as a whole is not a flashback which traces the development of matters leading to this death. Even though the individual scenes, episodes, or stories are told diachronically, the individual relationships between Lila and the different narrator roles as well as the novel as a whole are located in synchrony or, to be exact, outside of all time order. At the end, "everything is as if it had not happened" (G. 288) since it was only imagined, and it is this "I imagine" which can be called the leitmotiv or the dominant narrative mode of the novel. Camilla Huber, to give another example, who was murdered in an earlier episode which led to that amusing scene in court with Gantenbein as a blind witness (G. 244ff.), is alive in the very end, for it is she who is told the very last story of the novel, the story of the drowned man who almost managed "to drift off without a story" (G 288). The mimesis of the individual diachronic stories does not suspend the nonmimetic and achronic quality of the novel as a whole.

The fairy tale of Ali and Alil is placed in the center of the novel. It has a direct bearing on the relation between Gantenbein and Lila: blindness plays an important part in both. Ali, a young shepherd, takes as his bride the beautiful Alil whom her father sells at a low price because she is blind. A miracle doctor restores Alil's sight and she sees that Ali is not as handsome as many of the other shepherds. But she loves him nevertheless, "for he had given her all the colors of this world through his love, and she was happy and he was happy and Ali and Alil were the happiest couple at the edge of the desert" (G. 147). Alil had made for herself an image of Ali which she had to correct when she could see, but the "true" Ali was part of the "true" world which he had given to her: reciprocity between love and world view.

During a manicure, Gantenbein tells this story to Camilla Huber who, however, is disappointed since she wants to hear "true stories" and this particular one strikes her as a fairy tale. Gantenbein, therefore, invents a second part to his story: their happiness lasts for one year. Then Ali turns blind. But "no sooner had Ali turned blind than he no longer believed that she loved him, and every time that Alil left the tent, he became jealous." Ali begins to beat Alil and embraces another girl who comes to see him more and more often when Alil is not in the tent. When the miracle doctor also restores Ali's eyesight, Ali sees that Alil, who does not know of his recovery, goes to wash the tears off her face after Ali beat her and then slips back into his tent as the other girl.

Ali whose name is contained in Alil's—similar to Andri's which almost completely goes into Andorra—becomes jealous when his physical blindness sets in and lets his physical blindness turn into a blindness of the heart, which begins to destroy the image he had of Alil. He begins to make for himself a new image, an ugly one, an untrue one to which Alil, although under a false identity, begins to adjust: here, then, again the role playing as a result of image-making is quite in accordance with the passage from *Tagebuch 1946-1949* quoted above.

Alil is easily recognized as a palindrome of Lila, and the relationships of the two women to their respective men appears as inverse as their names. Whereas Lila's supposed unfaithfulness causes Gantenbein's jealousy and makes him pretend blindness, in order to see the "true" Lila, Ali turns blind and becomes jealous as a result of it, as he loses his image of Alil. Lila's acting is partially responsible for Gantenbein's jealousy and "blindness," Alil's acting is the result of Ali's blindness and jealousy.

All doubts that the Ali-Alil relationship is to be seen as a variation of the Gantenbein-Lila relationship vanish when one considers the fact that the contracted names of Lila and Alil—Lilalil (G. 174)—are inserted into the Philemon and Baucis episode which in itself is a variation of the Gantenbein-Lila relationship. The scene in which this "Lilalil" appears is also determined by love and jealousy. One night, Philemon as the old Gantenbein breaks into his wife's desk (a similar episode occurs in *Montauk* where the narrator remembers breaking into Ingeborg Bachmann's desk who I suspect had a great deal to do with Gantenbein[13]) and suddenly realizes that the love letters he is reading are his own, written when Lila was still Svoboda's wife. And the "Lilalil" which he finds in one of the letters reminds him of his once undoubting love: "Philemon, I say, you love her! Everything else is nonsense" (G. 174). This triple conditioning or dependency (Philemon-Baucis/Gantenbein-Lila/Ali-Alil) with the other "possibilities" (Enderlin-Lila as Svoboda's wife) as a backdrop on the one hand beautifully shows the complexity of the relationship between the narrator and his beloved woman; on the other hand it points at the artistry of storytelling and the great demands made on the reader of this novel.[14]

At the end of the "Lilalil" episode the narrator speaks of a primitive people, "where they decided by lot which man belonged to which woman." This belonging, however, only consisted in material care; eros and sex were completely separate from it, claims the narrator. What he seems to say, then, is that primitive man is free from the dilemma of love, jealousy, and promiscuity, thus betraying a certain romantic attitude which is always tinged by escapism and fatalism.

As there is constant interaction between the first two levels of image-making, the psychologically determined kind with its concomitant role playing and the auctorial variation of the "sketches of an I," the third level cannot be separated from the other two, either. If I am going to try to do this here anyway, it must be seen heuristically as an *epochë*.

The third level is that of the reader's image-making. As readers, we are given Gantenbein, Enderlin, and Svoboda as the three major possibilities of the narrator's I and Philemon and Ali as the two minor possibilities; we feel called upon to examine these possibilities, these images or portraits with their accompanying roles and stories as to their common or differing characteristics and to try to combine them into one essential story belonging to the one narrator hidden behind the several I's. We try to eliminate episodes and parts of stories which do not go together or even contradict one another, in order to make for ourselves a narrator image—and, of course, feel tempted to identify it with the true author Max Frisch. But the limits of image-making are reached where the psychological, interpersonal application of the second commandment as Frisch understands it is combined with the aesthetic aspect which characterizes the second and third levels: we should make for ourselves neither an image of a real person nor of a fictive one since there is no such thing as a unified character. Every character is made up of facets which correspond to the different roles played vis-à-vis different people. Stiller only wanted to become *one* other person; the narrator of *Gantenbein* tries out several different I's by experimenting with them like a scientist, putting them into different situations with different partners. One might criticize the author for the resulting style of storytelling with its interruptions, breaks, and shifts in perspective. Passages in *Tagebuch 1946-1949*, however, make it quite clear that the form of the novel is based on definite aesthetic concepts and on an all-encompassing weltanschauung. Frisch considers the aphoristic and the "skizze" (sketch, outline, first or rough draft) as appropriate for our contemporary world view which "is no more or not yet whole" (T. 118-19), and for this reason a work of literature which attempts perfection or wholeness appears to him "unethical" since only an open, provisional form can go with an open, nonfixed world view.

In light of Transactional Analysis, however, such relativism, such breaking up of traditional form, such violation of conventional or realistic storytelling, which Frisch shares with so many contemporary writers of fiction, appears much rather consistent with an aesthetic mimesis which is a true rendering of a psychologically enlightened view of man and his world. In connection with *Gantenbein*, reference has been made to the Picasso of the cubist period and the facet technique applied there.[15] This comparison certainly applies in some manner, but it is impossible to do optically what can be done verbally: to reunite in our imagination the parts of a disintegrating world, the fragments of a once whole personality which used to be "das höchste Glück der Erdenkinder" (Goethe), the different aspects of a world view in which "the opposite of a statement which has just overwhelmed us is no less convincing" (T. 119). Only "the mental eye" can see the disparate as one, even though this "seeing together" does not result in a seamless whole.

Mein Name sei Gantenbein as a novel whose locus is the imagination even in the sense of the imaginary, this novel of the "as if" (G. 131) as a novel made up of "stories which exist only from the outside" (G. 45), ends with these words:

> Everything is as if it had not happened.... It is a day in September, and when one comes back to light out of the dark and by no means cool tombs, we blink, so bright is the day;[16] I see the red soil of the fields above the tombs, far away and dark the autumnal sea, noon,

> everything is presence, wind in the dusty thistle, I hear the sounds of a flute, but it is not the Etruscan flutes in the tombs, it is the wind in the wires, in the rippling shadows of an olive-tree my car sits gray with dust and hot, snake heat in spite of the wind, but already September again: but presence and we sit at a table in the shade and eat bread until the fish is done, I put my hand around the bottle to check whether the wine (Verdicchio) is cold enough, thirst, then hunger, I enjoy life— (G. 288)

This "everything is as if it had not happened" reveals the novel as a whole as just a possibility and seems to be juxtaposed to the "true" life with its realities of dust and wind, of light and shadow, hunger and thirst. The narrator seems to have returned from the catacombs, ending the novel on a strong and positive note of affirmation of life, evoking the full reality of an Italian late-summer day and rejecting all speculations about the possibilities of an I, calling off the search for a character and its many roles. But then we notice the dash that is the last printed symbol of the text. And there seems to be no doubt that the absence of a period symbolizes the absence of an end to the novel. The words preceding that dash are not final either but allude to one of the possibilities which the novel leaves open and which leave the novel open, namely the possibility of "real" life which in all its reality is again and again confronted and put into doubt by that other life of the imagination, which stands in a constant relation of reciprocity with "real" life, in a relation of mutual conditioning and elucidation. The play *Biografie* of 1967 is another treatment of this interplay between reality and imagination, between an I and its nonrealized entelechies, as it were; *Man in the Holocene* so far is the last.[17]

In conclusion, then, one can say that Max Frisch's novel *Mein Name sei Gantenbein* represents a relatively early, although not the very first, thematization of what I have elsewhere called the principle of alterity.[18] In this, Frisch's novel precedes by a few years the emergence of reception aesthetics which I see as the critical stance analogous to the narrative strategy of openness, relativity, and nonfinality.[19] Frisch's novel with its pluralistic narrator and its reciprocity between different images and roles as well as its thematization of reader participation in its constitution represents a rejection of the auratic and "objective" view of the work of literature. Frisch denies that the one and only true meaning can be extrapolated from the text by the "right" reading, as do the receptionist critics, and points in the direction of that open novel by the uninformed narrator who becomes dominant in such later works as Böll's *Gruppenbild mit Dame* (*Group Portrait with Lady*), Christa Wolf's *Nachdenken über Christa T.* (*Quest for Christa T.*), or Siegfried Lenz's *Das Vorbild* (*An Exemplary Life*), to name only a few. Even though these and other works go further in the thematization of the constitution of the literary work by the reader and leave larger gaps which the reader must fill on his own, it is Max Frisch's *Mein Name sei Gantenbein* which can claim to be one of the first comprehensive and consistent thematizations of alterity.

1. (Frankfurt: Suhrkamp, 1950); from here on quoted in the text as "T." with page number. English version: *Sketchbook 1946-49*, tr. Geoffrey Skelton (New York: Harcourt, Brace, Jovanovich, 1977). The translations of all the quotations used in this article, however, are my own.

2. This view, for example, is expressed by Horst Steinmetz in *Max Frisch: Tagebuch, Drama, Roman* (Göttingen: Vandenhoeck & Ruprecht, 1973 [Kleine Vandenhoeck-Reihe 379], p. 27.

3. (Frankfurt: Suhrkamp, 1954). English translation: *I'm Not Stiller*, tr. Michael Bullock (New York; Vintage Books, 1962).

4. (Frankfurt: Suhrkamp, 1961). English edition: *Andorra*, tr. Michael Bullock (New York: Hill and Wang, 1964).

5. (Frankfurt: Suhrkamp, 1964); quoted hereafter according to the suhrkamp taschenbuch 286 (1975) as "G." with page number. English edition: *A Wilderness of Mirrors*, tr. Michael Bullock (New York: Random House, 1966).

6. The constitution of the novel by the reader as included in the narrative strategy I have called "thematization of alterity." I have discussed this concept at some length in several articles which appeared in *Germanisch-Romanische Monatsschrift* no. 4, 1979, *Colloquia Germanica* nos. 3-4, 1978, *Wirkendes Wort* no. 4, 1979, and the *University of Dayton Review* no. 2, 1978.

7. Interpretations of the novel as one of distrust and jealousy (R. Schroers and H. Vormweg) are refuted in light of my subsequent argument. *Mein Name sei Gantenbein* is much rather a novel about love and trust, at least efforts toward them. It is both logically and psychologically evident that distrust and jealousy are unavoidable complements of love and trust, especially in Frisch's antithetical mode of thinking and aesthetics where counterpositions are always included or considered.

8. Murray Krieger applied this split of each human being into person and persona(e), which was already familiar to the Greeks, to the activity of the literary critic in "The Critic as Person and Persona," *The Personality of the Critic* (*Yearbook of Comparative Criticism* 6), ed. Joseph P. Strelka (University Park: Pennsylvania State University Press, 1973), pp. 70-92. Krieger adduces Freudian concepts to his argument, whereas Frisch is more indebted to Jung.

9. In light of this relation between images, roles and stories, so-called true stories appear as uninteresting and naive. This simplistic attitude toward stories is shared by Camilla Huber with the bartender whom the narrator envies for having "an undoubting relation to his story." The narrator claims that "what someone has when he talks about himself, when he talks at all [are] models of experience—but no story" (G. 44-45).

10. Eric Berne, *Games People Play* (New York: Grove Press, 1964). Thomas A. Harris, *I'm OK—You're OK* (New York: Avon Books, 1973). Although Berne published the first papers in which he propounded his theory as early as 1957, he did not reach a wider public until 1964, with the publication of *Games People Play*. This was the same year *Gantenbein* appeared.

11. One could find here rather interesting and elucidating parallels with structural models of narrative works along the lines of information theory as Polish theoreticians in particular developed them. Kazimierz Bartoszyński, "Das Problem der literarischen

Kommunikation in narrativen Werken." *Sprache im technischen Zeitalter* 47 (1973): 202-24.

12. Enderlin is a mythologist. In connection with the sketchbook passage quoted above, in which Frisch spoke of the image- and role-creating power of myth and oracle, it is interesting that we learn about Enderlin "he can play no role" (G. 107). Scholarly findings are abstract, represent no images, and, therefore, have no image- and role-creating power.

13. Gerhard F. Probst, "Mein Name sei Malina: Nachdenken über Ingeborg B." *Modern Austrian Literature* 11 (1978), Nr. 1.

14. In many respects the narrative technique of *Gantenbein* seems to indicate on the part of its author an awareness of the issues raised during the debate on hermeneutics and criticism of ideology, triggered by the publication of Gadamer's *Wahrheit und Methode* in 1960, when Frisch began working on *Gantenbein*. Wittgenstein's concept of "language games" played an important part in that debate, and Max Frisch at the time was still close to Ingeborg Bachmann, who was very familiar with Wittgenstein's philosophy.

15. Examples for Picasso's cubist facet style would be the portraits of Ambroise Vollard (1909) and Daniel Henry Kahnweiler (1910).

16. This is an almost literal repetition of a passage in *Tagebuch 1946-1949* where in the *Schinz* sketch we read, "In the light, everything is as if it had never been" (T. 441).

17. (Frankfurt: Suhrkamp, 1967 [*Biografie*] and 1979 [*Holocene*]). English versions: *Biography: A Game*, tr. Michael Bullock (New York: Hill and Wang, 1969); *Man in the Holocene*, tr. Geoffrey Skelton (New York: Harcourt, Brace, Jovanovich, 1980).

18. If one considers Kafka's fiction—in particular his novels—as told by a narrator who does not comprehend the world he describes, thus as fiction which has no true center of consciousness and of reference, the reader, in his attempts "to understand" these novels, cannot duplicate the narrator's understanding of what he describes but must find his own key to this world, develop his own frame of reference. In this regard, Kafka's novels are determined by another understanding consciousness and are, thus, thematizations of alterity. (For a detailed discussion of Kafka from a point of view similar to the one indicated here, see Horst Steinmetz, *Suspensive Interpretation: Am Beispiel Franz Kafkas* (Göttingen: Vandenhoeck & Ruprecht, 1977.)

19. Hans Robert Jauss, whose essay entitled "Literary History as a Provocation of Literary Criticism," 1967, gave great impetus to reception aesthetics, describes the state of this branch of literary criticism in an article, "The Reader as an Instance of a New History of Literature," *Poetica* 7 (1975): 325-44, which together with papers by Karlheinz Stierle ("What Is Meant by Reception of Fictional Texts?" ibid., pp. 345-87) and Hans Ulrich Gumbrecht ("Consequences of Reception Aesthetics or Literary Criticism as Sociology of Communication," ibid., pp. 388-413), appeared under the general heading "Reception Aesthetics—Interim Report."

GERHARD F. PROBST

The Old Man and the Rain: *Man in the Holocene*

The title of this narrative, *Man in the Holocene*, initially puzzles the reader. It sounds like an account of the life conditions of prehistoric man. The original German title, however, contains a verb: *Der Mensch erscheint im Holozän* (Man appears or emerges in the holocene), which shifts the reader's expectation toward the evolutionary. But both German and English titles point at the generic, the entire species. Therefore, the reader is surprised to encounter an old man, a Herr Geiser,[1] who in the opening episode is seen trying to build a pagoda out of "Knäckebrot" (crisp bread). It is night, and there is thunder and rain. The old man is trapped in a remote Alpine valley in the Tessin or Ticino, the Italian-speaking part of southern Switzerland. It has been raining for days. "Not a night without thunderstorms and cloud-bursts" (11).[2] The only access road into the valley is being blocked by a collapsed support wall. There is no mail service, and due to power failure neither telephone nor television is working: Herr Geiser is almost completely cut off from the rest of the world.

What does Herr Geiser do in this calamity? He reads, reflects about the situation and checks on his supplies of food, firewood, and matches. But mainly he reads. He has a few novels which his deceased wife left him, but "novels are not suitable at all in these days" (16). Thus he turns to "Sachbücher": books on the history of the Tessin, a two-volume Swiss lexicon, the twelve-volume German Brockhaus encyclopedia, popular science books, gardening and hiking guides.[3] And he reads the Bible again, "which he has not read for a long time" (18). Herr Geiser not only reads these books, he makes excerpts and eventually clips entire articles from them, which he tacks to the paneling of his living room. When he runs out of space, he tapes his notes and clippings to all other available walls.

Gradually, as he reads these excerpts and clippings about the history and the legends of the Tessin, its geology and previous natural catastrophes, along with passages from the Bible, even the most unsuspecting reader must become aware of the fact that this narrative is more than just an account of an old man's predicament. He realizes that the title of the story with its reference to the emergence of modern man implies the complementary idea of man's extinction.[4] Juxtaposing Herr Geiser's apprehensions about the fate of the valley (will it disappear in the waters of an enormous lake or be buried under a huge mud slide?) with scientific descriptions of geologic epochs, surveys of the history of the region, and biblical accounts of the deluge, the narrator establishes a pattern which is to run all through the story: a skillful interweaving of several strands of thought and of three major attitudes, namely the scientific-scholarly, the religious, and the quotidian. This texture corresponds to the interrelation or even interdependence of the respective "protagonists"—Herr Geiser, the valley, the region, mankind, life on this planet, even the universe. It is proof of Max Frisch's great art how he achieves this complexity in a seemingly simple story about an old man. He does it by employing a narrative strategy which consists in interspersing the narration proper with certain signals that point beyond the scope of the story. He does not, however, become didactic or lead the reader by the hand, but rather gives him the satisfaction of discovering for himself the symbolism of the story.

The impression of simplicity is largely due to a style which alternates brief uncomplicated sentences—many of them one-liners—with longer pieces of narration and passages from the books consulted by Herr Geiser. But even these articles are presented in unpretentious language since they are taken from encyclopedias and other handbooks written for the non-specialist.

Herr Geiser thinks that novels are of little use in these days since they deal only "with people in their relation to themselves and to others" (16). But the real problem is man's relation to the forces of nature, and in novels people behave "as if the earth would remain the earth and the sea level would stay the same forever" (16). This is one of the reasons why Herr Geiser writes down his own observations of nature, copies and clips those passages dealing with the nature of lightning, with erosion, the formation of glaciers, the sequence of geologic epochs, and even the different types of thunder. And although it is not surprising that a man, particularly an old man—Herr Geiser is almost seventy-four—in a crisis should begin to think of his own death, the signals pointing to the death of man and the possible termination of life on this planet lead the reader to conclude that he is to see Herr Geiser's dilemma as the dilemma of *homo sapiens sub specie aeternitatis.*[5]

Herr Geiser's story, then, must be read as a parable. His seemingly practical measures, such as checking on his supplies of food, firewood, and matches which will be useless if the worst should happen, become symbolical of mankind's prudent considerations and actions directed at the problems of the day while the ones concerning the survival of mankind and the future of this planet are ignored.

The motivation for the narrative technique or structure characterized as an intertwining of several strands of thought or, to be more exact, one plot projected on a smaller background or screen—the valley—and simultaneously on three larger ones—mankind, the earth, even the universe—is very clever and convincing. Herr Geiser begins to feel the effects of aging in a loss of memory; hence his attempts to recall certain knowledge, mostly pertinent to his situation; hence the excerpting and clipping from books. Hence also the outward projection, as it were, of otherwise internalized information: tacking and taping those notes and clippings to the walls of his house, thus paradoxically surrounding himself with the bits of knowledge that he wants to remember.

The setting of the story is perhaps the most symbolical of anything that Max Frisch has written and reminds one of Ernest Hemingway's *Old Man and the Sea*. An old man water-bound in a remote Alpine valley is a very expressive symbol of the ever-increasing loneliness of old age. But whereas Hemingway stays completely within the framework of his tale, Frisch transcends it. Of course, in the broader sense of the word even Frisch just tells a story of an old man, but he intersperses his narrative with enough signals to make us surmise its symbolism. Hemingway's story line is continuous, his narrative manner objective. Frisch's story line is broken, sometimes blurred, his narrative manner alteristic.[6] And while Hemingway's old man is a simple and poor man in a paradigmatic existential situation, Frisch's old man is educated, well-to-do, part of the technological age, but in an equally paradigmatic existential situation and equally helpless against the forces of nature. Their names already tell the difference: Hemingway's fisherman is called Santiago and does not seem to have a last name; Frisch's "Pensionär" is never referred to without the attribute "Herr." His first name is never mentioned. We are not told what Herr Geiser was by profession before he retired to this valley, but he must have been director of some business firm (39, 124). And whereas Hemingway's old man quite literally fights for his life, first as he catches his fish and then as he tries to defend it against the sharks, Herr Geiser's concern for survival is largely intellectual. Herr Geiser does, however, make a real attempt to fight for his life—in a way.

One morning, Herr Geiser sets out to leave his valley and to cross over a mountain pass into the nearest valley where he could catch a bus to Locarno and from there to Basel where Herr Geiser lived before coming to the Tessin. Hiking in the mountains can always be dangerous, more so in the rain and the fog, and especially for an old man. Herr Geiser leaves his house before dawn. He has all the necessary equipment—rucksack, raincoat, umbrella, flashlight, magnifying glass, binoculars, map—but soon he, and so does the reader, realizes that some of this equipment is useless in the rain and fog (binoculars, for instance) and other items are too heavy. Although Herr Geiser knows the area, the rain and fog repeatedly cause him to lose his orientation; he finally continues more on instinct and is in constant danger of losing his footing and his life. Therefore, the rather laconic statement at the beginning of the episode, "Herr Geiser knows what he is doing" (89) in retrospect becomes more and more ironic.

The subsequent, almost Confucian pronouncement, "A road is a road even in the fog" (90) takes on a double meaning when it becomes apparent that Herr Geiser's mind grows more and more confused so that he does not quite know any more what he is doing and were he is going. Suddenly during his final descent into that other valley he turns back. The next day he suffers a stroke. Just before Herr Geiser reaches his house—it is past midnight by then—we read, "A road is a road even in the night" (107). This slight variation of the earlier motif with its evocation of Hermann Hesse's poem *Im Nebel* (In the Fog)[7] serves as a final signal to read Herr Geiser's mountain tour as symbolical action. One is tempted to think of religious symbolism. But Herr Geiser does not find his god on the mountain. There is no burning bush; just rocks, swollen mountain streams, and, in a rare dry spot, some ants. The mountain episode, thus, appears as symbolical action devoid of its traditional religious meaning—quite in agreement with Frisch's aesthetics.[8]

Additional signals for the reading of this episode lie in some other statements: "For the most time one does not think at all when walking" (101); "Sometimes Herr Geiser does think after all" (101); Herr Geiser briefly takes shelter in a mountain chapel; he looks down into an abyss where probably no human being has ever set foot and recites to himself the formula of the "golden section"; he tries to remember how the Alps were formed; he reflects about the fact that ants form states and recalls that the Romans invented and first built vaulted ceilings and roofs (is Herr Geiser perhaps an architect?). He thinks about the immense flood that would result from the melting of the Arctic ice—the Alps would rise from an ocean covering all of Europe. Then we read the sentence that Frisch chose for a title: "Man appears in the Holocene" (103). The "Umfeld" or "Bezugsfeld"[9] of all these statements, ideas, and actions seems to suggest that Herr Geiser's mountain tour must be read as a parable of man's journey through this world, alluding at the same time to the very small part which he plays—and not very well at that—in a lengthy tragicomedy.

To furnish additional signals for the reading of his narrative, particularly after the title has been set into context, the narrator follows up this report of the old man's hike in the rain and fog with a detailed discussion of the emergence of human life and the extinction of the dinosaurs. In preparation of it, there were some earlier remarks about a fire salamander which sought refuge in the house and when inspected under a magnifying glass reminded Herr Geiser of a dinosaur. The narrator dwells in particular on the tyrannosaurus rex, the most gigantic and terrible carnivore ever to terrorize the earth. His attributes are strangely reminiscent of man.

Two interpretive conclusions seem to be possible here: Man's destiny may turn out to be similar to that of the dinosaur—complete extinction—or he may be reduced in size and importance, although Frisch does not suggest any evolutionary connection between dinosaur and fire salamander (82-83).

There is a second episode thematically connected with Herr Geiser's mountain hike but showing the fewest digressions as far as straight storytelling is concerned. Herr Geiser remembers a mountain climb to the top of the Matterhorn, one of the most challenging peaks of the Swiss Alps, which fifty years ago he undertook with his now deceased older brother Klaus. The descent from the mountain, as always in mountaineering, proved to be much more difficult and dangerous than the ascent. Death was a constant companion lurking behind every turn and in every chasm.

Through the absence of digressions about geology, phylogeny, or even just the history of the Tessin, the symbolism of the episode is reduced and seems to evoke only the descent of old age. This, however, is in agreement with the general rhythm or movement of the narrative which began with an old man sitting in his living room, was gradually broadened in scope to include the entire valley and the canton, finally mankind, the planet earth, and even the universe, and which then, after that central and symbolically most expansive first mountain episode, is again narrowed down to the valley and the old man. His daughter has come to look in on him after his slight stroke which has paralyzed the lid of his left eye. There is some slight pressure on his left temple, but Herr Geiser's memory has apparently not deteriorated much, the pretendedly uninformed narrator tells us: he remembers his parents' first names, their birth dates, the name of the street in Basel where he was born, but the name of his youngest grandchild escapes him. There are still many notes and clippings which Herr Geiser thinks should be taped to the walls, but a draft of air blows them to the floor where they come to rest in meaningless confusion.

Repetition appears as the dominant trait shared by topic, theme, and structure of the narrative. Repetition is typical of old people's manner of thought, speech, and general behavior. In this regard, then, the repetition of the questions about death, biblical genesis, the "golden section," the history of the Tessin, the earth, the universe, but also the repetition of certain actions would be in character, as it were, with an old man. But repetition would at the same time allude to the cycles of nature, in microcosm as well as macrocosm, to the cyclical and repetitive which characterize the ontogeny of all living things when seen in the light of phylogeny.

It is here that the symbolic function of water must be mentioned. Not only is it of a pervasive presence in a very real sense, with its usefulness as well as destructiveness ("dam" and "deluge" would be the corresponding signals), but on the level of symbolism and, particularly in the context of German Geistesgeschichte, the Goethean "Wechseldauer" (permanence of change) and the Heraclitean *panta rhei* (All is in flux) must be considered.[10] Even the protagonist's name alludes to water.

But repetition is also an essential characteristic of musical composition and of narratives or other works of literature which employ this structural principle. Musical structure in literature goes with the episodic, the non-causal, and thematic, which we find so dominant in twentieth-century literature, especially in the expressionists.

Man in the Holocene can certainly be read and enjoyed as simply a story of an old man, almost the pathology of aging: the loss of memory (therefore the constant attempt to retrieve forgotten knowledge and the posting of notes and book clippings; doing unwise things such as taking a mountain tour in the fog and rain or cooking his cat after giving away all his frozen meat when the power failure temporarily made his freezer useless; cutting up his books and encyclopedias; repeating certain actions and sayings; living in the past, somewhat connected with his attempts to remember things). In the context of such a reading, all the references to history, geology, biology, and theology would be nothing but bits of knowledge that Herr Geiser tries to preserve or to recover. Even the title of the story would then allude to such knowledge only. But it would be a strange coincidence that all or much of this knowledge concern matters related to the life, survival, and death of man and of this planet. Or could Herr Geiser's choices be explained by his own general and particular situation, i.e., his age and the crisis caused by the rains? The last seven clippings reported by the narrator might provide an answer. They appear just before the end of the story, after all those pieces of paper had been blown to the floor.

There seems to be no other intrinsic motivation for presenting them at this juncture than their symbolism. They deal with the loss of fertile soil by erosion; the transplantation of the chestnut tree from Asia Minor to Greece, Rome, and the Alps, thus also to Herr Geiser's valley,[11] eschatology; cancer of the chestnut tree, first discovered, we learn, near New York City in 1904; the colonization of the Tessin by the Romans; and the symptoms of a brain stroke. Exactly in the middle of these clippings, between eschatology and cancer of the chestnut tree, the narrator places a definition of the philosophical concept of the "principle of coherence," according to which all being ("Das Seiende") is connected or related. This arrangement puts aging, the diseases of man and of civilizations into the context of the aging and the diseases of other parts of nature, at the same time, through the "principle of coherence," pointing beyond the boundaries of man and this earth. Mentioning the holocene again, the narrator signals the title of the story and alludes to the possible extinction of man.

There are two final points to be made here. The first concerns the relation between *Man in the Holocene* and other works by Max Frisch. It is no surprise that *Triptychon* and *Man in the Holocene* are closely related. Not only are they the two latest works published by Frisch—both of them deal with old age and death—but these two themes were already present in the *Tagebuch 1966-1971* as well as in *Montauk*. In the latter, brief mention is even made of *Man in the Holocene* as a work in progress. Frisch speaks of a narrative set in the Tessin, which "turned out a failure for the fourth time" because he feels that the "Erzähler-Position" (narrator position) is not convincing.[12] But besides the chronological proximity, *Triptychon* and *Man in the Holocene* have something else in common: the transcendence for which both Herr Geiser and the protagonists in *Triptychon* are searching reveals itself as an immanent transcendence. It is true that *Man in the Holocene* represents the cosmic extension, as it were, in which *Triptychon* as a play hardly succeeds—*Faust II* is the exception as well as the confirmation of this rule—but the search for that which transcends man's life characterizes both works. "Das also bleibt" (This then remains) are the final three words of *Triptychon*. And in typically antithetic Frisch style this statement implies its negation. For what remains is misunderstanding, reproach, guilt: nothing positive.

The end of *Man in the Holocene* is less pessimistic, at least on the surface or on the level of a realistic or factual reading of the text. The delugelike rain is over. Life in the valley has returned to normal: There is a blue sky, there are the white lines traced by airplanes above the mountains, butterflies, bees, and lizards in the sun; somebody is cutting trees with a chain saw, and the butcher's blond German wife is selling sausages and meats from her Volkswagen. "All in all a green valley, wooded as in the Stone Age. A dam is not planned. In August and September, at night, there are shooting stars and the hooting of an owl" (143). Life continues. There will be the same everyday routines. And men will keep hoping and waiting for the unusual, for happiness and good fortune (the folkloric symbol is the shooting star), and they will continue to be afraid of death (the traditional symbolism of the "Käuzchen," the screech owl which represents the very last word of the text). That which remains and transcends individual man in the one, mankind in the other work, is still of this world.

The second point concerns the relation between *Man in the Holocene* and Frisch's oeuvre as a whole. Are there thematic similarities? To mention the secondary theme first: Frisch's characters or protagonists often flee from the problems that confront them. Stiller does, as do Öderland, Faber, and Gantenbein in different ways. Herr Geiser tries to escape from his dilemma when he sets out on that strangely imprudent mountain-tour but returns to his house although he was close to his destination. This is strangely reminicent of Stiller who runs away from wife, friends, and job only to return and, after an initial resistance, to accept his former roles again.

But what about that dominant theme of "image-making" present in almost all of Max Frisch's works? Since normally with Frisch, image-making concerns the interhuman relationships and is closely related to his persistent topic of identity crisis, and since Herr Geiser is mostly by himself, image-making could only concern his former life and his memories. But this type of image-making with its effect on people's behavior towards each other certainly plays only a minor part in *Man in the Holocene*. But what other image-making is there? Man's image as it appears in the Bible? It is here that Frisch found this theme in the first place (Second Commandment), took it out of its religious context and psychologized it. What about man's image as it appears in the sciences? Or, going beyond all this, image-making in the sense of interaction between man and his environment? In the light of contemporary environmental concerns as well as the state and possibilities of nuclear physics, Frisch's theme of image making in its reciprocity and understood in a global or even universal sense would definitely apply to a narrative that shows man as a victim of nature. But man is not only a victim, he is also to quite an extent the maker of his world, a homo faber in a way different from, and at the same time similar to, Walter Faber, the engineer.

In closing, I want to return to an earlier remark in which I alluded to the musical structure of this narrative. I pointed out how the story developed and was broadened in scope from the old man to the valley, to the canton, to mankind, the planet earth and narrowed back down to the old man by introducing the appropriate signals in an acausal, theme-oriented way. I showed how in the very last, two-page paragraph the siege is over and life in the valley has returned to "normal." The seeming serenity of these final chords is broken, however, although very briefly, by four notes which evoke themes developed earlier. We hear of the cancer of the chestnut tree again, see a helicopter flying about in the valley and hear of passenger planes above the mountains. A remark about the changes in the glaciers turns all three signals into one direction: the threat of a global catastrophe caused by man. We remember an earlier passage dealing with the possibility of a second "deluge" created by the thawing of the Arctic ice (70, 103). And the beautiful white lines traced by airplanes on that blue sheet of sky above the mountains and their caps of ice and snow remind us that those white lines are potentially deadly since they contribute to the increase of carbon dioxide in our planet's atmosphere, creating the so-called greenhouse effect, a strangely and probably unintentionally sarcastic or paradoxical expression, resulting in a rise in the earth's temperature. The glaciers, the sky, and the chestnut tree still are beautiful. But underneath all this beauty and serenity an immense catastrophe is building up, and the narrator, to paraphrase T.S. Eliot, leaves the question open whether this world will end with a bang or with a whimper.

1. Frisch has always shown a predilection for symbolism or even punning in choosing his characters' names: Stiller/White, Öderland, Andri, Gantenbein/Enderlin, Ali, Lila, and Lilalil, Kürmann, Biedermann, just to name a few. "Geiser" alludes both to the Icelandic hot springs and to "Greis" (old man), maybe even "Geiss" ([mountain she-] goat). There is intrinsic reference to the former: Herr Geiser once took a trip to Iceland, which structurally plays an important part in the story (68ff.).

2. Numbers in parentheses refer to pagination in Max Frisch, *Der Mensch erscheint im Holozän: Eine Erzählung* (Frankfurt: Suhrkamp, 1979).

3. Somewhat tongue in cheek, Frisch imitates the manner of scholarly publications by supplying a bibliography. However, without naming the books from which Herr Geiser excerpts—at first with a pen and then with scissors—the reader would be incapable of that type of critical reading or "text concretization" described below.

4. Frisch's antithetical thinking to which I allude here always implies, or includes in the argumentation, the opposite of that which is stated. It could be called dialectic in a general way. It is well illustrated by his concept or theme of "image-making" discussed in my essay on the Gantenbein novel.

5. A few general remarks about Herr Geiser's excerpting technique may be in order here. A twofold selectivity can be observed. Not only are certain topics and articles chosen over others—obviously dependent on their relevance to Herr Geiser's existential situation as well as their inherent or intended symbolism—entire sections of the chosen articles are left out. The additional symbolic effect of this second type of selectivity sometimes is quite remarkable. One example must suffice. Under the heading "Mensch" (man or human being), the narrator reproduces verbatim from the Brockhaus encyclopedia passages dealing with man's ability to see himself as a subject in relation to an objective world (the *conditio sine qua non* for the text we are reading); man's attempt better to understand himself through divine beings, totems, spirits, or other alter egos; the extreme materialist view of man as a machine; man as a historical being shaped through traditions in the crafts, sciences, arts, morals, laws, and values; the difference between man and animal as to man's freer but at the same time problematic relation to his environment, characterized by his ability to project into the future ("man has a future"). The fact that this article on "Mensch" appears exactly in the middle of *Der Mensch erscheint im Holozän* (71-72), especially with the quotation concerning the future of man, can hardly be accidental and must be interpreted as an ironical implicit reference to an anthropocentric world view, to the title of the narrative, and to man's questionable chances of survival—antithetically even to the often invoked "Verlust der Mitte" (loss of the center) of modern man.

Left out from the "Mensch" article as it appears in the *Grosse Brockhaus* (7: 679 ff.) are the discussion of language, man's physical or somatic characteristics, the relationship between homo sapiens and other hominids as well as the history of the prehominids over the last five million years. The question arises why these passages are omitted. Do they distract from the main theme or themes? I would think so, especially since the "Mensch" article is directly preceded by a relatively long account of Herr Geiser's impressions of Iceland: large areas of almost complete barrenness reminding one of an "Urlandschaft" ("world before the creation of man," 70), enormous glaciers, volcanoes, lava, a new volcanic island rising out of the ocean and with birds as its first inhabitants. The account ends with the prophetic statement, "the fish will probably survive us, and the birds" (70), which is followed immediately by the "Mensch" article.

The "Bezugsfeld" (field of reference; see note 8) for all of these signals seems to be the future of man with implicit questions about those qualities and skills either enabling him to survive or contributing to his extinction. Language, however, or his relationship to other hominids or primates do not seem to be relevant in this regard. Therefore the gaps.

A final interesting point in this context concerns the difference in the "Bezugsfeld" (see above) of "Sachtext" (text dealing with factual information) and fictional text. What are the effects of incorporating—as Frisch does here—parts of a "Sachtext" into a fictional text? Are they mutual or one-directional? In other words, does the fictional text alter the quality of the "Sachtext" or vice versa? Obviously, facts remain facts whether they relate to history, geology, or biology. But the context in which they appear in a fictional text gives them a function other than the statement of facts: they point beyond their factuality.

6. See: Gerhard F. Probst, Alteristisches Erzählen: Beziehungen zwischen Struktur und Thematik der deutschen Nachkriegsliteratur, Wolfgang Elfe et al., eds., *Deutsche Exilliteratur-Nachkriegsliteratur. Akten des III. Exilliteratur-Symposiums der University of South Carolina (Jahrbuch für Internationale Germanistik* A 10) (Berne: Lang, 1981), pp. 88-95.

7. Seltsam, im Nebel zu wandern! / Einsam ist jeder Busch und Stein, / Kein Baum sieht den andern, / Jeder ist allein.

Voll von Freunden war mir die Welt, / Als noch mein Leben licht war; / Nun, da der Nebel fällt, / Ist keiner mehr sichtbar.

Wahrlich, keiner ist weise, / Der nicht das Dunkel kennt, / Das unentrinnbar und leise / Von allen ihn trennt.

Seltsam, im Nebel zu wandern! / Leben ist Einsamsein. / Kein Mensch kennt den andern, / Jeder ist allein.

Strange to walk in the fog! / Every bush and stone is lonesome, / no tree sees the other, / each is alone.

For me the world was full of friends / while my life was yet light; / now that the fog is falling, / none is in sight.

Truly, none is wise / who does not know the darkness / which inescapably and gently separates him from others.

Strange, to walk in the fog! / Life is loneliness. / No man knows the other, / each is alone.

8. This secularization of religious images or symbols is most obvious in Frisch's concept or theme of "image-making."

9. For the concepts of "Umfeld" and Bezugsfeld," see Karl Bühler, *Sprachtheorie* (Stuttgart: Gustav Fischer, 1965), pp. 154 ff., and Johannes Anderegg, *Fiktion und Kommunikation: Ein Beitrag zur Theorie der Prosa* (Sammlung Vandenhoeck) (Göttingen: Vandenhoeck & Ruprecht, 1973), p. 18.

10. I have discussed water symbolism extensively in my article "Conrad Ferdinand Meyers Gedicht Der römische Brunnen und Goethes Gesang der Geister über den Wassern," in *German Quarterly* 47 (1974): 233-44.

11. The name of the valley, Valle Onsernone, appears relatively late and almost as hidden away as the valley itself (67).

12. Max Frisch, *Montauk: Eine Erzählung* (Frankfurt: Suhrkamp, 1975), p. 21.

GERHARD F. PROBST

Max Frisch Bibliography

The following bibliography omits articles by, or about, Max Frisch which were published in daily newspapers only. Occasionally, a newspaper article is listed if it later appeared in a different form. Primary literature is listed in chronological order, including English translations; secondary literature, in alphabetical order. The latter is alphabetically arranged on two levels: subsections, according to the titles of the individual works treated and then within the different sections, according to the names of authors.

CONTENTS

PRIMARY LITERATURE
    Narrative Prose   178
    Plays   179
    Essays   179
    Abridged Editions, Collections, Revised Versions   179
    Recordings   181
    English Editions or Translations   181
    Articles, Prefaces, Epilogues   182
SECONDARY LITERATURE
    Books   188
        General   188
        Drama   189
        Narrative   190
        Individual Works   190
    Dissertations and Theses   191
    Articles, Interviews, Reviews   193
        General   193
        Drama in General   199
        Narrative in General   201
        Individual Works   202
            Als der Krieg zu Ende war   202
            Andorra   203
            Antwort aus der Stille   205
            Biedermann und die Brandstifter   205
            Bin oder Die Reise nach Peking   207
            Biografie: Ein Spiel   207
            Blätter aus dem Brotsack   209
            Der Mensch erscheint im Holozän   209
            Die Chinesische Mauer   209
            Die grosse Wut des Philipp Hotz   210
            Dienstbüchlein   210
            Die Schwierigen oder J'adore ce qui me brûle   210
            Don Juan oder Die Liebe zur Geometrie   211
            Graf Öderland   212

Homo faber 212
Mein Name sei Gantenbein 214
Montauk 217
Nun singen sie wieder 217
Santa Cruz. Eine Romanze 218
Schinz 218
Stiller 218
Tagebuch mit Marion, Tagebuch 1946-1949, Tagebuch 1966-1971 221
Triptychon 223
Wilhelm Tell für die Schule 223
Zürich-Transit 223
MUSICAL COMPOSITION
Die grosse Wut des Philipp Hotz 223

PRIMARY LITERATURE

Narrative Prose

Jürg Reinhart. Eine sommerliche Schicksalsfahrt: Roman aus Dalmatien. Stuttgart: Deutsche Verlagsanstalt, 1934.
Antwort aus der Stille. Erzählung aus den Bergen. Stuttgart: Deutsche Verlagsanstalt, 1937.
Blätter aus dem Brotsack. Tagebuch eines Kanoniers: Geschrieben im Grenzdienst 1939, Zürich: Atlantis, 1940.
J'adore ce qui me brûle oder Die Schwierigen: Roman. Zürich: Atlantis, 1943.
Bin oder Die Reise nach Peking. Zürich: Atlantis, 1945.
Marion und die Marionetten. Ein Fragment. Mit Holzschnitten von Hanns Studer. Basel: Linder, 1946 (Papillons-Handdrucke der Gryff-Presse 7).
Tagebuch mit Marion. Zürich: Atlantis, 1947.
Tagebuch 1946-1949. Frankfurt: Suhrkamp, 1950.
Stiller: Roman. Frankfurt: Suhrkamp, 1954.
Homo faber. Ein Bericht. Frankfurt: Suhrkamp, 1957.
Glossen zu Don Juan. Illustrationen von Walter Jonas. Viernheim, Zürich: Viernheim-Verlag, 1959.
Schinz. Skizze. Mit 5 Zeichnungen von Varlin. St. Gallen: Tschudy, 1959 (Die Quadrat-Bücher 7).
Mein Name sei Gantenbein: Roman. Frankfurt: Suhrkamp, 1964.
Zürich-Transit. Skizze eines Films. Frankfurt: Suhrkamp, 1966 (edition suhrkamp 161).
Wilhelm Tell für die Schule. Mit alten Illustrationen. Frankfurt: Suhrkamp, 1971.
Tagebuch 1966-1971. Frankfurt: Suhrkamp, 1972.
Glück: Erzählung. Mit drei Holzschnitten von Sven Knebel. Zürich: Brunnenturm-Presse, 1972.
Dienstbüchlein. Frankfurt: Suhrkamp, 1974 (suhrkamp taschenbuch 205).
Montauk. Eine Erzählung. Frankfurt: Suhrkamp, 1975.
Zitat. Mit 7 Holzdrucken von Gottfried Honegger, ed. Sybil Albers. Zürich: Verlag 3, 1976.

Der Mensch erscheint im Holozän. Eine Erzählung. Frankfurt: Suhrkamp, 1979.
Blaubart. Frankfurt: Suhrkamp. 1982.

Plays

Nun singen sie wieder. Versuch eines Requiems. Basel: Schwabe, 1946 (Premiere Zürich, 1945).
Santa Cruz. Eine Romanze. Basel: Schwabe, 1947 (Premiere Zürich, 1946).
Die Chinesische Mauer, Eine Farce. Basel: Schwabe, 1947 (Premiere Zürich, 1946).
Als der Krieg zu Ende war. Basel: Schwabe, 1949 (Premiere Zürich, 1949).
Graf Öderland. Ein Spiel in zehn Bildern. Frankfurt: Suhrkamp, 1951 (Premiere Zürich, 1951).
Don Juan oder Die Liebe zur Geometrie: Komödie in fünf Akten. Frankfurt: Suhrkamp, 1953 (Premiere Berlin and Zürich, 1953).
Herr Biedermann und die Brandstifter. Radio play. Hamburg: Hans-Bredow-Institut, 1956 (Hörwerke der Zeit 2; Broadcast Hamburg, 1953).
Biedermann und die Brandstifter. Ein Lehrstück ohne Lehre. Mit einem Nachspiel. Frankfurt: Suhrkamp, 1958 (Premiere Zürich, 1958).
Die grosse Wut des Philipp Hotz. Ein Schwank. Frankfurt: Suhrkamp, 1958 (Premiere together with *Biedermann* Zürich, 1958).
Andorra. Stück in zwölf Bildern. Frankfurt: Suhrkamp, 1961 (Premiere Zürich, 1961).
Biografie: Ein Spiel. Frankfurt: Suhrkamp, 1967 (Premiere Zürich, 1968).
Rip van Winkle. Radio play. Stuttgart: Reclam, 1969 (Broadcast München/Baden-Baden/Bremen, 1953).
Triptychon. Drei szenische Bilder. Frankfurt: Suhrkamp, 1978.

Essays

Öffentlichkeit als Partner. Frankfurt: Suhrkamp, 1967 (edition suhrkamp 209).
Errinnerungen an Brecht. Berlin: Friedenauer Presse, 1968 (appeared first in *Kursbuch 7*).
Dramaturgisches. Ein Briefwechsel mit Walter Höllerer. Berlin: Literarisches Colloquium, 1969 (LCB-Editionen 15).
Ansprache anlässlich der Verleihung des Friedenspreises des Deutschen Buchhandels. Frankfurt: Verlag der Buchhändler-Vereinigung, 1976 (also in *Zwei Reden zum Friedenspreis des Deutschen Buchhandels, 1976*; Max Frisch, *Wir hoffen*; Hartmut von Hentig, *Wahrheitsarbeit und Friede.* Frankfurt: Suhrkamp, 1976; edition suhrkamp 874).

Abridged Editions, Collections, Revised Versions

Die Chinesische Mauer (revised version), Frankfurt: Suhrkamp, 1955 (Premiere Berlin, 1955); production of unpublished second revised version Hamburg Schauspielhaus, 1965.
Graf Öderland (unpublished revised version, premiere Frankfurt, 1956).
Die Schwierigen oder J'adore ce qui me brûle: Roman (revised version of the 1943 novel, leaving out the first part "Reinhart oder Die Jugend"). Zürich: Atlantis, 1957.

Graf Öderland. Eine Moritat in zwölf Bildern (second revised version). Frankfurt: Suhrkamp, 1961 (Premiere Berlin, 1961).
Ausgewählte Prosa (ed. with epilogue by J. Kaiser). Frankfurt: Suhrkamp, 1961 (suhrkamp texte 6).
Erzählungen des Anatol Ludwig Stiller (*Stiller* excerpts with epilogue by W. Jens). Frankfurt: Suhrkamp, 1961 (suhrkamp texte 5).
Don Juan oder Die Liebe zur Geometrie (revised version). Frankfurt: Suhrkamp, 1962.
Geschichte von Isidor (in *Deutschland erzählt.* 46 Erzählungen, ed. B. v. Wiese, Frankfurt: Fischer, 1962; Fischer-Bücherei 500).
Stücke vol. 1 (Santa Cruz. Nun singen sie wieder. Die Chinesische Mauer. Als der Krieg zu Ende war—without original third act. Graf Öderland). Frankfurt: Suhrkamp, 1962.
Stücke vol. 2 (Don Juan oder Die Liebe zur Geometrie. Biedermann und die Brandstifter. Die grosse Wut des Philipp Hotz. Andorra). Frankfurt: Suhrkamp, 1962.
Dramen, with epilogue by W. Zeleny (Die Chineseische Mauer. Biedermann und die Brandstifter. Don Juan oder Die Liebe zur Geometrie. Andorra). Zürich: Schweizer Verlagshaus, 1967 (Neue Schweizer Bibliothek).
Biedermann und die Brandstifter (Zurich dialect version by Emil Bader). Wädenswil: Emil Bader, 1970.
Stücke 1 (as above, but with the so-called Version für Paris of *Graf Öderland*). Frankfurt: Suhrkamp, 1972 (suhrkamp taschenbuch 70).
Stücke 2 (as above, but with addition of *Biografie*). Frankfurt: Suhrkamp, 1973 (suhrkamp taschenbuch 81).
Frühe Stücke (Santa Cruz. Nun singen sie wieder). Frankfurt: Suhrkamp, 1966 (edition suhrkamp 154).
Stücke, with epilogue by J. Archipow (Nun singen sie wieder. Graf Öderland. Biedermann und die Brandstifter. Andorra). Leipzig: Reclam, 1973 (Reclams Universalbibliothek 430).
Aus einem Tagebuch und Reden, with epilogue by H. Kähler (from: Tagebuch 1946–1949. Ausgewählte Prosa. Öffentlichkeit als Partner). Berlin, DDR: Volk und Welt, 1974 (Volk-und-Welt-Spektrum 71).
Dienstbüchlein. Wilhelm Tell für die Schule. Zürich: Buchclub Ex Libris, 1975.
Meisterdramen (Nun singen sie wieder. Graf Öderland. Don Juan oder Die Liebe zur Geometrie. Biedermann und die Brandstifter. Andorra). Stuttgart: Europäische Buchgemeinschaft, 1975.
Stich-Worte. Ausgesucht von Uwe Johnson. Frankfurt: Suhrkamp, 1975.
Gesammelte Werke in zeitlicher Folge, ed. H. Mayer with collab. of W. Schmitz. Frankfurt: Suhrkamp, 1976. 6 vols.
  Vol. 1: 1931–1944. Kleine Prosaschriften. Blätter aus dem Brotsack. Jürg Reinhart. Die Schwierigen oder J'adore ce qui me brûle. Bin oder die Reise nach Peking.
  Vol. 2. 1944–1949: Santa Cruz. Nun singen sie wieder. Die Chinesische Mauer. Als der Krieg zu Ende war. Kleine Prosaschriften. Tagebuch 1946–1949.
  Vol. 3. 1949–1956: Graf Öderland. Don Juan oder Die Liebe zur Geometrie. Kleine Prosaschriften. Der Laie und die Architektur. Achtung: Die Schweiz. Stiller. Rip van Winkle.
  Vol. 4. 1947–1963. Homo faber. Kleine Prosaschriften. Herr Biedermann und die Brandstifter. Biedermann und die Brandstifter: Mit einem Nachspiel. Die grosse Wut des Philipp Hotz. Andorra.

Vol. 5. 1964-1967: Mein Name sei Gantenbein. Kleine Prosaschriften. Zürich-Transit. Biografie: Ein Spiel.
Vol. 6. 1968-1975: Tagebuch 1966-1971. Wilhelm Tell für die Schule. Kleine Prosaschriften. Dienstbüchlein. Montauk.

Gesammelte Werke in zeitlicher Folge (Werkausgabe Edition Suhrkamp in 12 volumes), ed. H. Mayer with collab. of W. Schmitz. Frankfurt: Suhrkamp, 1976.

Part 1: 1931-1944. 2 vols.
  Vol.1: Kleine Prosaschriften. Blätter aus dem Brotsack. Jürg Reinhart.
  Vol.2: Die Schwierigen oder J'adore ce qui me brûle. Bin oder Die Reise nach Peking.

Part 2: 1944-1949. 2 vols.
  Vol.1: Santa Cruz. Nun singen sie wieder. Die Chinesische Mauer. Als der Krieg zu Ende war. Kleine Prosaschriften.
  Vol.2: Tagebuch 1946-1949.

Part 3: 1949-1956. 2 vols.
  Vol.1: Graf Öderland. Don Juan oder Die Liebe zur Geometrie. Kleine Prosaschriften. Der Laie und die Architektur. Achtung: Die Schweiz.
  Vol.2: Stiller. Rip van Winkle.

Part 4: 1957-1963. 2 vols.
  Vol.1: Homo faber. Kleine Prosaschriften.
  Vol.2: Herr Biedermann und die Brandstifter. Biedermann und die Brandstifter: Mit einem Nachspiel. Die grosse Wut des Philipp Hotz. Andorra.

Part 5: 1964-1967. 2 vols.
  Vol.1: Mein Name sei Gantenbein.
  Vol.2: Kleine Prosaschriften. Zürich-Transit. Biografie: Ein Spiel.

Part 6: 1968-1975. 2 vols.
  Vol.1: Tagebuch 1966-1971.
  Vol.2: Wilhelm Tell für die Schule. Kleine Prosaschriften. Dienstbüchlein. Montauk.

Recordings

Max Frisch liest Prosa: Isidor (aus dem Roman *Stiller*). Der andorranische Jude (aus dem *Tagebuch 1946-1949*). Tonband (aus einem unveröffentlichten Roman). Zürich: Disco-Club, Europäischer Platten-Club, 1960 (Archiv der gesprochenen Dichtung der Schweizerischen Schiller-Stiftung).

Max Frisch liest Prosa: Isidor (aus dem Roman *Stiller*). Der andorranische Jude (aus dem *Tagebuch 1946-1949*). Tonband (Prosaskizze), Frankfurt: Suhrkamp, 1961.

Mein Name sei Gantenbein. Der Dichter liest aus seinem Roman. Hamburg: Deutsche Grammophon-Gesellschaft, 1965 (DGG. Literarisches Archiv).

Max Frisch: Wir hoffen. Rede zum Friedenspreis des deutschen Buchhandels 1976. Frankfurt: Suhrkamp, 1976.

English Editions or Translations

I'm Not Stiller, tr. Michael Bullock, London: Abelard-Schumann, 1958; Penguin Books, 1961; New York: Vintage, 1962.

Homo faber, tr. Michael Bullock. London: Abelard-Schumann, 1959; Penguin Books, 1974; New York: Harcourt, Brace, Jovanovich, 1971.
The Chinese Wall, tr. Harold Clurman. New York: Hill and Wang, 1961.
Three Plays (The Fire Raisers, Count Oederland, Andorra), tr. Michael Bullock. London: Methuen, 1962.
The Fire Raisers: a morality without a moral, with an afterpiece, tr. Michael Bullock. London: Methuen, 1962.
The Firebugs, a learning-play without a lesson, tr. Mordecai Gorelik. New York: Hill and Wang, 1963.
Biedermann und die Brandstifter, ed. Paul K. Ackermann. Boston: Houghton Mifflin, 1963.
Andorra, tr. Michael Bullock. London: Methuen, 1964; New York: Hill and Wang, 1964 (A Spotlight Drama Book, SD 7).
Andorra, ed. H.F. Garten. London: Methuen, 1964.
A Wilderness of Mirrors (Gantenbein), tr. Michael Bullock. London: Methuen, 1965; New York: Random House, 1966.
Graf Öderland. Eine Moritat in 12 Bildern, ed. George Salamon. New York: Harcourt, Brace and World, 1966.
Nun singen sie wieder, ed. W. F. Tulasiewicz and K. Scheible. London: Harrap, 1966.
Als der Krieg zu Ende war, ed. Stuart Friebert. New York: Dodd and Mead, 1967.
Three Plays (Don Juan, or The Love of Geometry; The Great Rage of Philip Hotz; When the War Was Over), tr. James L. Rosenberg. New York: Hill and Wang, 1967.
The Great Fury of Philip Hotz, tr. Michael Benedikt (in *Postwar German Theatre.* An Anthology of Plays, ed. M. Benedikt and G.E. Wellwarth. New York: Dutton, 1967.
Ausgewählte Prosa, ed. Stanley Corngold. New York: Harcourt, Brace and World, 1968 (edition suhrkamp in American text editions).
Four Plays (The Great Wall of China; Don Juan, or the Love of Geometry; Philipp Hotz's Fury; Biography: A Game), tr. Michael Bullock. London: Methuen, 1969.
Biografie: Ein Spiel, ed. Ulrich Weisstein. New York: Harcourt, Brace, Jovanovich, 1972 (edition suhrkamp in American text editions).
Biography: A Game, tr. Michael Bullock. New York: Hill and Wang, 1969.
Homo faber, ed. Paul K. Ackermann. Boston: Houghton Mifflin, 1973.
Now They Sing Again, in *The Contemporary German Theater,* ed. M. Roloff, tr. David Lommen. New York: Avon Books, 1972.
Montauk, tr. Geoffrey Skelton. New York: Harcourt, Brace, Jovanovich, 1976 (Helen and Kurt Wolff Books).
Sketchbook 1966-1971, tr. Geoffrey Skelton. New York: Harcourt, Brace, Jovanovich, 1974 (Helen and Kurt Wolff Books). London: Methuen, 1974.
Sketchbook 1946-1949, tr. Geoffrey Skelton. New York: Harcourt, Brace, Jovanovich, 1977 (Helen and Kurt Wolff Books).
"Man in the Holocene," tr. Geoffrey Skelton (in *New Yorker* 56, 19 May 1980).
Man in the Holocene. A Story, tr. Geoffrey Skelton. New York: Harcourt, Brace, Jovanovich, 1980 (Helen and Kurt Wolff Books).

Articles, Prefaces, Epilogues

Was bin ich? (in *Zürcher Student* 10, 1932-33).
Ich erwarte Post (in *Zürcher Student* 10, 1932-33).

Bibliography

Werkstudent (in *Zürcher Student* 11, 1933-34).
Vivant professores. Porträtchen in Worten (in *Zürcher Illustrierte* 28 April 1933).
Wie ich uns sehe: Ein Student über Studenten und Studentisches (in *Zürcher Illustrierte*, 28 April 1933).
Tage des Ruhmes. Skizze (in *Zürcher Illustrierte*, 1 Sept. 1933).
Zehn Schweizer über schweizerische Eigenart (in *Zürcher Illustrierte*, 27 Oct. 1933).
Menschen sehen dich an (in *Zürcher Illustrierte*, 5 Jan. 1934).
Ball (in *Zürcher Illustrierte*, 16 Feb. 1934).
Kurzgeschichte (in *Zürcher Illustrierte*, 27 April 1934).
Was ist eine Freundin? (in *Zürcher Illustrierte*, 1 June 1934).
Wann war ich am mutigsten? Eine Rundfrage und ihr Ergebnis (in *Zürcher Illustrierte*, 27 July 1934).
Eines Sommers. Kleine Feriengeschichte (in *Zürcher Illustrierte*, 3 Aug. 1934).
Vorbild Huber. Ein novellistischer Beitrag (in *Zürcher Illustrierte*, 31 Aug., 7, 14 September 1934).
Ist Kultur eine Privatsache? Grundsätzliches zur Schauspielhausfrage (in *Zürcher Student* 16, 1938-39).
Aus dem Taschenbuch eines Soldaten (in *Atlantis* 11, 1939).
Kunst der Erwartung. Anmerkungen eines Architekten (in *DU* 1, no. 5, 1941).
Von neuen Schweizerbüchern (in *Neue Schweizer Rundschau*, n.s. 9, 1941-42).
Albin Zollinger. Zu seinem Gedächtnis (in *Neue Schweizer Rundschau*, n.s. 9, 1941-42).
Blick in neue Schweizerbücher (in *Neue Schweizer Rundschau*, n.s. 9, 1941-42).
Anmerkungen zu neuen Schweizerbüchern (in *Neue Schweizer Rundschau*, n.s. 10, 1942-43).
Albin Zollinger als Erzähler. Zu seinem Todestag am 7. November (in *Neue Schweizer Rundschau*, n.s. 10, 1942-43).
Cécile Ines Loos: "Hinter dem Mond" (in *Neue Schweizer Rundschau*, n.s. 10, 1942-43).
Vom Arbeiten (in *Neue Schweizer Rundschau*, n.s. 11, 1943-44).
Nun singen sie wieder. Preface to the premiere (in *Programmhefte des Schauspielhauses Zürich*, 1944-45).
Notizen über Geträumtes (in *Programmhefte des Schauspielhauses Zürich*, 1944-45).
Die andere Welt (in *Atlantis* 17, 1945).
Santa Cruz. Preface to the premiere (in *Programmhefte des Schauspielhauses Zürich*, 1945-46).
Verdammen oder Verzeihen? (in *Neue Schweizer Rundschau*, n.s. 13, 1945-46).
Über Zeitereignis und Dichtung (in *Programmhefte des Schauspielhauses Zürich*, 1944-45).
Stimmen eines anderen Deutschland? Zu den Zeugnissen von Wiechert und Bergengruen (in *Neue Schweizer Rundschau*, n.s. 13, 1945-46).
Du sollst dir kein Bildnis machen (in *Schweizer Annalen* 3, 1946-47).
Death is so permanent (in *Neue Schweizer Rundschau*, n.s. 14, 1946-47).
Ferngesteuerte Ruinen (in *Athena* 2, nr. 8, 1946-47).
Zu Bert Brecht: Furcht und Elend des Dritten Reiches (in *Schweizer Annalen* 3, 1946-47).
Santa Cruz. Ein Vorwort (in *Programmhefte des Schauspielhauses Zürich*, 1945-46).
Wo spielt unser Stück? Brief an die Darstellerin einer Nebenrolle. On the occasion of the premiere of Die Chinesische Mauer (in *Programmhefte des Schauspielhauses Zürich*, 1946-47).
Drei Entwürfe zu einem Brief nach Deutschland (in *Die Wandlung* 2, 1947).

Kleines Nachwort zu einer Ansprache von Thomas Mann (in *Zürcher Student* 25, 1947).
Marion. Aus einem Skizzenbuch (in *DU* 7, nr. 3, 1947).
Was bin ich? (in *Schweizerspiegel* 23, nr. 10, 1948).
Als der Krieg zu Ende war. Preface to the premiere (in *Programmhefte des Schauspielhauses Zürich*, 1948-49).
Kultur als Alibi (in *Der Monat* 1, nr. 7, 1948-49).
Selbstanzeige (in *Atlantis Almanach 1949*. Zürich: Atlantis, 1948).
Friedrich Dürrenmatt. Zu seinem neuen Stück "Romulus der Grosse" (in *Die Weltwoche*, 6 May 1949).
Spanien: Im ersten Eindruck (in *Atlantis* 23, 1951).
Orchideen und Aasgeier. Ein Reisealbum aus Mexico, Oktober/November 1951 (in *Neue Schweizer Rundschau*, n.s. 20, 1952-53).
Glossen (in R.S. Gessner, *Sieben Lithographien*. Zürich: Private printing, 1952).
Unsere Arroganz gegenüber Amerika (in *Neue Schweizer Rundschau*, n.s. 20, 1952-53); also in Max Frisch, *Öffentlichkeit als Partner*).
Preface to L. Burckhardt and M. Kutter, *Wir selber bauen unsere Stadt*. Basel: Handschin, 1953).
Aus Notizen zu "Don Juan" (in *Programmhefte des Schauspielhauses Zürich*, 1952-53).
Cum grano salis. Eine kleine Glosse zur schweizerischen Architektur (in *Werk* 40, 1953).
Ist das Bühnenstück eine Lektüre? (in *Domino* 1, 1953).
Nachtrag zum transatlantischen Gespräch (in *Der Monat* 3, 1953).
Epilogue to H. Hearson and J.C. Trewin, *Euer Gnaden haben geschossen*, tr. H. Diessel. Zürich: Diogenes, 1954).
Begegnung mit Negern. Eindrücke aus Amerika (in *Atlantis* 26, 1954).
Firlefanz und Vision (in *Die Zeit*, 17 Sept. 1954).
Planung tut not; Diskussion um die neue Schweizerstadt (in *Die Weltwoche*, 29 April 1955).
Zur Chinesischen Mauer (in *Akzente* 2, 1955; also in *Programmhefte des Schauspielhauses Zürich*, 1955-56).
Der Laie und die Architektur (in *Merkur* 9, 1955).
Brecht als Klassiker (in *Dichten und Trachten* 6, 1955).
Achtung: Die Schweiz. Ein Gespräch über unsere Lage und ein Vorschlag zur Tat (co-authors L. Burckhardt and M. Kutter). Basel: Handschin, 1955.
Wiener Tagebuch (in *Deutsche Universitätszeitung* 10, 1955).
Die neue Stadt. Beiträge zur Diskussion (co-authors L. Burkhardt and M. Kutter). Basel: Handschin, 1956.
Vom Zu-Hause-Sein in unserer Zeit (lecture series of the Bavarian Broadcasting System, published in *Der Mensch in der Welt von heute und morgen*. Munich: Bremberger, 1956.
Kurzbiographie (in *Programmhefte der Städtischen Bühnen Frankfurt am Main. Schauspiel*, 1955-56; on the occasion of the premiere of the second version of "Graf Öderland").
Vom Umgang mit dem Einfall (ibid.).
Zu Graf Öderland (ibid.).
Brecht ist tot (in *Die Weltwoche*, 24 Aug. 1956).
Eine Chance der modernen Architektur vertan! (in *Die Weltwoche*, 14 Sept. 1956).
Soll Zürich einen Kopf haben? Neugestaltung der Seeuferpartie am Bürkli- und Bellevueplatz (in *Die Weltwoche*, 5 Oct. 1956).
Fort Worth. Die Stadt der Zukunft in Texas (in *Die Weltwoche*, 16 Nov. 1956).

Festrede zum Nationalfeiertag am 1. August 1957 im Industriequartier Zürich (in *Zürcher Woche*, 9 Aug. 1957; also in Max Frisch, *Öffentlichkeit als Partner*).
Notizen zu Biedermann und Hotz (in *Programmhefte des Schauspielhauses Zürich*, 1957-58).
Was ist komisch? (in *Programmhefte des Schauspielhauses Zürich*, 1957-58).
Man müsste Hände haben (in *Programmhefte des Schauspielhauses Zürich*, 1957-58).
Zur Uraufführung eines neuen Werkes (in *Die Weltwoche*, 21 March 1958).
Öffentlichkeit als Partner. Rede zur Eröffnung der Frankfurter Buchmesse 1958 (in *Börsenblatt für den deutschen Buchhandel* 14, 1958; also in Max Frisch, *Öffentlichkeit als Partner*).
Rede zur Verleihung des Georg-Büchner-Preises 1958 (in *Jahrbuch 1958 der Deutschen Akademie für Sprache und Dichtung Darmstadt*. Heidelberg: Lambert Schneider, 1959; also in Max Frisch, *Öffentlichkeit als Partner*; also under the title "Emigranten" in *Beiträge zum zwanzigjahrigen Bestehen der Neuen Schauspiel A.G. Zürich*. Zürich: Genossenschaftsdruckerei, 1958; also in *Club Voltaire, Jahrbuch für kritische Aufklärung* 1, 1963).
Preface to the *Catalogue of the Varlin Exhibit*. St. Gallen: Kunstmuseum, 1958.
Warum der Schriftsteller schreibt (in *Die Weltwoche*, 19 Dec. 1958).
Notiz zu Brecht (in Bertolt Brecht, *Drei Gedichte*: Erinnerung an Marie A., Legende von der Entstehung des Buches Taoteking auf dem Wege des Laotse in die Emigration, An die Nachgeborenen. With drawings by Beni Schalcher, ed. Bruno Margadant. Zürich: Schalcher, 1959).
Wie soll man neue Theater bauen? (in *Die Weltwoche*, 22 April 1960).
Das Lesen und der Bücherfreund (in *Das kleine Buch der hundert Bücher* 8, 1960; abridged version under the title "Unsere Gier nach Geschichten" in *Die Weltwoche*, 4 Nov. 1960).
Ihr grösstes künstlerisches Erlebnis. Silvesterumfrage *Weltwoche* an zwölf bekannte Persönlichkeiten (in *Die Weltwoche*, 30 Dec. 1960).
Die Schweiz ist ein Land ohne Utopie (in *Ex Libris* 15, 1960).
Nachruf auf Peter Suhrkamp (in *In memoriam Peter Suhrkamp*. Frankfurt: Suhrkamp, 1960).
Nachruf auf Albin Zollinger, den Dichter und Landsmann, nach zwanzig Jahren (in A. Zollinger, *Gesammelte Prosa* [Gesammelte Werke I]. Zurich: Atlantis, 1961).
Kleines Memorandum zu Graf Öderland (in Ludwig Mennel, Max Frisch. Aufrichtigkeit gegenüber dem Lebendigen, *Literatur-Revue*, 1961).
Meditationen über Freiheit und Vergangenheit (in *Deutsche Woche*, 10 May 1961).
Schriftsteller antworten ... (in *Die Zeit*, 10 Nov. 1961).
Anmerkungen zu Andorra (in *Programmhefte des Schauspielhauses Zürich*, 1961-62).
Werkbericht zum "Öderland 3" (in *Blätter des Schiller-Theaters Berlin*, 1961-62).
Das Paar (in *Jahresring*, 1961-62).
Notizen zu den Proben der Zürcher Aufführung von Andorra (in *Theater-Wahrheit und Wirklichkeit*. Freundesgabe zum 60. Geburtstag von Kurt Hirschfeld am 10. März 1962).
Exposé (in *Wettbewerb für einen Neubau des Schauspielhauses Zürich*. Zürich: Bauamt II der Stadt Zürich, 1963).
Teo Otto (in Teo Otto, *Skizzen eines Bühnenbildners*. St. Gallen: Tschudy, 1964; Quadratbücher 35).
Theater und Gesellschaft (in *Theater heute* 5, 1964).
Rede zum Tode von Kurt Hirschfeld (in *Theater heute* 5, 1964).

Ich schreibe für Leser (in *Dichten und Trachten* 24, 1964).
Der Autor und das Theater. Rede auf der Frankfurter Dramaturgentagung 1964 (in *Neue Rundschau* 76, 1965; also in Max Frisch, *Öffentlichkeit als Partner*).
Unbewältigte schweizerische Vergangenheit (in *Neutralität* 3, 1965; also in *Die Weltwoche*, 11 March 1966).
Ansprache zur Verleihung des Preises der Stadt Jerusalem (in *Die Weltwoche*, 23 April 1965).
Preface to Alexander J. Seiler, *Siamo italiani/ Die Italiener. Gespräche mit italienischen Arbeitern in der Schweiz*. Zürich: EVZ-Verlag, 1965 (also in *Die Weltwoche*, 10 December 1965).
Chinesische Mauer 1965 (in *Programmhefte des Deutschen Schauspielhauses in Hamburg*, 1964-65).
Grass als Redner (in *Die Zeit*, 24 Sept. 1965).
Überfremdung (in *Die Weltwoche*, 9 Sept. 1966).
Was steht zur Wahl (in *Zürcher Woche*, 4 March 1966).
Film als Einsicht (in "Abschied von gestern." Fünf Stimmen zu Alexander Kluges erstem Film, *Die Weltwoche*, 18 Nov. 1966).
Endlich darf man es wieder sagen. Eine Antwort an Emil Staiger (in *Die Weltwoche*, 23 Dec. 1966; also in *Sprache im technischen Zeitalter* 22, 1967 under the title "Eine Antwort an Emil Staiger"; also in Max Frisch, *Öffentlichkeit als Partner*).
Preface to G. Suter, *Die grossen Städte. Was sie zerstört und was sie retten kann*. Bergisch-Gladbach: Gustav Lübbe, 1966.
−nicht immer, aber oft−. Nachtrag zum Gespräch über Emil Staigers Rede, "Literatur und Öffentlichkeit" (in *Sprache im technischen Zeitalter* 22, 1967).
Notizen (in *DU* 27, 1967).
Griechenland 1967 (unter anderem) und wir (in *Die Weltwoche*, 2 June 1967).
Skizze (in Drei Begegnungen mit Günter Eich, *Merkur* 21, 1967).
Illusion zweiten Grades (in *Christ und Welt*, 19 Jan. 1967).
Schillerpreisrede (in Max Frisch, *Öffentlichkeit als Partner*).
Rede nach der Besetzung der Tschechoslowakei (in *Tschechoslowakei 1968*. Zürich: Die Arche, 1968; Edition "Arche Nova").
In eigner Sache. On the premiere of Biografie (in *Programmhefte des Schauspielhauses Zürich*, 1967-68).
Jemand hat sich geirrt (in *Zürcher Student* 46, 1968-69).
Schriftsteller, Johnson und Vietnam (in *Die Weltwoche*, 5 April 1968).
Demokratie ohne Opposition (in *Die Weltwoche*, 11 April 1968).
Politik durch Mord (in Martin Luther King. Die Ansprachen von Leopold Lindtberg, Max Frisch und Kurt Marti anlässlich der Kundgebung im Schauspielhaus Zürich vom 15. April 1968, *Die Weltwoche*, 26 April 1968).
Blick nach Osten (in *Die Weltwoche*, 24 May 1968).
Antwort auf Leserbriefe (in *Die Weltwoche*, 31 May 1968).
Die grosse Devotion (in *Die Weltwoche*, 12 July 1968).
Wieder Kalter Krieg (in *Die Weltwoche*, 30 Aug. 1968; also in *Dichten und Trachten* 30, 1968.
Die Prager Lektion (Max Frisch und Günter Grass, in *Die Zeit*, 25 Oct. 1968).
Wie wollen wir regiert werden? Zum ETH-Referendum (in *Die Weltwoche*, 13 Dec. 1968).
Was bin ich? (in *Schweizerspiegel* 23, nr. 10, 1968).

Theaterprobleme (unpublished address; excerpts have appeared in *Sechs moderne Theaterstücke*. Spectaculum 12. Frankfurt: Suhrkamp 1969; also in *Deutsche Zeitung/Christ und Welt*, 19 Jan. 1967 as "Illusion zweiten Grades").

Epilogue to Andrej D. Sacharow, *Wie ich mir die Zukunft vorstelle. Gedanken über Fortschritt, friedliche Koexistenz und geistige Freiheit*. Zürich: Diogenes, 1969.

Letter to Peter Suhrkamp and Gottfried Bermann Fischer of 17 May 1950 (in *Hermann Hesse–Peter Suhrkamp. Briefwechsel 1945-1959*. Frankfurt: Suhrkamp, 1969).

Letter to Stephan Kaiser of 23 Aug. 1955 (in St. K., *Die Besonderheiten der deutschen Schriftsprache in der Schweiz*, vol. 1, Duden Beiträge 30 a. Mannheim: Bibliographisches Institut, 1969).

Rede zum Zürcher Debakel (in *Theater heute* 9, 1970).

Dreigroschenoper ohne Songs. Ferngesteuerte Reisen: Notizen aus Berlin und Wien (in *Publik*, 25 Sept. 1970; also in *Städte 1945. Berichte und Bekenntnisse*, ed. Ingeborg Drewitz. Düsseldorf and Cologne: Diederichs, 1970).

So wie jetzt geht es nicht (in *Manifest 71*. Berne: Sozialdemokratische Partei der Schweiz, 1971).

G.H. Zur Person (in Gottfried Honegger, *Arbeiten aus den Jahren 1939-1971*. Teufen: Niggli, 1972).

Bundestagswahl: von aussen gesehen (in *Die Zeit*, 17 Nov. 1972).

Letter to Lucius Burckhardt and Markus Kutter of 19 June 1955 (in Th. Lengborn, *Schriftsteller und Gesellschaft in der Schweiz*. Frankfurt: Athenäum, 1972).

Rede für Bert Brecht (in Therese Giehse, *Ich hab nichts zum Sagen. Gespräche mit Monika Sperr*. Munich: Bertelsmann, 1973).

Die Schweiz als Heimat. Rede zur Verleihung des Grossen Preises der Schweizer Schillerstiftung, gehalten am 12. Januar im Zürcher Schauspielhaus (in *Nationalzeitung Basel*, 19 Jan. 1974).

Preface to *Max Frisch. Aus einem Tagebuch und Reden*. Volk und Welt Spektrum 71. Berlin: Volk und Welt, 1974.

Aus Sorge um die schweizerische Asylpolitik. Offener Brief an den Schweizerischen Bundesrat (in *Süddeutsche Zeitung*, 7 March 1974; also in *Frankfurter Rundschau*, 8 March 1974, under the title "Ein neues 'Schuldkonto' eröffnen? Offener Brief wegen der Chileflüchtlinge in der Schweiz").

Fragment aus einer Erzählung (in *Merkur* 28, 1974).

Epilogue to Verlagsgeschäfte und Moral. Max Frisch und Adolf Muschg zur Krise von Suhrkamp Zürich (in *Die Weltwoche*, 6 Nov. 1974).

Partei ergriffen (in *Jakob Bührer zu ehren. Eine Dokumentation*, in collaboration with W.M. Diggelmann, Max Frisch, A.A. Häsler, A. Muschg, H. Schneider, and R. Wespe, ed. Dieter Zeller. Basel: Z-Verlag, 1975).

Autobiographisches (in *Neue Rundschau* 86, 1975).

Nein, Mao habe ich nicht gesehen (in *Der Spiegel*, 9 Feb. 1976).

Abschied von der Biografie. Peter Rüedi sprach mit Max Frisch über dessen neues Stück Triptychon und sein Verhältnis zum Theater (in *Die Weltwoche*, 19 April 1978).

Verantwortung des Schriftstellers (Address delivered at the International PEN Club meeting in Stockholm in May 1978; in *Moderna Språk* 72, no. 3, 1978).

SECONDARY LITERATURE

Books

GENERAL

Baden, H.-J., *Poesie und Theologie*. Hamburg: Rauhes Haus, 1971.
Bänziger, H., *Frisch und Dürrenmatt*. Berne: Francke, 1960, 1976.
——, *Zwischen Protest und Traditionsbewusstsein*. Arbeiten zum Werk und zur gesellschaftlichen Stellung Max Frischs. Berne: Francke, 1975.
Beckermann, Th., ed., *Über Max Frisch*. Frankfurt: Suhrkamp, 1971 (edition suhrkamp 404).
Berger, R., and Diederichs, R., *Max Frisch: Bücher, Bilder, Dokumente*. Exhibition catalog and commentary. Zürich: Zentralbibliothek, 1977.
Dahms, E.M., *Zeit und Zeiterlebnis in den Werken Max Frisches:* Bedeutung und technische Darstellung. Berlin: de Gruyter, 1976 (Quellen und Forschungen zur Sprach- und Kulturgeschichte der germanischen Völker, n.s. 67).
Hanhart, T., *Max Frisch: Zufall, Rolle und literarische Form*. Interpretationen zu seinem neueren Werk. Kronberg/Ts.: Scriptor, 1976.
Hoffmann, F., *Der Kitsch bei Max Frisch*. Vorgeformte Realitätsvokabeln: eine Kitschtopographie, Bad Honnef: Keimer and Zurich: Hebsacker, 1979 (Keimers Abhandlungen zur deutschen Sprache und Kultur 2).
Jaeckle, E., *Der Zürcher Literaturschock*. Bericht. Munich: Langen-Müller, 1968.
Jurgensen, M., ed., *Frisch: Kritik-Thesen-Analysen*, Beiträge zum 65. Geburtstag. Berne: Francke, 1977.
Karasek, H., *Max Frisch*. Munich: Deutscher Taschenbuch-Verlag, 1976.
Lengborn, Th., *Schriftsteller und Gesellschaft in der Schweiz*: eine Studie zur Behandlung der Gesellschaftsproblematik bei Zollinger, Frisch und Dürrenmatt. Frankfurt: Athenäum, 1972.
Lusser-Mertelsmann, G., *Max Frisch: Die Identitätsproblematik in seinem Werk aus psychoanalytischer Sicht*. Stuttgart: Heinz, 1976 (Stuttgarter Arbeiten zur Germanistik 15).
Mayer, H., *Dürrenmatt und Frisch: Anmerkungen*. Pfullingen: Neske, 1963; new expanded edition, *Über Friedrich Dürrenmatt und Max Frisch*, 1977.
Merrifield, D.F., *Das Bild der Frau bei Max Frisch*. Freiburg: Becksmann, 1971.
Petersen, C., *Max Frisch*. Berlin: Colloquium, 1966 (Köpfe des XX. Jahrhunderts 44).
——, *Max Frisch*, tr. Ch. La Rue. New York: Ungar, 1972.
Schau, A., ed., *Max Frisch: Beiträge zur Wirkungsgeschichte*. Freiburg: Becksmann, 1971 (Materialien zur deutschen Literatur 2).
Schenker, W., *Die Sprache Max Frischs in der Spannung zwischen Mundart und Schriftsprache*. Berlin: de Gruyter, 1969 (Quellen und Forschungen zur Sprach- und Kulturgeschichte der germanischen Völker, n.s. 31).
Schmid, K., *Unbehagen im Kleinstaat*. Untersuchungen über C.F. Meyer, H.-F. Amiel, J. Schaffner, Max Frisch, J. Burckhardt. Zurich: Artemis, 1963.
Schäfer, W.E., *Anekdote, Antianekdote: Zum Stilwandel einer literarischen Form in der Gegenwart*. Stuttgart: Klett-Cotta, 1977 (Brecht, Frisch, and Wondraschek are treated).
Schmitz, W., ed., *Über Max Frisch II*. Frankfurt: Suhrkamp, 1976.
Schuchmann, M.E., *Der Autor als Zeitgenosse: Gesellschaftliche Aspekte in Max Frischs Werk* (Europäische Hochschulschriften I, 296). Frankfurt: Lang, 1979.

Schumacher, K., *"Weil es geschehen ist": Untersuchungen zu Max Frischs Poetik der Geschichte.* Königstein: Hain, 1979.
Stäuble, E., *Max Frisch: Ein Schweizer Dichter der Gegenwart.* Versuch einer Gesamtdarstellung seines Werkes. Amriswil: Bodensee, 1957; St. Gallen: Erker, 1971.
——, *Max Frisch: Gedankliche Grundzüge in seinen Werken.* Basel: Reinhardt, 1967, 1970.
Steinmetz, H., *Max Frisch: Tagebuch, Drama, Roman.* Göttingen: Vandenhoeck & Ruprecht, 1973 (Kleine Vandenhoeck-Reihe 379 S).
Stephan, P., *Dialog und Reflexion*: Modelle intersubjektiver Beziehungen im Werk Max Frischs. Berlin: Author, 1973.
Thranholm, M., *Fragmenter af rejsens mytologi: Odysseus-myten hos Homer og i den senborgerlige litteratur.* Copenhagen: Gyldendal, 1979.
Weisstein, U., *Max Frisch.* New York: Twayne, 1967.
Werner, M., *Bilder des Endgültigen, Entwürfe des Möglichen*: Zum Werk von Max Frisch. Berne: Lang, 1975 (Europäische Hochschulschriften, Reihe 1, Deutsche Literatur und Germanistik 111).
Wintsch-Spiess, M., *Zum Problem der Identität im Werk Max Frischs.* Zurich: Juris, 1965.

DRAMA

Biedermann, M., *Das politische Theater von Max Frisch.* Rheinfelden: Schäuble, 1974 (Theater unserer Zeit 13).
Durzak, M., *Dürrenmatt, Frisch, Weiss*: Deutsches Drama der Gegenwart zwischen Kritik und Utopie. Stuttgart: Reclam, 1972, 1973.
Geisser, H., *Die Entstehung von Max Frischs Dramaturgie der Permutation.* Berne: Haupt, 1973 (Sprache und Dichtung, n.s. 21).
Groot, G. de, *Zeitgestaltung im Drama Max Frischs. Die Vergegenwärtigungstechnik in 'Santa Cruz,' 'Die chinesische Mauer' und 'Biographie,'* (Amsterdamer Publikationen zur Sprache und Literatur, Bd. 33). Amsterdam: Editions Rodopi, 1977.
Jurgensen, M., *Max Frisch: Die Dramen,* Berne: Francke, 1968, 1976.
Karasek, H., *Max Frisch.* Velber: Friedrich, 1966, 1974 (Friedrichs Dramatiker des Welttheaters 17).
Knapp, G.P., ed., *Max Frisch. Aspekte des Bühnenwerks.* Berne: Lang, 1979 (Studien zum Werk Max Frischs, Band 2).
Köseoğlu, L., *Die Stellung der Frauenfiguren in den Dramen von Friedrich Dürrenmatt, Max Frisch und Hans Günter Michelsen bis 1968.* Hamburg: Author, 1974.
Neumann, G., Schröder, J., and Karnick, M., *Dürrenmatt, Frisch, Weiss*: 3 Entwürfe zum Drama der Gegenwart; with an introductory essay by G. Baumann. Munich: Fink, 1969.
Pickar, G.B., *The Dramatic Works of Max Frisch* (Europäische Hochschulschriften, Reihe 1, Bd. 182). Frankfurt: Lang, 1977.
Quenon, J., *Die Filiation der dramatischen Figuren bei Max Frisch.* Paris: Les Belles Lettres, 1975.
Schnetzler-Suter, A., *Max Frisch: Dramaturgische Fragen.* Berne: Lang, 1974 (Europäische Hochschulschriften, Reihe 1: Deutsche Literatur und Germanistik 100).
Weise, A., *Untersuchungen zur Thematik und Struktur der Dramen von Max Frisch.* Göppingen: Kümmerle, 1969 (Göppinger Arbeiten zur Germanistik 7).
Westphal, G., *Das Verhältnis von Sprechtext und Regieanweisung bei Frisch, Dürrenmatt, Ionesco und Beckett.* Würzburg: Gugel, 1964.

NARRATIVE

Baden, H.J., *Der Mensch ohne Partner*: Das Menschenbild in den Romanen von Max Frisch. Wuppertal-Barmen: Jugenddienst, 1966 (Das Gespräch 64).
Butler, M., *The Novels of Max Frisch*. London: Wolf, 1976.
Ellerbrock, J., *Identität und Rechtfertigung*: Max Frischs Romane unter besonderer Berücksichtigung des theologischen Aspektes. Hamburg: Author, 1976.
Jurgensen, M., *Max Frisch: Die Romane*. Interpretationen. Berne: Francke, 1970, 1976.
Knapp, G.P., ed., *Max Frisch: Aspekte des Prosawerks*. Berne: Lang, 1978.
Ullrich, G., *Identität und Rolle*: Probleme des Erzählens bei Johnson, Walser, Frisch und Fichte. Stuttgart: Klett, 1977 (Literaturwissenschaft und Gesellschaftswissenschaft 25).

INDIVIDUAL WORKS (arranged in alphabetical order of works treated)

Eckart, R., *Max Frisch: Andorra*. Munich: Oldenbourg, 1965 (Interpretationen für den Deutschunterricht).
Frühwald, W., and Schmitz, W., eds., *Max Frisch: Andorra, Wilhelm Tell:* Materialien, Kommentare. Munich: Hanser, 1977 (Reihe Hanser 243; Literatur und Kommentare 9).
Knapp, G.P., and Knapp, M. *Max Frisch: Andorra*. Grundlagen und Gedanken zum Verständnis des Dramas. Frankfurt, 1980.
Plett, P.C., ed., *Dokumente zu Max Frischs Andorra*. Arbeitsmaterialien Deutsch. Stuttgart: Klett, 1972.
Rosebrock, Th., *Erläuterungen zu Max Frischs Andorra und Biedermann und die Brandstifter*. Hollfeld/Obfr.: Bange, 1978 (Königs Erläuterungen 145).
Wendt, E., and Schmitz, W., eds., *Materialien zu Frischs Andorra*. Frankfurt: Suhrkamp, 1978 (edition suhrkamp 653).
Ravar, R., and Anrieu, P., *Le spectateur au théâtre* (recherche d'une méthode sociologique d'après Monsieur Biedermann et les incendiaires). Brussels: Institut de Sociologie Université Libre de Bruxelles, 1964.
Schmitz, W., ed., *Materialien zu Max Frisch*:Biedermann und die Brandstifter. Frankfurt: Suhrkamp, 1979.
Springmann, I., ed., *Max Frisch, Biedermann und die Brandstifter*. Erläuterungen und Dokumente. Stuttgart: Reclam, 1975 (Reclams Universalbibliothek 8129/8129a).
Kappler, A., *Erläuterungen zu Max Frischs Don Juan oder Die Liebe zur Geometrie*. Hollfeld/Obfr.: Bange, 1978 (Königs Erläuterungen und Materialien 25).
Geulen, H., *Max Frischs Homo faber: Studien und Interpretationen*. Berlin: de Gruyter, 1965 (Quellen und Forschungen zur Sprach- und Kulturgeschichte der germanischen Völker, n.s. 17).
Heidenreich, S., *Max Frisch: Homo faber*. Untersuchungen zum Roman. Hollfeld/Obfr.: Bange, 1977 (Analysen und Reflexionen 17).
Hoffmann, Chr., *Max Frischs Roman Homo faber, betrachtet unter theologischen Aspekten*. Frankfurt: Lang, 1978 (Theologie und Wirklichkeit, vol. 9).
Meurer, R., *Max Frisch: Homo faber*. Interpretationen. Munich: Oldernbourg, 1977 (Interpretationen für Schule und Studium).
Schmitz, W., *Max Frisch: Homo faber*. Materialien und Kommentare. Munich: Hanser, 1977 (Reihe Hanser 214; Literatur-Kommentare 5).

Botheroyd, P.F., *Ich und Er: First and Third Person Self-Reference and Problems of Identity in Three Contemporary German-Language Novels.* The Hague: Mouton, 1976 (On Grass's "Die Blechtrommel," Johnson's "Das dritte Buch über Achim" and Frisch's "Mein Name sei Gantenbein").
Gockel, H., *Max Frisch: Gantenbein. Das offen-artistische Erzählen.* Bonn: Bouvier, 1976 (Abhandlungen zur Kunst-, Musik- und Literaturwissenschaft 211).
Heidenreich, S., *Max Frisch: Mein Name sei Gantenbein, Montauk, Stiller.* Untersuchungen und Anmerkungen. Hollfeld/Obfr.: Bange, 1976 (Analysen und Reflexionen 15).
Kraft, M., *Studien zur Thematik von Max Frischs Roman "Mein Name sei Gantenbein"* Berne: Lang, 1969 (Europäische Hochschulschriften Reihe 1: Deutsche Literatur und Germanistik 23).
Ullrich, G., *Identität und Rolle*: Probleme des Erzählens bei Johnson, Walser, Frisch und Fichte (Das dritte Buch über Achim, Einhorn, Mein Name sei Gantenbein, Detlevs Imitationen 'Grünspan'). Stuttgart: Klett, 1977.
Groot, Cegienas de, *Zeitgestaltung im Drama Max Frischs:* Die Vergegenwärtigungstechnik in Santa Cruz, Die Chinesische Mauer und Biografie. Amsterdam: Rodopi, 1977 (Amsterdamer Publikationen zur Sprache und Literatur 33).
Naumann, H., *Der Fall Stiller, Antwort auf eine Herausforderung: Max Frischs "Stiller."* Rheinfelden: Schäuble, 1978.
Neis, E., *Erläuterungen zu Max Frisch: Stiller, Homo faber, Gantenbein.* Hollfeld/Obfr.: Bange, 1970 (Dr. Königs Erläuterungen zu den Klassikern 148).
Poser, Th., *Max Frisch, Stiller: Interpretationen.* Munich: Oldenbourg, 1977 (Interpretationen für Schule und Studium).
Schmitz, W., ed., *Materialien zu Max Frischs "Stiller,"* Frankfurt: Suhrkamp, 1978 (Suhrkamp-Taschenbücher 419, 2 vols.).
Kieser, R., *Max Frisch: Das literarische Tagebuch.* Frauenfeld: Huber, 1975.
Vin, D. de, *Max Frischs Tagebücher.* Studie über "Blätter aus dem Brotsack" (1940), "Tagebuch 1946-1949" (1950) und "Tagebuch 1966-1971" (1972) im Rahmen des Gesamtwerks (1932-1975). Cologne: Böhlau, 1977 (Forum Litterarum 10).

Dissertations and Theses

Alexander, L. R., Image and Imagery in Frisch's "Die Schwierigen." Diss. Michigan State University, 1970.
Baaske, J., Max Frisch als Dramatiker. Zum Problem der Gesellschaftskritik von der Position eines spätbürgerlichen Intellektuellen. State examination thesis Humboldt-Universität Berlin, 1962.
Braun, K., Die epische Technik in Max Frischs Roman "Stiller." Als Beitrag zur Formfrage des modernen Romans. Diss. Frankfurt, 1959.
Bui, H.N., Max Frischs Begriff "das wirkliche Leben." Diss. Munich, 1974.
Burger, H., Studien zur Erzähltechnik und Thematik bei Max Frisch. Diss. Brown University, 1971.
Burkhart, S.D., World War II in German Drama: The Individual Versus War (treating, among others, "Als der Krieg zu Ende war"). Diss. University of Cincinnati, 1969.
Butler, M., The Theme of Eccentricity in the Novels of Max Frisch. Diss. London, 1973.
Cock, M., The Presentation of Personality in the Novels of Max Frisch and Uwe Johnson. Diss. Oxford University, 1968.

Cordaro, L.T., Zum Problem der Entfremdung in den Romanen Max Frischs. Diss. City University of New York, 1979.
Eisenschenk, U., Studien zum Menschenbild in den Romanen vom Max Frisch. Diss. Vienna, 1971.
Federico, J.A., Metatheater. Self-consciousness and Role-Playing in the Dramas of Max Frisch, F. Dürrenmatt, and P. Handke. Diss. Ohio State University, 1976.
Gassmann, M., Max Frisch. Leitmotive der Jugend. Diss. Zurich, 1966.
Gramling, L.G., A Critical Analysis of Selected Dramatic Works of Max Frisch, and an Examination of Their Place in Contemporary German-language Drama. Diss. Catholic University of America, 1969.
Holley, J.F., The Problem of the Intellectual's Ethical Dilemma as Presented in Four Plays by Max Frisch. Diss. Tulane University, 1965.
Kiernan, D.J., Existentiale Themen bei Max Frisch. Die Existentialphilosophie Martin Heideggers in den Romanen Stiller, Homo faber und Mein Name sei Gantenbein. Diss. University of California at Berkeley, 1976.
Kilian, C.J.G., Die Gespaltenheit des Daseins bei Max Frisch. Pretoria, 1967.
Kingsbury, J., Crisis in the Novels of Max Frisch and H.E. Nossack. M. Litt. thesis Cambridge University, 1973.
Knapp, M., Elements of the Trivial and Their Transcendence in the Modern Novel: With an Emphasis on the Major Narrative Texts of Max Frisch. Diss. University of Utah, 1979.
Kopplow, H., Das dramatische Schaffen Max Frischs von den Anfängen bis zur Gegenwart. Diplomarbeit Rostock, 1966.
Lange, M.J., Zur Dimension der Zeit und des Raumes im Werk Max Frischs. Diss. Louisiana State University, 1973.
Levin, K.J.K., The Search for Lost Selves in Some Major Works of Samuel Beckett and Max Frisch. Diss. Indiana University, 1979.
McCormick, D., Max Frisch's Dramaturgical Development. Diss. University of Texas, 1973.
Martens, L., The Diary Novel and Contemporary Fiction: Studies in Max Frisch, Michel Butor, and Doris Lessing. Diss. Yale University, 1976.
Michot-Dietrich, H., Homo faber: Variations sur un thème de Camus. Diss. University of Michigan, 1965.
Omelaniuk, J., The Function and Significance of Dream Sequences in Max Frisch's Novels. Diss. University of Queensland, 1970.
Pollak, A. Die Don-Juan-Thematik bei Max Frisch. Eine Untersuchung zur Frage der Verarbeitung und Neugestaltung tradierten Stoffgutes. Diss. Vienna, 1975.
Pruszak, H.-J., Menschliche Existenz unter der Eigengesetzlichkeit der Lebensbereiche in Max Frischs Dramen. Eine verpflichtende Anrede an den glaubenden Menschen der Gegenwart. Diss. Humboldt-Universität Berlin, 1965.
Ramer, R.U., Studien über Rollen-Spiel und Flucht-Motiv im Gesamtwerk Max Frischs. Diss. Erlangen-Nürnberg, 1973.
Regnier, P.J.F., Real and Aesthetic Aspects of Modern Experience: Max Frisch and Norman Mailer, Diss. University of Wisconsin, 1974.
Rogers, E.L., A Study of Multiplicity Manifested in the Protagonists of Five Novels by Fyodor Dostoevsky, James Joyce, Hermann Hesse, and Max Frisch. Diss. University of North Carolina, 1974.
Ruppert, P., Existential Themes in the Plays of Max Frisch. Diss. University of Iowa, 1973.
Russell, Ch.R., Versions of the Contemporary Internalized Novel: Günter Grass, William Burroughs, Max Frisch, Alain Robbe-Grillet. Diss. Cornell University, 1973.

Salins, J.M., Zur Wirklichkeitsdarstellung in Max Frischs Werken. Diss. Rutgers University, 1969.
Schimanski, K., Max Frisch. Heldengestaltung und Wirklichkeitsdarstellung in seinem Werk. Diss. Leipzig, 1972.
Schröder, M., Max Frisch: die thematischen Elemente im Tagebuch und ihre Varianten in den Romanen. Diss. Vanderbilt University, 1973.
Schulze, Ch., Die Entwicklung des Dramatikers Max Frisch. Diplomarbeit Theaterhochschule Leipzig, 1958.
Seyd, A., Die Thematik des zweiten Weltkrieges in der Sicht des schweizer Dramatikers Max Frisch, dargestellt an seinen beiden Stücken Nun singen sie wieder und Als der Krieg zu Ende war. State examination thesis Jena, 1966.
Shantz, A.M., Max Frisch's Novel Stiller Compared with Hermann Hesse's Novel Steppenwolf. Diss. Bryn Mawr College, 1973.
Smith, E.Y., Crisis in the Novel: Max Frisch and Michel Butor. Diss. Indiana University, 1976.
Stemmler, W., Max Frisch, H. Böll und S. Kierkegaard. Diss. Munich, 1972.
Stiles, V.M., Dasein heisst keine Rolle spielen: eine Interpretation der Romane von Max Frisch. Diss. Cornell University, 1970.
Stine, L.J., Märchen and Sage Elements in the works of Max Frisch. Diss. Bryn Mawr College, 1977.
Trunz, F., Der kritische Realismus, erläutert an Hand von Andorra, einem Schauspiel von Max Frisch. Diplomarbeit Theaterhochschule Leipzig, 1965.
Wildbolz, A., Analyse und Interpretation der Zeitstruktur im modernen Theaterstück. Diss. Vienna, 1956.
Zakrison, G.W., The Crisis of Identity in the Works of Max Frisch. Diss. University of Nebraska, 1975.
Zehetbauer, V., Darstellung von Wirklichkeit als dramaturgisches Problem bei Max Frisch. Der Versuch einer Erhellung mit Hilfe der Unterscheidung von griechischem und hebräischem Denken. Diss. Mannhein, 1975.
Zeitz, B., Die Rechtsauffassung in der Dichtung von Max Frisch. Diss. Würzburg, 1972.
Zeller-Cambon, M., Max Frisch und Luigi Pirandello: eine Untersuchung zur thematischen und stilistischen Affinität ihrer Romane, Diss. Bryn Mawr College, 1976.
Zoll, R., Der absurde Mord in der deutschen und französischen Literatur. Diss. Frankfurt, 1961.
Zonta, R., Die zwischenmenschlichen Beziehungen im Werk von Max Frisch. Dargestellt am Problem der Liebe und Ehe. Diss. Innsbruck, 1973.

Articles, Interviews, Reviews

GENERAL

Ahl, H., Homo ludens, Homo faber-Homo sapiens. Max Frisch (in H.A., *Literarische Porträts*. Munich: Langen-Müller, 1962).
Ammer, S., Maks Fris Kao Moralist (in *Gledista*, Belgrade, Jan. 1969).
Anon., Das ist kein Grund zur Ruhe. Interview mit Max Frisch (in *Zürcher Student* 46, no. 4, 1968).
Anon., Die Notwehr erzeugt Werke. Spiegel-Interview mit dem Dramatiker Max Frisch (in *Der Spiegel*, 29 Jan. 1968).
Anon., Max Frisch. Literatur als Aufklärung. Zum 50. Geburtstag des Schweizer Schriftstellers und Dramatikers (in *Panorama*, May 1961).

Arnold, H.L., Gespräch mit Max Frisch (in H.L.A., *Gespräche mit Schriftstellern.* Munich: Beck, 1975; Beck'sche Schwarze Reihe 134).
Bach, H.L., and Bach, M., The Moral Problem of Political Responsibility: Brecht, Frisch, Sartre (in *Books Abroad* 37, 1963).
Bachmann, D., Heimat (in *Die Weltwoche*, 16 Jan. 1974).
Baden, H.J., Max Frisch: Religiöse Wandlung eines Schriftstellers (in *Stimmen der Zeit* 197, 1979).
Bänziger, H., Max Frisch: Der Protest eines Skeptikers (in *Universitas* 25, 1970; also in H.B., *Zwischen Protest und Traditionsbewusstsein*).
Barlow, D., 'Ordnung' and 'Das wirkliche Leben' in the Work of Max Frisch (in *German Life and Letters* 19, 1965-66).
Bautz, F.J., Ein unbequemer Zeitgenosse. Max Frisch und das Engagement an die Wahrhaftigkeit (in *Panorama*, Dec. 1958).
Beckman, H., Blick zurück auf Max Frisch (in *Rheinischer Merkur* 13, 1959).
Berchtold, A., L'oeuvre de Max Frisch (in *Suisse Contemporaine*, June 1949).
Bieneck, H., Max Frisch (in H.B., *Werkstattgespräche mit Schriftstellern*, Munich: Hanser 1962, 1976).
Bier, J. P., Zur Reprivatisierung der Literatur bei Max Frisch (in *Duitse kroniek* 29, 1977).
Bloch, P.A., Staatliche Literaturförderung? Gespräch mit Max Frisch (in P.A.B., ed., *Gegenwartsliteratur. Mittel und Bedingungen ihrer Produktion.* Berne: Francke, 1975).
—— and Bussmann, R., Gespräch mit Max Frisch (in P.A.B. and E. Hubacher, eds., *Der Schriftsteller in unserer Zeit. Schweizer Autoren bestimmen ihre Rolle in der Gesellschaft*, Berne: Francke, 1972).
—— and Schoch, B., Gespräch mit Max Frisch (in P.A.B., ed., *Der Schriftsteller und sein Verhältnis zur Sprache dargestellt am Problem der Tempuswahl*, Berne: Francke, 1971).
Brinkmann, H., Der komplexe Satz im deutschen Schrifttum der Gegenwart (bei Max Frisch und Günter Grass; in A. Haslinger, ed., *Sprachkunst als Weltgestaltung,* Festschrift für H. Seidler. Salzburg: Pustet, 1966; also in *Max Frisch: Beiträge zur Wirkungsgeschichte,* ed. Schau).
Burgauner, Chr., Versuch über Max Frisch (in *Merkur* 28, 1974).
Burger, H., Des Schweizer Autors Schweiz: Zu Max Frischs und Peter Bichsels Technik der Kritik an der Schweiz (in *Schweizer Monatshefte* 51, 1971).
Cauvin, M., Le chemin de Max Frisch (in *Etudes germaniques* 15, 1960).
Colberg, K., Max Frisch oder Die dritte Kraft des Gewissens (in *Die neue Schau* 13, 1952).
Cunliffe, W., Existentialist Elements in Frisch's Works (in *Monatshefte* 62, 1970; also in *Über Max Frisch II*, ed. Schmitz).
Demetz, P., Max Frisch (in P.D., *Die süsse Anarchie.* Skizzen zur deutschen Literatur seit 1945, Frankfurt: Ullstein, 1973. Ullstein Taschenbuch).
Edfeld, J., Max Frisch (in *Moderna Språk* 56, 1962).
Ehrhardt, M.-L., Auf der Suche nach Identität oder Die Gartenlaube für Männer. Eine Bemerkung zum Werk von Max Frisch (in H. Horn, ed., *Entscheidung und Solidarität.* Festschrift für Johannes Harder. Wuppertal: Hammer, 1973).
Eifler, M., Max Frisch als Zeitkritiker (in *Max Frisch. Aspekte des Prosawerks*, ed. Knapp).
Emmel, H., Parodie und Konvention: Max Frisch (in H.E., *Das Gericht in der deutschen Literatur des 20. Jahrhunderts.* Berne: Francke, 1963).

Esslin, M., Max Frisch (in M. Natan, ed., *German Men of Letters*, vol. 3, London: Wolff, 1964, 1968; also in M. Natan, ed., *Swiss Men of Letters*: Twelve Literary Essays. London: Wolff, 1970).

Falkenberg, H.-G., Leben und Werk Max Frischs (in *Blätter des Deutschen Theaters in Göttingen* 7, 1956-57).

Federspiel, J., Ein Brief an Max Frisch (in *Die Weltwoche*, 14 May 1971).

Fischer, J., Janowski, H.N., and Stammler, E., Rückzug auf die Poesie. Gespräch mit Max Frisch (in *Evangelische Kommentare* 1974).

Franzen, E., Über Max Frisch (in *Über Max Frisch*, ed. Beckermann; also in *Merkur* 12, 1958; also in E.F., *Aufklärungen*. Essays. Frankfurt: Suhrkamp, 1964).

Fringeli, D., *Von Spitteler zu Muschg. Literatur der deutschen Schweiz seit 1900*. Basel: Reinhardt, 1975).

Funke, H., Auf den Spuren von Max Frisch. Architektur, Städtebau und Provinzialismus in der Schweiz (in *Die Zeit*, 10 Sept. 1965).

Gerster, G., Der Dichter und die Zeit. Notizen zu Max Frisch (in *Neue literarische Welt* 3, 1952).

Gitermann, V., Rede anlässlich der Übergabe des Literaturpreises der Stadt Zürich an Max Frisch (in *Jahrbuch vom Zürichsee* 1958-59).

Gontrum, P., America in the Writings of Max Frisch (in *Pacific Coast Philology* 4, 1969).

Gross, H., Max Frisch und der Frieden (in *Text und Kritik* 47-48, 1975).

Gruenter, R., Der Künstler als 'démoralisateur.' Zum Zürcher Literaturstreit (in *Merkur* 21, 1967).

Gyurkó, L., Max Frisch (in L.G., *A német irodalom*. Budapest: Szépirodalmi Könyrkiadó, 1966).

———, Az i degember ès gépember. Max Frisch két regényhöse (in *Nagyvilág* 7, 1962).

Haberkamm, K., Max Frisch (in *Deutsche Literatur seit 1945 in Einzeldarstellungen*, ed. D. Weber. Stuttgart: Kröner, 1968, 1976; Kröners Taschenausgabe 832).

Haberl, F.P., Max Frisch: A Retrospective (in *World Literature Today* 51, 1977).

Häsler, A., Wir müssen unsere Welt anders einrichten. Gespräch mit Max Frisch (in *Die Tat*, 9 Dec. 1967; also in *Leben mit dem Hass. 21 Gespräche*, ed. A.H. Reinbek: Rowohlt, 1969).

Hagelstange, R., Verleihung des Georg-Büchner Preises an Max Frisch. Rede auf den Preisträger (in *Jahrbuch der Deutschen Akademie für Sprache und Dichtung Darmstadt* 1958; also in *Max Frisch: Beiträge zur Wirkungsgeschichte*, ed. Schau).

Harris, K., Die Sprache der menschlichen Beziehungen bei Max Frisch (in *Dichtung, Sprache, Gesellschaft*, ed. V. Lange and H.-G. Roloff. Frankfurt: Athenäum, 1971).

Hartmann, H., Der unbotmässige Schweizer. Max Frisch zum Fünfzigsten (in *Die Tat*, 13 May 1961).

Heissenbüttel, H., Max Frisch oder Die Kunst des Schreibens in dieser Zeit (in *Über Max Frisch*, ed. Beckermann).

Hentig, H. von, "Wahrheitsarbeit" und Friede: Rede auf Max Frisch zur Verleihung des Friedenspreises des Deutschen Buchhandels am 19. September 1976 (in M. Frisch and H.v. Hentig, *Zwei Reden zum Friedenspreis des Deutschen Buchhandels* (A,3).

Hinderer, W., "Ein Gefühl der Fremde." Amerikaperspektiven bei Max Frisch (in *Amerika in der deutschen Literatur. Neue Welt, Nordamerika, USA*. Wolfgang Paulsen zum 65. Geburtstag, ed. S. Bauschinger, H. Denkler, and W. Malsch, Stuttgart: Reclam, 1975).

Hirschfeld, K., Brief an Max Frisch (in *Die Weltwoche*, 19 May 1961).

Hoefert, S., Zur Sprachauffassung Max Frischs (in *Muttersprache* 73, 1963).

Hoffmann, Chr., Zehn Sätze zum Überleben (in *Deutsche Zeitung/Christ und Welt*, 5 Oct. 1973).
Holz, H.H., Max Frisch: engagiert und privat (in *Über Max Frisch*, ed. Beckermann).
Honsza, N., Identity and the Motif of the Mask in the Works of Max Frisch (in *Kwartalnik Neofilologiczny* 22. Warsaw 1975).
——, Die Identität im grossen Fragenkomplex. Max Frisch (in N.H., *Zur literarischen Situation nach 1945 in der BRD, in Österreich und in der Schweiz*, Acta Universitatis Wratislaviensis 214, 1974).
Horst, K.A., Notizen zu Max Frisch und Friedrich Dürrenmatt (in *Merkur* 8, 1954).
——, Max Frisch (in K.A.H., *Kritischer Führer durch die deutsche Literatur der Gegenwart*. Munich: Nymphenburger Verlagshandlung, 1962).
Ingold, F.Ph., Schwierigkeiten mit dem Vaterland (in *Schweizer Monatshefte* 54, 1974).
Ivernel, Ph., La tragi-comédie de l'intellectuel chez Frisch et Dürrenmatt (in *Langues modernes* 60, 1966).
Jacobi, J., Der Anti-Brecht (in *Die politische Meinung* 2, 1957).
Jacobs, W., Max Frisch (in W.J., *Moderne deutsche Literatur*: Portraits, Profile und Strukturen. Gütersloh: Signum, 1962; Signum Taschenbuch).
Jurgensen, M., Das Lebenswerk von Max Frisch und die Entwicklung seiner Schriften (in *Universitas* 32, 1977).
——, Die Entmythologisierung der Freiheit oder die Umschulung des Geistes (in *Schweizer Monatshefte* 51, 1971-72).
Kaiser, J., Max Frisch (in *Dichten und Trachten* 13, 1959).
——, Skizzen zum Bilde Frischs (in *Programmhefte des Schauspielhauses Zürich* 1961-62).
Kamnitzer, H., Die grosse Kapitulation (in *Neue deutsche Literatur* 3, 1959).
Kesting, M., Max Frisch (in *Handbuch der deutschen Gegenwartsliteratur*, ed. H. Kunisch in collaboration with H. Hennecke, Munich: Nymphenburger Verlagshandlung, 1965, 1969).
——, Max Frisch (in H.J. Schultz, ed., *Der Friede und die Unruhestifter*. Herausforderungen deutschsprachiger Schriftsteller im 20. Jahrhundert. Frankfurt: Suhrkamp, 1973; suhrkamp taschenbuch 145).
Kieser, R., An Interview with Max Frisch (in *Contemporary Literature* 13, 1972).
Kjaer, J., Max Frisch: Teori og praksis (in *Meddelelser fra gymnasiesklernes tysklaererforening* 47, 1972; also in German in *Orbis Litterarum* 27, 1972).
Knopf, J., Verlust der Unmittelbarkeit: Über Max Frisch und die "Neue Subjektivität" (in *Orbis Litterarum* 34, 1979).
Konstantinović, Z., Die Schuld an der Frau. Ein Beitrag zur Thematologie der Werke von Max Frisch (in *Frisch: Kritik, Thesen, Analysen*, ed. Jurgensen. Berne: Francke, 1977).
Krättli, A., "Jeder sei der Schatten des andern." Zu Karl Schmid und Max Frisch (in *Schweizer Monatshefte* 57, 1977-78).
Kurz, P.K., Identität und Gesellschaft. Die Welt des Max Frisch (in P.K.K., *Über moderne Literatur*: Standorte und Deutungen, vol. 2. Frankfurt: Josef Knecht, 1969).
Lembrikova, B., Max Frisch: kritik sovremennosti (in *Voprosy literatury* 11, 1967).
Lennartz, F., Max Frisch (in F.L., *Deutsche Dichter und Schriftsteller unserer Zeit*: Einzeldarstellungen zur Schönen Literatur in deutscher Sprache. Stuttgart: Kröner, 1959, Kröners Taschenausgabe 151).
Liersch, W., Wandlung einer Problematik (in *Über Max Frisch*, ed. Th. Beckermann).

Livingstone, R.S., Max Frisch (in *Australasian Universities Language and Literature Association Proceedings* 1, 1965).
——, The World-View of Max Frisch (in *Southern Review*: An Australian Journal of Literary Studies 1, 1965).
Lüthi, H.J., Max Frisch (in Kohlschmidt, W., ed., *Bürgerlichkeit und Unbürgerlichkeit in der Literatur der Deutschen Schweiz*. Berne: Francke, 1978.
Mangariello, M.E., El ansia de una vida auténtica y Latinoamérica en la obra de Max Frisch (in *Boletín de Estudios Germánicos* 9, 1972).
Mansilla, H.C.Z., Zwei Begegnungen in der Schweiz. Gedanken zu Gesprächen mit Max Frisch und Max Horkheimer (in *Frankfurter Hefte* 28, 1973).
Marchand, W., Max Frisch (in *Deutsche Dichter der Gegenwart*: Ihr Leben und Werk, ed. B.v. Wiese. Berlin: Schmidt, 1973).
Marti, K., *Die Schweiz und ihre Schriftsteller: die Schriftsteller und ihre Schweiz.* Zurich: EVZ-Verlag, 1966; Polis Zeitbuchreihe.
——, Zum Beispiel Max Frisch (in *Reformation* 14, 1964).
Mauranges, J.-P., Der Einfluss Thornton Wilders auf das literarische Schaffen von Friedrich Dürrenmatt und Max Frisch (in *Nordamerikanische Literatur im deutschen Sprachraum seit 1945*. Beiträge zur Rezeption amerikanischer Literatur, ed. H. Frenz and H. Lang. Munich: Winkler, 1973).
——, L'image de l'Amérique chez Max Frisch (in *Recherches germaniques* 7, 1977).
Mennemeier, F.N., Max Frisch: Poet und Moralist (in *Rheinischer Merkur*, 19 June 1962).
Meschini, B., Max Frisch (in *Der Schweizer Buchhandlungsgehilfe* 37, 1956).
Muschg, A., Vom Preis eines Preises oder Die Wohltat des Zweifels (in *Über Max Frisch II*, ed. Schmitz).
Musgrave, M.E., The Evolution of the Black Character in the Works of Max Frisch (in *Monatshefte* 66, 1974; also in German translation in *Materialien über Max Frischs Stiller*, ed. Schmitz).
Nakano, K., Über Max Frisch (in *Doitsu Bungaku* 34, 1965, in Japanese with German summary).
Oberholzer, O., Die Literatur der Gegenwart in der Schweiz (in *Die deutsche Literatur der Gegenwart. Aspekte und Tendenzen*, ed. M. Durzak. Stuttgart: Reclam, 1971).
Ossowski, R., Max Frisch (in R.O., ed., *Jugend fragt: Prominente antworten*. Berlin: Colloquium, 1975).
Praag, Ch. van, Montagetechnik bei Max Frisch als Element der Verfremdung (in *Etudes Germaniques* 34, 1979).
Raeber, K., Lieber schreiben als lesen. Eine Unterhaltung mit Max Frisch (in *Das Schönste* 8, 1962).
Rau, G., Max Frisch dramatique et romancier (in *Preuves* 90, 1958).
Reif, A., Die Machtinhaber müssen die Literatur fürchten. Ein Gespräch mit dem Schriftsteller Max Frisch (in *Die Tat*, 6 Jan. 1973).
Riese, C., The Imprisoned World of Max Frisch (in *Esquire* 58, 1962).
Rosengarten, W., Max Frisch (in *Schriftsteller der Gegenwart*, ed. K. Nonnemann. Olten: Walter, 1963; also in *Welt und Wort* 18, 1963).
Rüedi, P., Widerspruch im Widerspruch (in *Die Weltwoche*, 13 March 1974).
Salis, J.R. v., Unser Land als Gegenstand der Literatur. Zur Kontroverse zwischen Max Frisch und Otto F. Walter (in *Die Weltwoche*, 25 March 1966; also in J.R. v. S., *Schwierige Schweiz*. Zürich: Füssli, 1968).
Satonski, D., Homo Max Frisch (in *Kunst und Literatur* 14, 1966).

Schau, A., Dichtung der Permutation (in *Max Frisch: Beiträge zur Wirkungsgeschichte*, ed. Schau).

Scheible, K., Max Frisch und Friedrich Dürrenmatt: Betrachtungen über ihre Geisteshaltung und Arbeitsweise (in *Studies in German. In Memory of Andrew Louis*, ed. R.L. Kahn. Houston: Rice University Press, 1969; Rice University Studies 55).

Schenker, W., Mundart und Schriftsprache (in *Über Max Frisch*, ed. Beckermann; also in W. Sch., *Die Sprache Max Frischs in der Spannung zwischen Mundart und Schriftsprache*).

Schmid, K., Versuch über Max Frisch (in *Schweizer Annalen* 3, 1946–47).

Schroers, R., Max Frisch oder das Misstrauen (in *Christ und Welt*, 18 Sept. 1964).

Schwarz, Th., Die Kritik der bürgerlichen Gesellschaft bei Dürrenmatt und Frisch (in *Philologica* 18, 1966).

Serke, J., Nicht ohne Antwort. Ein Gespräch mit Max Frisch in Frankfurt (in *Frankfurter Rundschau*, 26 Jan. 1962).

Steinmetz, H., Auf dem Wege zum Klassiker? Oder wie Verlag und Kollege einem Autor in den Rücken fallen. Zu Uwe Johnsons Max Frisch. Stich-Worte (in *Frisch: Kritik, Thesen, Analysen*, ed. Jurgensen).

——, Max Frisch (in Dutch, in H.St., *Tijd en Werkelijkheid in de moderne Literatur*, Wassenaar: Servire, 1974).

Subiotto, A., The Swiss Contribution (in *The German Theatre: A Symposium*, ed. R. Hayman. New York: Barnes & Noble, 1975).

Suter, G., Die Schweiz und Max Frisch (in *DU* 27, 1967).

Tindemans, C., Max Frisch: Deeld en gelijkenis (in *Streven* 16, 1963).

Völker-Hezel, B., Fron und Erfüllung: Zum Problem der Arbeit bei Max Frisch (in *Revue des langues vivantes* 37, 1971).

Vogel, P.I., Und die Schweiz? Ein Interview mit Max Frisch (in *Neutralität* 2, 1964).

Vormweg, H., Die Renaissance des Barock: Hinweis auf einige Motive der modernen deutschen Literatur (in *Frankfurter Hefte* 21, 1966).

Wapnewski, P., Max Frisch: Von der durchschlagenden Wirkung eines Klassikers (in *Universitas* 31, 1976).

Weber, W., Max Frisch 1958 (in *Wirkendes Wort* 10, 1959; also in W.W., *Zeit ohne Zeit*: Aufsätze zur Literatur. Zurich: Manesse, 1959; also in *Bestand und Versuch. Schweizer Schrifttum der Gegenwart*, ed. B. Mariacher and F. Witz. Zurich: 1964).

Wehrli, M., Gegenwartsdichtung der deutschen Schweiz (in M.W., *Deutsche Literatur in unserer Zeit*. Göttingen: Vandenhoeck & Ruprecht, 1959; Kleine Vandenhoeck Reihe 73-74).

Werth, J., and Blanke, B., Interview mit Max Frisch (in *Frankfurter Rundschau*, 30 April 1966).

Whitton, K.S., The "Zürcher Literaturstreit" (in *German Life and Letters* 27, 1973–74).

Widmer, S., and Suter, G., Max Frisch und die Schweiz. Ein Briefwechsel zu "Unbehagen im Kleinstaat" (in *Die Weltwoche*, 10 May 1963).

Wolf, Chr., Max Frisch beim Wiederlesen oder: Vom Schreiben in der Ich-Form (in *Text und Kritik* 47–48, 1975; also in *Über Max Frisch II*, ed. Schmitz).

Zimmer, D.E., Noch einmal anfangen können. Ein Gespräch mit Max Frisch (in *Die Zeit*, 22 Dec. 1967).

Ziolkowski, Th., Max Frisch, Moralist without a Moral (in *Yale French Studies* 29, 1962).

Zoller, H., Max Frisch: Jerusalem-Preis 1965 (in *Die Weltwoche*, 23 April 1965).

Bibliography

DRAMA IN GENERAL

Anon., Morality Plays (in *Times Literary Supplement*, 11 Jan. 1963).

Allemann, B., Die Struktur der Komödie bei Frisch und Dürrenmatt (in *Das deutsche Lustspiel*, vol. 2, ed. H. Steffen. Göttingen: Vandenhoeck & Ruprecht, 1969; also in abbreviated form in *Über Max Frisch*, ed. Beckermann; also in *Positionen des Dramas*, ed. H.L. Arnold and Th. Buck. Munich: Beck, 1977; Beck'sche schwarze Reihe 163).

Archipow, J., Max Frisch auf der Suche nach der verlorenen Einheit (Postscript to Max Frisch, *Stücke*. Leipzig: Reclam, 1973).

Bachtler, E., Die Bühne als Seziertisch (in *Schweizer Illustrierte*, 29 Jan. 1968).

Brock-Sulzer, E., Überlegungen zur schweizerischen Dramatik von heute (in *Akzente* 3, 1956; also in *Max Frisch: Beiträge zur Wirkungsgeschichte*, ed. Schau).

———, Max Frisch (in *Welttheater*, ed. S. Melchinger and H. Rischbieter. Braunschweig: Westermann, 1962).

Elizalde, I., El teatro de Max Frisch (in *Arbor* 1972).

Esslin, M., Max Frisch (in *Plays and Players* 2, 1954).

Federico, J.A., The Hero as Playwright in Dramas by Frisch, Dürrenmatt, and Handke (in *German Life and Letters* 32, 1979).

Glaettli, W.E., Max Frisch, a New German Playwright (in *German Quarterly* 25, 1952).

Gontrum, P., The Influence of Thornton Wilder on Max Frisch (in *Proceedings of the Pacific Northwest Conference on Foreign Languages* 29, 1978).

Hammer, J.C., The Humanism of Max Frisch. An Examination of Three of His Plays (in *German Quarterly* 42, 1969).

Heidsieck, A., Absurdes und Groteskes im dramatischen Werk Max Frischs (in A.H., *Das Groteske und das Absurde im modernen Drama*. Stuttgart: Kohlhammer, 1969; Sprache und Literatur 53).

Heilman, R.B., Max Frisch's Modern Moralities (in *University of Denver Quarterly* 1, 1966).

Jotterand, F., Friedrich Dürrenmatt et Max Frisch à Paris (in *Perspectives du théâtre* 6, 1961).

Jurgensen, M., Symbols as Leitmotifs in the Dramas of Max Frisch (in *Journal of the Australasian Universities Language and Literature Association* 27, 1968).

———, Leitmotivischer Sprachsymbolismus in den Dramen Max Frischs (in *Wirkendes Wort* 18, 1968).

———, Die Welt auf Probe: Stichworte zum Drama Max Frischs (in *Max Frisch, Aspekte des Bühnenwerks*, ed. Knapp).

———, Max Frisch und seine Bühnendialektik. Von Chinesische Mauer bis Andorra (in *Universitas* 25, 1970; also in M.J., *Max Frisch. Die Dramen*; also in *Max Frisch: Beiträge zur Wirkungsgeschichte*, ed. Schau).

Karasek, H., Brechts Mittel ohne Brechts Konsequenzen. Über Fluchtwege vor der Wirklichkeit bei Dürrenmatt und Frisch (in *Theater heute*, Sonderheft Deutsches Theater 1945-70, Oct. 1970).

Kesting, M., Max Frisch. Nachrevolutionäres Lehrtheater (in M.K., *Panorama des zeitgenössischen Theaters*. Munich: Piper, 1969; also in *Max Frisch: Beiträge zur Wirkungsgeschichte*, ed. Schau).

Knapp, G.P., "Dass wir uns nur noch wiederholen": Jean-Paul Sartre und Max Frisch: Notizen zur literarischen Tradition (in *Max Frisch. Aspekte des Bühnenwerks*, ed. Knapp).

Knapp, M., "Die Frau ist ein Mensch, bevor man sie liebt, manchmal auch nachher." Kritische Anmerkungen zur Gestaltung der Frau in Frischtexten (in *Max Frisch. Aspekte des Bühnenwerks*, ed. Knapp).
Koebner, Th., Dramatik und Dramaturgie seit 1945 (in *Tendenzen der deutschen Literatur seit 1945*, ed. Th. K. Stuttgart: Kröner, 1971; Kröners Taschenausgabe 405).
Kuckhoff, A.-G., Postscript to *Max Frisch, Stücke*, Berlin, GDR: Volk und Welt, 1969.
Lübbren, R., Realismus im modernen Drama. Max Frisch, Friedrich Dürrenmatt, Samuel Beckett (in *Theater und Zeit* 5, 1957-58).
Mann, O., Das deutsche Drama des 20. Jahrhunderts (in O.M. and H. Friedmann, eds., *Deutsche Literatur im 20. Jahrhundert*, vol. 1. *Strukturen*. Heidelberg: Rothe, 1954, 1967.
Matthias, K., Die Dramen von Max Frisch. Strukturen und Aussagen (in *Literatur in Wissenschaft und Unterricht* 3, 1970; also in *Über Max Frisch II*, ed. Schmitz).
Maulnier, Th., Pirandello, Hochwälder, Frisch (in *Revue de Paris* 72, 1965).
Melchinger, S., Max Frisch (in *Die Zeit*, 17 April 1958).
Mennemeier, F.N., Liberaler Nachkriegshumanismus (in F.N.M., *Modernes deutsches Drama. Kritiken und Charakeristiken*. Vol. 2: *1933 bis zur Gegenwart*. Munich: Fink, 1975; Uni-Taschenbücher 425).
Müller, J., Max Frisch und Friedrich Dürrenmatt als Dramatiker der Gegenwart (in *Universitas* 17, 1962).
———, Max Frisch. Stücke. Bd. 1, 2 (in *Germanistik* 3, 1963).
Müller, K.-D., Das Ei des Kolumbus? Parabel und Modell als Dramenformen bei Brecht, Dürrenmatt, Frisch, Walser (in *Beiträge zur Poetik des Dramas*, ed. W. Keller. Darmstadt: Wissenschaftliche Buchgesellschaft, 1976).
Pache, W., Pirandellos Urenkel. Formen des Spiels bei Max Frisch und Tom Stoppard (in *Sprachkunst* 4, 1973).
Petersen, J.H., Frischs dramaturgische Konzeptionen (in *Max Frisch. Aspekte des Bühnenwerks*, ed. Knapp).
Pickar, G.B., From Place to Stage: An Evolution in the Dramatic Works of Max Frisch (in *Seminar* 9, 1973).
———, The Narrative Time Sense in the Dramatic Works of Max Frisch (in *German Life and Letters* 28, 1974-75).
———, The Emergence of the Narrator in the Dramatic Works of Max Frisch (in *Revue des langues vivantes* 41, 1975).
Plard, H., Der Dramatiker Max Frisch und sein Werk für das Theater der Gegenwart (in *Universitas* 19, 1964; also in *Max Frisch: Beiträge zur Wirkungsgeschichte*, ed. Schau).
———, Max Frisch, un théâtre de l'aliénation (in *Revue générale belge* 100, 1964).
Pryce-Jones, A., Max Frisch: The Sage of Bahnhofstrasse (in *Theatre Arts* 47, 1963).
Profitlich, U., "Verlorene Partien": Modelle des Misslingens im Drama Max Frischs (in *Max Frisch. Aspekte des Bühnenwerks*, ed. Knapp).
Quenon, J. Anthroponymie et caractérisation dans le théâtre de Max Frisch (in *Revue des langues vivantes* 39, 1973).
———, Die Filiation der dramatischen Figuren bei Max Frisch (in *Germanistik* 18, 1977).
Radimersky, G.W., Das Konzept der Geschichte in den Dramen Dürrenmatts und Frischs (in *Kentucky Foreign Language Quarterly* 13, 1966).
Rau, G., Max Frisch dramatique et romancier (in *Preuves* 90, 1958).
Sana, H., El teatro de Max Frisch (in *Indice*, 1970).
Schmitz, W., Frisch-Bilder: Linien und Skizzen der Forschung (in *Max Frisch. Aspekte des Bühnenwerks*, ed. Knapp).

Schrade, W., Frisch und Kafka auf Berliner Bühnen (in *Neue Literarische Welt* 4, 1953).
Schröder, J., Spiel mit dem Lebenslauf: Das Drama Max Frischs (in *Dürrenmatt, Frisch, Weiss*, ed. G. Neumann, J. Schröder, M. Karnick. Munich: Fink, 1969; also in *Über Max Frisch II*, ed. Schmitz).
Seidmann, P., Modern Swiss Drama. Frisch and Dürrenmatt (in *Books Abroad* 34, 1960).
Stauffacher, W., Die Leistung der Sprache: Zum Verhältnis von Wort und Geste im dramatischen Werk Max Frischs (in *Max Frisch. Aspekte des Bühnenwerks*, ed. Knapp).
Suter, G., Max Frisch: Ich habe Glück gehabt. Von "Nun singen sie wieder" zu "Andorra" (in *Die Weltwoche*, 3 Nov. 1961).
Thode, H.-G., Versuche mit ausgewählten Schauspielen von Max Frisch im Unterricht (in *Pädagogische Provinz* 15, 1961).
Weber, W., Zur Gesamtausgabe der Stücke von Max Frisch (in *Dichten und Trachten* 19, 1962).
Weisstein, U., Max Frisch's Stücke (in *Books Abroad* 37, 1963).
Wellwarth, G., Friedrich Dürrenmatt and Max Frisch: Two Views of the Drama (in *Tulane Drama Review* 6, 1962).
──, Max Frisch: The Drama of Despair (in G.W., *The Theater of Paradox and Protest: Development in the Avant-garde Drama*. New York: New York University Press, 1964).
Ziegler, K., Das moderne Drama als Spiegel unserer Zeit (in *Der Deutschunterricht* 13, 1961).
Zielkowski, Th., Contemporary German Drama (in *Books Abroad* 38, 1964).
Ziskoven, W., Max Frisch (in *Zur Interpretation des modernen Dramas: Brecht, Dürrenmatt, Frisch*, ed. R. Geissler. Frankfurt: Diesterweg, 1970).

NARRATIVE IN GENERAL

Adamson, C.L., The Contemporaneity of Max Frisch's Novels: Counter-Existentialism and Human Commitment (in *Wichita State University Bulletin* 49, 1973).
Arnold, A. Näher mein Ich zu Dir: Die Problematik des Alterns, des Sterbens und des Todes bei Max Frisch (in *Max Frisch. Aspekte des Prosawerks*, ed. Knapp).
Beckermann, Th., "Einmal möchte er es wissen": Zur Ästhetic des Engagements im Prosawerk von Max Frisch (in *Text und Kritik* 47-48, 1975).
Butler, M., Das Problem der Exzentrizität in den Romanen Frischs (in *Text und Kritik* 47-48, 1975).
Cock, M., "Countries of the Mind": Max Frisch's Narrative Technique (in *Modern Language Review* 65, 1970).
Corngold, St., Introduction to *Max Frisch, Ausgewählte Prosa*. New York: Harcourt, Brace & World, 1968 (edition suhrkamp in American text editions).
Cauvin, M., Max Frisch, l'absolu et le nouveau roman (in *Etudes germaniques* 22, 1967).
Eifler, M., Max Frisch als Zeitkritiker (in *Max Frisch. Aspekte des Prosawerks*, ed. Knapp).
Grimm, R., and Wellauer, C., Max Frisch. Mosaik eines Statikers (in *Zeitkritische Romane des zwanzigsten Jahrhunderts*, ed. H. Wagner, Stuttgart: Reclam, 1975).
Groot, C. de, Bildnis, Selbstbildnis und Identität in Max Frischs Romanen Stiller, Homo faber und Mein Name sei Gantenbein: Ein Vergleich (in *Amsterdamer Beiträge zur Neueren Germanistik* 9, 1979).
Hillen, G., Reisemotive in den Romanen von Max Frisch (in *Wirkendes Wort* 19, 1969).

Hoffmann, Ch., The Search for Self, Inner Freedom, and Relatedness in the Novels of Max Frisch (in *The Contemporary Novel in Germany: A Symposium*, ed. R. Heitner. Austin: University of Texas Press, 1967).

Honsza, N., Auf der Suche nach neuer Ich-Erfassung. Zur Kommunikativität und Applikation der Prosa von Max Frisch (in *Frisch: Kritik, Thesen, Analysen*, ed. Jurgensen).

———, Max Frisch und der moderne Schweizerische Roman (in *Beiträge zu den Fortbildungskursen des Goethe-Instituts*, 1969).

Jurgensen, M., Max Frisch: Die frühen Schriften (in *Max Frisch. Aspekte des Prosawerks*, ed. Knapp).

Kaiser, J., Max Frisch und der Roman. Konsequenzen eines Bildersturms (in *Frankfurter Hefte* 12, 1957; also in *Max Frisch, Ausgewählte Prosa*).

Mayer, H., Max Frischs Romane (in H.M., *Zur deutschen Literatur der Zeit*: Zusammenhänge, Schriftsteller, Bücher. Reinbek: Rowohlt, 1967; also in *Max Frisch. Aspekte des Prosawerks*, ed. Knapp).

Mayer, S., Die Funktion der Amerikakomponente im Erzählwerk Max Frischs (in *Max Frisch. Aspekte des Prosawerks*, ed. Knapp).

Mühll, Th.v.d., Schweizerische Prosaerzähler: Frisch, Moser, Welti, Hohl, Inglin (in *Neue Schweizer Rundschau*, 11, 1943).

Müller, J., Das Prosawerk Max Frischs: Dichtung unserer Zeit (in *Universitas* 22, 1967; also in *Max Frisch: Beiträge zur Wirkungsgeschichte*, ed. Schau; also in J.M., *Epik, Dramatik, Lyrik*).

Munteanu, R., Max Frisch si problemele romanului elvetian (in *Steaua* 23, 1972).

Rau, G., Max Frisch dramatique et romancier (in *Preuves* 90, 1958).

Reich-Ranicki, M., Über den Romancier Max Frisch (in *Neue Rundschau* 74, 1963; also in M.R.-R., *Deutsche Literatur in West und Ost: Prosa seit 1945*. Munich: Piper, 1963).

Rosenthal, E.Th., Die Erzählbarkeit von Bewusstseinszuständen: Capote, Frisch, Koeppen (in E.Th.R., *Das fragmentarische Universum. Wege und Umwege des modernen Romans*. Munich: Nymphenburger Verlagshandlung, 1970; Sammlung Dialog 43).

Stauffacher, W., Langage et mystère. A propos des derniers romans de Max Frisch (in *Etudes germaniques* 20, 1965; also in *Max Frisch: Beiträge zur Wirkungsgeschichte*, ed. Schau).

Stromšik, J., Das Verhältnis von Weltanschauung und Erzählmethode bei Max Frisch (in *Philologica Pragensia* 13, 1970; also in *Über Max Frisch II*, ed. Schmitz).

Ter-Nedden, G., Allegorie und Geschichte. Zeit- und Sozialkritik als Formproblem des deutschen Romans der Gegenwart (in *Poesie und Politik. Zur Situation der Literatur in Deutschland*, ed. W. Kuttenkeuler. Stuttgart: Kohlhammer, 1973; Sprache und Literatur 73).

Tindemans, C., Max Frisch: De Roman als zelf-verdediging (in *Dietsche Warande en Belfort* 110, 1965).

INDIVIDUAL WORKS
Als der Krieg zu Ende war

Anon. (bo), Als der Krieg zu Ende war: Notizen zu Max Frischs neuem Drama (in *Die Weltwoche*, 14 Jan. 1949).

Brock-Sulzer, E., Max Frisch: Als der Krieg zu Ende war (in *Schweizer Monatshefte* 28, 1948–49).

Butler, M., Das Paradoxon des Parabelstücks: Zu Max Frischs Als der Krieg zu Ende war und Graf Öderland (in *Max Frisch. Aspekte des Bühnenwerks*, ed. Knapp).
Korn, K., Als der Krieg zu Ende war. Gastspiel des dramatischen Kabinetts Baden-Baden (in *Die Zeit*, 6 April 1950).
Peters, W.A., Als der Krieg zu Ende war. Deutsche Erstaufführung in Baden-Baden (ibid.).
Scharff, E., Als der Krieg zu Ende war von Max Frisch (in *Die Volksbühne* 1, no. 2, 1951).
Spoerri, Th., Zu Max Frisch: Als der Krieg zu Ende war (in *Programmhefte des Schauspielhauses Zürich* 1948–49).

Andorra

Anon., Andorra von Max Frisch (in *Die Zeit*, 26 Jan. 1962).
Anon. (Leo), Wo liegt Andorra? (in *Die Zeit*, 2 Feb. 1962).
Anon. (G.W.v.L.). New York: Andorra, nicht gefragt (in *Die Bühne*, April 1963).
Anon. (R.M.), Andorra in Paris (in *Die Weltwoche*, 5 Feb. 1965).
Anon., Atrocity Stories. Andorra and Firebugs (in *Time*, 22 Feb. 1963).
Anon., Plays of Ideas. Andorra, Firebugs (in *Newsweek*, 25 Feb. 1963).
Arnold, A., Woyzeck in Andorra: Max Frisch und Georg Büchner (in *Max Frisch. Aspekte des Bühnenwerks*, ed. Knapp).
Aurin, K., Andorra: ein psychologisches Modell (in K.A., *Politische Psychologie*. vol. 3: Vorurteile. Ihre Erforschung und ihre Bekämpfung. Frankfurt: Europäische Verlagsanstalt, 1969; also in *Max Frisch: Beiträge zur Wirkungsgeschichte*, ed. Schau).
Bänziger, H., Andorra und die heile Welt (in *Frankfurter Hefte* 30, 1975; also in H.B., *Zwischen Protest und Traditionsbewusstsein*).
Biedermann, M., Politisches Theater oder radikale Verinnerlichung? Ein Vergleich der Stücke Biedermann und die Brandstifter und Andorra mit Biografie: Ein Spiel (in *Text und Kritik* 47–48, 1975).
Beckmann, H., Endlich ein Zeitstück! Max Frisch und der Jude von Andorra (in *Rheinischer Merkur*, 10 Nov. 1961).
Bondy, F., Gericht über die Schuldlosen. Oder: "Die Szene wird zum Tribunal." Zu S. Lenz' Die Zeit der Schuldlosen und Max Frischs Andorra (in *Der Monat* 14, Feb. 1962; also in *Max Frisch: Beiträge zur Wirkungsgeschichte*, ed. Schau).
Bovery, M., Mauern, die wir selber bauen (in *Die Tat*, 4 Nov. 1961).
Braun, H., Andorra in deutscher Sicht. Max Frisch in München (in *Rheinischer Merkur*, 26 Jan. 1962).
Brock-Sulzer, E., Andorra (in *Die Tat*, 4 Nov. 1961).
Brustein, R., German Guilt and Swiss Indictment (in *New Republic*, March 1963).
Bryden, R., Plaything (in *New Statesman*, 3 April 1964).
Cauvin, M., Max Frisch: Andorra (in *Etudes germaniques* 18, 1963).
Cwojdrak, G., Moral-Modell Andorra (in *Die Weltbühne* 21, 1966).
Davidowitz, I., It Can't Happen Here (in *Jerusalem Post*, 2 March 1962).
Enzensberger, H.M., Über Andorra (in *Programmheft Schauspielhaus Zürich*, 1961–62; also in *Max Frisch: Beiträge zur Wirkungsgeschichte*, ed. Schau).
Frühwald, W., Wo ist Andorra? Zu einem poetischen Modell Max Frischs (in *Beiträge zu den Ferienkursen des Goethe-Instituts für Deutschlehrer und Hochschulgermanisten aus dem Ausland*. Munich, 1966; also in *Über Max Frisch II*, ed. Schmitz).
Gellert, R., Paris: Andorra (in *New Statesman*, 7 Feb. 1964).
Gersch, W., Andorra: Inszenierung in der Volksbühne (in *Tribüne*, Berlin, GDR, 25 Feb. 1966).

Gessler, P., Zur Deutung von Max Frischs Andorra (in *Reformatio* 11, 1962).
Hampe, M., Wie die Aufführung entstand (in *Theater heute* 2, Nr. 12, 1961; also in *Max Frisch: Beiträge zur Wirkungsgeschichte,* ed. Schau).
Hegele, W., Max Frisch: Andorra (in *Der Deutschunterricht* 20, 1968; also in *Über Max Frisch,* ed. Beckermann).
Hewes, H., A Frisch Squall (in *Saturday Review,* 2 March 1963).
Hilty, M.R., Tabu Andorra (in *DU* 22, 1962).
Holz, H.H., Die Läuterung durch Einsicht (in *Panorama,* Dec. 1961).
Horst, K.A., Andorra mit anderen Augen (in *Merkur* 16, 1962).
Hüning, F., Pluralistische Textanalyse als kooperative Unterrichtsform, dargestellt am Beispiel von Max Frischs "Andorra," 1. Bild (in *Der Deutschunterricht* 25, 1973).
Jacobi, J., Andorra zum Beispiel (in *Die Zeit,* 17 Nov. 1961).
——, Fünf deutsche Bühnen im Spiegel von Max Frischs "Andorra." Aufführungen in München, Frankfurt, Düsseldorf, Hamburg und Berlin (in *Die Zeit,* 30 March 1962).
Karsch, W., Andorra (in W.K., *Wort und Spiel*: Aus der Chronik eines Theaterkritikers 1945-1962).
Kranz, H.B., Andorra wurde schnell abgesetzt: Max Frisch in New York (in *Frankfurter Rundschau* 60, 1963).
Krapp, H., Das Gleichnis vom verfälschten Leben (in *Programmheft der Städtischen Bühnen Frankfurt a.M.* 1961-62; also in *Spectaculum V*: Sechs moderne Theaterstücke. Frankfurt: Suhrkamp, 1962; also in *Max Frisch: Beiträge zur Wirkungsgeschichte,* ed. Schau; also in *Über Max Frisch II,* ed. Schmitz).
Kustow, M., No Graven Image (in *Encore* 9, 1962).
Liebermann, R., Andorra in New York (in *Neue Zürcher Zeitung,* 16 March 1963; also in *Max Frisch: Beiträge zur Wirkungsgeschichte,* ed. Schau).
Lohmann, C., Das Judenproblem im Literaturunterricht (in *Der Deutschunterricht* 18, 1966).
Meinert, D., Objektivität und Subjektivität des Existenzbewusstseins in Max Frischs Andorra (in *Acta Germanica* 2, 1967).
Okuda, K., Über Frischs Andorra und die Tragödie des Urteils (in *Quelle* 13, 1964).
Pesch, L., An der Wahrheit vorbei. Gedanken zu Max Frischs Andorra (in *Besinnung,* no. 1, 1963).
Petermann, G.A., Max Frisch und die Psychologie: Kritische Anmerkungen zu Interpretationen von Andorra (in *Max Frisch. Aspekte des Bühnenwerks,* ed. Knapp).
Pütz, P., Max Frischs "Andorra": Ein Modell der Missverständnisse (in *Text und Kritik* 47-48, 1975).
Riess, C., Mitschuldige sind überall: Eine Unterhaltung mit Max Frisch über sein neues Stück Andorra (in *Die Zeit,* 10 Nov. 1961).
Rischbieter, H., Andorra von Max Frisch in Zürich uraufgeführt. Das Stück–Der Kritiker über die Affürhung (in *Theater heute* 2, no. 2, 1961; also in *Max Frisch: Beiträge zur Wirkungsgeschichte,* ed. Schau; also in *Über Max Frisch II,* ed. Schmitz).
——, Andorra in München, Frankfurt und Düsseldorf (in *Theater heute* 3, 1962).
Schau, A., Modell und Skizze als Darbietungsform der Frischschen Dichtung, dargestellt an "Der andorranische Jude" (in *Studies in Swiss Literature,* ed. M. Jurgensen. Brisbane: University of Queensland, 1971; Queensland Studies in German Language and Literature 2).
Schlocker, G., Ausgeklügeltes Andorra. Max Frisch: Uraufführung in Zürich (in *Deutsche Zeitung,* 6 Nov. 1961; also in A. Schau, *Max Frisch: Beiträge zur Wirkungsgeschichte*).

Schmid, K., Max Frisch: Andorra und die Entscheidung (in K.S., *Unbehagen im Kleinstaat*).
Schumacher, E., Dramatik aus der Schweiz. Zu Max Frischs Andorra und Friedrich Dürrenmatts Die Physiker (in *Theater der Zeit* 17, 1962).
Seiser, R., Noch einmal: Andorra, Ein Lehrstück ohne Lehre (in *Die Christengemeinschaft* 34, 1962).
Stoop, B., A Play to Prick the Conscience (in *Christian Century*, 12 Sept. 1962).
Suter, G., Andorra: Zur Uraufführung des Stückes von Max Frisch am 2. November 1961 im Schauspielhaus Zürich (in *Die Weltwoche*, 10 Nov. 1961).
Thieberger, R., Andorra; nur ein Modell? (in *Max Frisch. Aspekte des Bühnenwerks*, ed. Knapp).
Torberg, F., Ein furchtbares Missverständnis (in *Forum* 8, 1961; also in F.T., *Gesammelte Werke in Einzelausgaben*, Munich: Langen/Müller, 1966, vol. 5: *Das fünfte Rad am Thespiskarren. Theaterkritiken*; also in *Max Frisch: Beiträge zur Wirkungsgeschichte*, ed. Schau).
———, Max Frischs Andorra (in *Encounter* 23, 1964).
Westecker, W., Andorra in und um uns. Max Frischs neues Stück uraufgeführt (in *Christ und Welt*, 8, Nov. 1961).
Whitcomb, R., Max Frisch's Andorra: National Bias and Critical Reception (in *Proceedings of the Pacific Northwest Conference on Foreign Languages*, 1972).
Wysling, H., Dramaturgische Probleme in Frischs Andorra und Dürrenmatts Besuch der alten Dame (in *Akten des 5. Internationalen Germanisten-Kongresses 1976*).

Antwort aus der Stille

Beriger, L., Max Frisch. Antwort aus der Stille (in *Das literarische Echo* 60, 1937).

(Herr) Biedermann und die Brandstifter

Biedermann, M., Politisches Theater oder radikale Verinnerlichung (under *Andorra*).
Blau, H., Shouting Fire in a Public Auditorium (in *Program of the San Francisco Actors' Workshop*, 28 Feb. 1964).
Blumer, A., and Kussler, R., Es ändert sich gar nichts–es muss sich was ändern: Zur Einführung in Max Frischs Biedermann und die Brandstifter und seine Behandlung im fremdsprachlichen Deutschunterricht (in *Deutschunterricht in Südafrika* 10, 1979).
Brewer, J., Max Frisch's Biedermann und die Brandstifter as the Documentation of an Author's Frustration (in *Germanic Review* 46, 1971; also in German translation in *Über Max Frisch II*, ed. Schmitz).
Brinkmann, H., Information und Realisierung (in *Studien zur Texttheorie und zur deutschen Grammatik. Festgabe für H. Glinz*, ed. H. Sitte and K. Brinker. Düsseldorf: Schwann, 1973).
Grenz, F., Diskussionsbeitrag zu Kusslers Methode, Frischs Biedermann zu unterrichten (in *Deutschunterricht in Südafrika* 10, 1979).
Heilman, R., Demonic Strategies: The Birthday Party and the Firebugs (in *Sense and Sensibility in Twentieth-Century Writing: A Gathering in Memory of W.V. O'Connor*, ed. B. Weber. Carbondale: Southern Illinois University Press, 1970).
Herms, D., Biedermann und die Brandstifter (in *Das deutsche Drama vom Expressionismus bis zur Gegenwart*, ed. M. Brauneck. Bamberg: Buchner, 1977).
Hewes. H., A Frisch Squall (see *Andorra*).
Hill, Ph., A Reading of the Firebugs (in *Modern Drama* 13, 1970).

Jäger, E.-M., Schwerin: Biedermann und die Brandstifter von Max Frisch (in *Theater der Zeit* 16, 1961).
Kahl, K., Frisch: Biedermann und die Brandstifter (in *Theater heute* 2, 1961).
Kaiser, J., Frisch aus Zürich (in *Frankfurter Hefte* 1958).
Karasek, H., Biedermann und die Brandstifter (in *Über Max Frisch*, ed. Beckermann).
Klose, W., Biedermann und die Brandstifter (in *Das Hörspiel im Unterricht*. Hamburg: Hans-Bredow-Institut, 1958, 1962).
Knust, H., Moderne Variationen des Jedermann-Spiels (in *Helen Adolf Festschrift*, ed. Sh. Z. Buehne, J. L. Hodge, and L. B. Pinto, New York: Ungar, 1968).
Koester, R., Everyman and Mammon: The Persistence of a Theme in Modern German Drama (in *Revue des langues vivantes* 35, 1969).
Krättli, A., Biedermann und die Brandstifter (in *Schweizer Monatshefte* 58, 1978).
Kranz, D., Im Herzen die Alten ... Biedermann und die Brandstifter von Max Frisch im Theater am Kurfürstendamm Berlin (in *Theater der Zeit* 14, 1959).
——, Biedermann und die Brandstifter (in *Sonntag*, 16 July 1961).
Kreutzer, H., Die Einbeziehung des Hörspiels in den Deutsch-Unterricht der Oberstufe (in *Der Deutschunterricht* 10, 1958).
Küsel, H., Rätsel, die uns aufgegeben sind. Die Brandstifter des Herrn B. (in *Die Gegenwart* 13, 1958).
Lewalter, Chr. E., Afterword (in Max Frisch, *Herr Biedermann und die Brandstifter*. Hamburg: Hans-Bredow-Institut, 1956).
Meinert, D., Das Absurde als Mittel der Verfremdung in Frischs Biedermann und die Brandstifter (in *Acta Germanica* 5, 1970).
Melchinger, S., Dar waren Etüden im neuen Stil. Max Frischs "Biedermann und Hotz" im Zürcher Schauspielhaus uraufgeführt (in *Die Zeit*, 17 April 1958); also in A. Schau, *Max Frisch: Beiträge zur Wirkungsgeschichte*).
Milfull, J., Der Tod in Salzburg? Biedermann und die Brandstifter. Frisch, Hofmannsthal, Brecht (in M. Jurgensen, *Frisch: Kritik, Thesen, Analysen*).
Mudrich, H., Frisch: Biedermann und die Brandstifter (in *Theater heute* 2, 1961).
Oliver, E., Burn Down the Blanchisserie (in *The New Yorker*, 23 February 1963).
Pickar, G., Biedermann und die Brandstifter: The Dilemma of Language (in *Modern Languages* 50, 1969).
Reding, J., Rückgrat aus Gummi gemacht. Biedermann und Hotz in Recklingshausen erfolgreich (in *Die Kultur* 13, 1965).
Riegel, P., Biedermann und die Brandstifter. Max Frischs "Jedermann 1958" (in *Blätter für den Deutschlehrer* 5, 1961).
Rode, R. O., Max Frischs Biedermann und die Brandstifter im Fremdsprachenunterricht (in *Deutschunterricht in Südafrika* 10, 1979).
Seller, P., Monsieur Biedermann et les incendiaires (in *Théâtre populaire* 31, 1958).
Stromšik, J., Biedermann und die Branstifter: Schwierigkeiten beim Schreiben eines Lehrstücks (in *Max Frisch. Aspekte des Bühnenwerks*, ed. Knapp).
Torberg, f., Biedermann und die Brandstifter, dazu: Die grosse Wut des Philipp Hotz (in F.T., *Das fünfte Rad am Thespiskarren*; also in *Max Frisch: Beiträge zur Wirkungsgeschichte*, ed. Schau).
Unseld, S., Gottlieb Biedermann: Nicht mehr davongekommen (in *Programmheft der Städtischen Bühnen Frankfurt a. M.*, 1958).
Weber, W., Zu Frischs Biedermann und die Brandstifter (in *Die Neue Zürcher Zeitung*, 3 May 1958; also in *Dichten und Trachten* 12, 1958; also in *Max Frisch: Beiträge zur Wirkungsgeschichte*, ed. Schau).

Weigel, H., Max Frisch. Biedermann und die Brandstifter (in H.W., *Tausendundeine Premiere*. Vienna: Wollzeilen, 1961).

Westecker, W., Lehrstück mit grotesken Stacheln. Max Frischs Biedermann und Hotz in Zürich uraufgeführt (in *Christ und Welt*, 18 January 1958).

Bin oder Die Reise nach Peking

Brock-Sulzer, E., Bin oder Die Reise nach Peking (in *DU*, July 1945).

Mayer, H., Bin oder Die Reise nach Peking (in H.M., *Dürrenmatt und Frisch*: Anmerkungen).

Pickar, G., Bin in Bin (in *South Central Bulletin* 29, 1969).

——, Bin oder Die Reise nach Peking: A Structural Study (in *Ball State University Forum* 17, 1976).

Schumacher, H., Zu Max Frischs Bin oder Die Reise nach Peking (in *Neue Schweizer Rundschau*, 13, 1945–46; also in *Über Max Frisch II*, ed. Schmitz).

Spycher, P., Nicht-gelebtes und gelebtes Leben in Max Frischs Bin oder die Reise nach Peking und Santa Cruz: Eine literarisch-psychologische Betrachtung (in *Max Frisch. Aspekte des Bühnenwerks*, ed. Knapp).

Staiger, E., Bin oder Die Reise nach Peking (in *Schweizer Monatshefte* 25, 1945; also in *Dichten und Trachten* 4, 1954).

Stine, L.J., Chinesische Träumerei, amerikanisches Märchen: Märchenelemente in Bin und Stiller (in *Max Frisch. Aspekte des Prosawerks*, ed. Knapp).

Biografie: Ein Spiel

Anon., Das zweifache Leben (in *Der Spiegel*, 16 Oct. 1967).

Anon., Abend mit Antoinette (ibid., 29 Jan. 1968).

Anon., Das andere Ich. Bemerkungen zum Stück (in *Programmhefte des Schauspielhauses Zürich* 1967-68).

Bänziger, H., Ab posse ad esse valet . . . Zu einem Zitat im Spiel Biografie (in *Frisch: Kritik, Thesen, Analysen*, ed. Jurgensen).

Beckmann, H., Max Frisch in der Probierstube. Hans Kürmanns Kür in der Biografie im Zürcher und Frankfurter Schauspielhaus (in *Rheinischer Merkur*, 9 March 1968).

Biedermann, M., Politisches Theater oder radikale Verinnerlichung (under *Andorra*).

Bradley, B., Max Frisch's Biografie: Ein Spiel (in *German Quarterly* 44, 1971; also in German translation in *Über Max Frisch II*, ed. Schmitz).

Brock-Sulzer, E., Max Frisch: Biografie: Ein Spiel (in *Die Tat*, 5 Feb. 1968).

Burgauner, C., Max Frisch, Biografie: Ein Spiel (in *Frankfurter Hefte* 23, 1968).

Drommert, R., Der Mann, der nicht wählen konnte (in *Die Zeit*, 9 Feb. 1968; also in *Max Frisch: Beiträge zur Wirkungsgeschichte*, ed. Schau, under the title "Über die Uraufführung in Düsseldorf").

Friebert, St., Max Frisch's New Play Biografie (in *Books Abroad* 42, 1968).

Gamper, H., Schwierigkeiten mit Frischs Biografie. Mögliche Lehren aus einer verhinderten Uraufführung (in *Zürcher Woche*, 6 Oct. 1967).

Gyssling, W., Spiel zwischen Schicksal und Zufall (in *Theater der Zeit*, 1968).

Ignee, W., Kürmann, Frisch und Noelte. Die Geschichte eines Fehlstarts (in *Der Monat* 20, 1968).

——, Darf man über Kürmann lachen? Die erste Probe von Max Frischs Biografie in Zürich (in *Christ und Welt* 6, 1968).

Ignee, W., "Ich hoffte auf ein gutes Stück." Noeltes Streit mit Frisch: Ein Gespräch mit dem Regisseur (in *Christ und Welt,* 6 Oct. 1967).
Jacobi, J., Der Mann, der nicht wählen konnte (in *Die Zeit,* 9 Feb. 1968; also in *Max Frisch: Beiträge zur Wirkungsgeschichte,* ed. Schau, under the title "Über die Uraufführung in Frankfurt").
Karasek, H., Die Premiere findet nicht statt. Max Frischs neues Stück Biografie wird vorerst nicht aufgeführt (in *Die Zeit,* 6 Oct. 1967).
Konstantinović, Z., Das diarische Ich im Bühnenwerk: Biographie: Ein Spiel (in *Max Frisch. Aspekte des Bühnenwerks,* ed. Knapp).
Leonhardt, R. W., Der Mann, der nicht wählen konnte (in *Die Zeit,* 9 Feb. 1968; also in *Max Frisch: Beiträge zur Wirkungsgeschichte,* ed. Schau, under the title "Über die Uraufführung in München").
Lindtberg, L, Was erwartet Max Frisch? (in *Christ und Welt,* 13 Oct. 1967).
Litten, R., Sein neues Stück. Was Max Frisch darüber im Gespräch verriet (in *Christ und Welt,* 30 June 1967).
Lorenzo, Uraufführung des Spiels Biografie von Max Frisch in Zürich (in *Schweizer Monatshefte* 47, 1967-68).
Lutz-Odermatt, H., Zum Ehe-Modell in Max Frischs Stück Biografie (in *Schweizer Rundschau* 67, 1968).
Marsillach, A., Mi versión de Biografie (in *Primer Acto* 111, 1969).
Mayer, S., Biografie: Ein Spiel: Stiller und/oder Gantenbein auf der Bühne (in *Max Frisch. Aspekte des Bühnenwerks,* ed. Knapp).
Melchinger, S., and Karasek, H., Max Frisch, Biografie: Ein Spiel (in *Theater heute* 9, no. 3, 1968).
Musgrave, M.E., Kürmann, His Wives, and "Helen, the Mulatta" in Max Frisch's Biografie: Ein Spiel (in *College Language Association Journal* 18, 1975).
Nieva, F., Biografie y otros problemas (in *Primer Acto* 111, 1969).
Obermüller, K., Biografie. Gedanken vor der Aufführung von Max Frischs neuem Stück (in *DU* 28, 1968).
Pickar, G.B., Max Frisch's Biografie: Image as 'Life-Script' (in *Symposium* 28, 1974).
Profitlich, U., Beliebigkeit und Zwangsläufigkeit: Zum Verhältnis von Frischs Schillerpreisrede und Biografie (in *Zeitschrift für Deutsche Philologie* 95, 1976).
Queizan, E., Una interpretación de Biografie (in *Primer Acto* 111, 1969).
Ruppert, P., Possibility and Form in Max Frisch's Biography: A Game (in *Modern Drama* 1975).
Schärer, B., Die Bedeutungslosigkeit des Privaten. Zur Uraufführung von Max Frischs Biografie im Schauspielhaus Zürich (in *Die Weltwoche,* 9 Feb. 1968).
Schwab-Felisch, H., Die erfolgreiche Biografie (in *Merkur* 22, 1968; also in *Max Frisch: Beiträge zur Wirkungsgeschichte,* ed. Schau).
Stone, M., Der abgehalfterte Faust. Max Frischs Biografie als geistiges Bonbon in Berlin (in *Christ und Welt,* 12 April 1968).
Stromšik, J., Biografie Maxe Frische (in *Časopis pro moderní filologii* 50, 1968).
Tank, K.L., Schachspiel mit Shakespeare und Hannes Kürmann (in *Sonntagsblatt,* 11 Feb. 1968).
Torberg, F., Das Leben ändern, nicht die Welt. Uraufführung der Biografie von Max Frisch in Zürich (in *Max Frisch: Beiträge zur Wirkungsgeschichte,* ed. Schau).
Weisstein, U., Introduction (in Max Frisch, *Biografie: Ein Spiel,* New York: Harcourt, Brace, Jovanovich, 1972).
Zimmer, D.E., Der Mann, der nicht wählen konnte (in *Die Zeit,* 9 Feb. 1968; also in

Max Frisch: Beiträge zur Wirkungsgeschichte, ed. Schau, under the title "Über die Uraufführung in Zürich").

Blätter aus dem Brotsack

Beckmann, H., Max Frisch unter Waffen (in *Rheinischer Merkur,* 4 Dec. 1964).
Jaeggi, U., Die gesammelten Erfahrungen des Kanoniers Max Frisch (in *Text und Kritik* 47-48, 1975).
Weber, W., Blätter aus dem Brotsack. Zur Neuausgabe von Max Frischs Aufzeichnungen aus dem Grenzdienst 1939 (in W.W., *Tagebuch eines Lesers.* Olten: Walter, 1966).

Der Mensch erscheint im Holozän

Bollinger, B., Max Frisch und das Phänomen des Alterns. Versuch über die Erzählung Der Mensch erscheint im Holozän (in *Schweizer Monatshefte* 59, no. 7, 1979).
Goetz, R.M., Alter ohne Revolte (in *Merkur* 33, 1979).
Jenny, U., Über Max Frisch: Der Mensch erscheint im Holozän. Herrn Geisers Naturkatastrophe (in *Der Spiegel,* 7 May 1979).

Die Chinesische Mauer

Brock-Sulzer, E., Die Chinesische Mauer (in *Schweizer Monatshefte* 26, 1946-47).
――, Die Chinesische Mauer (in *Die Tat,* 23 Oct. 1946).
――, Die Chinesische Mauer (ibid., 14 Nov. 1954).
Creutz, L, Kleinbürger angesichts der Zukunft. Ein Zeitstück am Kurfürstendamm (in *Die Weltbühne* 1955).
Durzak, M., Max Frisch und Thornton Wilder, Der vierte Akt von The Skin of Our Teeth (in *Frisch: Kritik, Thesen, Analysen,* ed. Jurgensen).
Gontrum, P., Max Frisch's Die Chinesische Mauer: A New Approach to World Theater (in *Revue des langues vivantes* 36, 1970).
――, Max Frisch's The Chinese Wall (in *Proceedings: Pacific Northwest Conference on Foreign Languages,* ed. J. Mordaunt. Victoria, B.C.: University of Victoria, 1968).
Horst, K.A., Zur Chinesischen Mauer (in *Merkur* 8, 1954).
Hubacher, E., Die neue Chinesische Mauer. Ein Welttheater unserer Zeit in Gestalt einer Farce (in *Die Volksbühne* 23, 1955).
Jacobi, J., Die Chinesische Mauer. Farce von Max Frisch. Deutsches Schauspielhaus Hamburg (in *Die Zeit,* 5 March 1965).
Jacobi, W., Max Frisch, Die Chinesische Mauer: Die Beziehungen zwischen Sinngehalt und Form (in *Der Deutschunterricht* 13, 1961; also in *Max Frisch: Beiträge zur Wirkungsgeschichte,* ed. Schau).
Jacobs, W., Historischer Gespensterreigen. Die Chinesische Mauer von Max Frisch am Hamburger Schauspielhaus (in *Frankfurter Rundschau,* 3 March 1965).
Kaiser, G., Max Frischs Farce Die Chinesische Mauer (in *Über Max Frisch,* ed. Beckermann).
Karsch, W., Max Frisch: Die Chinesische Mauer (in W.K., *Wort und Spiel,* under *Andorra*).
Luft, Fr., Max Frisch, Die Chinesische Mauer (in F.L., *Stimme der Kritik.* Berliner Theater seit 1945. Velber: Friedrich 1961, 1965).
Muschg, W., Die Chinesische Mauer. Zur Uraufführung von Max Frischs Komödie (in *Programmhefte des Schauspielhauses Zürich* 1946-47).
Teichmann, H., Der Intellektuelle und der Machtstaat. Zur Uraufführung von Max Frischs Die Chinesische Mauer (in *Pädagogische Provinz* 15, 1961).

Torberg, F., Die Chinesische Mauer (in *Forum* 3, 1956).
Unseld, S., Notizen (in *Programmheft des Staatstheaters Kassel* 9, 1958).
———, Die Chinesische Mauer (in *Nationaltheater Mannheim. Bühnenblatt für die 178. Spielzeit*, nos. 7, 8).
Vielhaber, G., Im Revoluzzer-Schick. Wiederum Max Frischs Chinesische Mauer bei den Ruhrfestspielen (in *Frankfurter Rundschau*, 28 May 1968).
Wagner, K., Die Chinesische Mauer in Hamburg (in *Theater heute*, no. 4, 1965).
Wagner, M., Timeless Relevance: Max Frisch's The Chinese Wall (in *Modern Drama* 16, 1973).
Waldmann, G., Das Verhängnis der Geschichtlichkeit. Max Frisch: Die Chinesische Mauer (in *Wirkendes Wort* 17, 1967; also in *Über Max Frisch II*, ed. Schmitz; also in *Max Frisch: Beiträge zur Wirkungsgeschichte*, ed. Schau).
Ziskoven, W., Max Frisch. Die Chinesische Mauer (in *Zur Interpretation des modernen Dramas. Brecht, Dürrenmatt, Frisch*. Frankfurt: Diesterweg, 1978).

Die Grosse Wut des Philipp Hotz

Dütsch, A., Zwei neue Stücke von Max Frisch (under *Biedermann*).
Melchinger, S., Das waren Etüden im neuen Stil. Max Frischs Biedermann und Hotz im Zürcher Schauspielhaus uraufgeführt (under *Biedermann*).
Reding, J., Rückgrat aus Gummi gemacht (under *Biedermann*).
Torberg, F., Biedermann und die Brandstifter, dazu: Die grosse Wut des Philipp Hotz (under *Biedermann*).
Weber, W., Zu Frischs Biedermann und die Brandstifter (under *Biedermann*).
Westecker, W., Lehrstück mit grotesken Stacheln. Max Frischs Biedermann und Hotz in Zürich uraufgeführt (under *Biedermann*).

Dienstbüchlein

Becker, R., Milde Stärkung (in *Der Spiegel*, 25 March 1974).
Bondy, F., Max Frisch und der Aktivdienst (in *Schweizer Monatshefte* 1974).
Hilty, H. R., Ein Buch aktiver Erinnerung (in *Über Max Frisch II*, ed. Schmitz).
Jaeggi, U., Die gesammelten Erfahrungen des Kanoniers Max Frisch (under *Blätter aus dem Brotsack*).
Kaiser, J., Max Frischs Kritik an einem Kanonier (in *Über Max Frisch II*, ed. Schmitz).
Kohlschütter, A., Helvetische Malaise (in *Die Zeit*, 5 April 1974).
Krämer-Badoni, R., Ich beklage mich nicht . . . (in *Deutsche Zeitung/Christ und Welt*, 9 March 1974).
Leisi, E., Die Kunst der Insinuation (in *Über Max Frisch II*, ed. Schmitz).
Salis, J. R. von, Schweigen war die Regel (in *Die Weltwoche*, 10 April 1974; also in *Über Max Frisch II*, ed. Schmitz).
Schmidt, A., Die Armee der Vaterlandsbesitzer (in *Frankfurter Rundschau*, 16 March 1974).
Tank, K.L., Durchgemogelt und dienstbuchlich (in *Deutsches Allgemeines Sonntagsblatt*, 10 March 1974).
Wallmann, J.P., Max Frischs Dienstbüchlein (in *Neue deutsche Hefte* 21, 1974).

Die Schwierigen oder J'adore ce qui me brûle

Beckmann, H., Blick zurück auf Max Frisch. Zu seinem ersten Roman Die Schwierigen (in *Rheinischer Merkur*, 2 May 1958).

Gasser, M., Agenda (in *Die Weltwoche*, 5 June 1957).
Korrodi, E., Ein Roman von Max Frisch. J'adore ce qui me brûle oder Die Schwierigen (in *Über Max Frisch II*, ed. Schmitz).
Kulp, M., Die Schwierigen (in *Reclams Romanführer*, ed. J. Beer. Stuttgart: Reclam, 1963, vol. 2, Reclams Universalbibliothek 8862-8879).

Don Juan oder Die Liebe zur Geometrie

Anon., Max Frisch: Don Juan oder Die Liebe zur Geometrie. Premiere 5. Mai 1953 im Schauspielhaus Zürich (in *Die Weltwoche*, 8 May 1953).
Bachmann, D., Der Unentschiedene. Zur Aufführung von Don Juan oder Die Liebe zur Geometrie von Max Frisch im Zürcher Schauspielhaus (in *Die Weltwoche*, 5 June 1964).
Brock-Sulzer, E., Don Juan oder Die Liebe zur Geometrie (in *Die Tat*, 8 May 1953).
——, Max Frisch: Don Juan oder Die Liebe zur Geometrie (in *Die Tat*, 2 June 1964).
Dietrich, M., Preface to *Don Juan. Theater der Jahrhunderte*, ed. J. Schondorff. Munich: Langen-Müller, 1967.
Franz, H., Der Intellektuelle in Max Frischs Don Juan und Homo faber (in *Zeitschrift für Deutsche Philologie* 90, 1971; also in *Über Max Frisch II*, ed. Schmitz).
Gnüg, H., Das Ende eines Mythos: Max Frischs Don Juan oder Die Liebe zur Geometrie (in H.G., *Don Juans theatralische Existenz. Typ und Gattung*. Munich: Fink, 1974; also in *Über Max Frisch II*, ed. Schmitz; also in *Die deutsche Komödie. Vom Mittelalter bis zur Gegenwart*, ed. W. Hinck. Düsseldorf: Bagel, 1977).
Gontrum, P., Max Frisch's Don Juan. A New Look at a Traditional Hero (in *Comparative Literature Studies* 2, 1965).
Hoffmann-Ostwald, D., Berlin, Maxim-Gorki-Theater: Don Juan oder Die Liebe zur Geometrie von Max Frisch (in *Theater der Zeit* 4, 1967).
Horn, P., Zu Max Frischs Don Juan oder Die Liebe zur Geometrie (in *Frisch: Kritik, Thesen, Analysen*, ed. Jurgensen).
Humm, R. J., Max Frisch steht Rede (in *Die Weltwoche*, 22 May 1953).
Ingen, F. J. van, Configuraties van Don Juan in het Werk van Max Frisch (in *Handelingen van het eenendertigste Nederlands Filologencongres*: Gehouden te Utrecht op Woendsdag 5, donderdag 6 en vrijdag 7 april 1972, Amsterdam: Holland University Press, 1974).
Kieser, R., and Guilloton, D. Starr, Faustische Elemente in Max Frischs Don Juan oder Die Liebe zur Geometrie (in *Max Frisch. Aspekte des Bühnenwerks*, ed. Knapp).
Kopelev, L., Poraženie rassudka: forčestvo razuma. Maks Friš, Don Žuan, ili ljubov 'k geometrii (in *Teatr Moskva* 28, 1967).
Krättli, A., Don Juan oder Die Liebe zur Geometrie (in *Programmhefte des Schauspielhauses Zürich* 1963-64).
Kuby, E., Don Juans Liebe zur Geometrie ist klein (in *Frankfurter Hefte* 6, 1953).
Matthews, R., Theatricality and Deconstruction in Max Frisch's Don Juan (in *Modern Language Notes* 87, 1972).
Rötzer, H. G., Frischs Don Juan: Zur Tradition eines Mythos (in *Arcadia* 10, 1975).
Rüf-Gebert, P., Zu Max Frischs Don Juan oder Die Liebe zur Geometrie (in *Schweizer Rundschau* 53, 1953; also in *Max Frisch: Beiträge zur Wirkungsgeschichte*, ed. Schau).
Ruppert, P., Max Frisch's Don Juan: The Seductions of Geometry (in *Monatshefte* 67, 1975).
——, Max Frisch's Don Juan: The Paradigm of His Intellectual Anti-Hero (in *Germanic Notes* 7, 1976).

Stössinger, F., Schauspielhaus Zürich: Max Frischs Don Juan oder Die Liebe zur Geometrie (in *Die Tat*, 8 May 1953).
Vogtmann, M., Frischs Don Juan oder Die Liebe zur Geometrie (in *Theater heute* 2, 1961).
Weickert, Ch., Max Frisch-Erstaufführung in der DDR. Don Juan oder Die Liebe zur Geometrie (in *Die Tat*, 10 Dec. 1966).
Wendt, E., Frischs Don Juan oder Die Liebe zur Geometrie (in *Theater heute* 3, 1962).
Werner, J., Ein trauriger Held. Vorgeschichte und thematische Einheit von Max Frischs Don Juan oder Die Liebe zur Geometrie (in *Sprachkunst* 8, 1977).
Wollenberger, W., Max Frisch, Don Juan oder Die Liebe zur Geometrie (in *Zürcher Woche*, 5 June 1964).

Graf Öderland

Anon., Max Frisch, Graf Öderland (in *Christ und Welt*, 16 Aug. 1951).
Biedermann, M., Graf Öderland in Beziehung zu seiner Umwelt: Eine Untersuchung (in *Max Frisch. Aspekte des Bühnenwerks*, ed. Knapp).
Butler, M., Das Paradoxon des Parabelstücks: Zu Max Frischs Als der Krieg zu Ende war und Graf Öderland (under "Als der Krieg zu Ende war").
Colberg, K., Max Frisch: Graf Öderland (in *Schweizer Monatshefte* 30, 1950-51).
Dürrenmatt, F., Brief an Max Frisch über Graf Öderland (in H. Bänziger, *Frisch und Dürrenmatt*).
———, Eine Vision und ihr dramatisches Schicksal (in *Die Weltwoche*, 16 Feb. 1951; also in F.D., *Theaterschriften und Reden*, ed. E. Brock-Sulzer. Zurich: Verlag der Arche, 1966; also in *Über Max Frisch*, ed. Beckermann).
Jacobi, H., Zu Graf Öderland (in *Die Zeit*, 22 Feb. 1951).
Kaiser, J., Öderländische Meditationen. Porträt eines Stückes und einer Aufführung (in *Frankfurter Hefte* 11, 1956).
Karsch, W., Graf Öderland (in W.K., *Wort und Spiel*, under *Andorra*).
Knapp, G.P., Angelpunkt Öderland: Über die Bedeutung eines dramaturgischen Fehlschlages für das Bühnenwerk Frischs (in *Max Frisch. Aspekte des Bühnenwerks*, ed. Knapp).
Rischbieter, H., Max Frisch, Graf Öderland; monströse Moritat (in *Theater heute* 2, no. 11, 1961).
———, Wendt, E., and Koegler, H., Versuch, Bilanz zu ziehen. Berliner Dramaturgie (in *Theater heute* 3, no. 12, 1963).
Rüf, P., Graf Öderland, eine Moritat von Max Frisch (in *Schweizerische Rundschau* 1951).
Salamon, G., Introduction to Max Frisch, *Graf Öderland. Eine Moritat in 12 Bildern*, New York: Harcourt, Brace & World, 1966; edition suhrkamp in American text editions.
Salis, J.R.v., Zu Max Frischs Graf Öderland (in J.R.v.S., *Schwierige Schweiz*. Zurich: Füssli, 1968).
Schmid, K., Notizen (in *Programmheft Schauspielhaus Zürich*, 1951).
Suter, G., Graf Öderland mit der Axt in der Hand. Zur Uraufführung der letzten Fassung von Graf Öderland, eine Moritat von Max Frisch. Berliner Festwochen 1961 (in *Die Weltwoche*, 6 Oct. 1961; also in *Über Max Frisch*, ed. Beckermann).

Homo faber

Alleman, B., Max Frisch und Homo faber (in *Hessischer Rundfunk*, 20 Oct. 1957).

Bibliography

Basler, O., Der neue Frisch (in *Die Tat*, 29 Nov. 1957).
Bialik, W., Der Zufall als Strafe im Roman Homo faber von Max Frisch (in *Studia Germanica Posnaniensia* 4, 1975).
Bicknese, G., Zur Rolle Americas in Frischs Homo faber (in *German Quarterly* 42, 1969; also in *Deutschlands literarisches Amerikabild*, ed. A. Ritter. New York: Olms, 1977).
Bradley, B., Max Frisch's Homo faber. Theme and Structural Devices (in *Germanic Review* 41, 1966).
Brandt, Th., Homo faber (in *Deutsche Rundschau* 81, 1958).
Butler, M., The Dislocated Environment: The Theme of Itinerancy in Max Frisch's Homo faber (in *New German Studies* 4, 1976).
Christiaens, J., Homo faber (in *Leuvense Bijtragen* 55, 1966).
Enzensberger, H.M., Vergebliche Brandung der Ferne. Eine Theorie des Tourismus (in *Merkur* 12, 1958).
Farner, K., Homo frisch (in *Die Weltbühne*, 1 Jan. 1958).
Franz, A., Max Frisch: Homo faber (in *Bücherei und Bildung* 9, 1957).
Franz, H., Der Intellektuelle in Max Frischs Don Juan und Homo faber (under *Don Juan*).
Franzen, E., Homo faber (in *Merkur* 12, 1958; also in E.F., *Aufklärungen. Essays*).
Friedrich, G., Die Rolle der Hanna Piper. Ein Beitrag zur Interpretation von Max Frischs Roman Homo faber (in *Studia neophilologica* 49, 1977).
Geissler, R., Max Frischs Homo faber (in R.G., *Möglichkeiten des modernen deutschen Romans*. Frankfurt: Diesterweg, 1962, 1976).
Haberkamm, K., Il était un petit navire. Anmerkungen zur Schiffsmotivik in Max Frischs Homo faber (in *Duitse kronick* 29, 1977).
Haerdter, R., Das Fatum und der Zufall (in *Die Gegenwart* 12, 1957).
Hartung, R., Eine moderne Tragödie. Max Frisch Homo faber (in *Neue deutsche Hefte* 42, 1958).
Hasters, H., Das Kamera-Auge des Homo faber (in *Diskussion Deutsch* 9, 1978).
Henze, W., Die Erzählhaltung in Max Frischs Roman Homo faber (in *Wirkendes Wort* 11, 1961; also in *Max Frisch: Beiträge zur Wirkungsgeschichte*, ed. Schau).
Herzog, B., Von den Liebesromanen älterer Herren (in *Schweizer Rundschau* 60, 1960).
Hildebrand, R., Max Frischs Homo faber (in *Mädchenbildung und Frauenschaffen* 9, 1959).
Horst, K.A., Neuer Wein in alten Schläuchen (in *Jahresring* 58-59, 1958).
Ihlenfeld, K., Homo faber (in K.I., *Zeitgesicht. Erlebnisse eines Lesers*. Witten: Eckart, 1961).
Ingen, F. van, Max Frischs Homo faber zwischen Technik und Mythologie (in *Amsterdamer Beiträge zur neueren Germanistik* 2, 1973).
Jens, W., Max Frisch und Homo faber (in *Die Zeit*, 9 Jan. 1958; also in *Max Frisch: Beiträge zur Wirkungsgeschichte*, ed. Schau).
Kaiser, G., Max Frischs Homo faber (in *Schweizer Monatshefte* 38, 1958-59; also in *Max Frisch: Beiträge zur Wirkungsgeschichte*, ed. Schau; also in *Über Max Frisch II*, ed. Schmitz).
Knapp, M., Der "Techniker" W. Faber: Zu einem kritischer Missverständnis (in *Germanic Notes* 8, 1977).
Kulp, M., Homo faber (in *Reclams Romanführer*, ed. J. Beer, vol. 2).
Latta, A.D., Walter Faber and the Allegorization of Life: A Reading of Max Frisch's Novel Homo Faber (in *Germanic Review* 54, 1979).
Liersch, W., Wandlung einer Problematik (in *Neue Deutsche Literatur* 7, 1958; also in *Über Max Frisch*, ed. Beckermann).

Michot-Dietrich, H. Meursault et Faber: Vaincus ou vainqueurs? Une comparaison entre L'Etranger et Homo faber (in *Archiv für das Studium der Neueren Sprachen und Literaturen* 213, 1976).
Müller, K.-D., Der Zufall im Roman. Anmerkungen zur erzähltechnischen Bedeutung der Kontingenz (in *Germanisch-Romanische Monatsschrift*, 28, 1978).
Müller, G., Europa und Amerika im Werk Max Frischs. Eine Interpretation des Berichts Homo faber (in *Moderna Språk* 62, 1968).
Neis, E., Homo faber (in E.N., *Erläuterungen zu Max Frisch: Stiller, Homo faber, Gantenbein*).
Praag, Ch. van, Der Schicksalsweg des Regeltechnikers Homo faber. Ein antithetischer Roman (in *Duitse kroniek* 29, 1977).
Pütz, P., Das Übliche und das Plötzliche. Über Technik und Zufall in Homo faber (in *Max Frisch. Aspekte des Prosawerks*, ed. Knapp).
Roisch, U., Max Frischs Auffassung vom Einfluss der Technik auf den Menschen: nachgewiesen am Roman Homo faber (in *Weimarer Beiträge* 13, 1967; also in U.R. and G. Jäckel, *Struktur und Symbol*, Halle/Saale: Mitteldeutscher Verlag, 1977; also in *Über Max Frisch*, ed. Beckermann; also in *Max Frisch: Beiträge zur Wirkungsgeschichte*, ed. Schau).
——, Afterword (in Max Frisch, *Homo faber, Ein Bericht*, Berlin, GDR: Volk und Wissen, 1973).
Salis, J.R.V., Zu Max Frischs Homo faber (in J.R.v.S., *Schwierige Schweiz*, under *Graf Öderland*).
Schmidtmann, K., Mondfinsternis mit Sabeth. Tragödie eines Technikers in Max Frischs Homo faber (in *Rheinischer Merkur*, 25 Oct. 1957).
Schürer, E., Zur Interpretation von Max Frischs Homo faber (in *Monatshefte* 59, 1967).
Suter, G., Homo faber. Ein Bericht von Max Frisch (in *Die Weltwoche*, 1 Nov. 1957).
Waidson, H.M., Max Frisch: Homo faber (in *Twentieth Century German Literature*, ed. A. Closs. New York: Barnes & Noble, 1969).
Weber, W., Max Frisch 1958 (in W.W., *Zeit ohne Zeit*).
Wehrli, M., Gegenwartsdichtung der deutschen Schweiz (in *Deutsche Literatur in unserer Zeit*. Mit Beiträgen von W. Kayser et al. Göttingen: Vandenhoeck & Ruprecht, 1959; Kleine Vandenhoeck Reihe 73-74).
Weidmann, B., Wirklichkeit und Erinnerung in Max Frischs Homo faber (in *Schweizer Monatshefte* 44, 1964-65).
Westecker, W., Zwei Romane von Max Frisch. Die Scheiternden. Der technische und der künstlerische Mensch (in *Christ und Welt*, 5 Dec. 1957).

Mein Name sei Gantenbein

Arnold, H. L., Möglichkeiten nicht möglicher Existenzen. Zu Max Frischs Roman Mein Name sei Gantenbein (in *Eckart-Jahrbuch*, ed. K.L. Tank. Witten: Eckart, 1964-65).
Baumgart, R., Othello als Hamlet (in *Der Spiegel*, 2 Sept. 1964; also in *Über Max Frisch*, ed. Beckermann).
Beckmann, H., Entwürfe zu einem Ich (in *Rheinischer Merkur*, 4 Sept. 1964).
Bier, J.P., Mein Name sei Gantenbein. Ein Beitrag zur Deutung von Max Frischs letztem Roman (in *Revue des langues vivantes* 33, 1967).
Birmele, J., Anmerkungen zu Max Frischs Roman Mein Name sei Gantenbein (in *Monatshefte* 60, 1968; also in *Max Frisch: Beiträge zur Wirkungsgeschichte*, ed. Schau).
Blöcker, G., Max Frischs Rollen (in G.B., *Literatur als Teilhabe*. Kritische Orientierungen zur literarischen Gegenwart. Berlin: Argon, 1966).

Butor, H., Entwürfe zu einem Ich. Der neue Roman von Max Frisch: Mein Name sei Gantenbein (in *Sonntagsblatt*, 20 Sept. 1964).
Cauvin, M., Max Frisch, l'absolu et le nouveau roman (in *Etudes germaniques* 22, 1967; also in *Max Frisch: Beiträge zur Wirkungsgeschichte*, ed. Schau; also in German translation in *Über Max Frisch II*, ed. Schmitz).
Clements, R., The European Literary Scene (in *Saturday Review*, 26 Dec. 1964).
Cunliffe, W.G., Die Kunst, ohne Geschichte abzuschwimmen (under *Stiller*).
Emrich, W., Die "goldenen Früchte" der Literaturkritik (in *Die Welt der Literatur*, Oct. 1964; also in W.E., *Polemik*. Frankfurt: Athenäum, 1968).
Farner, K., Mein Name sei Frisch (in *Sinn und Form* 18, 1966).
Grözinger, W., Der Roman der Gegenwart: Freiheit des Lesers (in *Hochland* 57, 1964).
Hamm, P., Entwürfe zu einem späten Ich. Zu Max Frischs Mein Name sei Gantenbein (in *Die Weltwoche*, 16 Oct. 1964).
Hartung, R., Max Frisch: Mein Name sei Gantenbein (in *Neue Rundschau* 75, 1964).
Heise, H.-J., Ein grosses Arsenal menschlicher Möglichkeiten. Zu einem neuen Roman von Max Frisch (in *Die Tat*, 7 Aug. 1964).
Heissenbüttel, H., Ein Erzähler, der sein Handwerk hasst? Zu Max Frischs drittem (*sic*) Roman: Mein Name sei Gantenbein (in *Die Welt der Literatur*, 3 Sept. 1964).
Holthusen, H.E., Ein Mann von fünfzig Jahren (in *Merkur* 18, 1964; also in H.E.H., *Plädoyer für den Einzelnen*. Kritische Beiträge zur literarischen Diskussion. Munich: Piper, 1967; also in *Max Frisch: Beiträge zur Wirkungsgeschichte*, ed. Schau).
Iggers, W., Max Frisch, Mein Name sei Gantenbein (in *Books Abroad* 29, 1965).
Ihlenfeld, K., Max Frisch: Mein Name sei Gantenbein (in *Neue Deutsche Hefte* 105, 1965).
Joho, W., Spiel mit Möglichkeiten (in *Neue deutsche Literatur* 13, 1965).
Jurgensen, M., Mein Name sei Gantenbein (in *Max Frisch: Beiträge zur Wirkungsgeschichte*, ed. Schau).
Kähler, H., Max Frischs Gantenbein-Roman (in *Sinn und Form* 17, 1965; also in *Über Max Frisch*, ed. Beckermann).
Krättli, A., Max Frisch: Mein Name sei Gantenbein (in *Schweizer Monatshefte* 44, 1965).
Kraus, W., Mein Name sei Gantenbein (in *Wort in der Zeit* 10, 1964).
Kurz, P.K., Vorstellungen gegen das Wahre. Zur Diskussion um Max Frischs Gantenbein (in *Sonntagsblatt*, 4 Oct. 1964).
——, Mein Name sei Gantenbein (in *Stimmen der Zeit* 175, 1964).
Leber, H., Mein Name sei Gantenbein. Notizen zur jüngeren Literatur in der Schweiz (in *Wort in der Zeit* 11, 1965).
Manthey, J., Prosa des Bedenkens (in *Frankfurter Hefte* 20, 1965).
Marchand, W.R., Max Frisch, Mein Name sei Gantenbein (in *Zeitschrift für deutsche Philologie* 87, 1968; also in *Über Max Frisch*, ed. Beckermann).
Mayer, H., Mögliche Ansichten über Herrn Gantenbein. Anmerkungen zu Max Frischs neuem Roman (in *Die Zeit*, 25 Sept. 1964; also in *Über Max Frisch II*, ed. Schmitz; also in H.M., *Über Dürrenmatt und Frisch*).
——, Prof. Herzog: ein amerikanischer Gantenbein? (in *Die Zeit*, 7 May 1965).
Masini, F., Il mio nome sia Gantenbein di Max Frisch (in F.M., *Itinerario sperimentale nella letteratura tedesca*. Parma: Studium Parmense, 1970).
Merrifield, D.F., Max Frischs Mein Name sei Gantenbein: Versuch einer Strukturanalyse (in *Monatshefte* 60, 1968; also in *Max Frisch: Beiträge zur Wirkungsgeschichte*, ed. Schau).
Neis, E., Gantenbein (in E.N., *Erläuterungen zu Max Frisch*).

Petersen, J.H., Wirklichkeit, Möglichkeit und Fiktion in Max Frischs Roman Mein Name sei Gantenbein (in *Max Frisch. Aspekte des Prosawerks*, ed. Knapp).
Probst, G.F., Du sollst dir kein Bildnis machen. Überlegungen zu Max Frischs Roman Mein Name sei Gantenbein (in *Colloquia Germanica*, nos. 3-4, 1978).
Reich-Ranicki, M., Plädoyer für Max Frisch. Zu dem neuen Roman Mein Name sei Gantenbein und Hans Mayers Kritik (in *Die Zeit*, 2. Oct. 1964; also in M.R.-R., *Literatur der kleinen Schritte*, Munich: Piper, 1967 and Frankfurt: Ullstein, 1971; also in *Über Max Frisch II*, ed. Schmitz).
Schaub, M., Un événement: le nouveau roman de Frisch (in *Journal de Genève*, Dec. 1964).
Schneider, P., Mängel der gegenwärtigen Literaturkritik (in *Neue Deutsche Hefte* 107, 1966.
Schober, O., Max Frisch: Mein Name sei Gantenbein. Spiegelungen des Rollenverhaltens im Roman (in *Der deutsche Roman im 20. Jahrhundert* 2, 1976).
Schroers, R., Max Frisch oder das Misstrauen (in *Christ und Welt*, 18 Sept. 1964; also in *Max Frisch: Beiträge zur Wirkungsgeschichte*, ed. Schau).
Seeba, H. C., "Erfahrung" und "Geschichte" bei Max Frisch (in H.C.S., *Kritik des ästhetischen Menschen*. Bad Homburg: Gehlen, 1970).
Stauffacher, W., Gantenbein: une nouvelle forme romanesque (Réponse à M. Cauvin in *Etudes Germaniques* 22, 1967; also in *Max Frisch: Beiträge zur Wirkungsgeschichte*, ed. Schau).
Stiles, V. M., Max Frischs Roman Mein Name sei Gantenbein: "Spiel mit Varianten" (in *Modern Language Studies* 10, 1979).
Stone, M., Max Frisch oder der Konjunktiv im Hirn (in *Christ und Welt*, 18 Sept. 1964; also in *Max Frisch: Beiträge zur Wirkungsgeschichte*, ed. Schau).
Stromšík, J., Max Frisch, Mein Name sei Gantenbein: Eine Interpretation (in *Acta Universitatis Carolinae. Philologica Germanistica Pragensia* 5, 1968).
Suter, G., Dreieckskomödie im Spiegelsaal. Zum neuen Buch von Max Frisch (in *Zürcher Woche*, 4 Sept. 1964).
Tindemans, C., Max Frisch: der roman als zelfverdediging (in *Dietsche Warande en Belfort* 110, 1965).
Toman, C., Bachmanns Malina und Frischs Gantenbein, Zwei Seiten des gleichen Lebens (in *Die Tat*, 24 Aug. 1974).
Villain, J., Gantenbein: Flucht aus der Geschichte in Geschichten oder: Das Unbehagen im Wirtschaftswunder (in *Der Sonntag*, 14 March 1965).
Vin, D. de, Max Frisch: Mein Name sei Gantenbein. Eine Interpretation (in *Studia Germanica Gandensia* 12, 1971).
——, "Mein Name sei Gantenbein" van Max Frisch: Over de struktuur van een hedendaagse roman (in *Handelingen van het eenendertigste Nederlands Filologencongres*: Gehouden te Groningen op Woensdag 1, donderdag 2 en vrijdag 3 april 1970. Groningen: Wolers-Noordhoff, 1971).
Vogel, W., Zur Besprechung von Max Frischs neuem Roman Mein Name sei Gantenbein in domino No. 57 (in *domino* 58, 1964).
Vormweg, H., Othello als Mannequin (in *Der Monat* 17, 1964; also in H.V., *Die Wörter und die Welt*, Neuwied: Luchterhand, 1968, under the title "Max Frisch oder Alles wie nicht geschehen").
Weber, W., Max Frisch, Mein Name sei Gantenbein (in W.W., *Tagebuch eines Lesers*. Olten: Walter, 1966).

Montauk

Arnold, H.L., Erzählung vom Gelingen eines Scheiterns. Max Frischs Montauk (in *Frankfurter Rundschau*, 24 Jan. 1976).

Bachmann, D., Auf der Suche nach Gegenwart. Die Erzählung Montauk: nicht nur ein neues Buch, sondern auch ein neuer Max Frisch (in *Die Weltwoche*, 1 Oct. 1975).

Baden, H.J., Max Frischs Lebensbericht (in *Lutherische Monatshefte* 14, 1975).

Bänziger, H., Leben im Zitat. Zu Montauk: ein Formulierungsproblem und dessen Vorgeschichte (in *Max Frisch. Aspekte des Prosawerks*, ed. Knapp).

Beckmann, H., Kein Name für eine Schuld. Max Frisch mag nicht mehr erfinden (in *Rheinischer Merkur*, 10 Oct. 1975).

Blöcker, G., and Schwab-Felisch, H., Max Frischs Konfessionen (in *Merkur* 29, 1975).

Chiusano, I.A., Romanzo come un diario: Montauk di Max Frisch (in *Fiera Letteraria* 7, 1976).

Gockel, G., Montauk. Eine Erzählung (in *Duitse kronick* 29, 1977).

Hagelstange, R., Rastlose Neugier auf sich selbst (in *Welt am Sonntag*, 28 Dec. 1975).

Hartung, R., Schreibend unter Kunstzwang. Zu der autobiographischen Erzählung Montauk von Max Frisch (in *Die Neue Rundschau* 86, 1975; also in *Über Max Frisch II*, ed. Schmitz).

Hofe, G. vom, Zauber ohne Zukunft. Zur autobiographischen Korrektur in Max Frischs Erzählung Montauk (in *Euphorion* 70, 1976).

Johnson, U., Zu Montauk (in *Über Max Frisch II*, ed. Schmitz).

Karasek, H., Bekenntnisse auf Distanz (in *Der Spiegel*, 29 Sept. 1975).

Knapp, G.P., Noch einmal: Das Spiel mit der Identität. Zu Max Frischs Montauk (in *Max Frisch. Aspekte des Prosawerks*, ed. Knapp).

Krättli, A., Leben im Zitat. Max Frischs Montauk (in *Schweizer Monatshefte* 55, 1975; also in *Über Max Frisch II*, ed. Schmitz).

Mayer, H., Die Geheimnisse jedweden Mannes. Leben, Literatur und Max Frischs Montauk (in *Deutsche Zeitung*, 21 Nov. 1975; also in *Die Weltwoche*, 7 Jan. 1976; also in *Über Max Frisch II*, ed. Schmitz; also in H.M., *Über Friedrich Dürrenmatt und Max Frisch*).

Michaelis, R., Love Story–und mehr. Die Erzählung Montauk und das Lesebuch Stich-Worte (in *Die Zeit*, 19 Sept. 1975).

Müller-Salget, K., Max Frischs Montauk: eine Erzählung? (in *Zeitschrift für Deutsche Philologie* 97, 1978).

Nöhbauer, H.F., Ein Autor stellt sich aus. Max Frisch liefert mit seiner Erzählung Montauk Intimes für die Bestsellerliste (in *Bücherkommentare*, no. 6, 1975).

Prawer, S., In and Out of Character (in *Times Literary Supplement*, 2 Jan. 1976).

Stauffacher, W., Diese dünne Gegenwart. Bemerkungen zu Montauk (in *Frisch: Kritik, Thesen, Analysen*, ed. Jurgensen).

Wapnewski, P., Hermes steigt vom Sockel: Gedanken zu Max Frisch in Montauk (anlässlich des 15. Mai 1976; in *Merkur* 30, 1976).

Wallmann, J.P., Max Frischs autobiographische Erzählung Montauk (in *Die Tat*, 7 Nov. 1975).

Nun singen sie wieder

Anon., Max Frisch: Nun singen sie wieder (in *Die Tat*, 1 April 1945).

Anon., Nun singen sie wieder (in *Die Bühnenkritik* 5, 1947).

Brock-Sulzer, E., Nun singen sie wieder (in *Schweizer Monatshefte* 25, 1945–46).

Butzlaff, W., Die Darstellung der Jahre 1933-1945 im deutschen Drama (in *Der Deutschunterricht* 16, 1964).
Horwitz, K., Zur Inszenierung von Nun singen sie wieder (in *Programmhefte des Schauspielhauses Zürich* 1944-45).
Pechel, J., Nun singen sie wieder. Versuch eines Requiems. Theaterstück von Max Frisch (in *Deutsche Rundschau* 71, 1948).
Pleister, W., Nun singen sie wieder (in *Die Schule* 2, 1947).
Suter, G., Max Frisch. Von Nun singen sie wieder zu Andorra (in *Die Weltwoche*, 3 Nov. 1961).
Th., Max Frisch: Nun singen sie wieder (in *Programmhefte des Schauspielhauses Zürich* 1944-45).
Tulasiewicz, W.F., and Scheible, K., Introduction (in Max Frisch, *Nun singen sie wieder. Versuch eines Requiems.* London: Harrap, 1966).
Ziskoven, W., Nun singen sie wieder. Versuch eines Requiems (in *Zur Interpretation des modernen Dramas: Brecht, Dürrenmatt, Frisch*, ed. R. Geissler. Frankfurt: Diesterweg, 1978; also in *Max Frisch: Beiträge zur Wirkungsgeschichte*, ed. Schau).

Santa Cruz. Eine Romanze

Anon., Max Frisch Santa Cruz (in *Die Weltwoche*, 18 April 1947).
Brock-Sulzer, E., Max Frisch Santa Cruz (in *Die Tat*, 9 March 1946).
——, Santa Cruz (in *Schweizer Monatshefte* 26, 1946-47).
Diederichsen, D., Dramen-Lese (in *Bücherei und Bildung*, no. 1, 1962).
Feiler, M. Chr., Im Münchner Residenztheater: Santa Cruz und die niederen Bühnen weihen (in *Münchner Merkur*, 8 Oct. 1951).
Geering, A., Max Frisch: Santa Cruz (in *Schweizer Monatshefte* 27, 1947-48).
Hilpert, H., Santa Cruz. Aus einem Vortrag (in *Programmheft des Schauspielhauses Zürich* 1945-46).
——, Bemerkungen zu Santa Cruz (in *Blätter des Deutschen Theaters in Göttingen*, 1956-57).
Hilty, H. R., Prolegomena zum modernen Drama (in *Akzente* 5, 1958).
Reindl, L. E., Über Santa Cruz (in *Blätter des Deutschen Theaters Konstanz*, no. 2, 1948-49).
Schaefer, H.-L., Max Frisch: Santa Cruz. Eine Interpretation (in *Germanisch-Romanische Monatsschrift* 20, 1970; also in *Über Max Frisch II*, ed. Schmitz).
Spycher, P., Nicht-gelebtes und gelebtes Leben in Max Frischs Bin oder Die Reise nach Peking und Santa Cruz: Eine literarisch-psychologische Betrachtung (in *Max Frisch. Aspekte des Bühnenwerks*, ed. Knapp).

Schinz

Weisstein, U., Max Frischs Schinz (in *Books Abroad* 35, 1961).

Stiller

Bänziger, H., Der Steppenwolf und Stiller. Zwei Fremdlinge innerhalb der bürgerlichen Welt (in *Materialien zu Max Frischs Stiller*, ed. Schmitz; also in H.B., *Zwischen Protest und Tradition*).
Basler, O., Max Frisch: Stiller (in *Neue Schweizer Rundschau*, 22, 1954-55).
Bauer, E., Max Frischs Stiller. Vorschläge zur Erarbeitung im Unterricht (in *Materialien zu Max Frischs Stiller*, ed. Schmitz).
Beckmann, H., Die eigene Wirklichkeit (in *Rheinischer Merkur*, 26 Nov. 1954).

Böschenstein, H., Stiller: ein neuer Menschentyp (in *Materialien zu Max Frischs Stiller*, ed. Schmitz; also in H.B., *Der neue Mensch*. Die Biographie im deutschen Nachkriegsroman. Heidelberg: Rothe, 1958).
Bonnin, G., Stiller: Swiss Don Quichote (in *Studies in Swiss Literature*, ed M. Jurgensen. Brisbane: University of Queensland 1971; Queensland Studies in German Language and Literature 2).
Braem, H.M., Leidenschaft der Freiheit (in *Deutsche Rundschau* 81, 1955).
Braun, K., Max Frischs Stiller: Sprache und Stil: Zwei Beispielanalysen (in *Materialien zu Max Frischs Stiller*, ed. Schmitz; also in K.B., *Die epische Technik in Max Frischs Roman Stiller*. Als Beitrag zur Formfrage des modernen Romans, Diss. Frankfurt 1959).
——, Der Erzähler in Max Frischs Stiller (ibid.).
——, Die vertikale und horizontale Gliederung der Geschichte in Max Frischs Roman Stiller (ibid.).
——, Die Tagebuchform in Max Frischs Stiller (ibid.).
Butler, M., Die Funktion von Stillers Geschichten: Isidor (in *Materialien zu Max Frischs Stiller*, ed. Schmitz; also in M.B., *The Novels of Max Frisch*).
——, Rolf: Die Zweideutigkeit der Ordnung (ibid.).
Cases, C., Max Frischs Stiller (in C.C., *Saggi e note di letteratura tedesca*. Torino: Einaudi, 1963, German translation by Fr. Kollmann under the title *Stichworte zur deutschen Literatur*. Kritische Notizen. Vienna: Europa-Verlag, 1969).
Demetz, P., Das Schweizer Establishment und Anatol Ludwig Stiller (in *Materialien zu Max Frischs Stiller*, ed. Schmitz; also in P.D., *Die süsse Anarchie*. Skizzen zur deutschen Literatur seit 1945, Frankfurt: Ullstein, 1970, 1973).
Deschner, K., Max Frisch. Stiller und andere Prosa (in K.D., *Talente, Dichter, Dilettanten*. Wiesbaden: Limes, 1964).
Dürrenmatt, Fr., Stiller. Roman von Max Frisch. Fragment einer Kritik (in F.D., *Theaterschriften und Reden*. Zürich; Verlag der Arche, 1966; also in *Über Max Frisch*, ed. Beckermann; also in *Materialien zu Max Frischs Stiller*, ed. Schmitz).
Frank, C., Will nicht Stiller sein (in *Frankfurter Hefte* 11, 1956).
Franzen, E., Über Max Frischs Stiller oder Der gescheiterte Traum vom neuen Ich (in E.F., *Aufklärungen*, under *Homo faber*).
Frühwald, W., Parodie der Tradition. Das Problem literarischer Originalität in Max Frischs Roman Stiller (in *Materialien zu Max Frischs Stiller*, ed. Schmitz).
Gontrum, P., The Legend of Rip van Winkle in Max Frisch's Stiller (in *Studies in Swiss Literature*, ed. Jurgensen; also in German translation in *Materialien zu Max Frischs Stiller*, ed. Schmitz).
Haerdter, R., Mr White und die Wahrheit (in *Die Gegenwart* 9, 1954).
Harris, K., Stiller: Ich oder Nicht-Ich? (in *German Quarterly* 41, 1968; also in an abridged version under the title Die Kierkegaard-Quelle zum Roman Stiller in *Materialien zu Max Frischs Stiller*, ed. Schmitz).
Helmetag, Ch., The Image of the Automobile in Max Frisch's Stiller (in *Germanic Review* 47, 1972; also in German translation in *Materialien zu Max Frischs Stiller*, ed. Schmitz).
Henning, M., Die Ich-Erzähler als Medium der Verfremdung in Max Frischs Stiller (in M.H., *Die Ich-Form und ihre Funktion in Thomas Manns Doktor Faustus und in der deutschen Literatur der Gegenwart*. Tübingen: Niemeyer, 1966).
Hesse, H., Über Max Frischs Stiller (in *Die Weltwoche*, 19 Nov. 1954; also in H.H., *Gesammelte Werke*, vol. 12: *Schriften zur Literatur* 2. Frankfurt: Suhrkamp, 1970).

Hinderer, W., Ein Gefühl der Fremde. Amerikaperspektiven in Max Frischs Stiller (in *Materialien zu Max Frischs Stiller*, ed. Schmitz; also in *Amerika in der deutschen Literatur*, ed. S. Bauschinger. Stuttgart: Reclam, 1975).

Holl, O., *Der Roman als Funktion und Überwindung der Zeit*: Zeit und Gleichzeitigkeit im deutschen Roman des 20. Jahrhunderts. Bonn: Bouvier, 1968).

Horst, K. A., Bilderflucht und Bildwirklichkeit (in *Merkur* 9, 1955; also in *Max Frisch: Beiträge zur Wirkungsgeschichte*, ed. Schau).

Ihlenfeld, K., Stiller (in K.I., *Zeitgesicht*, under *Homo faber*).

Jens, W., Afterword (in Max Frisch, *Erzählungen des Anatol Ludwig Stiller*; also in *Über Max Frisch*, ed. Beckermann; also in *Materialien zu Max Frischs Stiller*, ed. Schmitz.).

Kayser, W., Wer erzählt den Roman? (in *Neue Rundschau* 68, 1957; also in W.K., *Die Vortragsreise*. Berne: Francke, 1958).

Karmasin, H., Schmitz, W., and Wünsch, M., Kritiker und Leser: Eine empirische Untersuchung zur Stiller-Rezeption (in *Materialien zu Max Frischs Stiller*, ed. Schmitz).

Kieser, R., Das Tagebuch als äussere Struktur: Stiller (in *Materialien zu Max Frischs Stiller*, ed. Schmitz; also in R.K., *Max Frisch: Das literarische Tagebuch*).

Koch, Th., Auf den Spuren Dostojewskijs (in *Die Zeit*, 2 Dec. 1954).

Kohlschmidt, W., Selbstrechenschaft und Schuldbewusstsein im Menschenbild der Gegenwartsdichtung. Eine Interpretation des Stiller von Max Frisch und der Panne von Friedrich Dürrenmatt (in *Das Menschenbild in der Dichtung*, ed. A. Schaefer. Munich: Beck, 1965; Beck'sche Reihe 34; also in W.K., *Konturen und Übergänge*. Berne: Francke, 1977; also in *Materialien zu Max Frischs Stiller*, ed. Schmitz; also in *Max Frisch: Beiträge zur Wirkungsgeschicte*, ed. Schau).

Kulp, M., Stiller (in *Reclams Romanführer*, ed. J. Beer, under *Die Schwierigen*).

Links, R., Stiller. Afterword (in *Max Frisch: Stiller*. Berlin, DDR: Volk und Welt, 1975; also in *Materialien zu Max Frischs Stiller*, ed. Schmitz).

Lusser-Mertelsmann, G., Selbstflucht und Selbstsuche. Das 'Psychoanalytische' in Frischs Stiller (in *Materialien zu Max Frischs Stiller*, ed. Schmitz).

——, Die Höhlengeschichte als symbolische Darstellung der Wiedergeburt (ibid.).

Manger, P., Kierkegaard in Max Frisch's Novel Stiller (in *German Life and Letters* 20, 1966–67).

Marti, K., Das Bildnis und die Schweize (in K.M., *Die Schweiz und ihre Schriftsteller – Die Schriftsteller und ihre Schweiz*. Zurich: EWZ-Verlag, 1966; Polis Zeitbuchreihe 28; also in *Materialien zu Max Frischs Stiller*, ed. Schmitz).

——, Das zweite Gebot im Stiller von Max Frisch (ibid.; also in *Kirchenblatt für die reformierte Schweiz*, 5 Dec. 1957).

Mayer, H., Anmerkungen zu Stiller (in H.M., *Dürrenmatt und Frisch*; also in *Über Max Frisch*, ed. Beckermann; also in *Materialien zu Max Frischs Stiller*, ed. Schmitz).

Milanowska, H., Der Erzählenstandpunkt als Mittel zur Bestimmung des Erzählers im Roman Stiller von Max Frisch (in *Studia Germanica Posnaniensia* 1, 1971).

Musgrave, M. E., The Evolution of the Black Character in the Works of Max Frisch (under "General Articles").

Nizon, P., Und Stiller? (in P.N., *Diskurse in der Enge. Aufsätze zur schweizer Kunst*. Berne: Kantelaber, 1970; Zurich: Benziger, 1973; also in *Materialien zu Max Frischs Stiller*, ed. Schmitz).

Pender, M., The Role of the "Staatsanwalt" in Max Frischs Stiller (in *German Life and Letters* 32, 1979).

Pfanner, H., Stiller und das Faustische bei Max Frisch (in *Orbis Litterarum* 24, 1969; also in *Max Frisch: Beiträge zur Wirkungsgeschicte*, ed. Schau).

Pickar, G.B., "Kann man schreiben, ohne eine Rolle zu spielen?" Zur Problematik des fingierten Erzählens in Stiller (in *Max Frisch. Aspekte des Prosawerks*, ed. Knapp).
Plant, R., The Past Was a Dead Burden (in *Saturday Review*, 12 April 1958).
Rychner, M., Stiller (in *Die Tat*, 27 Nov. 1954).
Salyámosy, M., Anatol Stillers Spanienerlebnis (in *Annales Universitatis Budapestinensis, Sectio Philologica Moderna* 5, 1974).
Schimanski, K., Der Konflikt zwischen Individuum und Gesellschaft in Max Frischs Stiller (in *Materialien zu Max Frischs Stiller*, ed. Schmitz; also under "Dissertations and Theses").
Schonauer, F., Roman des modernen Ich (in *Christ und Welt*, 13 Jan. 1958).
Schmitz, W., Zur Entstehung von Max Frischs Roman Stiller (in *Materialien zu Max Frischs Stiller*, ed. Schmitz).
Staiger, E., Stiller. Zu dem neuen Roman von Max Frisch (in *Max Frisch: Beiträge zur Wirkungsgeschichte*, ed. Schau).
Steinmetz, H., Roman Als Tagebuch: Stiller (in H. St., *Max Frisch: Tagebuch, Drama, Roman*, under "General Books"; also in *Materialien zu Max Frischs Stiller*, ed. Schmitz).
Stine, L.J., Chinesische Träumerei: amerikanisches Märchen. Märchenelemente in Bin und Stiller (under *Bin*).
Tank, K.L., Schuld: ein Weg zur Wirklichkeit. Stiller: ein Roman wider die Selbstreflexion (in *Sonntagsblatt*, 16 Jan. 1955).
Unseld, S., Ein neuer Roman von Max Frisch (in *Morgenblatt für Freunde der Literatur*, 23 Sept. 1954).
Wahl, R., Max Frisch: Stiller (in *Münchner Merkur*, 2 March 1955).
Weideli, W., Stiller ou le Malaise Helvétique (in *Adam* 27, no. 275, 1959).
Westecker, W., Zwei Romane von Max Frisch (under *Homo faber*).
White, A., Max Frisch's Stiller as a Novel of Alienation, and the nouveau roman (in *Arcadia* 2, 1967; also in German translation in *Materialien zu Max Frischs Stiller*, ed. Schmitz).
Wünsch, M., Stiller: Versuch einer strukturalen Lektüre (in *Materialien zu Max Frischs Stiller*, ed. Schmitz).
Zeller-Cambon, M., Max Frischs Stiller und Luigi Pirandellos Mattia Pascal: Die Odyssee zu sich selbst (in *Frisch: Kritik, Thesen, Analysen*, ed. Jurgensen).
Zimmermann, W., Max Frisch: Stiller (W.Z., *Deutsche Prosadichtungen unseres Jahrhunderts. Interpretationen für Lehrende und Lernende*, vol. 2. Düsseldorf: Schwann, 1969).

Tagebuch mit Marion, Tagebuch 1946-1949, Tagebuch 1966-1971

Anon., Max Frisch: Tagebuch 1946–49 (in *Die Weltwoche*, 27 Oct. 1950).
Anon., Prospects of the Suicide Society (in *Times Literary Supplement*, 29 Sept. 1972).
Bachmann, D., Nachdenken über Max Frisch (in *Die Weltwoche*, 19 April 1972).
Bänziger, H., Max Frischs neues Tagebuch als Dokument der Zeit (in *Universitas* 28, 1975; also in H.B., *Zwischen Protest und Traditionsbewusstsein*).
Beckmann, H., Blitzartige Zugriffe (in *Rheinischer Merkur*, 21 April 1972).
Bernardi, E., Max Frisch e il romanzo-diario (in *Annali della Facoltà di Lingue e Letterature stranieri di Ca' Foscari* 6, 1967).
Boerner, P., *Tagebuch*. Stuttgart: Metzler, 1969 (Sammlung Metzler 85).
Bondy, F., Frisch's best-selling 'Diary' (in *New York Times*, 7 April 1972).
Boveri, M., Tagebuch 1966-1971 (in *Neue Rundschau* 83, 1972).
Burgauner, Chr., Zwei Interessen und zwei Instanzen (in *Frankfurter Hefte* 27, 1972).

Cann, A., Dos diarios (in A.C., *A partir de Heliand*. Cordóba, Argentina: Universidad Nacional, 1964).
Gilman, R., Sketchbook 1966-1971 (in *New York Times*, April 1972).
Hartung, R., Versuch, ein Meisterwerk zu beschreiben (in *Die Zeit*, 5 May 1972).
Henningsen, J., Jeder Mensch erfindet sich eine Geschichte: Max Frisch und die Autobiographie (in *Literatur in Wissenschaft und Unterricht* 4, 1971).
Hiltbrunner, H., *Alles Gelingen ist Gnade*. Tagebücher. Zurich: Artemis, 1958.
Hilty, H.R., Ein Buch aktiver Erinnerung (in *Über Max Frisch II*, ed. Schmitz).
Jurgensen, M., Die Erfindung eines Lesers (in *Frisch: Kritik, Thesen, Analysen*, ed. Jurgensen; also in M.J., *Das fiktionale Ich*. Untersuchungen zum Tagebuch. Berne: Francke, 1979).
Karsunke, Y., Das sprechende Pferd (in *Frankfurter Rundschau*, 10 June 1972).
Kieser, R., Man as His Own Novel: Max Frisch and the Literary Diary (in *Germanic Review* 47, 1972).
——, Das Tagebuch als Idee und Struktur (in *Max Frisch. Aspekte des Prosawerks*, ed. Knapp).
Krättli, A., Über literarische Gegenwart. Mit Randnotizen zum Tagebuch 1966-1971 von Max Frisch (in *Schweizer Monatshefte* 52, 1972-73).
Krolow, K., Exemplarische Besinnung (in *Zeitwende*, 5 May 1959; also in *Dichten und Trachten* 13, 1959).
Kuby, E., Der Wächter (in *Frankfurter Hefte* 6, 1951).
Kuhn, Chr., Der Dichter und sein Tagebuch (in *DU* 24, 1964).
Kurczaba, A., The Diary and the Struggle for Expression: Frisch's Blätter aus dem Brotsack, Tagebuch 1946-1949, and Tagebuch 1966-1971 (in A.K., *Gombrowicz and Frisch. Aspects of the Literary Diary*. Bonn: Bouvier, 1980; Abhandlungen zur Kunst-, Musik- und Literaturwissenschaft, Band 295).
Kurz, P.K., Tagebuch als 'kombattande Resignation' (in *Bücherkommentare* 3, 1972; also in *Stimmen der Zeit* 189, 1972, under the title "Aus Berzona nichts Neues").
Mast, H., Tagebuch mit Marion von Max Frisch (in *Neue Schweizer Rundschau*, 15, 1947-48).
Mayer, H., Die Schuld der Schuldlosen (in *Der Spiegel*, 12 June 1972; also in H.M., *Über Friedrich Dürrenmatt und Max Frisch*).
Petersen, J., Der Gerechte (in *Deutsche Zeitung/Christ und Welt*, 12 May 1972).
Pulver, E., Mut Zur Unsicherheit. Zu Max Frischs Tagebuch 1966-1971 (in *Frisch: Kritik, Thesen, Analysen*, ed. Jurgensen).
Reich-Ranicki, M., Der Klassiker der Skizze (in *Die Zeit*, 5 May 1972).
Rüedi, P., Tagebuch für Mitglieder (in *Sonntags-Journal*, 29-30 April 1972).
Rüst, Th. G., Gesammeltes aus fünf Jahren zum Menschen und zur Zeit (in *zs/impuls*, no. 2, May 1972).
Schafroth, H.F., Bruchstücke einer grossen Fiktion: Über Max Frischs Tagebücher (in *Text und Kritik* 47-48, 1975).
Schimanski, K., Ernst genommene Zeitgenossenschaft: subjektiv gespiegelt (in *Weimarer Beiträge* 20, 1974; also in *Über Max Frisch II*, ed. Schmitz).
Schmolze, G., Max Frisch. Tagebuch 1966-1971 (in *Zeitwende/Die neue Furche* 43, 1972).
Schumacher, H., Max Frisch. Tagebuch 1946-49 (in *Neue Schweizer Rundschau*, 18, 1950-51).
Tank, K.L., Max Frisch. Tagebuch 1966-1971 (in *Deutsches Allgemeines Sonntagsblatt*, 23 April 1972).

Wallmann, J.P., Max Frischs neues Tagebuch (in *Die Tat*, 8 July 1972; also in *Neue deutsche Hefte* 113, 1972).
Wapnewski, P., Tua res. Zum Tagebuch II von Max Frisch (in *Merkur* 26, 1972, also in *Über Max Frisch II*, ed. Schmitz).
Woog, E., Max Frischs Tagebuch (in *Neutralität* 10, no. 9, 1972).

Triptychon

Bormann, A. von, Theater als Existenz-Erfahrung? Die Wende von Max Frisch zum christlichen Laienspiel (in *Max Frisch. Aspekte des Bühnenwerks*, ed. Knapp).
Burgauner, Chr., Max Frisch: Triptychon (in *Frankfurter Hefte* 34, no. 2, 1979).
Matt, P.V., Max Frischs mehrfache Hadesfahrt. Aus Anlass des Stückes Triptychon (in *Neue Rundschau* 89, no. 4, 1978).
Rüedi, P., Die lange Ewigkeit des Gewesenen. Max Frisch schrieb sin Stück vom Tod, das nicht gespielt wird (in *Deutsche Zeitung/Christ und Welt*, 12 April 1978).
Schmitz, W., Zu Max Frisch: Triptychon: Drei szenische Bilder (in *Max Frisch. Aspekte des Bühnenwerks*, ed. Knapp).

Wilhelm Tell für die Schule

Bachmann, D., Saison für Tell (in *Die Weltwoche*, 30 July 1971).
——, Das war Frischs Geschoss (in *Die Zeit*, 24 Dec. 1971).
Baumgart, R., Wilhelm Tell: ein ganz banaler Mörder (in *Über Max Frisch II*, ed. Schmitz).
Berchtold, A., Wilhelm Tell im 19. und 20. Jahrhundert (in *Tell. Werden und Wandern eines Mythos*, ed. E. Stunzi. Berne: Hallwag, 1973).
Flaschka, H., Wilhelm Tell für die Schule als verfremdeter Klassiker (in *Diskussion Deutsch* 9, 1978).
Habe, H., Die Helden im Eimer (in *Die Welt am Sonntag*, 7 Nov. 1971).
Jenny, U., Max Frisch: Wilhelm Tell für die Schule (in *Hessischer Rundfunk* 1 April 1972).
Jurgensen, M., Die Entmythologisierung der Freiheit oder Die Umschulung des Geistes (in *Schweizer Monatshefte* 51, 1972).
Muschg, A., Apfelschuss war nicht verlangt (in *Über Max Frisch II*, ed. Schmitz; abridged version in *Der Spiegel*, 9 Nov. 1971).
Schröder, J., Wilhelm Tell für die Schule als Max Frisch für die Schule (in *Max Frisch. Aspekte des Prosawerks*, ed. Knapp).
Schultz, U., Das war Frischs Geschoss (in *Deutsche Zeitung/Christ und Welt*, 13 Aug. 1971).
Steiner, J., Brauchbare Schweiz (in *Sonntags-Journal*, 10-11 July 1971).

Zürich-Transit

Ohly, H.W., "Ich hatte das Bedürfnis, in ein neues Medium einzusteigen" (in *Evangelischer Filmbeobachter* 18, 1966).
Zanetti, G., Epilog zu einem Film von Max Frisch (in *Zürcher Woche*, 17 Dec. 1965).

MUSICAL COMPOSITION

Lang, Max, *Die grosse Wut des Philipp Hotz*, grotesque opera in one act by Max Frisch, music by Max Lang, partitura 1960 (microfilm at Schweizer Landesbibliothek).

Frisch's Biographical Data

15 May 1911	Max Rudolf Frisch is born in Zurich to Franz Bruno Frisch, architect, and Karolina née Wildermuth.
1924–1930	He attends the Kantonale Realgymnasium Zürich (Public Grammar School of the Canton of Zurich).
1931–1933	He is enrolled at Zurich University, majoring in German Studies. His father's death forces him to leave school and to earn a living.
1933–1936	Max Frisch works as a free-lance journalist, travels abroad for the first time: Prague, Budapest, Dalmatia, Istanbul, Greece.
1936–1941	Financially supported by a friend, Max Frisch enrolls at the Eidgenössische Technische Hochschule Zürich (Federal Technical University of Zurich), majoring in Architecture.
1938	Receives Conrad Ferdinand Meyer Prize of the City of Zurich.
1939–1945	Periodical military service in the Swiss artillery.
1942	Max Frisch opens his own architectural office in Zurich.
1946	Trips to Germany and Italy.
1947	Trips to Berlin and Prague.
1948	Trips to Breslau (Wroclaw), Paris, Prague, Vienna, and Warsaw. Repeated meetings with Brecht in Zurich.
1949	Max Frisch completes his first major architectural project: the municipal swimming pool Letzigraben in Zurich.
1951	Receives Rockefeller Grant for Drama.
1951–1952	One-year's stay in the United States and Mexico.
1954	Max Frisch closes his architectural office to devote full-time to writing. He takes up residence at Männedorf near Zurich.
1955	Receives Wilhelm Raabe Prize of the City of Braunschweig, Germany.
1956	Trips to the United States, Mexico, and Cuba.
1957	Travels in Arab countries.
1958	Receives Georg Büchner Prize of the German Academy of Language and Literature at Darmstadt. Receives Charles Veillon Prize of the City of Zurich.
1959	Max Frisch moves to Uetikon on the Lake, Switzerland.
1960–1965	He lives in Rome, Italy.

Biographical Data

1962	Receives Art Prize in Literature of the state of Northrhine-Westphalia, Germany.
1965	Receives Literature Prize of the City of Jerusalem.
	Receives Schiller Prize of the state of Baden-Württemberg, Germany.
	Max Frisch moves to Berzona in the Canton of Tessin (Ticino) in southern Switzerland.
1966	First trip to the USSR.
1968	Second trip to the USSR.
1969	Trip to Japan.
1970-1971	Winter in New York, lecturing at Columbia University.
1971-1972	Winter in New York.
1972-1973	Winter in Berlin.
1973-1974	Winter in Berlin.
1974	Receives Grand Prize of the Swiss Schiller Foundation.
1975	Trip to China.
1976	Receives Peace Prize of the German Book Trade.
1980-1981	Residing in New York.

Contributors

HANS BÄNZIGER is professor of German at Bryn Mawr College.
JAY F. BODINE was professor of German at the University of Kentucky.
KLAUS JEZIORKOWSKI is professor of German at Johann Wolfgang Goethe-Universität in Frankfurt am Main.
MANFRED JURGENSEN is professor of German at the University of Queensland, Australia.
ROLF KIESER is professor of German at the Graduate Center and Queens College, City University of New York.
WULF KOEPKE is professor of German at Texas A & M University.
MARIAN E. MUSGRAVE is professor of English and director of black studies at Miami University (Ohio).
GERHARD F. PROBST is professor of German at Transylvania University and professor of English at the Technische Universität Berlin (West).
HORST STEINMETZ is professor of German at the University of Leiden (Netherlands).
LINDA J. STINE is lecturer in German at Bryn Mawr College.

www.ingramcontent.com/pod-product-compliance
Lightning Source LLC
Chambersburg PA
CBHW032041150426

43194CB00006B/377